COGNITIVE PSYCHOLOGY

The Study of Knowing, Learning, and Thinking

COGNITIVE PSYCHOLOGY

The Study of Knowing, Learning, and Thinking

Barry F. Anderson

Portland State University

ACADEMIC PRESS

New York   San Francisco   London

A Subsidiary of Harcourt Brace Jovanovich, Publishers

Figures 81 and 82 from THE ROLE OF SPEECH IN THE
REGULATION OF NORMAL AND ABNORMAL BEHAVIOR
by Alexander R. Luria. Permission of Liveright, Publishers.
Copyright 1961 Pergamon Press, Ltd.

ACADEMIC PRESS, INC.
111 Fifth Avenue, New York, New York 10003

United Kingdom Edition published by
ACADEMIC PRESS, INC. (LONDON) LTD.
24/28 Oval Road, London NW1

Library of Congress Cataloging in Publication Data

Anderson, Barry F
    Cognitive psychology.

    Bibliography: p.
    Includes index.
    1. Cognition.   2.   Learning, Psychology of.
3. Thought and thinking.   I. Title.   [DNLM: 1. Cognition.   2. Psychology.   BF121 A545c]
BF311.A589   153   74-17967
ISBN 0-12-057850-6

To Lillian, my mother

Contents

Preface

This book presents cognitive psychology, not as simply another subject coordinate with perception, learning, and thinking, but as a view that comprehends and integrates these areas. For many years, it has been experimental psychology that has held together perception, learning, and thinking, doing so largely on the basis of a common methodology. However, the experimental method, while continuing to be of great importance in these areas, is no longer unique to them, and methods other than the experimental method are making important contributions to them. At the same time, the growth of knowledge in these areas is making it increasingly feasible to present them as related on a more substantive basis. Out of the current flux in the definition of courses in these areas, cognitive psychology seems to be emerging in a role that at least complements the old role of experimental psychology. What has always been common to perception, learning, and thinking is a concern with the processes of knowing, an empirical approach to epistemology. This book attempts to develop that theme.

I see this book as usable in two ways. It can be used, as I have used it in the past, as the sole text for a one-term course in cognitive psychology. I expect that this is the way in which it will be used most frequently. However, it can also be used, as I intend to use it in the future, as a unifying text for a year sequence in cognitive psychology, supplemented each term by a text or set of readings in perception, learning, or thinking. In this latter use, not only can the various areas of cognitive psychology be related to a common framework, but the common framework and the more specific treatments can be tested against one another, leading to a more active questioning of each.

Acknowledgments

I would like to raise a glass in appreciation to Robert Bjork, to David Elmes, to Mark Lepper, to Gerald Murch, to James Paulson, to Kelyn Roberts, to David Wrench, and to Benson Schaeffer, for sharing their fine minds with me and thus helping to make this book a far better one than I could have written alone; to my publisher, for exercising editorial imagination and editorial wisdom, each at the right time; and to Mary Foon, for handling administrative matters with exceptional competence during the year I was in Greece. I would also like to present a special bouquet to my family, Aliki, Delia, and Erik, for understanding that some of the most important things in life require very hard work over a very long period of time. Σᾶς ἀγαπῶ πολύ.

COGNITIVE PSYCHOLOGY

The Study of Knowing, Learning, and Thinking

INTRODUCTION

part I

Knowing, Learning, and Thinking

chapter 1

> *Many of the characteristics of human intelligence can be anticipated on the basis of general considerations.*

Knowing takes many forms. This is true not only across different species but within the human species, as well. We perceive, we know intuitively, and we reason. There is no simple answer to the question, "How do we know?"

Consider a person learning to perceive a new object.

> The student being introduced for the first time to microscopic techniques in a course in histology is told to look for the *corpus luteum* in a cross-sectional slide of rabbit ovary. He is told with respect to its defining attributes that it is yellowish, roundish, of a certain size relative to the field of the microscope, etc. He finds it. Next time he looks, he is still "scanning the attributes." But as he becomes accustomed to the procedure and to the kind of cellular structure involved, the *corpus luteum* begins to take on something classically referred to as a *Gestalt* or configurational quality. Phenomenologically, it seems that he no longer has to go through the slow business of checking size, shape, color, texture, etc. Indeed "corpus luteumness" appears to become a property or attribute in its own right [Bruner, Goodnow, & Austin, 1962, p. 46].

3

Or consider a person thinking creatively.

> Permit me a rough comparison. Figure the future elements of our combinations as something like the hooked atoms of Epicurus. During the complete repose of the mind, these atoms are motionless, they are, so to speak, hooked to the wall; so this complete rest may be indefinitely prolonged without the atoms meeting, and consequently without any combination between them.
>
> On the other hand, during a period of apparent rest and unconscious work, certain of them are detached from the wall and put in motion. They flash in every direction through the space (I was about to say the room) where they are enclosed, as would, for example, a swarm of gnats or, if you prefer a more learned comparison, like the molecules of gas in the kinematic theory of gases. Then their mutual impacts may produce new combinations.
>
> What is the role of the preliminary conscious work? It is evidently to mobilize certain of these atoms, to unhook them from the wall and put them in swing. . . . The mobilized atoms are therefore not any atoms whatsoever; they are those from which we might reasonably expect the desired solution [Poincaré, 1913, pp. 387ff.].

Or consider a person making a decision. Here, the decision is whether to buy a cast iron stove or a sheet metal stove to heat a summer cabin in Maine.

> Initially, the person decided on a cast iron stove because it looked more handsome and rugged, would hold the heat longer, and was not as hazardous as the sheet metal stove. However, when he tried to purchase a cast iron stove, he found that the price of new stoves was too high (about $50.00), and that the few second hand stoves available were the wrong shape or size. Thus, budgetary and aesthetic interests blocked the action. A friend then urged him to purchase a sheet metal stove; this could be done for only $5.00. The friend argued that such a stove was not dangerous in the summertime when it would not be crammed with wood. Furthermore, the sheet metal stove was more useful in the summer since it would rapidly take the chill off the cabin and would not retain heat into midday. In spite of all the arguments for a sheet metal stove, the person could not bring himself to buy such a stove because of its poor looks. He associated the handsome ruggedness of a cast iron stove with the coast of Maine and the character of its people. He had a strong interest in having the stove "fit with its surroundings." Finally, however, he brought himself around to also liking the sheet metal stove. He accomplished this by stressing the fact that Maine lobstermen often used sheet metal stoves in their cabins on the offshore islands. Thus, the sheet metal stove came to represent the hardy ingenuity of the Maine lobstermen and took on an "it's not handsome but it sure works" quality where the ugliness of the stove actually added to its charm. The sheet metal stove was immediately purchased [DeRivera, 1968].

Or, finally, consider a person thinking in a distorted fashion.

> I am surprised that anyone as well educated as you must be . . . would stoop to such a depth as to torture helpless little cats in the pursuit of a cure for alcoholics. . . . Instead why not torture the

drunks . . . if such people are weaklings the world is better off without them. . . . My greatest wish is that you have brought home to you a torture that will be a thousand fold greater than what you are doing to the little animals. . . . I'm glad I am just an ordinary human being . . . with a clear conscience, knowing I have not hurt any living creature [Masserman, 1946].

We wish to inquire about human intelligence. There are many paths by which we could enter the vast body of relevant material. Since no one of them possesses the virtues of all, we shall take not one, but two. First, in this chapter, we shall begin with the general and abstract, asking what intelligence is and what characteristics we might reasonably expect any knowing system, human or nonhuman, living or nonliving, to have. In this, we shall be particularly concerned with complex knowing systems functioning in the complex world in which man finds himself. Then, in the main part of the book, we shall begin again, but at the beginning this time, asking how physical energies are transduced into nervous impulses at the sensory surfaces, how preliminary organization is imposed on these nervous impulses, how the incoming patterns of activity establish contact with memory and alter memory, and, finally, how the results are made use of in constructing and evaluating alternative courses of action. First, then, some general principles.

Constancy, Variation, and Adaptation

All systems require a certain amount of constancy (Ashby, 1956, 1960). This is true of systems as diverse as the air–water cycle, ionization reactions, caterpillars, and democracy. Temperatures sufficiently extreme to freeze or vaporize all water would disrupt the air–water cycle, and an increase in violence could bring down a democracy. Systems retain their integrity only within a limited range of conditions; extreme conditions will destroy them.

Yet our world is not constant. Our world is a kaleidoscope of physical energies that change season by season, day by day, hour by hour, and minute by minute. Conditions may vary greatly, and systems are often destroyed as a consequence.

In such a variable world, adaptive systems are far more likely to survive. An adaptive system is a system that confronts environmental change by attempting to nullify either the change or its effects (Ashby, 1956, 1960). In nature, only living systems are adaptive (see Sommerhoff, 1969; Von Bertalanffy, 1956). A ther-

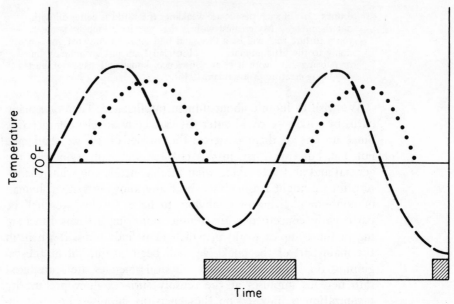

FIGURE 1. *A simple adaptive system: The achievement of constancy in a variable world. The dashed line represents the variable external conditions (in this case, the outside temperature); the dotted line represents the more nearly constant internal conditions (the inside temperature); and the shaded areas represent the adaptive response (in this case, turning on the heat).*

mostat is a simple example of an artificial adaptive system (see Figure 1); when the temperature falls below a certain level, the thermostat responds by turning on the heat and thus corrects its environment. An adaptive system produces a better fit between itself and its environment by changing one or the other or both. Changing the environment is referred to as *assimilation,* and changing oneself is referred to as *accommodation* (Piaget, 1952a). One assimilates the environment to oneself, or one accommodates oneself to the environment. In eating an apple, for example, a person accommodates by opening his mouth, chewing, and secreting digestive juices. At the same time, he assimilates the apple by grinding it up and digesting it.

Adaptation in Species

Individuals and species adapt by means of different mechanisms (see Sommerhoff, 1969). Species adapt by reproductive variation and differential survival, each generation producing a variety of offspring and only the best-adapted of these surviving to contribute to the next generation. Thus, each generation tends to have the characteristics of those individuals in its parents' generation that survived long enough to reproduce, and the species moves slowly toward a better fit to the environment.

Changes produced by the mechanisms of reproductive variation and differential survival are fixed in the gene code and remain constant throughout the life of an individual system; examples are the evolution of lungs and fur. However, some of these fixed features contribute to the capacity of the individual system for change during its life, features ranging from the very capacity for responding to the capacities for learning and thinking.

Adaptation in Individuals

Whereas reproductive variation and differential survival is the means by which species adapt, responding is the means by which individual systems adapt. Individual systems may respond so as to produce internal or external changes. In animals, responses that produce internal changes tends to be involuntary—for example, reducing perspiration and increasing metabolism when the surroundings become colder. And responses that produce external changes tend to be voluntary. External changes are produced by locomotion, by manipulation, or, vicariously, by communication—for example, going south for the winter, building a shelter, or asking that more wood be put on the fire.

Adaptive systems necessarily possess three kinds of mechanisms, however rudimentary. They must have a *receptor mechanism* to detect changes in the world; they must have an *effector mechanism* in order to do something about these changes; and they must have a mechanism that *connects* receptor states to effector states (Ashby, 1956, 1960; MacKay, 1956).

These general considerations give us reason to expect to find certain features when we encounter human intelligence. We can expect to find mechanisms for detecting important changes in the world, mechanisms for responding to these changes, and connecting mechanisms. Moreover, we can expect that the nature of the connection will be such as to ensure that the responses will have the effect of nullifying at least certain of the important changes or their consequences.

Variation, Covariation, and Knowledge

We have already encountered the concept of variation. The world is not constant. Energies vary from place to place and from time to time. Some places are warm, and some are cold; some places are rich in food, and others are scarce of food.

In addition to variation, however, there is also covariation. Although energies are not stable, the ways in which they change are. It is covariation that makes knowing, learning, and thinking possible. By covariation we mean order, lawfulness, structure, correlation, contingency. To say that things covary is simply to say that they tend to change together. Certain changes in the environment tend to predict certain changes in a given system—for example, extreme cold will kill a living system. And certain changes in the environment tend to predict certain other changes in the environment—for example, the falling of the leaves predicts cooler days, and the appearance of blossoms predicts warmer days (see Figure 2). An adaptive system necessarily represents co-variation.

Because adaptive systems take account of covariation in the world, they may be considered to be knowing systems. Knowledge may be broadly defined as a pattern of internal states (for example, neural in animals, electronic in computers) each of which corresponds to some state in the world. Note that knowledge by this definition may or may not correspond to the external *pattern*; and, of course, where it does correspond, it may do so to any degree. Note also that the internal states need not in any way resemble the external states, as the ancient Greeks once thought they did: We can know about light without having lights inside our heads, and we can know about sound without sounds echoing in our brains. Finally, knowledge by this definition may be innate or learned and may be conscious or unconscious.

We have seen that any world in which there is variation and covariation may give rise to knowing systems. But our world is also complex, and environmental complexity makes certain design features valuable in knowing systems. Let us take our first step, then, from the general to the particular, in this case to our particular world, and see what features it might make desirable.

Environmental Complexity and Information Reduction

Our world is complex in that there are many sources of variation. This complexity poses certain problems. Consider the plight of a hunter who has caught a rabbit, eaten it, and found it satisfying. What knowledge should he store in memory after this experience? He could remember that "Small, furry creatures that

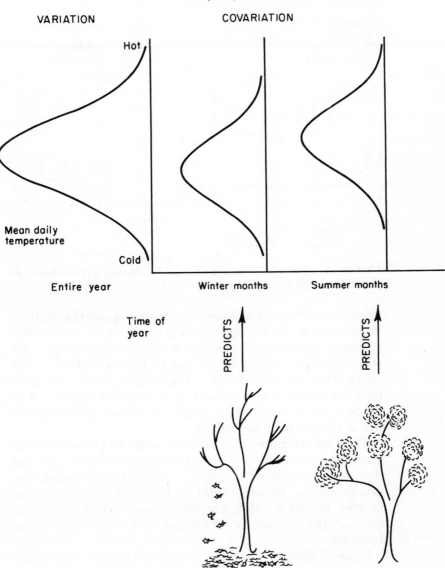

FIGURE 2. *Variation and covariation.*

are white, have long ears, and are sitting on rocks facing trees are good to eat." The trouble with such a representation is that many of these variables are irrelevant: Small, furry creatures that are black or brown, that have short ears, and that are sitting in the grass are also good to eat. Not all the variables are relevant. A hunter who has included the irrelevant variables of color, ear length, and specific location and orientation might bypass many

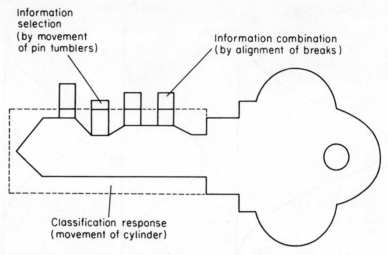

FIGURE 3.   *A simple artificial mechanism for selecting and combining information in stimulus classification.*

an edible creature in the hopes of encountering one that matches his description. He has specified a class that is so limited that he might not encounter another member in his lifetime. Another possibility would be for the hunter to remember that "furry things are good to eat." The trouble here is that more than this one variable is relevant; if he does not remember that the thing he ate was small, he might try to catch something that will, in the end, catch and eat him.

There are many sources of variation in our world, and, for most predictions, many are relevant and many are irrelevant. The fact that we live in a world in which many but not all variables are usually relevant for any prediction has three important consequences. In such a world, it is advantageous (*a*) to select information,* (*b*) to combine information, and (*c*) to resample information.

Figure 3 illustrates a simple artificial device that both selects and combines information, a lock. The pin tumblers respond selectively to the width of the key at various points. They do not respond to its color or its temperature or its electrical properties. The information from the four pin tumblers is combined by the align-

---

* Information is related to variation in a very precise way (Attneave, 1959; Garner, 1962). We say that the six faces of a die, taken together, present us with more variation than do the two sides of a coin, taken together, but that knowledge of which face of a die has come up presents us with more information than does knowledge of which side of a coin has come up. Both information and variation increase with the number of alternative possibilities.

ment or nonalignment of the breaks that divide each pin tumbler in two. If the breaks are in line, the cylinder will turn, indicating that the key has been "recognized."

Information Selection

We select and combine information in such a way as to reduce information (see Posner, 1964). Reducing information means reducing many possibilities to few possibilities—for example, by classifying plants as edible or inedible, we reduce many different types of plants to just two, and by classifying animals as dangerous or not dangerous, we again reduce many possibilities to just two.

There are two kinds of value in selecting relevant, and rejecting irrelevant, sources of information. One, the fewer the sources of variation that are processed, the less is the burden on the information-processing system. Indeed, any system that is simpler than its environment, that is, whose capacity for variation is less than the variation in its environment, is necessarily an information-reducing system. Furthermore, selecting even less information than can be handled at capacity can free certain information-processing systems for attention to other tasks. Two, the fewer the irrelevant sources of variation that are contained in an internal representation, the greater is its generality. Only if the hunter who has caught the rabbit ignores at least specific location and orientation, will his knowledge be sufficiently broad to be of use on more than a very limited number of occasions. Indeed, in a world which, if Heraclitus was right, never repeats itself, it would seem necessary to reject some information if either the individual system or the species is to be able to benefit at all from experience. Because we may "never step into the stream twice," irrelevant differences between one occasion and the next must be disregarded if the lessons of the past are ever to be applied to the present.

Degree of Covariation and Relevance. Although random selection of information would satisfy these purposes, it would not be likely to do so in the most useful way. It is far more adaptive to give preference to sources of variation that predict events relevant to survival and that predict them well. We shall refer to these two characteristics of a source of variation as relevance and degree of covariation, respectively.

Degree of covariation refers to the extent to which knowledge of the status of one source of variation improves one's ability to predict the status of another source of variation. For example, the call of an animal predicts its proximity with greater certainty than does the presence of its tracks in the earth. Other things being equal, it is more adaptive to give preference to those sources of variation that covary highly with the events they predict.

Relevance refers to the extent to which the event predicted is important to the continued existence of the system. The call of a rhinoceros is more relevant to a man's survival than is the call of a songbird. The relevance, importance, or significance of any covariation is counted ultimately in terms of effects on the system. Thus, the relevance of covariation between the environment and the system, itself, is immediate and clear—for example, fire burns. The relevance of covariation among environmental events, however, is indirect; such covariation is relevant only to the extent that it permits prediction of environmental events that do have direct effects on the system—for example, smoke predicts fire, and fire burns. The capacity to predict will make no contribution to survival unless the chain of prediction ultimately terminates in changes within the system, itself.

Thus, we should expect an adaptive system of any sophistication to represent in some way both degree of covariation and relevance.

Information Combination

In those cases where information from more than one source is relevant to a given prediction, it is at least desirable, and sometimes essential, to combine this information in generating a prediction. Information can be combined in two ways, corresponding to the two ways predictor variables can be related. Predictor variables can combine additively, or they can interact, and different design features are best suited to combining information in each case.

Additive Combinations. Predictors are additive when the predictive value of each is the same at all levels of the other. For example, in judging the ripeness of an apple, the color of different parts of the apple are at least approximately additive, or independent, predictors of ripeness. The redder any given part of an apple is, the riper the apple is likely to be, regardless of the color of other parts. Similarly, the sizes of different body parts are at least approximately additive predictors of the strength of an adversary. Fairly simple mechanisms will suffice when predictors can be treated as independent. The ripeness of an apple can be judged from an overall impression of its redness, without specifically taking different parts into account (something like a light meter with a red filter could do the job), and the strength of an adversary can similarly be judged from an overall impression of its size. When predictors are nearly additive, combining them and basing the prediction on the equivalent of a sum or an average has the effect of reducing random error in prediction. Note that information reduction is involved here; many different apples will be judged as having the same degree of ripeness.

Interactive Combinations. Predictors are interactive when the predictive value of each is different at different levels of the other. For example, light may be safe when it is steady (from the sun) but potentially harmful when it is flickering (from a fire); amount of light and steadiness of light interact.

Consider the situation confronted by a man living in a part of Africa inhabited by lions, gorillas, ground squirrels, and the deadly poisonous snake, the black mamba. If we classify these animals according to just two variables, color and size, we obtain the table in Figure 4. The lion and the mamba have been double-starred because they are quite dangerous to man, whereas the ground squirrel and even the shy gorilla are harmless and need not be feared. Note that information reduction is involved, because four kinds of animals, lion, squirrel, gorilla, and mamba, are reduced to two, dangerous and harmless. Color and size are not additive here, for the predictive value of color is not the same for animals of different sizes: Among small animals, the black ones are dangerous, but, among large animals, it is the brown ones that are dangerous. (One could not represent degree of dangerousness by, for example, assigning values of 0 to small, 1 to large, 0 to brown, and 1 to black and then simply adding these, for this would inaccurately yield $0 + 0 = 0$ for squirrel, $0 + 1 = 1$ for mamba, $1 + 0 = 1$ for lion, and $1 + 1 = 2$ for gorilla.) These predictors interact.

A primitive example of a mechanism that responds to interactions is a frog's "bug detector" (Lettvin, Maturana, McCulloch,

	Brown	Black
Large	LION**	GORILLA
Small	SQUIRREL	MAMBA**

FIGURE 4. *Interactive predictors.*

& Pitts, 1959). Certain neurons in the frog's visual system are wired so that they respond only to objects that are small and dark and moving. It is not that moving objects simply produce a low rate of firing in such neurons and that smallness and darkness combine additively to increase the rate of firing. There is no firing at all unless all three properties are present.

When we encounter human intelligence, we can expect to find mechanisms for handling both additive and interactive predictors.

Information Resampling

A consequence of information reduction is that prediction is not perfect, and a consequence of imperfect prediction is that it is adaptive to resample information in order to update predictions. Where there are more relevant sources of covariation than a limited-capacity system can take into account, it will be inaccurate in predicting the consequences of its responses. When prediction of the consequences of responses is not adequate for a given purpose, monitoring those consequences directly by means of a feedback control system will tend to enhance their adaptive effect (Bellman, 1964).

Feedback control systems are to be contrasted with open control systems (see Figure 5). In open control, an initiating stimulus determines the response, regardless of the effects of the response. In feedback control, the response is guided by its effects. Open control systems are often called ballistic systems; a ballistic missile, such as a bullet, is one that is simply aimed and fired. Feedback control systems are often called guided systems; a guided missile is corrected in its course many times after it has

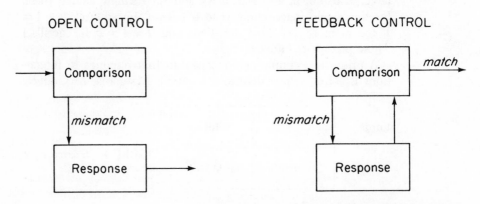

FIGURE 5.   *Open control and feedback control systems.*

been released. The reason a guided missile is more accurate than a ballistic missile is that many more sources of covariation than the sender has knowledge of affect the course of a missile's flight.

The basic difference between open and feedback control systems can be seen in subjects attempting to point at a target while wearing displacing prisms. Subjects who are not permitted to see their own hands miss the target by an amount equal to the angle of the prism, indicating open control; while subjects who are permitted to see their own hands eventually point to the target, indicating feedback control (Mittelstaedt, 1964).

The advantages of feedback control are so great that it is difficult to find examples in nature of open control systems. But one example is the releasing response of the mated female tick (Hinde, 1966). The tick climbs to the tip of a bush and waits there, perhaps for months, until the smell of butyric acid, a product of mammalian skin glands, causes her to release her grip and drop from the branch. There is no opportunity to use feedback here, because there is no possibility of correcting the response. Another example is the striking response in mantids (Hinde, 1966). Open control is employed here, because the time to process feedback would be longer than the time it would take the forelegs to reach the prey. Feedback control, as we shall see, is important, not only at the level of overt behavior, but also at the level of conceptual behavior.

From the point of view of the species, an adaptive system may be considered to be a guided system. The genetic code cannot know all the influences that will act upon an organism during its life. Rather than "throw" it into life with a preprogrammed sequence of responses, the genetic code equips it with capacities for sensing environmental conditions and responding appropriately to them, which tends to keep the organism "on course." Thus, the same powerful principle, information resampling, operates on both large and small scales (see Sommerhof, 1969).

In this section, we have seen that, because human intelligence functions in a complex world, we can expect to encounter mechanisms for selecting, combining, and resampling information. Moreover, we can expect that the mechanisms for selecting information will take degree of covariation and relevance into account and that the mechanisms for combining information will, in concert, at least, be capable of dealing with both additive and interactive predictors. While remaining at a general level, we have been able to add a number of specifications to our characterization of human intelligence. We shall be able to do this one more time.

Internal Complexity and Organization

We took our first step from the general to the particular by considering the type of world in which man functions: a complex world. We take our second step from the general to the particular by considering the type of knowing system that man is: a complex system. We shall consider two kinds of complexity and two kinds of organization. The fact that human intelligence consists of a large number of components requires hierarchical organization, and the fact that human intelligence is capable of complex sequences of operation requires organization into representational and executive systems. We begin with hierarchical organization.

Hierarchical Organization

The argument of this section is that human intelligence, because of its large number of components, consists of a hierarchy of levels of intelligence. By a hierarchy we mean an arrangement in which components of a low order are brought together to form components of a higher order, which may in turn be brought together to form components of a still higher order. First, we must begin by distinguishing among levels of intelligence.

Levels of Intelligence: Knowing, Learning, and Thinking. Adaptive systems may be classified on the basis of their levels of intelligence. *Intelligence* may be defined as the capacity of a system for modifying its knowledge (see Bellman, 1964). The capacity to fix a temporary pattern of internal states we call *learning.* Temporary patterns of internal states can arise in either of two ways. When they reflect current receptor states, they are the result of experience. When they do not correspond to current receptor states, but are generated on an internal basis, they are the product of thought. Thus, it is the generation of a temporary pattern of internal states that we call *thinking.* If a forager discovers a new root vegetable and finds that it is good to eat, he has learned. If he considers the possibility that he might plant some of these and get them to grow as a crop, he has thought. On the basis of intelligence, we may distinguish three levels of adaptive systems (see Sommerhof, 1969). Level I systems only know; they have no intelligence. Level II systems know and learn; they have some intelligence. And Level III systems know, learn, and think; they have a high degree of intelligence.

In Level I systems, change in knowledge, if it is to take place, must be effected by some external agent. In living systems, this is accomplished by reproductive variation and differential survival. Knowledge modified in this way corresponds to the world of the system's ancestors. This is perfectly adequate in a world that does not change from generation to generation, and innate knowledge actually possesses certain advantages: It does not require a capacity for learning, and it does not require time for learning. Level I systems can adapt to fairly rapidly changing worlds by maturing rapidly and producing large numbers of offspring; the fruit fly, for example, can adapt even to seasonal variations by means of the mechanism of reproductive variation and differential survival. Level I includes plants, as well as animals. Plants grow toward light and water; the Mimosa withdraws when touched; and the Venus Flytrap closes on its prey.

In Level II systems, knowledge is, to some extent, acquired after the system has been constructed, and to that extent, it corresponds to the world of the system's own experience. "Prewired" knowledge we call instinct, and "postwired" knowledge we call memory. Memory is important in a changing world, and an extensive memory is essential in the rapidly changing world that man has created. Level II is believed to include only animals, and perhaps not even the simplest of these. There is no clear evidence of even primitive forms of learning below the coelenterates (for example, sea anemones, jellyfish, hydras) (Razran, 1971).

In Level III systems, a further advance in adaptability is possible. By reorganizing experience, it is possible for a system to see beyond experience and anticipate a future that is quite unlike the past. This is what man does when he takes steps to avoid world famine, irreversible destruction of the environment, or nuclear warfare, none of which he has ever experienced. Level III seems to include only mammals and seems to be developed to a high level only in the primates, most notably, of course, humans.

Knowing, Learning, and Thinking in Man. Like all adaptive systems, man knows, and much of his knowledge is innate. Like other higher animals, he learns. And, like other mammals, he thinks. To illustrate these levels, let us consider the processing of stimulus information. Mechanisms for both selecting and combining information exist at each of the three levels.

At Level I, information is selected by man's range of sensitivities and by stimulus control of attention. He is sensitive to informative sources of energy, particularly to light and sound, which carry information over great distances. And he is insensitive to uninformative sources of energy, such as the infrared light produced by the temperature of the eye and the low-frequency sounds produced by the blood rushing through the ear (von Békésy, 1967). He attends reflexively to changes in his environment, to rapid motion, a sudden sound, an unusual smell (Sokolov, 1963a,b). These are likely to be informative, for changes often predict further changes.

At Level II, information is selected that has proved to be of significance in the experience of the individual. Thus, on the very same walk, a botanist will notice some things, and a geologist, others; and things that one can readily discriminate will appear indistinguishable to the other.

Though secondary perception and associative memory seem to select information in similar ways, they seem to function somewhat differently in combining information. Secondary perception combines information about features to form descriptions of things. For example, what at one time are all seen simply as grasses may later, on the basis of additional information about such features as color and leaf shape, be seen as many different kinds of grasses. Secondary perception combines information in a way that divides the world into a world of many particular things. Associative memory, on the other hand, combines information about things to form groups of things. Some kinds of grasses are remembered as being sweet to the taste, and others as bitter. Associative memory combines information in a way that puts the many things of perception together into groups of intuitively related things. It is thus that such things as butterfly, garden, summer, and sunshine come to seem to belong together.

Secondary perception seems designed to handle interacting variables, and associative memory to handle additive variables. Coupled together, as they are, they seem capable of handling a wide range of problems. Consider again the problem of the lions, gorillas, ground squirrels, and mambas. The strategy of perception is to divide. We do not perceive simply brownness, blackness, largeness, and smallness; we perceive lions, gorillas, ground squirrels, and mambas. The strategy of associative memory is to join. A fear response is associated with the perception of a lion and the perception of a mamba, thus grouping these two animals together as equivalent. Note that the fear response could equally readily have been associated with any subset of the four stimuli. The perceptual strategy of dividing the world up into particular things makes no assumption as to how variables combine. Associations, on the other hand, seem to be at least approximately additive. If we consider the presence or absence of each animal as a derived variable (derived by the processes of perception), then the presence or absence of lions and the presence or absence of mambas would seem to be treated by associative memory as at least approximately additive. A lion coming onto the scene would produce fear, whether there is a mamba around or not, and it would increase the initial level of fear by very roughly the same amount in either case.

At Level III, information is both selected and combined by means of rules. The rule, "When the lake has melted and the Great Star rises from the top of the mountain, it is time to offer seeds to the Earth Spirit," tells us both what information to select and how to combine it. The lake must have melted, *and* the Great Star must have risen from the top of the mountain. Rules can represent either additive or interactive combinations and can do so with great elegance and precision.

These three levels of intelligence seem to be hierarchically related in man, with Level III processes superimposed on Level II processes and Level II processes superimposed on Level I processes (Piaget, see Flavell, 1966.) We learn about what we have sensed and attended to, and we think about what we have learned. The question is, "Why is the organization hierarchical?" Simon's (1969) parable of Hora and Tempus suggests an explanation in a most entertaining way.

> There once were two watchmakers, named Hora and Tempus, who manufactured very fine watches. Both of them were highly regarded, and the phones in their workshops rang frequently—new customers were constantly calling them. However, Hora prospered, while Tempus became poorer and poorer and finally lost his shop. What was the reason?
>
> The watches the men made consisted of about 1000 parts each. Tempus had so constructed his that if he had one partly assembled and had to put it down—to answer the phone, say—it immediately fell to pieces and had to be reassembled from the elements. The better the customers liked his watches, the more they phoned him and the more difficult it became for him to find enough uninterrupted time to finish a watch.
>
> The watches that Hora made were no less complex than those of Tempus. But he had designed them so that he could put together subassemblies of about ten elements each. Ten of these subassemblies, again, could be put together into a larger subassembly; and a system of ten of the latter subassemblies constituted the whole watch. Hence, when Hora had to put down a partly assembled watch in order to answer the phone, he lost only a small part of his work,

and he assembled his watches in only a fraction of the man-hours
it took Tempus [pp. 90–91].*

The argument applies all the more strongly in the case of human intelligence, which is certainly more complex than Hora and Tempus's watches. It should thus be no surprise that it, too, is organized hierarchically. Consider how human intelligence must have been constructed. In evolution, genetic variation corresponds to assembly, and fertilization corresponds to the ringing of the telephone. If the changes produced by genetic variation do not result in a set of adaptive subassemblies by the time fertilization occurs, they will not be likely to be transmitted through many generations. Evolution selects for design features that not only contribute to the continued existence of a system but also do so fairly soon after they have made their appearance. Evolution takes little account of promises. Thus, human intelligence consists of Level I subassemblies organized together into larger assemblies by Level II processes, which are finally organized into still larger systems of thought at Level III (Piaget, see Flavell, 1963).

This cannot be the entire explanation of the hierarchical organization in human intelligence, however, for it often happens in evolution that provisional solutions are dropped out after more adaptive ones have been achieved: After all, man has lost his gills and his tail. Hierarchical organization must continue to be of value to the individual system. It is understandable that it should be, because, not only is nature a builder in constructing man, but man is a builder in constructing representations of the world, and hierarchical organization seems to be of value in the process of construction, generally. Indeed, a microgenesis seems to be involved in every complex cognitive act (Flavell & Draguns, 1957). Information is first processed by subsystems that are most primitive evolutionarily, producing results that are of some value to the system, just as they were of some value to its ancestors. These results are then processed further by subsystems that are more recent evolutionarily, producing results that are of greater value to the system, just as they were of greater value to its ancestors. Once again, we encounter a principle so powerful that it seems to apply both at the level of the species and at the level of the individual system. The first was information resampling; the second is hierarchical organization.

* Reprinted from *The Sciences of the Artificial* by H. A. Simon, by permission of the M.I.T. Press, Cambridge, Massachusetts. © 1969 The M.I.T. Press.

Representational–Executive Organization

In the foregoing, we were concerned with internal complexity, defined in terms of number of components. We saw that a large number of components requires hierarchical organization. Here, we are concerned with a different definition of internal complexity, in terms of the kinds of sequences of operation possible.

The argument begins with the observation that man generates sequences of ideas and behaviors that involve dependencies that operate over arbitrary distances. For example, the verb agrees in number with the singular subject in each of the following sentences:

The box is red.

The box of pins is red.

The box of pins, tacks, and paperclips is red.

In the second and third sentences, a singular verb is selected even though its immediate antecedents are a plural noun in the one case and a series of plural nouns in the other. The dependency in number operates over arbitrary distances.

Animals below man demonstrate the same capacity, though on a more limited scale, in performing double alternations (Hunter, 1920). The double-alternation task requires the animal to respond twice to the right and then twice to the left in order to obtain food. Here also, the correct response depends on more than just the preceding response.

Such complex sequences require something more than hierarchical organization. They require control processes to ensure completion of a plan (Bever, Fodor, & Garrett, 1968; Chomsky, 1957, 1959; Lashley, 1951). Associations among representations (in the example, "box"—"is") would seem to be inadequate by themselves, for arbitrarily long sequences can be embedded between the associated terms without disturbing the dependency. Indeed, associations among representations would not seem to be involved at all in judging such sequences as, *Colorless green ideas sleep furiously*, to be grammatical (Chomsky, 1957). Such judgments must be judgments about sequences of executive control processes (here, adjective–adjective–noun–verb–adverb), rather than judgments about sequences of representations, for such sequences as "colorless green" and "green ideas" are quite unfamiliar. We shall expand on the notion of representation–executive organization when we come to the executive system.

This ends our general systems introduction to human intelligence. From the fact that man is an adaptive system, we shall expect that he will have capacities for sensing and acting upon the environment and a mechanism for relating these, and we shall expect that this mechanism will be such as to nullify at least certain of the sensed changes or their effects. From the fact that he is adapted to a complex world, we shall expect that he will have capacities for selecting, combining, and resampling information, and we shall expect that the mechanisms for selecting information will take account of degree of covariation and relevance and that the mechanisms for combining information will be able to handle both additive and interactive variables. Finally, from the fact that he is, himself, complex, we shall expect that his intelligence will consist of representational and executive systems and that these will be hierarchically organized.

THE REPRESENTATIONAL SYSTEM

SYSTEM

part II

Primary Perception

chapter 2

Information is received by the senses, processed by a variety of analyzers, and formed into an analogue model of the world.

The story of how man knows the world begins at the sensory surfaces, the interface between the knower and the known, where physical energy is transformed into neural activity, to be treated as information. That is where this chapter will begin. To yield a perceptual world that is both organized and meaningful, however, information selected by the senses must be combined. It must be collated both within the present and with the past. Starting with the isolated fragments of the world that have managed to get through the few sensory openings in our nervous system, we must now attempt to construct some representation of what the world out there might be like. This chapter is concerned with how feature analyses and analogue processes collate information within the present. The following chapter will take up the problem of how current information is collated with that in memory.

Let us begin by looking briefly at physical energy and sensory experience. Different kinds of physical energy produce the various sensory qualities, and different amounts of physical energy produce different degrees of sensory intensity.

Kind of Energy and Sensory Quality

Information selection begins with selective sensitivity (von Békésy, 1967). Man is not sensitive to all that goes on about him. He looks out at the world through a limited number of openings in his nervous system. It is important to be aware of the selective nature of our sensitivity, for much of subsequent cognitive processing is predicated on the assumptions of our sense receptors. Not until we come to the processes of reasoning, in the latter half of the book, will we encounter processes that are capable of rising above these assumptions and questioning them.

It is important to note that, whereas our sensory system is generally quite adaptive, it involves only Level I mechanisms and thus is adapted to the world of our ancestors. Because the distribution and significance of physical energies have recently changed in certain important respects, our sensory system has become out of date. Chemicals that are very harmful to us pollute the air and water and contaminate our food, yet many of these chemicals are colorless, odorless, and tasteless. Unfortunately, the inability to see, smell, or taste these chemicals has consequences, not only for sensation and perception, but also for thought and judgment. It is much easier to get people concerned about pollutants that they can sense than about pollutants that they cannot sense. The following point made by Sir Francis Bacon (1952) in his discussion of the "idols of the mind" is as applicable in our day as it was in his:

> But by far the greatest impediment and aberration of the human understanding proceeds from the dullness, incompetency, and errors of the senses; since whatever strikes the senses preponderates over everything, however superior, which does not immediately strike them. Hence contemplation mostly ceases with sight, and a very scanty, or perhaps no regard is paid to invisible objects [*Novum Organum*, Book I, Paragraph 50].

Let us be more specific about the limitations of the senses. The most important sources of energy to which man is sensitive are electromagnetic, mechanical, chemical, and gravitational. He cannot detect nuclear bonding energy or magnetic energy, at all; and, although he can detect electrical energy, this probably occurs by way of direct effects on the nerves, rather than by way of specialized receptors (Uttal, 1969).

Not only is man sensitive to only certain kinds of energy, but his sensitivity is restricted to a narrow range within each kind. The electromagnetic spectrum (see Figure 6) extends from cosmic rays, with wavelengths as short as 4/10,000,000,000 inch (10 nm), to radio waves as long as 18 miles (over 28×10^{12} nm), yet man is sensitive only to the wavelengths between 16 millionths of an inch (400 nm, violet) and 32 millionths of an inch (700 nm, red), a tiny window, indeed.

The reason the eye does not respond to wavelengths greater than 700 nm may be that the eyeball, itself, like all warm bodies, emits infrared radiation, and this has no predictive value. Our sensitivity to long wavelengths stops at the very point that radiation from the eyeball begins; in a dark room, we can detect just the faintest trace of redness (von Békésy, 1967).

The situation is similar for acoustic stimuli. Man is sensitive only in the range from 20 to 20,000 Hz (see Figure 7). The reason the ear does not respond to frequencies below 20 Hz may be that blood rushing through the ear produces acoustic stimuli with frequencies below this point, and these, like infrared radiation from the eyeball, have no predictive value (von Békésy, 1967).

With respect to chemical stimuli, the number of different

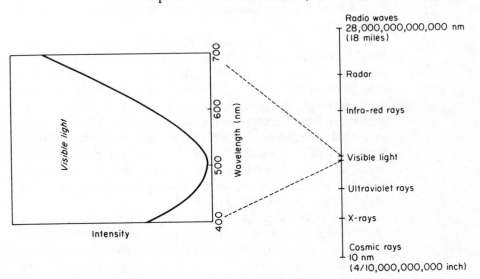

FIGURE 6. *The range of visual sensitivity.*

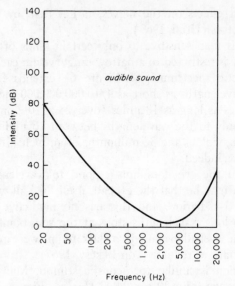

FIGURE 7. *The range of auditory sensitivity.*

chemicals is truly staggering, yet we respond to only four primary tastes: sweet, sour, salt, and bitter (Pfaffman, 1959). And we respond to only about six primary odors: fragrant, putrid, fruity, spicy, burned, and resinous (Adey, 1959; Henning, 1924). Though no quantitative statement of the number of chemical differences to which we are not sensitive seems possible, the number must be enormous.

Why is it that we look out at the world through so few windows? One reason must have to do with costs. Different instruments are required for detecting different kinds of energy, and even for detecting different forms of what is essentially the same kind of energy. As a thermometer is needed to detect subtle, random molecular activity and a microphone to detect more vigorous, patterned molecular activity, so also are warm and cold receptors needed for detecting the former and a cochlea for detecting the latter. Since it is costly, in terms of both evolutionary time and genetic capacity, to add sensory instruments, it is not likely that a great many will be evolved.

Another reason must have to do with benefits. Sources of variation that have no survival value in themselves and that do not even covary highly with those that do are, in the interests of simplification and generality, best not detected. We have seen that certain ranges of electromagnetic and acoustic energy fall in this category. Perhaps nuclear bonding and magnetic energy do also. Even sources of variation that have predictive value, in themselves, might not be worth detecting if they covary so highly with other predictors that they add little to overall accuracy in prediction. A fire already gives a flickering yellow light, a crackling noise, warmth, and its own special odor. Do we need any more information in order to identify it?

It is useful to distinguish between primary and secondary sensory qualities. The qualities that differ from sense to sense are what Locke called secondary qualities. They are presumed to be properties of the observer, and not of the world. Only qualities that can be detected by more than one sense, what Locke called primary qualities, are attributable to the world. (The logic here is that of converging operations; see Bridgeman, 1927.)

The secondary qualities, color, tone, odor, and the like, present us with a profound mystery, having to do with the very relationship between the objective and subjective worlds. The problem is this: How can the same kind of neurons produce the experience of red in one part of the brain and the fragrance of roses in another? We have no answer.

The primary qualities are intensity, duration, and location, corresponding to energy, time, and space (Boring, 1933). They seem easier to understand than the secondary qualities. All modalities respond to differences in intensity and duration, because all individual receptors respond in these ways. The greater the stimulating energy, the more vigorously each receptor responds; and the longer the energy continues, the longer each receptor continues to respond. And most modalities respond to differences in location, because they have a number of receptors in different spatial locations.

Let us now consider what may be the most primitive of the primary qualities, and what is certainly the best understood, sensory intensity.

Amount of Energy and Sensory Intensity

Intensity must be a very primitive sensory response, for a graded response to different amounts of energy is found even in protozoa (Alpern, Lawrence, & Wolsk, 1967). In man, it is certainly a highly refined one. Our range of sensitivity to quantitative differences seems to be much better than our range of sensitivity to qualitative differences. In the cases of vision and audition, at least, it seems virtually complete. The eye is sensitive to as few as 20 quanta of light (Corso, 1967); and the ear is sensitive to about the same amount of sound energy (Geldard, 1953), just slightly more than is produced by the random activity of air molecules. In the case of olfaction, also, sensitivity is great; odors can be detected for concentrations as low as a few parts per million. The upper ends of the various ranges of sensitivity seem to be set only by tissue damage and destruction of the sense organ.

If we present stimuli at varying energy levels and measure the magnitude of the response to each, either by asking the subject how intense each seems to be (Stevens, 1960) or by measuring activity at the receptor, itself (Fuortes, 1958), we can plot what is called a psychophysical function (see Figure 8).

If we consider only those judgments that seem to be based simply on stimulus intensity, rather than time or space, two functions seem to be obtained. Brightness, loudness, and smell show decreasing functions, and temperature, pressure, heaviness, and shock follow increasing functions (Stevens, 1960). On the log–log plot in Figure 8, an exponent of 1.0 represents a linear function; a given increment in physical energy produces the same increment in sensory intensity, no matter what the initial level of physical energy. Exponents less than 1.0 represent decreasing

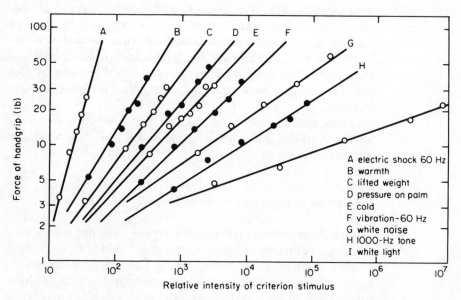

FIGURE 8. *Psychophysical functions. The exponents are as follows:* A = 3.5, B = 1.6, C = 1.45, D = 1.1, E = 1.0, F = .95, G = .6, H = .6, I = .33. [*Taken, with permission, from S. S. Stevens, "The psychophysics of sensory function,"* American Scientist, 1960, **48**, 226–253.]

functions; a given increment in physical energy produces a smaller increment in sensory intensity, the higher the initial level of physical energy. Exponents greater than 1.0 represent increasing functions; a given increment in physical energy produces a larger increment in sensory intensity, the higher the initial level of physical energy.

It has been suggested (von Békésy, 1967; Osgood, 1953) that the decreasing psychophysical function constitutes another mechanism for information selection. It seems to be an adjustment of the distance senses to the fact that the amount of physical energy decreases as a function of the square of the distance. A cracking twig in the distance may be as relevant to survival as one nearby, yet the amount of acoustic energy that it adds to the background energy is considerably less. The decreasing psychophysical function takes this into account.

The increasing psychophysical function also appears to be a mechanism for information selection. The increasing psychophysical function seems to be found only for senses that reflect conditions at the body surface or within the body. These senses would seem to be concerned with relevance, as well as covariation, for high amounts of energy applied to the body may damage it. Thus, increments at high initial levels become increasingly important to detect. The increasing psychophysical function takes this into account.

To yield a perceptual world that is both organized and meaningful, information selected by the senses must be combined. The first step in this process involves the innate mechanisms of feature analysis.

Preliminary Feature Analyses

Information passed on by the receptors is combined by a hierarchy of processes. The first set of processes is primary perception. It seems to be based on innate, prewired mechanisms and thus to be at Level I. These mechanisms, in the case of vision, seem to be located in the intermediate and ganglionic layers of the retina (see Figure 9), and in the superior colliculus, the lateral geniculate nucleus of the thalamus, and the visual cortex (see Figure 10). Primary perception is fast and crude and results in a wholistic percept. Primary mechanisms analyze features of brightness, color, slope, length, and motion, and present to the executive system a global figure–ground pattern for further processing.

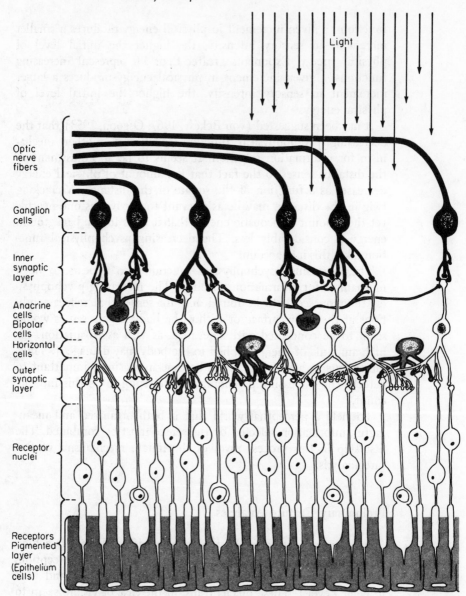

Light

Optic
nerve
fibers

Ganglion
cells

Inner
synaptic
layer

Anacrine
cells
Bipolar
cells
Horizontal
cells

Outer
synaptic
layer

Receptor
nuclei

Receptors
Pigmented
layer
(Epithelium
cells)

FIGURE 9.   *The retina. [Taken, with permission, from P. H. Lindsay and D. A. Norman,* Human information processing *(New York: Academic Press, 1972), p. 178.]*

Since perceptual processes are best understood in the case of vision, this discussion is couched primarily in terms of the visual system, but findings about other systems will be brought in where

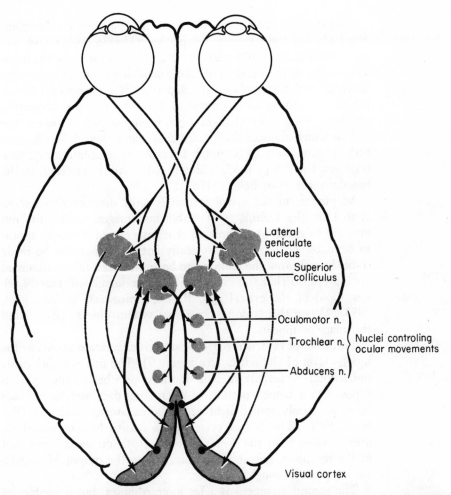

FIGURE 10.   *The visual system.* [*Taken, with permission, from P. H. Lind-say and D. A. Norman,* Human information processing (*New York: Academic Press, 1972*), *p. 170.*]

they present interesting comparisons. First, we shall consider the precortical and cortical mechanisms for feature processing.

Precortical Mechanisms

The precortical mechanisms involved in vision are the retina, the superior colliculus, and the lateral geniculate. Let us begin with the retina.

Adaptation in the Retina. The retina accomplishes the functions of adaptation and contrast. Adaptation (Helson, 1964) and contrast (von Békésy, 1967) are very widespread cognitive mechanisms. They seem to be found in all sense modalities and to occur centrally, as well as peripherally. Adaptation is a mechanism for rejecting invariance, and contrast is a mechanism for amplifying variation. That which changes much is emphasized at the expense of that which changes little, since only where there is much variation is there likely to be much covariation. Adaptation and contrast are, thus, both mechanisms of information selection, in the broader sense (von Békésy, 1967).

Adaptation in the visual system is most dramatically demonstrated by the technique of stabilizing images. Ordinarily, our eyes are in constant motion, so that images which would appear to be stable on the retina are really not. An image can be made stable by reflecting the stimulus to be viewed off a mirror mounted on the eye, so that the movements of the image will exactly follow those of the eye (Riggs, Ratliff, Cornsweet, & Cornsweet, 1953). When this is done, the visual system quickly adapts, and the image disappears.

Two lines of evidence suggest that this adaptation occurs in the bipolar layer of the retina (see Figure 9). The first is rather easily understood. Sensitivity to light is the same whether the retina is exposed to a striped pattern of alternating dark and light bands or to an evenly spread light of the same average intensity (Pribram, 1971). This is true even though sensitivity is measured for areas smaller than the bands. Thus, adaptation must occur, not at the receptors, but at some point where the output of individual receptors is brought together.

The second argument is a bit more complex, but it enables us to locate the site of adaptation more precisely. An electrode is placed outside the eye to record potentials generated by the retina, in the form of an electroretinogram. The electroretinogram includes two components: a small *a*-wave and a larger *b*-wave. It is the *b*-wave that we are interested in, for it adapts in the same way the percept does. When circulation to all of the retina except the receptors is cut off, the *b*-wave is destroyed. Thus, the *b*-wave, and the mechanism of adaptation, lie somewhere beyond the receptors, in the bipolar or ganglionic layers of the retina. When the ganglionic layer is destroyed, the *b*-wave remains. Hence, the *b*-wave and the mechanism of adaptation would seem to depend on the bipolar layer of the retina (Pribram, 1971).

It should be pointed out that there is nothing quite comparable to the retina for the other sensory systems. The retina is an outgrowth of the brain, a kind of satellite computer, that has no counterpart in any other modality, with the possible exception of audition. Yet it may be possible to generalize these findings about adaptation to other sensory systems if we go no farther than to hazard the guess that adaptation is the first mechanism of primary perception beyond the receptors in all modalities.

Contrast in the Retina. Contrast seems to be the next mechanism of primary perception. Some unwanted information has been eliminated from further consideration, and what remains must now be cleaned up for further processing. The signals, at this point, are rather noisy; they contain random perturbations introduced by the medium of transmission and by the system, itself. Such diffuse signals are sharpened by systems of lateral inhibition (von Békésy, 1967). A point of light is seen as a point of light, even though it scatters light over a large area of the retina; a pure tone is heard as a pure tone, even though it causes the entire basilar membrane to vibrate; and a vibrating point is felt as a point, even though it causes a large area of skin to vibrate.

Mechanisms of contrast occur, in vision, as early as the ganglionic layer of the retina. The receptive field of a single ganglion cell can be mapped by recording the activity of the cell while a stimulus is moved over the retina. Two patterns emerge (see Figure 11): on-center cells are fired by light in the centers of their receptive fields and inhibited by light in their surrounds, and off-center cells are inhibited by light in the centers of their receptive fields and fired by light in their surrounds. In both cases, the receptive field is divided into a center and a surround, which affect the ganglion cell in opposite ways (Rodieck, 1965). The effect of such cells is to enhance contours, to exaggerate the differences between areas differing in brightness.

Color in the Retina. The retina appears to contain three kinds of light-sensitive pigments: one with its peak sensitivity in the blue region, one with its peak sensitivity in the green region, and one with its peak sensitivity in the yellow region (MacNichol, 1964). This accounts for the fact that three wavelengths are all that is needed to produce all the colors in the visible spectrum (Young, 1801).

ON-CENTER

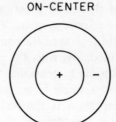

OFF-CENTER

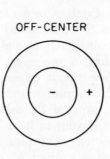

FIGURE 11. *Receptive fields of on-center and off-center ganglion cells.*

+ indicates region of excitatory fibers
- indicates region of inhibitory fibers

The Superior Colliculus and the Lateral Geniculate. The superior colliculus and the lateral geniculate nucleus of the thalamus lie enroute from the retina to the visual cortex (see Figures 10 and 12). Little is known about them. In lower vertebrates, the superior colliculus is the main terminus of the optic nerve (Milner, 1970). In mammals, it seems to process spatial information. Schneider (1967/1968) has shown that, in the hamster, the superior colliculus mediates spatial discrimination. And Bitterman (1960) has presented evidence which indicates that spatial discrimination is more primitive phylogenetically than form discrimination.

The thalamus (see Figure 12) seems to be the highest stimulus–response correlation center in animals lacking a developed cerebral cortex (Riklan & Levita, 1969). In animals that do have a developed cerebral cortex, the thalamus and the cortex seem to work closely together. The thalamus contains three kinds of nuclei: sensory nuclei, arousal nuclei, and association nuclei. It is only the sensory nuclei that are of concern to us here. The most important of these are the lateral geniculate nuclei, which process visual information, and the medial geniculate nuclei, which process auditory information.

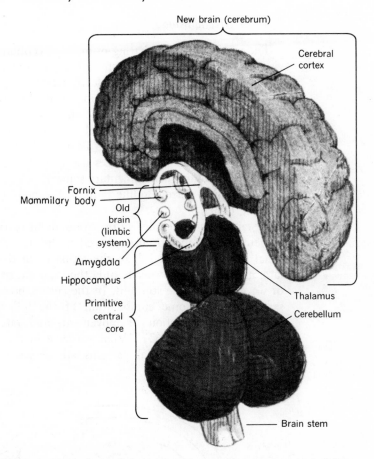

FIGURE 12.   *The brain.* [*Adapted from p. 34 of* Introduction to psychology, *Fifth Edition, by E. R. Hilgard, R. C. Atkinson, and R. L. Atkinson, copyright, 1971, by Harcourt Brace Jovanovich, Inc., and reproduced with their permission.*]

Single-cell recordings indicate that the lateral geniculate nuclei in monkeys mediate brightness and color discrimination (Wiesel & Hubel, 1966). Evidence exists (DeValois & Jacobs, 1968) that this is accomplished by "on" and "off" processes; some cells are activated by short wavelengths but inhibited by long wavelengths. This is consistent with a postulated organization into black–white, blue–yellow, and red–green opponent processes (Hering, 1920). Some such organization may account for the fact that red–green color blind persons can still see yellow; whereas loss of red and green processes in the retina could not account for this, loss of a red–green opponent process in the lateral geniculate could.

Cortical Mechanisms

The cortical areas mediating primary perception seem to be the visual, auditory, and somesthetic areas (see Figure 13). Damage to these areas produces deficits clearly related to primitive perceptual mechanisms, such as blind spots in the visual field, silent regions in the auditory area, or difficulty in discriminating patterns (Milner, 1970). A person deprived of the visual area cannot see patterns at all; he is object-blind (Teuber, 1960). Electrical stimulation in the visual area produces flashes of light; in the auditory area, buzzing and other elementary sounds; and in the somesthetic area, itching in corresponding parts of the body (Penfield & Rasmussen, 1950).

By far the most detailed information about cortical mechanisms of perception comes from single-cell recordings. To obtain an optimal response from a cell in the retina or in the lateral geniculate, it is necessary to specify only the location, size, and intensity or wavelength of the stimulus. In the cortex, however, it is necessary to specify some combination of the following properties: length, slope, direction of movement, and rate of movement (Hubel & Wiesel, 1962). What we have in the cortex are local pattern analyzers. Spatial patterns are detected by length and

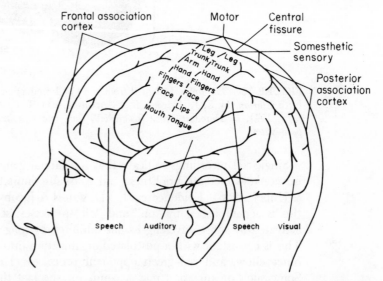

FIGURE 13. *The cerebral cortex.* [*From p. 451 of* Elements of psychology, *Second Edition, by David Kretch, Richard S. Crutchfield, and Norman Livson. Copyright © 1958 by David Krech and Richard S. Crutchfield. Copyright © 1969 by Alfred A. Knopf, Inc. Reprinted by permission of the publisher.*]

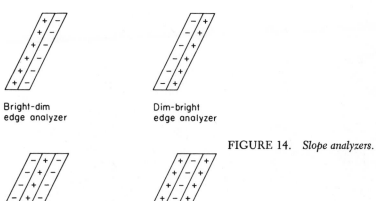

Bright-dim
edge analyzer

Dim-bright
edge analyzer

FIGURE 14.   *Slope analyzers.*

Slit analyzer

Line analyzer

+ indicates region of excitatory fibers
− indicates region of inhibitory fibers

slope analyzers, and temporal patterns, by motion analyzers. Analyzers that are specific with respect to retinal position feed into analyzers that are more general in that their response is independent of retinal position. These analyzers appear to be innate (Hubel & Wiesel, 1963). It is important to note that information from the two eyes has come together by this point (Morgan, 1965). These local pattern analyzers respond more vigorously when the stimuli are viewed with both eyes than when they are viewed with only one eye (Hubel & Wiesel, 1962). The receptive fields of four types of slope analyzers are shown in Figure 14, and a simple wiring diagram for the construction of a slope analyzer out of on-center units is shown in Figure 15.

Because the two eyes are processed separately before the cortex is reached, the aftereffects of stimulation processed precortically do not transfer from one eye to the other. You can demonstrate this for yourself quite easily. Cover one eye with your hand for a minute or so, to dark adapt it, and then place this book flat on the table. Now hold this page up, perpendicular to the book, so that the page's edge touches your nose. Your left eye will then be viewing the preceding page and your right eye the following one. The page seen by the eye that was covered will appear lighter than the one seen by the other eye. Brightness adaptation is lateral and does not transfer from one eye to the other. The same is true for color adaptation.

Lateral effects can also be observed in other systems; for exam-

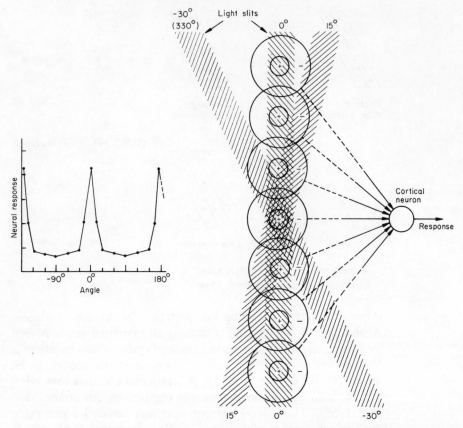

FIGURE 15. *The construction of a slope analyser out of on-center units.* [*Taken, with permission, from P. H. Lindsay and D. A. Norman,* Human information processing (*New York: Academic Press, 1972), p. 101.*]

ple, temperature adaptation is lateral. The effect can be obtained by immersing one hand in hot water and one in cold water for a while and then putting both in the same luke-warm water. The luke-warm water will seem cool to the hand that was in the hot water and warm to the hand that was in the cold water.

But adaptation also occurs at the level of the cortex. Because information from the two eyes has come together by the time the cortex is reached, aftereffects of stimulation of the cortical analyzers are central and do transfer from one eye to the other. Motion aftereffects are, perhaps, the most dramatic. If you roll on the grass and then stop, the world will seem to spin around in the opposite direction; if you stare at a waterfall for a minute or so and then look at the cliff next to it, a portion of the cliff that is about the width of the waterfall will appear to move upward

(Adams, 1834). These effects transfer from one eye to the other; that is, if the adapting stimulus is presented to one eye, the after-effect can be obtained in the other eye. The aftereffect is stronger in the adapted eye, however, indicating that some of these complex analyzers occur before information from the two eyes is brought together.

Slope aftereffects also transfer binocularly. These are called figural aftereffects. If a person fixates a curved inspection line for a minute or so and then looks at a straight test line, the test line appears curved in the opposite direction (Gibson, 1933). If, after fixating a straight inspection line, he looks at a straight test line that forms a slight angle with it, the test line appears rotated away from the inspection line (Gibson, 1937). These effects are easier to obtain if the stimuli are viewed through a rolled-up piece of paper, or reduction tube.

Precortical–Cortical Interaction

Minsky (1970) has suggested that the brain represents the world essentially in terms of a line drawing, as in a coloring book, and then fills in brightness and color information later. A study by Murch (1972) suggests that this view is correct. His study is based on the McCullough effect (McCullough, 1965). This effect is obtained by presenting a field of green and black vertical stripes, a field of red and black horizontal stripes, a field of green and black vertical stripes, and so forth, in temporal alternation. Afterward, a field of white and black vertical stripes will appear reddish, and a field of white and black horizontal stripes will appear greenish. What Murch showed is that aftereffects of the slope stimulation transfer from one eye to the other but aftereffects of the color stimulation do not. Apparently, the cortical analyzers represent only slope information (a coloring-book representation), and continuing input from the precortical mechanisms, presumably the lateral geniculate, is necessary in order to fill color in. The McCullough effect has also been obtained using motion instead of slope (Stromeyer & Mansfield, 1970), and motion, but not color, aftereffects transfer binocularly (Murch, 1974).

Garner's (1970; Garner & Felfoldy, 1970) notion of the integrality of stimulus dimensions seems relevant here. Integrality is the extent to which stimulus dimensions tend to be processed together, presumably because of the way the perceptual system is innately organized. Two criteria of integrality are based on speed classification tasks, and a third on a similarity judgment task.

Assume that you are given a deck of cards, half with large circles

on them and half with small circles on them, and you are asked
to sort them quickly into two piles, one for the large circles and
one for the small circles. Your sorting time is recorded. You are
now given a second deck of cards in which all the cards with large
circles are marked with red and all those with small circles are
marked with blue. We say that size and color are redundant in this
case (see Figure 16), because if you know the size you can infer
the color, and if you know the color you can infer the size. You
are asked to sort this second deck, again on the basis of size. The
question is, Will the redundant color dimension help you; will it
enable you to sort more quickly? The answer depends on whether
color and size are presented in an integral or a nonintegral fashion.
If it is the circles themselves that are colored, the redundant color
dimension will facilitate sorting more than if it is an area adjacent

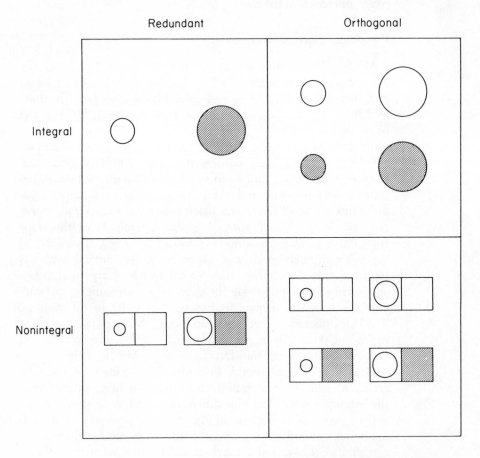

FIGURE 16. *Redundancy, orthogonality, and integrality.*

to each circle that is colored (see Figure 16). This gives us one criterion of integrality: Dimensions A and B are considered to be integral to the extent that making B redundant with A facilitates sorting on A (Garner & Felfoldy, 1970).

Now, assume that you are given a third deck of cards. In this deck also, half the cards have large circles on them and half small circles, and half are marked with red and half with blue. But now half of the cards with each size of circles are marked with red, and half with blue. We say that size and color are orthogonal in this case (see Figure 16), because knowing the size tells you nothing about the color and knowing the color tells you nothing about the size. You are also asked to sort this deck on the basis of size. The question this time is, will the orthogonal color dimension interfere with sorting; will it force you to sort more slowly than when no color dimension was present? Again, the answer depends on whether color and size are presented in an integral or a nonintegral fashion. The orthogonal color dimension will interfere with sorting more if it is integral with size than if it is nonintegral. This gives us a second criterion of integrality: Dimensions A and B are considered to be integral to the extent that making B orthogonal to A interferes with sorting on A (Garner & Felfoldy, 1970).

A third criterion of integrality is based on a task involving judgments of similarity. Assume that you are asked to give a number reflecting the similarity of a large red circle and a small red circle, and another number reflecting the similarity of a large red circle and a large blue circle. In the first case, the stimuli differ in size only, and, in the second case, they differ in color only. Let us say that you judge the large red circle and the small red circle to differ by 2 units, and the large red circle and the large blue circle to differ by 3 units. The question here is, what number will you give when asked to compare the small red circle and the large blue circle, which differ along two dimensions? Once more, the answer depends on integrality. If the stimuli are integral, they will differ by $\sqrt{2^2 + 3^2} = 3.6$ units (the distance along the hypoteneuse in a two-dimensional Euclidean space). If they are nonintegral, they will differ by $2 + 3 = 5$ units (the distance around the corner in a two-dimensional city-block space). This gives us a third criterion of integrality: Dimensions A and B are considered to be integral to the extent that they combine according to a Euclidean, rather than a city-block, metric (Garner & Felfoldy, 1970; Hyman & Well, 1968).

Integrality seems to be a matter of degree. Some dimensions, such as the hue and saturation of a single patch, seem to be integral by all of these criteria. Others, such as the hue of one patch and the saturation of another or the diameter of a circle and the angle of the enclosed radius, seem to be nonintegral by all of these criteria. Still others, such as the horizontal and vertical location of a dot, seem to be optionally integral, in that they are treated as integral where integrality is facilitating and as nonintegral where integrality would be interfering.

Presumably, these various degrees of integrality will eventually be explainable in terms of where in the visual system information from the two dimensions is combined. Hue and saturation both seem to be processed precortically, in the lateral geniculate, and they are highly integral. Information from different figures and information from size and angle within a single figure would, as we shall see, seem to be processed beyond the cortical analyzers, and both are highly nonintegral. There is some indication that spatial information may be handled both precortically, in the superior colliculus, and cortically; and this may account for its optional status.

The Analogue Model

Primary perception seems to create an analogue model of the world, in which a great deal of information is processed in parallel. Analogue processes are to be contrasted with digital processes. A slide rule is an analogue mechanism, and a desk calculator is a digital one. A graph or a model is an analogue representation of a system; a table of numbers or an equation is a digital one. A digital process assumes discrete states; the final digit on a desk calculator, for example, can be a 1 or a 2, but nothing in between. An analogue process can, in principle, at least, vary continuously from one state to another; a slide rule can be set anywhere between 1 and 2. Moreover, analogue processes often process information in parallel, while digital processes often process information serially. A wind tunnel model, for example, takes many factors into account simultaneously, in a continuous fashion; while a simulation on a digital computer has to deal with one factor at a time, in a discrete fashion. Although we shall see evidence for digital, serial processes in later chapters, primary perception seems to be analogue and parallel. The analogue model represents things and locates them in time and space.

The Perception of Things

We perceive things. But what is a thing? A thing would seem to be a collection of properties that cohere in space and time, that are perhaps also similar, and that interact in predicting other properties. Both primary and secondary perceptual processes seem to be required to represent a thing fully.

Consider a face. The energies from a face are spatially and temporally contiguous and tend to be similar in terms of brightness, color, slope, and motion. Thus, as we shall see shortly, they would tend to be grouped together in the analogue model. We tend to partition the world on the basis of spatiotemporal contiguity and similarity without information as to the predictive value of such partitions. The assumption of a system that does this is that contiguity and similarity lumps are predictive lumps.

The analogue model appears to combine predictors by adding or averaging them. This is a satisfactory solution to the problem of combining information if the predictors are additive, and proximity and similarity of properties would seem to be additive predictors of at least the fact that we are confronted with a thing of some sort. However, they would seldom be additive predictors of what kind of thing we are confronted with and, hence, of what other things might be expected to follow. While determination of thingness seems to be accomplished by primary perception, secondary perception seems to be required for more precise identification of a thing.

Several lines of evidence point to the special importance of contour in primary perception. When a continuous brightness gradient is superimposed on a uniformly lighted, textureless field (a ganzfeld, see Figure 17), the gradient is not perceived. But,

FIGURE 17. A *ganzfeld*. [*Taken, with permission, from D. Krech and R. S. Crutchfield*, Elements of psychology (*New York: Knopf, 1958*), *p. 85.*]

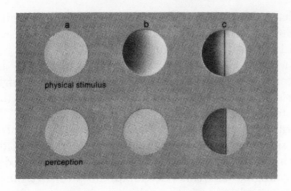

FIGURE 18. *Assimilation within a contour.* [*Taken, with permission, from D. Krech and R. S. Crutchfield,* Elements of psychology (*New York: Knopf, 1958*), p. 86.]

when a contour (a line) is placed across the direction of the gradient, the field suddenly appears to be divided, at the contour, into a uniform dark gray portion and a uniform light gray portion (see Figure 18) (Avant, 1965). Of course, if the surface is textured, brightness gradients will be perceived.

The rule seems to be that assimilation occurs within a contour and contrast occurs across a contour. It should be noted that both assimilation and contrast, in this sense, are examples of assimilation, in the broader sense in which it is opposed to accommodation. Both distort incoming information so that it will fit better the information-processing requirements of the system. Though this use of terms is somewhat confusing, this is the accepted terminology, and the context should make clear which sense of assimilation is intended.

It is presumably this same mechanism of assimilation within an area marked off by a contour that accounts for the fact that a solid green lawn appears solid green, when we have green receptors only near the center of our visual field and no color receptors at all in the periphery. Without such a mechanism, the lawn would appear green only near the center and gray at the periphery. This seems to be the "coloring book" mechanism again. It is presumably this same mechanism that accounts for filling in of the blindspot, that part of the retina through which the optic nerve passes and which, therefore, contains no light-sensitive cells.

You can demonstrate the blind spot and filling in of the blind spot on yourself by looking at Figure 19. Close your right eye and fixate the X in Figure 19a. By moving the page toward and away from you, you can find a distance where the square will disappear. At this distance, the square is falling on the blind spot in the retina of your left eye. Close your right eye again, and fixate the X in Figure 19b. You will find that there is no distance that will produce a break in the bar. Even though, at the same dis-

×

(a)

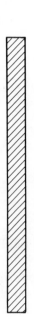

                                                        ×

(b)

FIGURE 19.   *A simple demonstration of assimilation within a contour.*

tance as in the first demonstration, a portion of the bar falls on the blind spot and is not detected. It is guessed in at a higher stage by the mechanism of assimilation.

Contour analysis seems to involve innate mechanisms. Both children who have not seen any line drawings for the first year of life (Hochberg & Brooks, 1962) and nonliterate peoples who have never seen line drawings (Gibson, 1969) can identify line drawings of familiar objects on first seeing them. Another fact that points to the same conclusion is that, in the history of art (Gregory, 1970) and in the development of drawing in children, line drawings precede shaded drawings.

We seem to group similar contours together as parts of the same object or thing. Grouping by proximity and by similarity

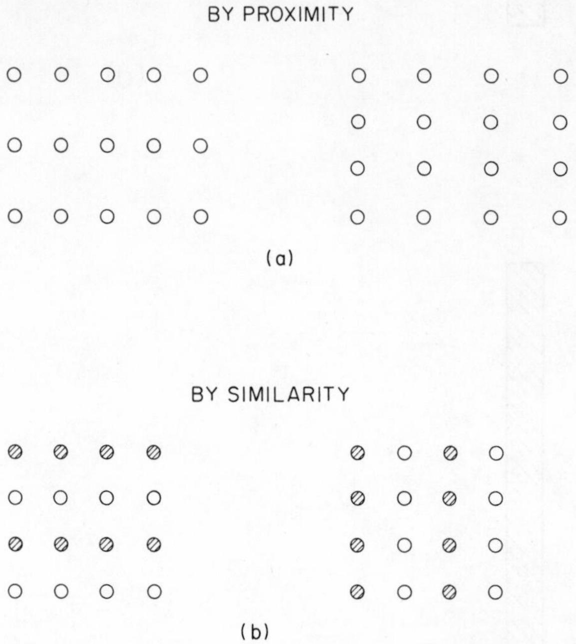

BY PROXIMITY

(a)

BY SIMILARITY

(b)

FIGURE 20.   *Perceptual grouping by proximity and similarity.*

is illustrated in Figure 20. In Figure 20a, near items are perceived as "going together," thus yielding the appearance of rows on the left and columns on the right. In Figure 20b, similar items are perceived as going together, yielding the appearance of rows on the left and columns on the right (Wertheimer, 1958).

Similarity can be defined in many ways. Items may be similar in brightness, as in Figure 20b, or in color, shape, or motion. Grouping by color is what is involved in color blindness tests. A page is filled with dots of several colors forming the background and dots of a single color being arranged in the shape of a numeral. Normal people can see the numeral, but color-blind people cannot. An important point with respect to contour is that grouping of color will not occur, even for normal people, if the colors fill uniform areas so that there is no brightness gradient. The colors must be presented as dots, which contrast in brightness with the white surface of the page. Without these contours, the effect is the same as in the ganzfeld without a contour.

That grouping can occur on the basis of similarity of motion is easy to see. When a group of people moves through a stationary crowd, the people in the group seem to cohere as a perceptual

○ △ ○ △

○ △ ○ △   FIGURE 21. *Perceptual grouping by "shape."*

○ △ ○ △

○ △ ○ △

unit. Similarly, clouds or birds moving by one another at different altitudes cohere as perceptual units.

The situation becomes more complex in the case of shape. Figure 21 demonstrates grouping on the basis of what is often presumed to be shape. But this grouping could be on the basis of length, slope, or angle, and need not be on the basis of overall shape. Olson and Attneave (1970) attempted to isolate the factors of length, slope, and angle. They found grouping on the basis of length (or texture density—it does not seem possible to unconfound these factors) and slope, but not on the basis of angle. Their slope and angle stimuli are shown in Figure 22. Slope yielded phenomenal grouping and fast reaction times in identifying the odd quadrant; angle yielded no phenomenal grouping and slow reaction times in identifying the odd quadrant. It is important to note that Olson and Attneave took the care to control average slope in constructing their angle stimuli, so that angle, itself, had to be discriminated. The reason grouping is obtained in Figure 21 is, apparently, not because triangles and circles can be represented at

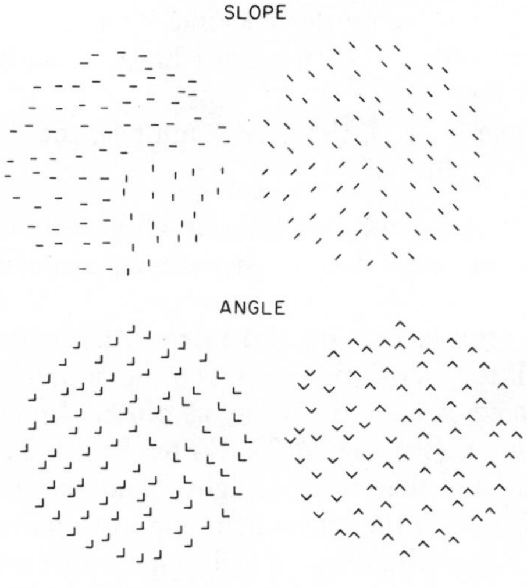

SLOPE

ANGLE

FIGURE 22. *Perceptual grouping by slope but not angle. [Taken, with permission, from R. K. Olson and F. Attneave, "What variables produce similarity grouping?" American Journal of Psychology, 1970, 83, 1–21.]*

the level of primary perception, but because triangles and circles differ in their average slopes.

Beck (1967) has shown that brightness and slope differences combine additively in determining strength of grouping. This is consistent with the notion of parallel processing in an analogue system.

The Perception of Time and Space

Things are located in time and space, and primary perception seems to represent the three dimensions of space and the time dimension in a single analogue model. Indeed, nowhere do the analogue properties of primary perception seem to show up so clearly as in the perception of time and space.

Apparent movement provides a most instructive example. Apparent movement is what makes motion pictures appear to move. The simplest demonstration of apparent movement is produced by flashing two lights successively in a dark room. The temporal interval is crucial. If the interval is too short, both lights will appear to flash simultaneously; and, if the interval is too long, the appearance will be of one light flashing and then a second light flashing. At the optimal interval, however, the appearance will be of a single light coming on in the position of the first light, moving to the position of the second light, and going off. Intensity and distance are also important. These relations are expressed in Korte's laws (Korte, 1915):

(*a*) The greater the distance between the two lights, the greater must be the intensity or the greater the time interval.

(*b*) The greater the intensity, the greater must be the distance or the less the time interval.

(*c*) The greater the time interval, the greater must be the distance or the less the intensity.

Thus, spatial, temporal, and intensity factors are all important. The rapid calculation of all these factors suggests an analogue mechanism.

Quality as well as intensity factors are also represented in this analogue model. Thus, all the factors that we saw to be important in grouping seem to be represented. Quality factors can be demonstrated by using three lights (see Figure 23; Korte, 1915). The center light is flashed first, and then the side lights. The question is, to which of the side lights will the center light appear to move? If one side light is closer than the other, it will appear to move to the closer one, demonstrating grouping by proximity (see Fig-

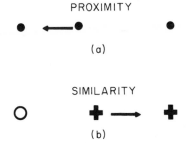

PROXIMITY

(a)

SIMILARITY

(b)

FIGURE 23. *Proximity and simi-larity in apparent motion. [Taken, with permission, from A. Korte, "Kinema-toskopische Untersuchungen, "Zeit-schrift für Psychologie, 1915, 72, 194–296.]*

ure 23a). If one side light is the same shape as the center light and the other a different shape, the center light will appear to move to the position of the identically shaped light, demonstrating grouping on the basis of something like similarity of slope (Figure 23b).

Finally, the third dimension, depth in space, is also represented in this model. This is suggested by the demonstration illustrated in Figure 24, where following presentation of 1 by 2 gives the impression of rotation into the third dimension. It is also suggested by an experiment that asks whether it is retinal distance or inferred (actual) distance in three-dimensional space that is important in Korte's laws (Corbin, 1942). These two kinds of distance can be separated experimentally by presenting the stimuli in a plane that is not normal to the line of sight, as in Figure 25. When this is done, the optimal time interval for apparent movement turns out to be the one that corresponds to the inferred (actual) distance between the lights in three-dimensional space.

Corbin (1942) also asked a similar question of grouping. We have seen that grouping occurs on the basis of proximity. We can ask, then, whether it is proximity in terms of retinal distance or proximity in terms of inferred distance in three-dimensional space that is important. These two kinds of distance can be separated, as before, by presenting dots in a plane that is not normal to the line of sight, as in Figure 26. If the dots are arranged so that they would be grouped in rows on the basis of retinal distance and in columns on the basis of inferred distance, they will be perceived in columns.

This much tells us that primary perception is capable of repre-

FIGURE 24. *Depth in apparent motion.*

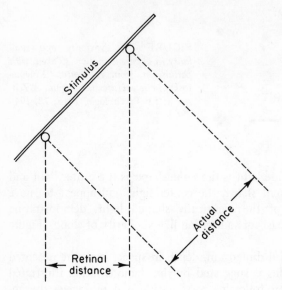

Observer

FIGURE 25. *Retinal and inferred distance in apparent motion.*

senting three-dimensional space. But it is obviously also capable of representing two-dimensional space. What factors determine whether a stimulus will be represented as two-dimensional or three-dimensional in primary perception? The answer seems to be simplicity: Where alternative perceptual organizations are possible, the simpler will tend to be perceived. Let us see what this means.

The principle of simplicity seems to be quite general, applying to the dominance of one two-dimensional organization over another, as well as to the dominance of a three-dimensional organization over a two-dimensional one. Figure 27a could be perceived as being composed of the elements shown in Figure 27b, or it

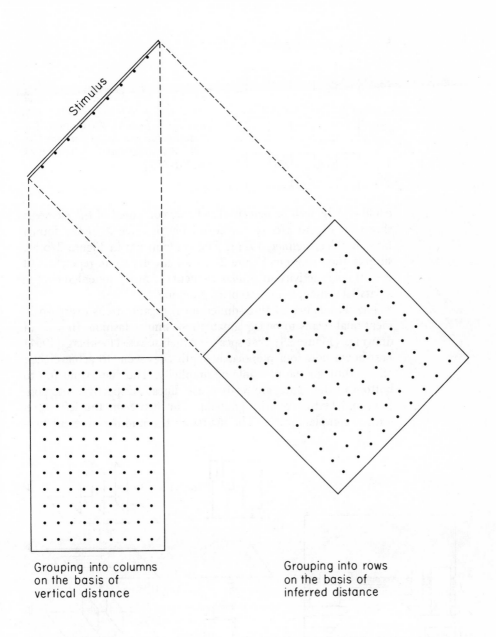

Grouping into columns
on the basis of
vertical distance

Grouping into rows
on the basis of
inferred distance

FIGURE 26.   *Retinal and inferred distance in perceptual grouping.*

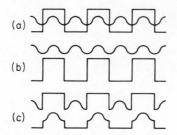

(a)

(b)

(c)

FIGURE 27. *Simplicity in two-dimensional perception. [Taken, with permission, from M. Wertheimer, "Untersuchungen zur Lehre von der Gestalt,"* Psychologisches Forschung, 1923, **4**, 301–350.]

could equally well be perceived as being composed of the elements shown in Figure 27c, yet we invariably perceive it in the former fashion (Wertheimer, 1923). The components in Figure 27b are simpler than those in Figure 27c; they involve more repetition. It is as though activity in similar elements is mutually enhancing in a parallel system, as in perceptual grouping.

The dominance of three-dimensional organizations over two-dimensional seems to be explainable in a similar fashion. In a set of drawings (Figure 28) that speak for themselves, Hochberg (1964) has shown how four monocular depth cues seem to achieve their effects through the principle of simplicity. The cues, from top to bottom in the figure, are relative size, linear perspective, interposition, and texture–density gradient. The figure on the left represents a complete scene. The figures in the middle represent two-

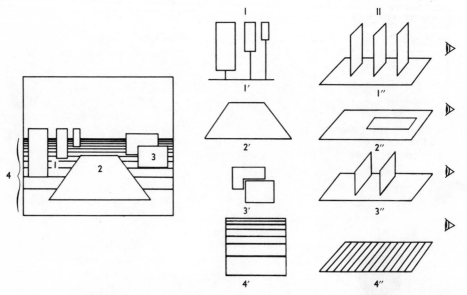

FIGURE 28. *Simplicity in three-dimensional perception: The monocular cues for depth.* [*Taken, with permission, from J. E. Hochberg,* Perception (*Englewood Cliffs, New Jersey: Prentice-Hall, 1964), p. 88.*]

dimensional interpretations of portions of the scene, and the figures on the right represent three-dimensional interpretations of the same portions of the scene. In every case, the three-dimensional interpretation is simpler. There are reasons for believing that interposition involves mechanisms of secondary perception, and, consequently, it will be discussed in the next chapter.

An effect which appears quite similar may, in fact, be due to a quite different mechanism. A line drawing of all 12 edges of a cube (see Figure 29) can be perceived either three-dimensionally, as a cube, or two-dimensionally, as simply a pattern of lines on the page (Kopfermann, 1930). Many drawings similar to Figure 29 are possible. Hochberg and Brooks (1960), using cubes and other figures, have shown that the strength of the three-dimensional organization is a function of the extent to which it results in a reduction in number of angles, different angles, and continuous lines.

While it seems possible to understand the Hochberg (1964) examples (with the probable exception of interposition) in terms of something no more complex than uniformity of texture density or uniformity of line length, the Hochberg and Brooks (1960) results point rather definitely to angles as being important in the determination of three-dimensionality. Similarly, Attneave (1972) has obtained suggestive evidence that, in the perception of orientation in three-dimensional space, the tendency to equalize angles is stronger than the tendency to equalize lengths. The problem here is that simplicity in the perception of angles would seem to imply parallel processing of angles, yet the findings of Olson and Attneave (1970) indicate that angles are not processed in parallel.

Actually, there are two mechanisms which could account for simplicity in perception. One is that simplicity is inherent in perception, that the parallel, analogue processes of perception tend, as we have suggested, toward an end state of simplicity (Mach, 1959). The other is that simplicity is inherent in the world and that the simplicity in perception is no more than a reflection of this; a variety of retinal patterns are produced by a single stimulus, and we have learned to infer a single stimulus on the basis of such patterns (Brunswick, 1954; Gibson, 1950). It turns out to be very difficult to decide between these views (Attneave,

 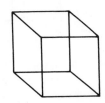

FIGURE 29. *Another demonstration of simplicity in three-dimensional perception. [Taken, with permission, from H. Kopfermann, "Psychologische untersuchungen uber die Wirkung zweidimensionaler Darstellungen korperlicher Gebilde," Psychologisches Forschung, 1930, 13, 293–364.]*

1972). Actually, they are not mutually exclusive. One possibility is that such elementary cues (Hubel & Wiesel, 1962, 1968) as brightness, motion, length, and slope tend toward a simple organization in the analogue model on the basis of innate principles of organization, while angle and more complex cues tend to lead to simple inferences on the basis of experience. In any case, we shall consider inference on the basis of complex cues in the next chapter.

The principle of simplicity seems to apply also when information is integrated across successive moments in time. If a wire cube is rotated (see Figure 30), the impression of depth is inescapable. This is called the *kinetic depth effect*. The effect is obtained even if the wire form is rotated between a light source and a rear-projection screen, so that only the two-dimensional shadow appears on the screen, and it is obtained even with nonsense shapes (Wallach & O'Connell, 1953). It is apparently simpler to see one figure moving in three-dimensional space than to see many different figures moving into one another in two-dimensional space.

What seems to be involved here is the motion parallax cue to depth. Motion parallax can be demonstrated by moving your head from side to side. Near objects move farther than distant objects, yielding a gradient of motions, comparable to a texture–density gradient (Gibson, 1950). Perhaps it is simpler to perceive a single displacement at different distances in three-dimensional space than many different displacements in two-dimensional space.

Yet motion parallax does not seem that much different from binocular parallax. Motion parallax can be demonstrated in another way, one which makes it easier to understand its relationship to binocular parallax. Instead of moving your head from side to side, open and close your eyes alternately. This will produce apparent movement. Again, near objects appear to move farther than distant objects. Binocular parallax occurs when you leave both eyes open. The subjective impression produced by binocular parallax is not the same as that produced by motion parallax, so there must be important differences. Yet the principle of simplicity would

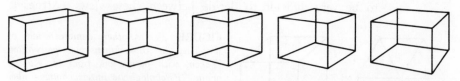

FIGURE 30. *Simplicity in three-dimensional perception: Motion cues. Taken, with permission, from J. E. Hochberg,* Perception *(Englewood Cliffs, New Jersey: Prentice-Hall, 1964), p. 93.]*

seem to be involved in both cases. It would certainly seem simpler to use both eyes to construct a single perceptual world than to construct a different perceptual world with each eye. The gradient of retinal disparities may function much like a texture–density gradient in creating an impression of depth. It is important to note that information from the two eyes has been brought together by the time the motion analyzers are reached (Morgan, 1965) and that the capacity to use both motion parallax and binocular parallax cues for depth appears to be innate (Bower, 1964; Gibson, 1969).

A kind of bilateral parallax can occur in other sense modalities. If two identical tones are presented in immediate succession, one to each ear, a single tone will be heard that appears to come from the side of the head to which the first tone was presented. Indeed, the most important basis for screening out irrelevant auditory input, as at a cocktail party, is the primary cue of location (Cherry, 1953). This is why it is so difficult to sort out different voices on a monaural tape recorder or with a single hearing aid. Bilateral parallax has also been obtained with touch (von Békésy, 1967). If two fingers are stimulated by the same series of tactile clicks, but with a difference in the time of arrival of the clicks, the sensation will be experienced as coming from the region between the fingers. A similar effect can be obtained by stimulating the two knees in the same fashion. The experience in these latter two cases is, needless to say, a strange one.

Adaptation Level and the Primary Constancies

Both the primary constancies and adaptation level have to do with the apparent magnitudes of sensory properties of things; and, in both cases, these magnitudes seem to be perceived in relation to a background magnitude, or adaptation level. Let us begin with primary constancy, which seems to be a special case, and then consider adaptation level, which seems to be the general case.

Constancy, in general, refers to the fact that perceived properties of objects appear more nearly constant over certain changes in the environment than are the energies that strike the receptor surfaces. The constancies most frequently studied are brightness, color, size, and shape. These seem to fall into two categories, however.

Brightness constancy and color constancy seem to have to do with magnitudes; the property being judged and the change in the environment both relate to amount of energy. Brightness constancy is illustrated by the fact that snow seems white and coal black, whether in sunlight or moonlight. Light energy is being judged, and it is light energy that changes from day to night. Color constancy is illustrated by the fact that the sky in a color photograph seems pale blue, the leaves green, and the apples red, whether it is viewed outdoors or in the yellowish light of a tungsten bulb. From the point of view of a color unit anywhere in the system, however, this is the same as light energy; to a red unit, a red light is a high-energy stimulus, and a blue light is a low-energy stimulus. Thus, color constancy may also be regarded as a magnitude constancy.

Although a similar argument can be applied to the case of length and slope analyzers, the status of both size and shape constancy appears to be mixed, and both are better discussed in the next chapter.

Brightness constancy has been measured under conditions where the brightness of the target and the brightness of the background were known precisely (Wallach, 1948). In the experiment depicted in Figure 31, the subject's task was to adjust the brightness of the central disk on the right until it appeared to match that of the central disk on the left. The results were simple: Over a wide range of conditions, the stimuli were judged as being of the same brightness when the ratio of the intensity of the disk to the intensity of the surround was the same in both stimuli. This mechanism cannot be perfect, however, for snow does appear brighter in the sunlight than in the moonlight. While comparable studies have not been done for color constancy, it is presumed that the same underlying mechanism is involved.

In the perception of magnitudes, as in the perception of time

FIGURE 31.   *Brightness constancy.*

and space, a kind of simplicity seems to be achieved. We perceive fewer brightnesses and hues than strike our sensory surfaces. And, in both the perception of magnitudes and the perception of time and space, some kind of parallel processing would seem to be involved, which enables parts to be perceived in relation to the wholes in which they are contained.

Adaptation-level effects differ from constancy effects only in including a memory component. Adaptation level is illustrated by the fact that the outdoors seems very bright when you come out of a dark place. Here, also, the part is perceived in relation to the whole, but the whole includes a memory of prior stimulation. While this memory lingers, an object that previously seemed middle gray will now seem brighter. Once the memory has faded, however, the middle gray object will again appear middle gray, and we will be left with brightness constancy. Adaptation-level effects would seem to be the more inclusive category, with the primary constancies being special cases in which the memory component has fallen to zero.

The same principle seems to apply to what has been called the transposition of relations. Let us say, for example, that a person learns that dark berries are good to eat and white berries are not. Let us say that he learns this during the day, when the dark berries reflect 10 units of light energy and the white berries reflect 100. If he goes out berry picking in the evening when the dark berries put out 1 unit and the white berries 10, he will continue to pick the dark berries. If he simply responded to the uncorrected stimulus, he would have picked the white berries in the evening, because they, like the berries he found good during the day, reflected 10 units of light energy. We say that this person has transposed relations; he learned the relationship "darker," and he picked the darker berries both during the day and during the evening. We can be more precise than this, however.

The mathematical theory of adaptation level (Helson, 1964) has been applied to this general problem with remarkable success (Zeiler, 1963). Let us see how this is done, but simplifying the mathematics somewhat. To express the berry-picking situation in terms of adaptation level, say that the average amount of light energy is 40 during the day and 4 in the evening. Then the dark berries are represented by a ratio of $10/40 = .25$ during the day and a ratio of $1/4 = .25$ at night. What our friend learned during the day was that berries whose intensity was 1/4 the adaptation level are good, and what he picked in the evening were berries whose intensity was 1/4 the adaptation level, the same ratio and the same berries.

But this is simply brightness constancy. Let us see how memory can be added to the adaptation level. Assume that a subject is shown three different stimuli, with the values 1, 2, and 3, and that he learns to choose the middle one. (The numbers 1, 2, and 3 simply represent three different sensory magnitudes, for example, three different brightnesses, three different loudnesses, or three different weights.) The adaptation level will be $(1 + 2 + 3)/3 = 2$. The ratio of the positive stimulus will, therefore, be $2/2 = 1.00$. What the subject has learned to do, according to the theory, is to select a stimulus with a ratio of 1.00.

Assume that the subject is then shown three different stimuli, with the values 4, 5, and 6. The question is, which will he choose? In computing the adaptation level here, we must take into account not only these stimuli but also the preceding stimuli whose effect on the current adaptation level is still felt. What we need is a weighted average of the adaptation level that 4, 5, and 6 alone would produce and the adaptation level that 1, 2, and 3 alone would produce. Since the effects of 1, 2, and 3 are in a fading memory system, they will be weighted less, the longer it has been between training and testing. Let us arbitrarily weight them as follows:

$$AL = .75(5) + .25(2) = 4.25.$$

The resulting stimulus ratios will then be .94, 1.18, and 1.41. The subject will pick the stimulus with the ratio closest to 1.00, which, in this case, is the least intense stimulus. Transposition has failed in this case. Such failure would not be predicted by the simple notion that the subject learns the relation "middle" (Kohler, 1929), which, as we shall see later, would seem to require executive operations. The reason for the failure is that the subject was not given time to adapt fully to the new stimuli. He is still partially adapted to the training stimuli.

Let us see what happens when the temporary memory for the training stimuli has faded. The weighting will then be as follows:

$$AL = 1.00(5) + 0(2) = 5.$$

The resulting stimulus ratios will then be .8, 1.0, and 1.2, and the subject will pick the intermediate stimulus, since its ratio now equals the positive training ratio of 1.0. Transposition has succeeded in this case. In cases such as this, the theory thus predicts failure of transposition on an immediate test, but transposition on a delayed test. Such results have been obtained (Rudel, 1957; Thompson, 1955).

The mechanism that computes adaptation level seems to do

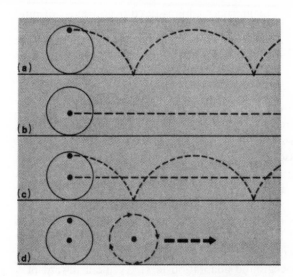

FIGURE 32. *The partitioning of motion.* [*Taken, with permission, from D. Krech, R. S. Crutchfield, and N. Livson,* Elements of psychology, *2d ed.* (*New York: Knopf, 1969*), *p. 225.*]

more than just compute an overall adaptation level. What it seems to do is compute an overall adaptation level for the scene, then separate adaptation levels for components of the scene. We have already encountered a good example of this process. When there is no contour in the ganzfeld, a single average is computed. When there is a contour, an average is computed for each side of the contour (see page 46), and, as Wallach's work suggests, each of these adaptation levels is perceived in relation to the overall adaptation level.

This partitioning of adaptation levels can also be seen in the case of motion perception. If one point, as in Figure 32a, moves in a cycloidal path and another point, as in Figure 32b, moves in a straight-line path, they will be perceived, as in Figure 32d, as having a common forward motion, and (a) will be seen as describing a circle with respect to this common motion. Similarly, if one point (a) moves in a circular path and another (b) moves in a vertical path, (a) and (b) will appear to move up and down together, with (a) appearing to move toward and away from (b) in a horizontal path (Johansson, 1950). As Hochberg (1957) describes it,

> In general, a "figural hierarchy" of motion is perceived: first, a static background; next, and in reference to this, the common motion; and highest, the components of motion relative to the common motion [p. 79].

Partitioning of adaptation levels seems also to occur in the perception of reward magnitude by rats. Consider the following two sequences of reward magnitudes administered over a series of nine trials.

> *Series A:* 1 5 5 1 1 5 1 5 5
> *Series B:* 1 1 1 1 1 1 1 1 5

In the first case, the animal receives a 1-gm reward on the first trial, a 5-gm reward on the second trial, and so on. In the second case, the animal receives a 1-gm reward on each of the first eight trials and then is suddenly switched to a 5-gm reward on the last trial. The first case is like the ganzfeld without the contour. The animals compute a single overall adaptation level and respond on the basis of the average amount of reward (Hulse & Firestone, 1964; Logan, Beier, & Ellis, 1955). The second case is like the ganzfeld with the contour; a sharp change appears after the eighth trial. The animal begins to compute a new adaptation level after this change; however, this new adaptation level is perceived in relation to the background adaptation level. While a reward of 5 has a value of $5/3.0 = 1.67$ for the animals in the first case, the same reward has a value of $5/1.0 = 5.00$ for the animals in the second case. (The adaptation level of 3.0 was obtained by adding up 1, 5, 5, 1, 1, 5, 1, 5, and dividing by 8, and the adaptation level of 1.0 was obtained by adding up 1, 1, 1, 1, 1, 1, 1, 1, and dividing by 8.) The animals in the second case show what has been called an "elation" effect (Crespi, 1944; Zeaman, 1949), performing more vigorously for the new food reward. Similarly, "depression" effects are observed if small rewards follow a run of large rewards. The first case illustrates assimilation; new stimuli are computed in with the old average. The second case illustrates contrast; new stimuli are computed into a new average, which is perceived in relation to the old.

A final word of caution is in order with respect to adaptation level effects. Whereas adaptation level effects seem to be clearly primary perceptual processes, it is not clear just where in a discussion of primary perception they should be considered, and the present placement should be regarded as somewhat arbitrary. As we have already seen, some aftereffects are lateral and some central, and it may well be that the principle of adaptation level is expressed in a variety of mechanisms.

Very-Short-Term Memory

We shall find it convenient to distinguish among four levels of memory: a very-short-term, or iconic, memory (VSTM), a short-term, or working, memory (STM), an intermediate-term memory

(ITM), and a long-term memory (LTM). (See Wickelgren, 1970.) Long-term memory is the locus of permanent changes in knowledge (Level II), and STM is where knowledge is rearranged (Level III). Both will be considered in later chapters. Inter-mediate-term memory, if there is, indeed, such a system, retains a temporary context for about a week. We shall consider it later, also. Our present concern is only with VSTM.

There actually seem to be a number of VSTMs. As with adaptation level, there may be no one "place" to discuss VSTM. An experiment by Hochberg (1968) points to a number of VSTMs in the visual mode. Hochberg moved a cross, as in Figure 33, behind a window at different rates, so that only one angle comprising the cross was visible during any given frame. With very rapid succession, the successive frames fused; thus, 1 (⌐) followed by 2 (⌐) yielded a "+." At slower rates (about 5 frames per second), a square is often perceived moving around behind the window; a form is constructed, and this construction is not influenced by instructions. At still slower rates (about 1–2 frames per second), a cross is perceived, and this construction is influenced by instructions. The first effect occurs before things are located in time and space, and the second effect occurs after this point. The third effect, because it is influenced by instructions, seems to be a matter of secondary perception. It will be discussed in the next chapter.

An experiment by Treisman (1964) makes a similar distinction for the auditory mode. She presented a message to each ear and ensured that the subject would attend to one ear and ignore the other by requiring the subject to repeat aloud the message coming in the ear to be attended to (a process called shadowing). The messages were identical, but one was ahead of the other. The

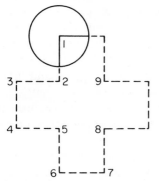

Form presented to the mind's eye
by sequential views of right angles

FIGURE 33. *Hochberg's cross.* [*From "In the mind's eye" by Julian Hochberg, in* Contemporary theory and research in visual perception *edited by Ralph Norman Haber. Copyright © by Holt, Rinehart and Winston, Inc. Reprinted by permission of Holt, Rinehart and Winston, Inc. P. 322.*]

subject noticed the identity only if the message to the unattended ear led by 1.3 sec or less or if the message to the attended ear led by 4.3 sec or less. In both cases, the message was in a very unstable memory system and quickly lost, but it appears that two systems, with different durations, were involved.

A considerable amount of research has been done on the duration of VSTM, but, because this research does not make it possible to identify the particular VSTM system involved, it will not be reviewed here. Hochberg's and Treisman's results indicate that, in any case, the duration is very brief.

Three general conclusions have emerged from research on VSTM that seem to be particularly noteworthy.

(1) The duration of VSTM is increased by increasing stimulus intensity and stimulus duration and by decreasing the intensity of surrounding stimuli (Neisser, 1967). Very short-term memory systems seem to be the only ones that are affected in this way by these variables.

(2) The duration of auditory VSTM is greater than that of visual VSTM (Morton, 1970; Neisser, 1967). Perhaps this is because auditory patterns are primarily temporal, while visual patterns are primarily spatial.

• (3) The capacity of VSTM, although it has never been measured adequately, would seem to be quite great (Averbach & Sperling, 1961). In the case of visual VSTM, what subjects report is that the entire scene seems to be there, and this may be the case. Indeed, if VSTM is an analogue memory, it may not even be useful to talk about capacity.

The Determinants of Attention

We have seen that the analogue processes of primary perception combine information to yield a unitary representation of a world of objects located in time and space and corrected for certain variations in background conditions. They also select information for further processing. Some areas stand out as figures, and others recede to form a ground. The interesting question is, What is seen as figure and what as ground? What, in the terms that primary perception deals with, has nature found to be important to process further?

We should expect that the features that demand attention would meet two requirements: (1) The energies should be likely to have predictive value; and (2) the events they predict should have important consequences for the system. These are the familiar factors of degree of covariation and relevance.

In some cases, attention seems to be demanded by rather specific inputs that are directly related to the system's functioning—for example, flying insects, in the case of frogs (Lettvin *et al.*, 1959); certain moving objects, in the case of ducklings (Hess, 1959); and sexual stimuli in the case of many animals (Hinde, 1966). The list could be extended indefinitely.

The more interesting cases are where attention is demanded by general characteristics of the stimulating energies. There appear to be two such characteristics. One is amount of energy. We attend to bright lights, loud sounds, and strong odors. Things that generate a great amount of energy—large objects, near objects, and large numbers of objects—are likely to have considerable relevance to survival. Not only are they likely to be sources of great potential impact on the system, but they are also likely to be close at hand and to require an immediate response. Furthermore, great amounts of energy, by themselves, can damage a system. It is clearly the relevance factor that is operating in the case of amount of energy.

It is a bit puzzling to compare greater attention to high levels of energy with lesser sensory discrimination at high levels of energy, the decreasing psychophysical function. While primary perception seems to treat the greater of two stimulating energies as the more important, the distance senses seem to treat such differences as less important, the greater the stimulating energy. While these two design principles are not in direct conflict, they seem difficult to reconcile in any intuitively satisfying way.

The other general characteristic of the stimulating energies that demands attention is change in amount or kind of energy (Sokolov, 1964). Things that change are likely to tell us about other things that change. Only where there is variation can there be covariation and, hence, the possibility of predicting anything, of significance to the system or not.

Spatial change seems to be the most important factor determining visual figure–ground organization. Of two areas, the smaller will tend to be seen as the figure. In Figure 34, the shape composed of the narrower segments is more often seen as figure (Oyama, 1960). It is true that moving areas tend to be seen as figures, but, even here, it is the spatial organization that appears to be fundamental. A stationary rock will be seen as figure against the ground of a moving stream.

The effects of change cannot be explained in terms of energy. We cannot say that the only reason thunder catches our attention

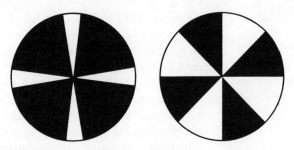

FIGURE 34. *The influence of area on figure–ground organization.* [*From "Figure–ground dominance as a function of sector angle, brightness, hue, and orientation" by T. Oyama, in* Journal of Experimental Psychology, 1960, **60,** *299–305. Copyright (1960) by the American Psychological Association. Reprinted by permission.*]

and stands out as figure against the ground of other sounds has to do with amount of energy and that change is unimportant, for a reduction in sound energy will also command attention (Sokolov, 1964), as when the singing of the birds of the chirping of the crickets suddenly stops. Nor would it seem that the effects of energy can be explained in terms of change, for attention seems more likely to be directed, and directed longer, to increases than decreases in energy. It is easier to ignore whispering than shouting.

The notion that change is important in determining what will be seen as figure is consistent with a theme that runs through all analogue processes: Parts are perceived in relation to the wholes they belong to. One must have an overall appreciation of the scene in order to appreciate which parts represent changes.

Consciousness

The results of primary processing enter consciousness. The best guess at the present as to the locus of consciousness would place it in the cerebral cortex. A well-developed cerebral cortex is the single anatomic feature that most markedly distinguishes the higher animals from the lower. In man, 9 billion of the 12 billion neurons in the entire brain are located in the cerebral cortex (Hilgard *et al.*, 1971), and there are 6000–60,000 synapses per cortical neuron (Lindsay & Norman, 1972). We shall consider two arguments that locate consciousness in the cortex, one having to do with the reticular activating system and the other having to do with graded potentials.

The reticular activating system (RAS) is a reticulum, or network, of sensory fibers that arises in the brainstem and projects widely over the cortex. This system seems to awaken the cortex into consciousness in preparation for incoming information. Stimulation of the RAS awakens a sleeping animal and alerts an animal that is already awake (Lindsley *et al.*, 1950), and stimulation of the RAS improves cortical resolution as measured by both the smallest interstimulus interval that produces two distinct cortical responses (Lindsley, 1958) and the amount of information that can be obtained from a brief tachistoscopic exposure (Fuster, 1958). Destruction of the RAS produces an animal that is comatose (Morgan, 1965); and anesthetic drugs that produce unconsciousness appear to act by depressing the RAS (Hilgard & Bower, 1966). Although stimuli still evoke electrical responses in the cortex of a comatose subject, the subject is unaware of them. Thus, the RAS seems to be essential to consciousness, and the locus of consciousness seems to be in the cerebral cortex.

The second argument for locating consciousness in the cerebral cortex is based on the properties of graded potentials. Pribram (1971) has provided this argument. He calls attention to the difference between action potentials and graded potentials. When low voltages are placed across a neuron, the dendrites and cell body respond in a graded manner (see Figure 35), the magnitude of the response being a direct function of the stimulating voltage; and the response does not propagate along the neuron. Such a response is a graded potential. Above a certain threshold voltage, the axon

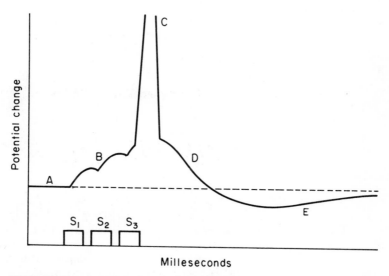

FIGURE 35. *Graded and action potentials. S = stimulation; A = resting potential; B = summated graded potentials; C = action potential; D = negative afterpotential; E = positive afterpotential.*

responds in an all-or-none manner (see Figure 35), the magnitude of the response being constant and not a function of the stimulating voltage; and the response does propagate itself along the length of the axon. Such a response is an action potential.

Action potentials and graded potentials are presumed to be related in the following manner. Graded potentials wax and wane in the dendrites and cell body until the threshold of the action potential is reached. (Graded potentials have actually been observed fluctuating rhythmically in the absence of action potentials.) The neuron then fires, and the action potential travels the length of the axon, releasing transmitter substances at the various synapses. These transmitter substances cross the synapses and set up graded potentials in other neurons. The graded input combines algebraically with the ongoing graded activity, increasing or decreasing (depending on whether the synapse is excitatory or inhibitory) the probability of firing in these neurons.

The patterns of graded activity are presumed to be the locus of consciousness. Graded potentials have been found to be correlated with rhythms recorded simultaneously from aggregates of cortical neurons, which are thought to be responsible for EEG activity (electroencephalograph brain wave patterns recorded at the scalp),

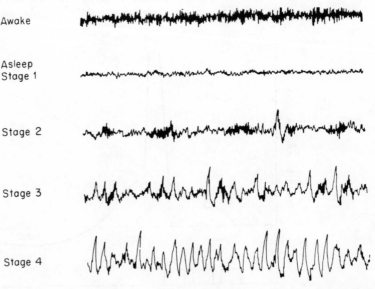

FIGURE 36. *Electroencephalograms for various states of consciousness.*
[*From page 147 of* New directions in psychology 2, *edited by Frank Barron, William C. Dement, Ward Edwards, Harold Lindman, Lawrence D. Phillips, and James and Marianne Olds. Copyright © 1965 by Holt, Rinehart and Winston, Inc. Reprinted by permission of Holt, Rinehart and Winston, Inc.*]

and changes in EEG activity are associated with changes in states of consciousness (see Figure 36).

Pribram suggests that the graded potentials compute spatial neighborhood actions among neurons and, to some extent, temporal interactions, by a continuous, analogue process. This raises the question as to whether such analogue properties as grouping, simplicity, adaptation level, and attention to change are consequences of the way in which graded potentials interact, and hence properties of consciousness, or whether they are consequences of the way in which both graded potentials and action potentials interact in complex nerve nets, and hence properties of both conscious and unconscious processes. We shall return to this question in the next chapter.

Primary perception presents us with a matrix of things located in time and space and calls our attention to certain of these things. We could respond directly to these percepts, as lower organisms seem to do, but, in order to handle complex and novel interactions among features, greater articulation is required, and for this we need additional mechanisms. These are the mechanisms of secondary perception.

Secondary Perception

chapter 3

The analogue model is refined and supplemented and presented as an information display to the executive system.

Secondary perception adds detail to the objects roughed out by primary perception. It does this by selecting and combining features and relating these to what is already in memory. The mode of selecting, combining, and relating that is adaptive in a particular instance has to be learned. Initially, this learning seems to require executive processes, but, with practice, it seems to proceed quite automatically.

We located primary perception in certain precortical structures, such as the retina and the sensory nuclei of the thalamus, and in the projection areas of the cortex. Secondary perception seems to involve the posterior association area (see Figure 13). The effect of damaging the posterior association area is to produce agnosia, an inability to recognize formerly familiar objects. A monkey with damage in the visual association area will put a lighted match in his mouth over and over again, apparently unable to learn the significance of the visual percept (Kluver & Bucy, 1938). Humans with similar damage are unable to recognize friends by sight (Terzian & Dalle Ore, 1955) and unable to see the humor in cartoons (Milner, 1954). Though it is not clear to what extent these effects are perceptual and to what extent they are simply associative, stimulation of the area surrounding the visual projection area produces images of remembered scenes (Gregory, 1973, p. 68), effects that are clearly perceptual.

Subcortically, secondary perception may involve the association nuclei of the thalamus, at least during the early stages of learning. The association nuclei are believed to coordinate the anterior and posterior association areas of the cortex (Riklan & Levita, 1969; Smith, 1965; Truex & Carpenter, 1964). It is of interest that both the association nuclei of the thalamus and the anterior and posterior association areas of the cortex are areas which show marked development in primates and particularly marked development in man (Smith, 1965).

The Distinction between Primary and Secondary Perception

By way of introduction, let us examine briefly three kinds of evidence that suggest a distinction between primary and secondary perception; phylogenetic, ontogenetic, and microgenetic. Phylogenesis refers to the evolution of a species; more primitive organisms seem to perceive only those properties that we have identified with primary perception: brightness, location, size, motion, and slope; more advanced ones also perceive shape and other complex patterns. Ontogenesis refers to the development of an individual organism; the infant first perceives only the properties processed by primary perception and then, after a period of learning, also perceives complex patterns. Microgenesis refers to the growth of a single percept; in any perceptual act, primary feature analysis precedes the processes of secondary perception. Let us examine the evidence for each of these statements.

Phylogenetic Evidence

The arthropods are capable of discriminating depth, size, and looming (a rapid increase in size, as from an approaching object; Gibson, 1969). Spatial discrimination occurs earlier than form discrimination (Bitterman, 1960). Brightness constancy has been found in fish (Burkamp, 1923) and hens (Katz & Ravesz, see Forgus, 1966), yet shape constancy has been obtained only with difficulty even in rats (Fields, 1932; Forgus, 1954). In higher animals, depth, size, and looming appear to be processed by subcortical mechanisms (Gibson, 1969).

Ontogenetic Evidence

In the phenomenon of imprinting, ducks are hatched with a tendency to follow a moving object that contrasts with its surroundings, ordinarily its mother. Only these primary properties are innate, however; a more precise representation of its mother (it will initially follow objects as diverse as a duck, a man, or a red watering can) awaits experience (Hess, 1959; Lorenz, 1935). Similarly, chickens tend to flee when a silhouette resembling a hawk (short neck and long tail) is passed overhead, but not when a silhouette resembling a goose (long neck and short tail) is passed overhead (Tinbergen, 1951). Although this ability to discriminate shape was once thought to be innate, it is now known to require experience (Schleidt, 1961).

In man, responses to depth, size, and looming appear to be present at birth (Gibson, 1969). Eye movements of neonates follow moving objects well, thus demonstrating figure–ground perception, but do not search systematically within an object, thus failing to demonstrate detailed perception within the figure (Hebb, 1949; Salapatek & Kesson, 1966). While they fixate a vertex, they do not scan along the edges from one vertex to another (Zinchenko & Tarskonov, 1963; see Figure 37). Motion parallax seems to be effective in the early discrimination of depth (Bower, 1965; Gibson,

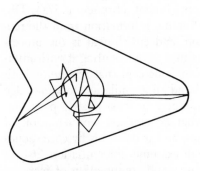

Trajectory of eje movements
of three year old in familiarization with figure (20 seconds)

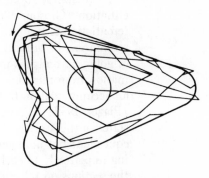

Trajectory of eye movements
of six year old in familiarization
with figure (20 seconds)

FIGURE 37. *Eye movements in three- and six-year-old children. [Taken, with permission, from V. P. Žinchenko, van Chzhi-Tsin, and V. V. Tarskonov, "The formation and development of perceptual activity," Soviet Psychology and Psychiatry, 1963, 2, 3–12.]*

1969) but not perspective (Bower, 1965). And, while brightness constancy changes only from 30 to 44% (a change of 14%) between the ages of 3 and 14, shape constancy changes from 15 to 60% (a change of 45%) in the same period of time (see Forgus, 1966). (100% constancy represents the case where a given object is judged to have the same properties despite changes in viewing conditions, for example, the same brightness despite changes in illumination or the same shape despite changes in orientation.)

Microgenetic Evidence

The properties processed by primary perception appear first in tachistoscopic presentation. If a picture is flashed briefly, it is not an isolated feature or two that is perceived, but a roughing out of the scene into patterns of brightness; what is first seen is a blob of a particular intensity, size, and location (Freeman, 1929). An unpatterned bright field will mask (that is, block the perception of) a previously presented letter stimulus only if presented within 80 msec, but a pattern will produce masking as long afterward as 180 msec (Spencer, 1969). Finally, reducing exposure time improves brightness constancy but destroys shape constancy (see Forgus, 1966).

Selection of Features

There appear to be two aspects to secondary perception: differentiation (Gibson, 1969) and enrichment (Bruner, 1957a). Differentiation is the process of extracting information from the representation in primary perception, and enrichment is the process of going beyond this information and supplementing it with information from memory. The result is a percept that represents both an accommodation to the world and an assimilation to knowledge (Piaget, 1952a). To be adaptive, a percept must relate a particular state of the world to a somewhat generalized representation of equivalent but nonidentical states, and it does this by corresponding imperfectly to each. We shall examine differentiation first, in the sections on selection of features and combination of features; then we shall consider enrichment, in the section on going beyond the information given.

Two questions about the differentiation, or accommodation, aspect of secondary perception have aroused considerable interest. The first has to do with information selection, with the size of the units in which information is obtained from primary perception. Do we match templates or test features? In the former case, the entire figure would be matched against a unitary representation, or template, in memory; in the latter, portions of the figure would be matched against part representations. The second question has to do with information combination, with whether features, if it is features that are processed, are processed at the same time or one after the other. Is processing parallel or serial?

There seems to be considerable evidence against template matching and for feature testing. First, the similarity relations among stimuli, as measured by both the tendency to make the same response to different stimuli (as confusion errors in learning tasks or as correct responses in transfer tests) and ratings of similarity, seem to be better accounted for by a feature model. Figure 38 shows how a template for an **A** could fit an **R** better than a somewhat different **A** and thus misidentify both. It would seem that an **A** is defined in terms of a collection of features (horizontal, diagonals, symmetry, etc.), rather than as an intact spatial pattern (Neisser, 1967). Template-matching processes are used by dollar-bill changers and by the machines that read numbers on bank checks, yet they are able to function well only because their input is constant. In the variable world in which the human perceptual apparatus has to function, a feature-processing system would seem far more adaptive.

Gibson (1969) has analyzed the letters of the alphabet into features such as horizontal, vertical, right oblique, and left oblique (see Figure 39). She has also shown that the greater the number of features two letters have in common, the more likely they are to be confused.

Earlier, Jakobson and Halle (1956) had analyzed phonemes into features (see Figure 40), such as vocalic–nonvocalic, nasal–oral, and tense–lax, and Wickelgren (1966) had successfully predicted confusions on the basis of their analysis. Certain facts suggest that

Template for **A**

Fits some **R**'s

FIGURE 38.   *Errors in template matching.* [*Adapted from "Pattern recognition by machine" by O. G. Selfridge and U. Neisser, in* Scientific American, *1960,* **203,** *60–68. Copyright © (1960) by Scientific American, Inc. All rights reserved.*]

Better than some **A**'s

Features	A	E	F	H	I	L	T	K	M	N	V	W	X	Y	Z	B	C	D	G	J	O	P	R	Q	S	U
Straight																										
horizontal	+	+	+	+		+	+								+				+							
vertical		+	+	+	+	+	+	+	+	+					+		+	+				+	+			
diagonal /	+							+	+		+	+	+	+	+											
diagonal \	+							+	+	+	+	+	+	+	+								+	+		
Curve																										
closed																+		+			+	+	+	+		
open V																				+						+
open H																	+		+	+					+	
Intersection	+	+	+	+		+	+						+			+						+	+	+		
Redundancy																										
cyclic change																										
symmetry	+	+		+	+		+	+	+		+	+	+	+		+	+	+			+					+
Discontinuity																										
vertical	+		+	+	+		+	+	+	+					+							+	+			
horizontal		+	+			+	+								+											

FIGURE 39. *Distinctive features of letters of the English alphabet.* [From page 88 of Principles of perceptual learning and development *by E. J. Gibson. New York: Appleton, 1969. Copyright © 1969 Meredith Corporation.*]

the mechanisms for processing phonemic distinctions are innate. For example, only 15 to 20 such distinctions are needed to describe the phonetics of all languages (Chomsky & Halle, 1968), and categorical perception of phonemes appears to be present in infants by at least the age of 4 weeks (Eimas, Siqueland, Jusczyk, & Vigorito, 1971). Yet, these mechanisms are also obviously affected by experience, for adults have great difficulty in processing phonemic distinctions that are not employed in their native tongue (Lenneberg, 1967).

On the basis of a rational analysis, Guzmán (1968) has suggested a number of features that might be important in the visual

	o	a	e	u	ə	i	l	ŋ	ʃ	ʃ̂	k	ʒ	ʒ̂	g	m	f	p	v	b	n	s	θ	t	z	ð	d	h	#
1. Vocalic/non-vocalic	+	+	+	+	+	+	+	−	−	−	−	−	−	−	−	−	−	−	−	−	−	−	−	−	−	−	−	−
2. Consonantal/non-consonantal	−	−	−	−	−	−	+	+	+	+	+	+	+	+	+	+	+	+	+	+	+	+	+	+	+	+	−	−
3. Compact/diffuse	+	+	+	−	−	−		+	+	+	+	+	+	−	−	−	−	−	−	−	−							
4. Grave/acute	+	+	−	+	+	−								+	+	+	+	+	−	−	−	−	−	−				
5. Flat/plain	+	−		+	−																							
6. Nasal/oral								+	−	−	−	−	−		+	−	−	−	−	+	−	−	−	−				
7. Tense/lax									+	+	+	−	−	−			+	+	−		+	+	+	−	−	−	+	−
8. Continuant/interrupted									+	−	−	+	−	−		+	−	+	−		+	+	−	+	+	−		
9. Strident/mellow										+	−		+	−		+		−			+	−		+	−			

FIGURE 40. *Distinctive features of English phonemes.* [Reprinted from On human communication *by E. C. Cherry, by permission of The M.I.T. Press, Cambridge, Massachusetts. © 1965 The M.I.T. Press. P. 40.*]

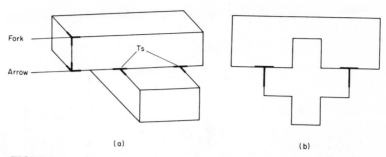

Fork

Arrow

Ts

(a)   (b)

FIGURE 41. *Arrows, forks, and Ts as features in secondary perception.*

identification of rectilinear three-dimensional objects. In Figure 41a, "arrows" indicate that the two enclosed surfaces are part of the same figure, "forks" indicate that the three enclosed surfaces are part of the same figure, and "Ts" indicate that one figure is occluded by another. Such an analysis is not sufficient, however, as Chapanis and McCleary (1953) have shown. In Figure 41b, the "Ts" would lead to the perception of the lower shape extending behind the upper one. The perception that is usually reported is of a cross extending over a rectangle, and this would seem to require a principle of simplicity (Attneave, 1972). Secondary perception operates on the output of primary perception.

If we put two of Guzmán's arrows together, we obtain the higher-order pattern in Figure 42a, and, if we put two of his forks together, we obtain the higher-order pattern in Figure 42b. Together, these constitute the classic Müller–Lyer illusion. Although the two horizontal lines are identical in length, the bottom one appears longer.

Gregory (1963) has provided an explanation for this illusion based on the assumption that arrows and forks arranged in this manner constitute higher-order cues to depth. The double-arrows are seen as outside corners (see Figure 43); they indicate that the connecting line is the nearest part of the figure. The double forks are seen as inside corners (see Figure 44); they indicate that the connecting line is the most distant part of the figure. This illusion, along with a large number of similar ones, is presumed to be a consequence of the fact that the mechanism of size constancy

(a)

FIGURE 42. *An illusion produced by double arrows and double forks.*

(b)

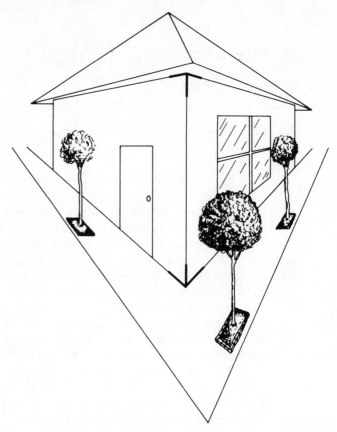

FIGURE 43.   *Double arrows as outside corners.*

produces a difference in perceived size for identical retinal images perceived as being at different distances.

This explanation of the Müller–Lyer illusion is supported by the finding that the Müller–Lyer figures are actually seen as shapes in depth when presented as luminous lines in the dark, where there are no conflicting depth cues from the page, and by the finding that that angle of the forks and arrows which produces the strongest sense of depth also produces the strongest illusion (Gregory, 1973). That the Müller–Lyer illusion is an illusion of secondary perception is indicated by the fact that it is weak in cultures that are exposed to few rectilinear forms (Segal, Campbell, & Herskovitz, 1966).

We have seen that primary perception is analogue, representing dimensions as continua. Secondary perception, in marked contrast, represents a much more limited number of positions along the same dimensions. Information is digitalized as it is coded

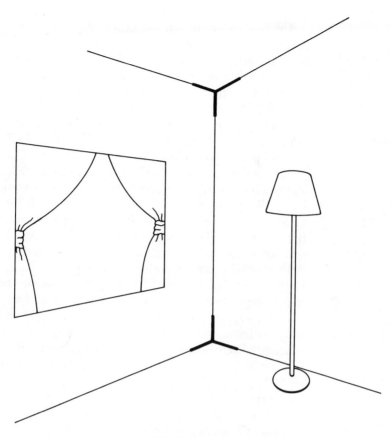

FIGURE 44.   *Double forks as inside corners.*

into the features of secondary perception. Gibson's (1969) and Jakobson and Halle's (1956) features exemplify the limiting case, where only two positions are represented on each dimension. A variety of intermediate cases are revealed in studies of absolute judgment.

Absolute judgment is to be contrasted with comparative judgment. In a comparative judgment experiment, two stimuli are presented simultaneously or in immediate succession, and the subject is asked to make some judgment comparing them, for example, to say "same" or "different." This procedure yields a scale of just-noticeable differences (jnd's) that number in the thousands for such dimensions as brightness and loudness. Comparative judgment seems to involve comparing a current stimulus with information in VSTM. The fact that so many comparative judgments are possible is consistent with the notion that the capacity of VSTM is very great.

Absolute judgment, on the other hand, seems to involve comparing a current stimulus with information in LTM. In an absolute judgment experiment, a single stimulus is presented, and the subject is asked to name it, for example, "middle C," "1½ ounces," or "98.6°F." The number of absolute judgments that can be made along a single dimension is extremely limited. We can make absolute judgments of about five loudnesses (Garner, 1953), six pitches (Pollack, 1952, 1953), three curvatures (Miller, 1956), and from 10 to 15 positions on a line (Miller, 1956).

Absolute judgments are affected by discriminability. They are affected both by discriminability produced by increasing the spacing of the stimuli along the dimensions on which they differ and, even more markedly, by discriminability produced by increasing the number of dimensions on which they differ. The effect of spacing along a single dimension has sometimes (for example, Pollack, 1953) been reported as having only slight effects, but Hartman (1954) showed that the effects can be considerable if sufficient practice is given. In all, he employed four sets of nine pure tones separated by either 50, 100, 200, or 500 mels.[1] Training was continued for seven weeks. He found, for example, that, whereas reliable absolute judgments could be made of only about three stimuli separated by 50 mels, reliable absolute judgments could be made of about five stimuli separated by 300 mels. We would expect practice to be important in secondary perception.

Lockhead (1970) found that increasing the separation of stimuli in a two-dimensional space, as well as in a one-dimensional space, increases the number of absolute judgments that are possible. The fact that these dimensions (lightness and loudness, in one condition, and roughness and hue, in another) were not only nonintegral but from different modalities seems to locate the effect beyond primary perception.

The effect of adding dimensions is much greater. For 1, 2, 3, and 4 dimensions, the span of absolute judgment is 6, 20, 37, and 64, respectively (see Figure 45; Attneave, 1959; Miller, 1956). The important point here is that such a gain in absolute judgment does not require integral dimensions. The dimensions may be as unrelated as lightness and loudness or roughness and hue (Lockhead, 1970).

In secondary perception, we seem to make better use of a little information on a lot of dimensions than a lot of information on a few dimensions. It is more helpful to say that a person is tall, dark,

---

[1] A mel is a measure of pitch. At 60 dB, A 1000-Hz tone has a pitch of 1000 mels, and a tone of 10,000 Hz has a pitch of only 3000 mels.

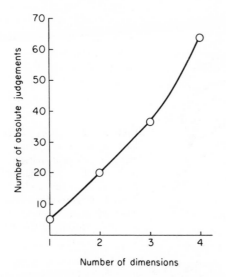

FIGURE 45. *Number of absolute judgments as a function of stimulus dimensionality.*

and handsome, than to say that he is 73.064 inches tall. Information seems to be digitalized as it passes from primary to secondary perception. It is undoubtedly only because naturally occurring stimuli ordinarily differ on so many dimensions that we can identify so many faces, animals, cars, and chess patterns. The "absolute pitch" of musicians might seem to constitute an exception, but there is evidence (Bachem, 1950) that musicians with "absolute pitch" do not make judgments along the single continuum of frequency. The stimuli they are judging are multidimensional; they are not pure tones, but differ in timbre as well as pitch, and musicians make use of this property. This is undoubtedly why they often have "absolute pitch" for only one or two instruments.

We might conclude this section on the selection of features by noting a particularly interesting consequence of feature selection: the effectiveness of what are called supernormal stimuli. These are stimuli that combine the defining features of a class of stimuli in an exaggerated form, and thus represent nothing at all like an average, schema, or template of the naturally occurring objects. Cartoon drawings of objects (see Figure 46) are recognized more rapidly than are either accurate line drawings or photographs (Fraisse & Elkin, 1963; Ryan & Schwartz, 1956). This is probably why bird books and anatomy books do not use photographs, which would be perfect templates, but drawings in which the distinctive features are slightly exaggerated. It is interesting to consider that the mechanism involved here might be at least one mechanism involved in the production of human ideals and aesthetic stand-

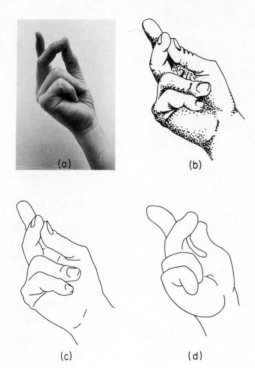

(a)   (b)

(c)   (d)

FIGURE 46. *Enhancement of features. Part (a) is a photograph; (b) is a shaded drawing; (c) is a line drawing; and (d) is a cartoon. [Taken, with permission, from T. A. Ryan and C. B. Schwartz, "Speed of perception as a function of mode of representation,"* American Journal of Psychology, 1956, **69**, 60–69.]

ards. Beautiful women and handsome men are not so much averages as collections of features in exaggerated form.

Combination of Features

The second question about the differentiation, or accommodation, aspect of secondary perception has to do with the combination of features. Are they processed serially or in parallel?

The difference between serial and parallel processing of features may be understood in terms of an analogy with voting. If feature tests are compared with voters, then parallel processing is like a voice vote, and serial processing is like a roll call vote. While in a roll call vote reaction time increases linearly with the number of voters (features tested), in a voice vote it is approximately independent of the number of voters (features tested). (For a more precise treatment, see Egeth, 1966.)

The distinction between serial and parallel processing is the one with which we shall be concerned in this section; however, it is important also to distinguish between sequential and nonsequential processing (Neisser, 1967). Whereas serial processing is like a roll call vote, sequential processing is like decisions in a chain of command. In a roll call vote, all voters are queried (all features tested), regardless of how earlier voters voted. In decision-making in a chain of command, the decision at one stage determines whether and where the matter will be routed for further processing (whether and what additional features will be tested). Serial processing may be either sequential or nonsequential, though parallel processing is necessarily nonsequential. It is often assumed that serial processing is sequential in the human brain. We shall see in a later chapter that this is not always the case; hence, we must be alert to the fact that these two distinctions are not identical but are concerned with different kinds of evidence.

Serial Processing

The most readily observable indication that serial processing occurs at some level in perception is the fact that our eyes roam serially about a scene we are looking at. Not only do our eyes move from figure to figure; they also move about within a figure (see Figure 37).

Minsky (1961) has argued from general considerations for the desirability of serial processing, at least at relatively advanced levels in processing. If the description of a scene is accomplished by the repeated application of a fixed set of pattern-recognition techniques, it will be possible to obtain arbitrarily complex descriptions from a fixed-complexity mechanism. For example, by repeated application of a chair-recognizer and a table-recognizer, one could describe an unlimited variety of scenes: a table; a chair; a table and a chair; two chairs; a chair on a table; and so forth.

An observation that the reader should be able to make easily for himself suggests that stimulus processing is, at least in some cases, serial, even within a figure. Look at Figure 47. You may notice, especially if you have never seen the figure before, that for a mo-

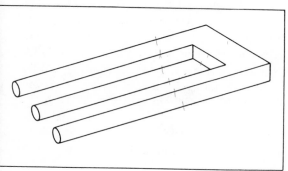

FIGURE 47. *An impossible object.*

ment it appears normal enough. It actually takes a moment to realize that the components cannot be assembled into any consistent structure. Incidentally, this second step, as we should expect of secondary perception, is dependent on learning; shown the impossible object in Figure 47, together with a consistent figure that both begins and ends with two legs, and a consistent figure that both begins and ends with three legs, young children cannot reliably indicate which one "has something wrong with it" (Coleman, 1973).

The most direct evidence for serial processing comes from studies that vary the number of stimulus features that have to be processed and examine the effect on reaction time. At first glance, two kinds of studies appear to fall in this category. In one kind (for example, the Neisser, Anderson and Johnson, Lindsay and Lindsay, and Hawkins studies to be discussed shortly), the number of stimulus features that must be processed is varied rather directly, and the number of alternative responses is held constant. This is the kind of study with which we shall be concerned here. In the other kind of study (for example, the Hick, Hyman, and Neisser studies to be discussed later), the number of alternative responses is varied, but one is never clear as to the precise effect this has on the number of stimulus attributes that must be processed. It appears that response selection is the important factor determining reaction time in studies of this latter kind (Keele, 1973), and they will therefore be discussed in a later chapter.

Let us begin with a study by Neisser (1963). Neisser devised an ingenious technique for eliminating the effect of overt responding on reaction time. He had subjects scan lists of letters for target letters and measured the time it took to reject nontargets. Subjects looked down a large number of lists for, for example, the letter Z. Each list contained one Z, but its position would vary from list to list. The rate at which having to go farther down the list and reject additional letters adds to the reaction time provides a measure of the time it takes to decide that a letter is not a Z. This additional time involves no time for selecting and activating a response, because no response is made to rejected letters.

When a Z is embedded in a list of curvilinear letters, such as O, D, U, G, Q, and R, something like a test for curvilinearity would seem sufficient to identify a letter as a non-Z. However, when the Z is embedded in a list of rectilinear letters, such as I, V, M, X, E, and W, no single test would seem to suffice, and additional tests would presumably be needed. Neisser found, as we might expect, that the time required to decide that a letter is not a Z is greater in the second case. (We shall consider other aspects of this study in a later chapter.)

Anderson and Johnson (1968) obtained evidence for both parallel and serial processing with stimuli that were both simpler and more well defined than Neisser's. Their stimuli were horizontal rows of contiguous square cells. The rows varied in length, and each cell could be either black or white. Thus, we may represent the stimuli by binary numbers, such as 0, 101, 11010, 00100010, and so on, where the 0s represent white cells and the 1s represent black cells. Their procedure was to present two stimuli, one immediately following the other, and to measure the time required for a subject to indicate whether they were the same or different, the two stimuli being compared always being identical with respect to length. The times we shall be concerned with are the times required to indicate that two identical stimuli were the same.

The results, over a large number of stimuli, in a number of experiments, can be summarized quite simply in terms of a "runs code." The runs code for a stimulus is the number of runs (uninterrupted sequences) of black cells it contains. The lengths of the runs are unimportant. Thus, the following stimuli would have runs codes of 1: 1, 11111111, 11100, 00010; and the following stimuli would have runs codes of 2: 1011, 1010, 11111101, 1000010.

Reaction time is simply a linear function of the runs code. The fact that the length of the runs is unimportant suggests that the cells within a run are processed in parallel, perhaps by a brightness summator or a length detector. The fact that the number of runs is linearly related to reaction time suggests that this parallel test is applied serially to the various runs in a stimulus.

An interesting additional finding was that a correction for symmetry is required. The corrected runs code for a symmetrical stimulus is equal to the uncorrected runs code for half the stimulus. Thus, the following stimuli all have corrected runs codes of 1: 101, 01010, 11111111. It is not clear what kind of mechanism would be able to account for this intriguing finding, but it may be important to note that only symmetry about the vertical axis was examined.

Lindsay and Lindsay (1966) also obtained evidence for both parallel and serial processing with well-defined stimuli. In addition, they obtained evidence for a practice effect. Their study is complex, but well worth the effort required to understand it.

Lindsay and Lindsay's stimuli consisted of geometric figures (see Figure 48) that differed on five binary dimensions: background (light or dark), border (present or absent), shape (rectangle or

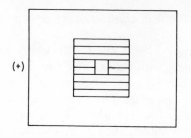 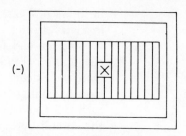

FIGURE 48. *The "+" and "−" stimuli used by Lindsay and Lindsay. (Note: The "+" stimulus appeared on a 60% gray background, and the "−" stimulus appeared on a 10% gray background.)* [From *"Reaction time and serial versus parallel information processing"* by R. K. Lindsay and J. M. Lindsay, in Journal of Experimental Psychology, 1966, **71**, 294–303. Copyright (1966) by the American Psychological Association. Reprinted by permission.]

square), stripes (vertical or horizontal), and × (present or absent). All 32 possible stimuli were used.

The subject was required to respond "+" to the dark, no-border, square, horizontal, no-× stimulus; "−" to the light, border, rectangle, vertical, × stimulus; and "0" to all others. The "+" and "−" stimuli were each presented 210 times, and each of the 30 "0" stimuli was presented seven times, for a total of 210. Reaction time measures were taken.

The results are shown in Figure 49. Each stimulus has been represented by a binary number. The five digits indicate background, border, shape, stripes, and ×, in that order. Zeros indicate values associated with the "−" stimulus, and ones indicate values associated with the "+" stimulus. Thus, a 0 in the first position indicates a light background color, and a 1 indicates a dark background color. 00000 and 11111 represent the "−" and "+" stimuli, respectively.

Notice the "0" stimuli in Figure 49. Of these, the longer reaction times occur to the −−0−0 and −−1−1 stimuli, the stimuli where the shape and × dimensions were both like the "−" stimulus or both like the "+" stimulus. Let us see how this might be explained. Assume that the "0" stimuli are processed serially and that the first two dimensions checked are shape and ×. If these are 01 or 10, the stimulus must be a "0," and testing can be terminated. If, on the other hand, these are either 00 or 11, testing must be continued. This assumption accounts for the data, and we conclude that the features of the "0" stimuli were processed serially, beginning with shape and ×. We shall consider the rest of Figure 49 very shortly.

Stimulus	Mean RT in milliseconds	Errors
00000	597	582
00001	761	48
00010	685	81
00011	639	13
00100	663	12
00101	663	18
00110	651	18
00111	704	17
01000	696	46
01001	670	11
01010	639	11
01011	621	11
01100	639	74
01101	729	39
01110	672	18
01111	791	185
10000	822	138
10001	707	17
10010	690	33
10011	701	13
10100	630	9
10101	690	34
10110	675	22
10111	741	108
11000	677	13
11001	672	7
11010	645	11
11011	651	12
11100	661	11
11101	752	100
11110	664	23
11111	617	495

FIGURE 49. *Reaction times and errors obtained by Lindsay and Lindsay. [Taken, with permission, from R. K. Lindsay and J. M. Lindsay, "Reaction time and serial versus parallel information processing,"* Journal of Experimental Psychology, 1966, **71**, 294–303.]

Perceptual Set as Affecting Order of Coding. Where processing is serial, order of processing provides one mechanism for the operation of perceptual set. Perceptual set refers to the effects of such factors as context, motivation, and instructions on perception. These factors may affect perception by affecting the order of serial coding. This is shown clearly in some experiments by Harris and Haber (1963) and Haber (1964a). Their stimuli differed in color, shape, and number, and they trained their subjects to code them either in terms of objects (for example, one red triangle, three blue stars) or in terms of dimensions (for example, red blue, triangle star, one three). Sometimes a set was established by telling the subject that a correct report on one of the dimensions, say color, was ten times as important as any other. Such a set improved accuracy for the dimensions coders, who could easily rearrange the order in which they coded the dimensions, but had little effect on the objects coders, who could not vary the order of coding and always coded in the order of English syntax. The effect appears to be a perceptual effect, rather than a response effect, that is, an effect on order of coding, rather than order of report, for even when dimensions coders were forced to report the dimensions in an order inconsistent with the set, set improved performance.

Parallel Processing

The following phenomenological description suggests that serial processing may give way to parallel processing with practice.

> The student being introduced for the first time to microscopic techniques in a course in histology is told to look for the *corpus luteum* in a cross-sectional slide of rabbit ovary. He is told with respect to its defining attributes that it is yellowish, roundish, of a certain size relative to the field of the microscope, etc. He finds it. Next time he looks, he is still "scanning the attributes." But as he becomes accustomed to the procedure and to the kind of cellular structure involved, the *corpus luteum* begins to take on something classically referred to as a *Gestalt* or configurational quality. Phenomenologically, it seems that he no longer has to go through the slow business of checking size, shape, color, texture, etc. Indeed, "corpus luteumness" appears to become a property or attribute in its own right [Bruner, Goodnow, & Austin, 1962, p. 46].

This is what appears to have happened to the "+" and "−" stimuli in Lindsay and Lindsay's experiment. Let us return to Figure 49. The fastest reaction times are to the "+" and "−" stimuli. This is inconsistent with a serial processing model. In order to identify either of these stimuli, it is necessary to check all five dimensions, for, even if the first four have turned out to be 1s, for example, the last might be a 0 and thus make the stimulus a "0," rather than a "+." In order to identify a "0" stimulus, on the other hand, it is necessary to check dimensions only until both a 0 and a 1 have been noted, for any stimulus that has both a 0 and a 1 is necessarily a "0" stimulus. If dimensions are checked serially throughout, then the reaction times to the "+" and "−" stimuli should be the longest, not the shortest. We conclude from this that the features of the "+" and "−" stimuli were processed in parallel. The fact that the "+" and "−" stimuli were each presented 30 times as often as each of the "0" stimuli, taken together with the fact that processing seems to be parallel in the former case and serial in the latter, suggests that processing tends to become parallel with extended practice.

Perhaps the reason that processing tends to become parallel with practice is that simple stimulus features (for example, slope) that are redundant with complex stimulus features (for example, shape) are eventually processed by simple analyzers that can operate in parallel (Neisser, 1967). It would be interesting to know something about the roles of cortical and postcortical processes in parallel and serial processing. The interesting possibility suggests itself that parallel processing is accomplished entirely by cortical processes, while serial processing also involves postcortical control mechanisms.

Going beyond the Information Given

Differentiation made perception more complex, by adding features and thus increasing the number of percepts and decreasing their perceived similarity. It thus made perception correspond more closely with the world. Enrichment makes perception simpler, by increasing the similarity between the current percept and the memories of past percepts. Whereas differentiation made perception correspond more closely with the world, enrichment makes perception correspond more closely with the system's knowledge. Enrichment is the process of going beyond the information given (Bruner, 1957a) and supplementing it with information from memory. The same yellow–orange is judged as more yellow when it is presented in the shape of a banana than when it is presented in the shape of an orange (Adams, 1923; Bruner, Postman, & Rodrigues, 1951). More red has to be added to the background to make a reddish heart-shaped stimulus disappear than to make an identically reddish triangle disappear (Harper, 1953). The "droodles" in Figure 50 actually look different when you know that the one on the left represents a soldier and a dog going behind a

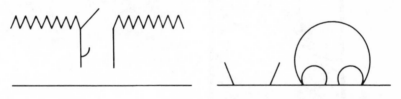

FIGURE 50.   *Droodles.*

fence, and the one on the right represents a washerwoman from behind.

Enrichment is a result of interpretation. We interpret perceptual data as particular things, and we assume more about these things than meets the eye. Bruner and Potter (1964) have shown how premature attempts to identify a stimulus can produce interpretations that actually delay final identification. They presented subjects with out-of-focus slides of common objects and scenes and asked them to try to identify the slides as they were gradually brought into focus, different groups of subjects being started at different degrees of initial focus. Their principal finding was that those who started the farthest out of focus required the highest degree of final focus for correct identification. Presumably, new perceptual data tended to be assimilated to erroneous interpretations based on the earlier degrees of focus, rather than being accommodated to by more veridical interpretations.

It is the interpretation in secondary perception, rather than the data in primary perception, that is stored in long-term memory.

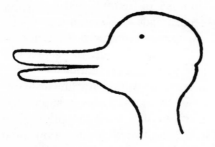

FIGURE 51. *Two ambiguous pictures.* [*The wife/mother-in-law figure is taken from E. G. Boring, H. S. Rangfeld, and H. P. Weld,* An introduction to psychology (*New York: Wiley, 1930*).]

Wiseman and Neisser (1971) found that fragmented pictures are very difficult to recognize on a second presentation if they do not receive an interpretation on the first presentation, and Clark, Carpenter, and Just (1972) found that ambiguous pictures, such as the duck/rabbit and wife/mother-in-law pictures (Figure 51), are almost impossible to reinterpret on the basis of information in LTM. That is, if you see the first picture as a duck and then are told that you can also see a rabbit there, you will almost certainly be able to see the rabbit eventually by looking at the picture, but you will almost certainly not be able to see it by examining your mental image of the picture. Hunter (1957) showed that modification of the interpretation in LTM can interfere with later perceptual recognition. He had subjects "wait" in a room with a poster in it, then brought them into another room and had them either describe the poster or perform a control task, and, finally, showed them the poster that had been in the waiting room and asked them whether it was the one they had seen before. Those who had attempted to describe the poster were more likely to say that it was not, often defending their judgment by noting details that they had mentioned in their recall but that were not in the poster.

Perceptual Set as Affecting Manner of Coding. Enrichment provides a second mechanism for the operation of perceptual set. The first mechanism was order of coding; this one is manner of coding. By priming one memory process or another, such factors as context, motivation, and instructions can affect the manner in which sensory input is coded.

We are likely to perceive what we have strong associative strength for. Associative strength, as we shall see in the next chapter, is influenced by frequency and arousal, corresponding to co-variation and relevance. As a consequence, perceptual set of this kind leads us to see what we have seen in the past and what is relevant to our needs.

Frequency

In reading the word **FR*Q**NCY**, it is easy to guess in the missing letters. Though this is a related phenomenon, it is not the one we are concerned with here—unless you actually saw the **E, U,** and **E.** We are concerned with effects on perception, on what is perceived, not on what is simply known in some other way.

In perceptual filling-in, frequently encountered features seem actually to be perceived in the absence of sensory input. For example, a triangle with a missing vertex, if flashed briefly, is often seen as a complete triangle (Bobbitt, 1942). In perceptual compromise, frequently encountered features are perceived along with conflicting sensory input. For example, a red ace of spades, if flashed briefly, will often be seen as a color that is a fusion of the expected black and the actual red (Bruner & Postman, 1949). In still other cases, infrequently encountered features may not be perceived even in the presence of sensory support. For example, a woman in a bathing suit, standing on her head on top of a bale of cotton in an otherwise ordinary dock scene is seldom seen (Haber, personal communication). As another example, you you probably failed to see the extra "you" in this sentence.

A particularly important example of perceptual filling-in is segmentation in the perception of speech. There are usually no breaks between words in the acoustic stimulus for speech perception, a fact which, until recently, has made the problem of designing a computer model of speech perception altogether intractable. What man seems to do and what modern computer programs do (Eden, 1962; Halle & Stevens, 1959) in perceiving speech is to fill in probable organization on the basis of past experience.

Halle and Stevens's program attempts to fit entire words or phrases to the incoming acoustic flow. When a fit is obtained, the breaks between words are thus automatically established. Human speech perception seems to operate in a similar way, so that we hear segments where there are no segments. If a single word is repeated over and over again, it may first be heard as "stress, stress, stress," then suddenly change to "rest, rest, rest," then suddenly change again to "tress, tress, tress" (Warren & Gregory, 1958). The change is abrupt, from one interpretation to another without any awareness of an uninterpreted stimulus.

The words that are tried out are selected on the basis of context in Halle and Stevens's program, and this is undoubtedly true for humans, as well. The perception of language, like secondary perception in general, relies on context for resolving ambiguity. Words presented against a masking background of white noise, for example, are easier to perceive when they occur in sentences (Miller, Heise, & Lichten, 1951).

Arousal

Relevance to the system, as well as covariation, seems to be represented in secondary perception, although the evidence is scant. We should begin by making a distinction between arousal and value. Arousal is simply excitement; while value is a response that is, in some sense that we shall examine more closely later, positive or negative. Both positively and negatively valued stimuli produce arousal. The position we shall take is that the representational system responds only to arousal; associative strength tends to be high for both positive and negative stimuli. The executive system, on the other hand, distinguishes between positive and negative value, guiding us toward the beneficial and away from the harmful.

Thus, we should expect that both positive and negative stimuli would be readily perceived. This is referred to as a *vigilance effect*. According to Blum (1954), vigilance effects should be more difficult to observe in the case of negative stimuli. Vigilance should obtain until the stimulus begins to have effects at the conscious level, and then perceptual defense should take place, as the executive system begins to reject what is negatively valued. He performed an experiment which seems to demonstrate both effects. On each trial, four pictures of a dog were flashed simultaneously, and the subject was to indicate in which position a particular picture appeared. In some cases, the target picture showed the dog engaged in neutral behavior; and, in others, it showed the dog engaged in emotionally laden behavior, for example, licking its genital area. At exposures well below the threshold of conscious perception, vigilance effects were observed; that is, the critical pictures were more often correctly located than the neutral ones. At exposures approaching the threshold of conscious perception, defense effects were observed; that is, the critical pictures were less often correctly located than the neutral ones. Because perceptual defense seems to involve the executive system, we shall consider it in the second part of the book.

Analogue Properties Again

Several lines of evidence suggest that, with practice, learned aspects of perception come to be handled by the same mechanisms that produce analogue properties in primary perception. We have already seen that serial processing may give way to parallel processing with practice. There are other, presumably related, effects of practice: Information in LTM seems to be act in concert with information contained in the current stimulus in the perception of things, in the perception of time and space, in the computation of adaptation level and the constancies, and in the activation of attention. Let us consider briefly each of these points.

That "thing perception" is determined by information in the current stimulus and information in LTM acting in concert is suggested by many of the so-called physiognomic properties of perception (Hochberg, 1957; Werner & Wapner, 1952). Beauty, for example, may indeed lie in the eye of the beholder (and, moreover, may be greatly dependent on learning), yet the beholder has the immediate impression that it is inherent in the object. The same is true for friendliness and hostility, prestige, humorousness, and a variety of other traits. A particularly clear example is the expressive qualities of music, which, as any westerner who has listened to Chinese music might guess, are at least partly learned, and yet which seem to the enculturated to be properties of the music, itself.

That the perception of space and time is determined by information in the current stimulus and information in LTM acting in concert is suggested by certain effects obtained with rotating trapezoids and with trapezoidal rooms. We have seen that the kinetic depth effect operates with nonsense shapes and does not appear to require experience (Wallach & O'Connell, 1953). If a trapezoid is rotated, however, it appears to oscillate, instead of rotate. The effect seems to derive from the assumption that the figure is a rectangle, which causes cues to be interpreted in a misleading fashion. This assumption seems to be at least in part learned, for the effect is not so great among primitive peoples who live in an "uncarpentered" world that lacks rectangles (Allport & Pettigrew, 1957).

The trapezoidal room of Figure 52, when viewed with one eye through a peephole, appears to be rectangular, thus providing misleading cues as to distance and size. Primary mechanisms of organizational simplicity are undoubtedly involved here, but an experiment by Kilpatrick (1954) suggests that learning is also quite

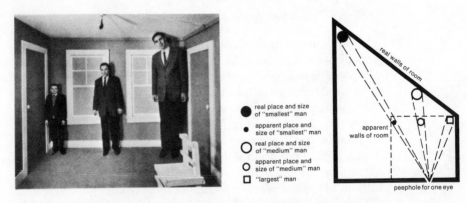

FIGURE 52. *The trapezoidal room.* [*Taken, with permission, from* D. Krech, R. S. Crutchfield, *and* N. Livson, Elements of psychology, 2d ed. (*New York: Knopf, 1969*), *pp.* 211, 212.]

important. After exploring the trapezoidal room by tracing around it with a stick and bouncing a ball against the walls (or by watching someone do these things), subjects began to perceive the trapezoidal room as trapezoidal. What is more, this training transferred to a rectangular room, so that they then perceived it as trapezoidal.

Stimulus factors and memory factors also seem to cooperate in producing the perception of apparent movement. Jones and Bruner (1954) flashed either a stick figure or a nonsense figure (see Figure 53) successively in two different places, so as to produce apparent movement. Subjects reported that the stick figure moved farther and faster than the nonsense figure.

FIGURE 53. *Stick figure and nonsense figure used by Jones and Bruner.* [*Taken, with permission, from E. E. Jones and J. S. Bruner, "Expectancy in apparent visual movement,"* British Journal of Psychology, 1954, **45**, 157–165.]

Several observations suggest that information in LTM is important in producing adaptation level and constancy effects. The same laboratory weights are judged heavier by watchmakers than by weight lifters. And the same people are judged shorter by tall people than by short people (Hinckley & Rethlingshafer, 1951), lighter by dark-skinned people than by light-skinned people (Marks, 1943), and younger by old people than by young people (Rethlingshafer & Hinckley, 1963).

Adaptation level seems to bear an important relation even to human happiness (Parducci, 1968). This is presumably why we take for granted the many good things that we have, the ability to see, the ability to walk, the company of friends. We have adapted to these aspects of our life. It may be for a related reason that we tend to view life competitively, partitioning of adaptations rendering what two people have in common less important than the difference between what each has.

We have seen that the constancies are affected by experience. Here again, there seems to be a great similarity between learned and unlearned effects.

Finally, change from what is in LTM, as well as from what is in the less stable memory systems, can activate attention. If a friend's hair or clothes or weight is different from what it was some time ago, you may notice it immediately, though sometimes you know simply that something has changed without being able to specify just what it is. The first night after one of the elevated railway lines in Chicago had been shut down, many people awakened and called the police, at about the time that a train would usually have gone by, to report that there was a loud noise or that something "big" had happened, though they did not know what. We shall consider this effect in greater detail in the next chapter.

Thus, the final stage in secondary perception, after practice, may be the same as the final stage in primary perception: activity in a complex neural net that terminates in a pattern of interacting graded potentials and consciousness. To say that secondary perception builds on the output of primary perception (Hebb, 1949; Neisser, 1967) seems to be right in one sense and wrong in another. It seems to be right in that the prewired feature processors lead into learned processes that combine their outputs. But it seems to be wrong in that learned processes, as well as unlearned ones, are ultimately affected by the same innate analogue mechanisms.

Are these analogue mechanisms based on graded potentials or action potentials? This is a question we raised in the last chapter. Pribram (1971) has suggested that the old truth of psychology that practice makes the conscious unconscious might be explained by assuming that, as the processing of arrival impulses into departure impulses becomes more efficient, there will be less time, and presumably less need, for the waxing and waning of graded patterns. Amount of graded activity should thus decline with practice, and amount of consciousness with it.

This view could account for the fact that the output of primary and secondary perception are blended in consciousness, at least after some practice. Patterns of action potentials based on innate connections would swiftly activate patterns of action potentials based on well-learned connections before any pattern of graded potential activity is ever built up. Yet it would not seem to shed any light on the question of whether the analogue properties are properties of graded potentials or simply properties of complex neural nets that hold regardless of whether the neurons are interacting by means of action potentials or graded potentials.

Percepts, Hallucinations, Eidetic Images, and Memory Images

Our information-processing system is not simply an "upstream" device, but one in which higher processes can act back upon lower processes (Bruner, 1970). Perceptual patterns can be activated, not only by sensory input, but by executive activity, as well.

An image is a perceptual experience that occurs in the absence of sensory stimulation. Let us begin by distinguishing afterimages, which are effects in primary perception, from images in secondary perception. The most important difference is that images in secondary perception are subject to executive control, whereas afterimages are not. Hallucinations, eidetic images, and memory images can all be activated by appropriate instructions, whereas afterimages can be induced only by prolonged stimulation. Another difference is that images in secondary perception last for days, months, or years, whereas afterimages last only seconds or minutes. A particularly intriguing difference is that images in secondary perception decrease in size and afterimages increase in size as distance is increased.

This last point requires explanation. Imagine a candle 1 foot in front of your eyes, and then imagine the same candle across the room. These are images in secondary perception, and the distant image should seem much smaller than the near one, as a distant candle would seem smaller than a near candle (see Figure 54a). Now fixate on the X in Figure 55 for about a minute, and then look at the white page just inside the cover of this book. The whiteish psi you should see is an afterimage (it helps to blink a few times to see the afterimage), and it should get larger, not smaller, as you move the book away from you, following Emmert's (1881) law (see Figure 54b). Apparently, the mechanisms that show afterimage effects are located before the analogue model of space, and the mechanisms that produce images in secondary perception are located after the analogue model of space.

While hallucinations, eidetic images, and memory images are all subject to executive control, the nature of this control is different for hallucinations. We can make eidetic images and memory images come and go at will and, in the case of memory images at least, even alter them freely. But, subjectively, we seem to have no control over hallucinations. Perhaps this is why they, unlike eidetic images and memory images, tend to be confused with reality.

Despite subjective appearances, however, we do have control over hallucinations. Hallucinations can be modified by reinforcement, like other responses (Fairweather, Sanders, Maynard, Cressler, & Jennings, 1967), and they can be controlled by hypnotic instructions. The difference between hallucinations and other images may be that hallucinations are controlled by automatic, subordinate executive mechanisms, while the control of eidetic images and memory images resides in the superordinate executive system. But such distinctions are a topic for later discussion.

Both positive hallucinations, seeing something that is not there, and negative hallucinations, not seeing something that is there, can be induced hypnotically. The following reports from subjects

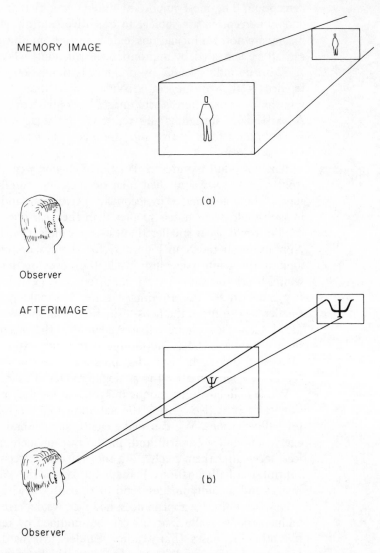

MEMORY IMAGE

(a)

Observer

AFTERIMAGE

(b)

Observer

FIGURE 54. *The effect of projection distance on the sizes of memory images and afterimages.*

hypnotically instructed to hallucinate a mosquito, a positive hallucination, shed an interesting light on the relationship between hallucinations and percepts.

> SUBJECT A: I know very well there wasn't a mosquito in the room but when I was told it would bother me I felt an overpowering need to act as if it were. But I didn't feel it and I didn't hear it.

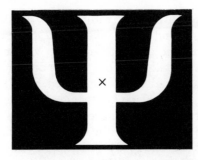

FIGURE 55. *An inspection figure for producing an afterimage.*

SUBJECT B: When you told me there was a mosquito I heard him right away and felt him buzzing around my face. Looking back at it now the buzzing wasn't really very clear, but at the time it didn't occur to me that there wasn't a real mosquito [Shor, 1965].

Hypnosis seems to be an effect on the executive system, and we shall consider it later. In the case of Subject A, the effect seems to have stopped there; it affected his actions but not his perception. In the case of Subject B, however, the executive system seems to have wrought a change in perception. It would be interesting to know whether such changes produce afterimages and whether these transfer binocularly, for this would tell us how far back "downstream" executive control extends. Unfortunately, little progress has been made on this question (Erickson, 1941; Hibler, 1941).

While eidetic images and memory images are alike in the preceding respects, they differ in others (Haber, 1964; Jaensch, 1925; Kluever, 1928). For example, it has been reported that memory images seem to be located inside the head, but that eidetic images, like afterimages, seem to be located outside the head, even conforming to the shape of objects on which they are projected. The most striking and demonstrable difference, however, is in the amount of detail represented. Eidetic images enable subjects to count the buttons on a shirt or to report the letters in a foreign word weeks after seeing the stimulus.

Stromeyer (1970; Stromeyer & Psotka, 1970) has provided a particularly convincing demonstration of the great detail in eidetic images, using stereoscopic dot patterns. A stereoscopic pair of dot patterns is constructed by (*a*) selecting any random pattern of dots for one member of the pair and then (*b*) deriving the other member of the pair from the first by systematically displacing certain dots certain specified distances. When one member of such a pair is presented to one eye and the other to the other eye, a three-dimensional form with dotted surfaces is seen standing out from a dotted background. Taken separately, each member of such a pair is simply a random pattern with no special characteristics; the special characteristics have to do with the relationship between them. Stromeyer has found an eidetiker who can view one member of such a stereoscopic pair with one eye, wait several hours, view the other member with the other eye, and then identify the particular three-dimensional form represented by their combination. The appellation "photographic memory" certainly seems a fitting description of such a performance.

Several lines of evidence point to the similarity between memory images and percepts. Perky (1910) had subjects imagine things, like a banana, on a blank screen and describe the images. On some trials, she projected a faint picture of the target object on the screen from behind. Her main finding was that subjects often could not discriminate between a percept and a self-generated image; they would describe the projected picture, thinking that it was an image they had produced themselves.

Posner (1969) has shown that the reaction time for deciding that "A" and "A" are the same (physical identity) is faster than that for deciding that "A" and "a" are the same (name identity). What is more to the present point he also showed that the reaction time for deciding that an "A" and an imagined "A" are the same is equal to that for physical identity. Apparently, the image of an "A" functions very much like the percept of an "A" in this respect.

Finally, Brooks (1967, 1968) has obtained evidence which suggests that the comprehension of spatial information involves the same system as visual perception. Subjects were given two types of messages: spatial and nonspatial. An example of a spatial message would be: "In the starting square put a 1. In the next square to the *right* put a 2. In the next square *up* put a 3. . . ." An example of a nonspatial mesage would be: "In the starting square put a 1. In the next square to the *quick* put a 2. In the next square *slow* put a 3. . . ." The messages were presented either visually, to be read, or aurally. The subject's task was to repeat the message immediately after its presentation. The results showed superior recall for the spatial message when it was heard, rather than read. (The reverse was true for the nonspatial message.) Apparently, reading makes demands on the same system that is used to retain spatial information.

Perception and Thought

The mechanisms of perception, and here we shall not attempt to distinguish between primary and secondary perception, can affect thought when our eyes are open and when our eyes are closed. When our eyes are open, perception serves as an external memory (Newell & Simon, 1972). When our eyes are closed, at least in the sense of our not attending to our environment, perception provides us with the images of our internal memory.

External Memory

We use external memory when we take notes, underline books, use paper and pencil for calculations, or move pieces on a chessboard. The virtues of external memory are its unlimited capacity and indefinite duration (Newell & Simon, 1972). The chief difficulty with external memory is retrieval time (Newell & Simon, 1972): It is much quicker, for example, to retrieve your telephone number from internal memory than to retrieve it from the external memory of a telephone book.

We tend to rely on external memory a great deal in our thinking; our thinking tends to be stimulus bound. It is, consequently, often restricted by the dominant perceptual organization, by the way the problem is presented in perception. Duncker (1945) showed this in two different experiments.

In one, he employed the two-string problem (Maier, 1930). The two-string problem requires that two strings suspended from the ceiling be tied together, with the strings having been placed sufficiently far apart that you cannot simply take one in your hand and walk over and reach the other. There are two solutions to this problem, a swinging solution and an anchoring solution. In the swinging solution, the subject ties a weight on the end of one of the strings and swings it; while holding on to the other string, he catches the swinging string on the near swing. In the anchoring solution, the subject ties one of the strings to a chair and pushes the chair as close to the other string as he can; then he simply goes and gets the other string. Duncker introduced this problem to subjects through the use of three different drawings (see Figure 56). What he found was that subjects who saw drawing (a) were more likely to use the anchoring solution than those who saw either (b) or (c).

In the other experiment, Duncker used a problem which required that a cork be used for the solution or one which required that a matchbox be used for the solution. He presented the materials in two perceptually quite different ways: with the critical object isolated or with the critical object perceptually embedded. Thus, the cork was either lying next to a bottle or inserted in the bottle, and the matchbox was either placed next to some matches or filled

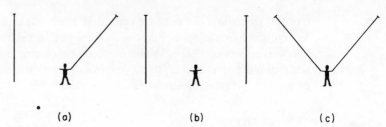

(a)   (b)   (c)

FIGURE 56. *Three different perceptual representations of the two-string problem. [Taken, with permission, from K. Duncker, "On problem-solving,"* Psychological Monographs, 1945, **58** (5) (*Whole No. 270*), 23.]

with the matches. What he found was that it is much more diffi-cult to retrieve a perceptually embedded object from external mem-ory and use it in the solution of a problem. This is apparently because we do not attend to it (Glucksburg & Danks, 1968; Glucks-burg & Weisberg, 1966). A similar effect has also been observed in animals. It is easier for a chimp to see that a stick can be used to rake a banana in from outside his cage when the stick is isolated than when it is the branch of a tree (Kohler, 1925).

Finally, the dependence of thought on perceptual factors has been demonstrated in children, using Piaget's conservation task (Piaget & Inhelder, 1962). If water is poured from a narrow beaker

Start

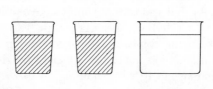

Unscreened pouring   Screened pouring

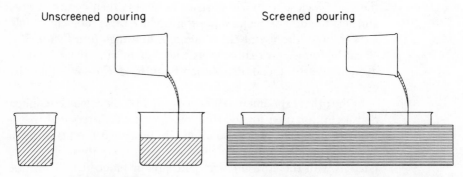

FIGURE 57. *Screened and unscreened pouring in the testing of conserva-tion.*

into a wide one (see Figure 57), children below the age of about 7 fail to see that the quantity of water is unchanged, or conserved. One important source of the difficulty seems to be organization in external memory; the children are likely to say that there is less water in the wide beaker because the water is lower, or more because it is wider. Their thought is dominated by the appearance of things. If a screen is placed before the beakers during the pouring operation, many children approaching the age of conservation who would otherwise have failed the task now succeed, reporting correctly that the amount of water is unchanged by the pouring (Bruner *et al.*, 1966). Because the mechanisms of conservation are executive, we shall consider conservation in greater detail in the second part of the book.

In a later chapter, when we discuss problem-solving strategies, we shall consider some techniques for overcoming the restricting effects of perceptual organization on problem solving, and even using them to advantage.

Memory Images

We have already considered the nature of memory images and some of the factors that influence them. What remains to be discussed is the role that memory images play in thought. There seem to be two kinds of memory images: verbal and nonverbal (Paivio, 1971). A comparison of verbal and nonverbal memory images is of particular interest in the light of findings regarding hemispheric specialization. It seems that the left half of the brain, which controls the right side of the body, performs a verbal function and that the right half, which controls the left side of the body, performs a nonverbal function. Perhaps this is what has led poets to speak of the "right hand of reason" and the "left hand of intuition" (Bruner, 1964).

One line of evidence for hemispheric specialization comes from reaction-time studies. Reaction time for identifying verbal material, such as letters and numbers, is faster when the material is presented to the right ear or the right half of the visual field, and reaction time for identifying nonverbal material, such as pitch patterns and dot or line patterns, is faster when the material is presented to the left ear or the left half of the visual field (Milner, 1971). Similar reaction-time studies show that familiar faces (easy to verbalize) are processed by the left hemisphere, while unfamiliar faces (difficult to verbalize) are processed by the right hemisphere; and slopes of 0°, 45°, and 90°, which are easy to verbalize as "vertical," "diagonal," and "horizontal," are processed by the left hemisphere, while the more difficult to verbalize intermediate slopes are processed by the right hemisphere (Rizolatti, Umilta, & Berlucchi, 1971; Umilta *et al.*, 1972).

The most dramatic demonstrations of hemispheric specialization, however, involve cutting the corpus callosum, the great cable of fibers that connects the two hemispheres. This operation has been performed for medical reasons on some humans. With the corpus callosum cut, the right hand becomes a strictly verbal hand, for the right (nonverbal) side of the brain can no longer tell the left side of the brain, by way of the corpus callosum, what to make it do. Similarly, the left hand becomes a strictly nonverbal hand. If a subject with his corpus callosum cut is asked to match shapes, he can do so with his left hand but not with his right. If he is asked to point to the names of objects, he can do so with his right hand but not with his left (Sperry, 1964; Sperry & Gazzaniga, 1967).

It is important to point out that the right hemisphere is not completely incapable of handling verbal materials. It is, after all, capable of understanding simple experimental instructions, and it can even spell simple words, like "hat," by manipulating large cut-out letters out of sight with the left hand (Milner, 1970).

With this distinction in mind, let us look now at verbal and nonverbal memory images. Nonverbal images seem to be specialized for handling spatial information, and verbal images for handling order information (Paivio, 1971).

Nonverbal Memory Images. Nonverbal memory images, at least visual ones, seem to be organized spatially. Taylor and Posner (1968) presented subjects with three uppercase letters in alphabetical order, followed by a probe letter that was either in uppercase (physical identity) or in lowercase (name identity). The subject's task was to indicate whether the probe letter was among the original three. In the case of physical identity, reaction times were fastest when the matching letter was adjacent to the probe, suggesting a spatial basis for search. In the case of name identity, reaction times were fastest when the matching letter was on the left, suggesting search on the basis of a list in associative memory. The difference was most dramatic when the interval between presentation of the original three letters and presentation of the probe letter was short, though it was still present at an interval of 3 sec, the longest that Taylor and Posner examined.

The spatial organization in visual images seems to make them especially easy to recall. The most dramatic example of this is eidetic imagery, which we have already considered. Closely related are the mnemonic techniques used by professional memory experts (Hunter, 1957), which make possible such feats as remembering *pi* carried to 30 decimal places for decades (Luria, 1968).

Asch (1968; Asch, Ceraso, & Heimer, 1960) seems to have provided the clearest laboratory demonstration of this effect. Asch's experiments demonstrate a difference between what might be called unitizing and associating, a difference that may be taken as marking the boundary between this chapter and the next. Subjects are given pairs of items like those in Figure 58 to recall immediately. The members of a pair are either placed next to one another as separate figures, as the teardrops that are placed next to the dotted line, or drawn together as part of the same figure, as the teardrops that are drawn with a dotted line. What Asch found was that almost exactly twice as many unitized pairs as associated pairs were produced in free recall and that the components of a unitized pair were almost always either recalled together or forgotten together. It seems as though the spatial organization serves as a kind of "glue" to hold features together.

The subjects in Asch's experiment had no special eidetic capacities. Apparently, anyone can be trained to use memory images to unitize items, instead of associating them, and thus to increase his memory capacity. Wallace *et al.* (1957), by simply instructing subjects to visualize both members of each pair together in the same image, got subjects to the point where they actually learned 500 pairs with one trial per pair and with a recall accuracy of 99%. Even without training, however, ordinary subjects use images, as indicated by the fact that words are easier to recall the more concrete they are, that is, the more readily images can be associated to them (Paivio, 1971).

The special "glue" of memory images may not always be a boon, however, for it can hinder analytic thought. Shepard, Hovland, and Jenkins (1961) presented both integral and nonintegral stimuli (see Figure 59) for classification. When the correct classification was triangles versus circles, for example, subjects with the nonintegral stimuli would state simply that one class consisted of triangles and the other of circles. Subjects with the integral stimuli, on the other hand, would frequently state that one class consisted of large and small triangles and the other of large and small circles. These two statements of the concept specify exactly the same partition of the stimuli, but the latter is unnecessarily complex in that it includes reference to the irrelevant variable, size. Perception has combined the dimensions so well that it is difficult to select out only what is relevant.

Despite this limitation, the analogue properties of perception

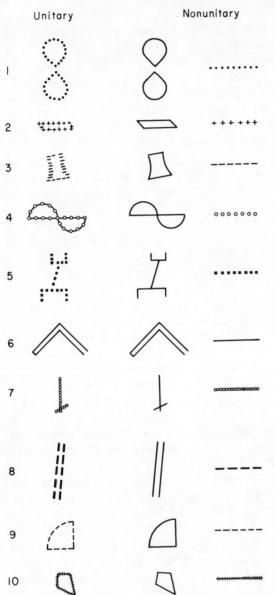

Unitary   Nonunitary

FIGURE 58.   *Unitary and nonunitary stimulus pairs used by Asch, Ceraso, and Heimer.* [From "Perceptual conditions of association" by S. E. Asch, J. Ceraso, and W. Heimer, in Psychological Monographs, 1960, **74** (Whole No. 490), 11. Copyright (1960) by the American Psychological Association. Reprinted by permission.]

seem to make it very useful as a medium for conducting "mental experiments" (Barnett, 1957) in problem solving and creative thinking, a kind of "sandbox in the head" (Attneave, 1972).

Piaget (see Ginsburg & Opper, 1969) has described the early stages in the development of the capacity to conduct such mental experiments, a stage of static images and a stage of dynamic

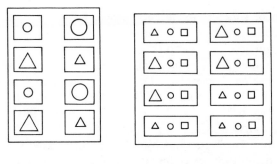

Integral   Nonintegral

FIGURE 59. *Integral and nonintegral stimuli used by Shepard, Hovland, and Jenkins.* [*From "Learning and memorization of classifications" by R. M. Shepard, C. I. Hovland, and H. M. Jenkins, in* Psychological Monographs, *1961, 75 (Whole No. 517). Copyright (1961) by the American Psychological Association. Reprinted by permission.*]

images. Before the age of 7, a child can do no more than reproduce images of things he has actually seen, and only static images at that. If he is shown the blocks in the upper left of Figure 60 and then shown the top block being displaced to the position in the upper right of Figure 60, he can neither draw the final position from memory nor recognize it when it is shown to him. At around 4 or 5, he tends to produce and select drawings like A, B, C, and D, and, at around 6, he tends to produce and select drawings like F and G. The ability to use dynamic images to reproduce what he has seen and to anticipate what he has not—displaced blocks, bent lines, folded shapes—comes at around 7 years of age. This is the

Movement of blocks

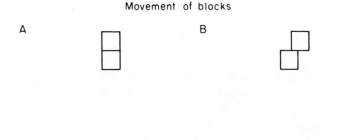

Drawing of blocks

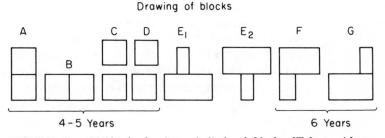

FIGURE 60. *Children's drawings of displaced blocks.* [*Taken, with permission, from H. Ginsburg and S. Opper,* Piaget's theory of intellectual development *(Englewood Cliffs, New Jersey: Prentice-Hall, 1969), p. 156.*]

age of the advent of concrete operations, which, as we shall see later, involve a good deal of organization in the executive system. From this age on, mental images can be a great aid to thought.

We shall have more to say about such "mental experiments" when we get to the executive system. For now, we wish to focus on the "sandbox," itself. Two points can be made. One is that the "sandbox" seems to be truly analogue. Shepard and Metzler (1971) presented pairs of solid objects constructed by joining cubes and asked subjects whether one object could be rotated into the other. When the objects were the same in this sense, reaction time was a precise linear function of the difference in orientation, increasing 16 msec for each degree of rotation. The function was almost exactly the same whether the rotation was in depth or in the picture plane.

The second point is that, as we might well expect, nonverbal information is more accessible to the analogue model than is verbal information. This was shown in an experiment by Anderson and Johnson (1966b). They presented subjects with information in either a verbal or a nonverbal form and then posed a problem whose solution required making use of the information. While the same number of subjects in both conditions reported manipulating imaginal representations of the problem, imaging was positively correlated with solution frequency only for those subjects who had received the critical information in a nonverbal form. As a consequence, more subjects solved the problem in the nonverbal condition.

Verbal Memory Images. There is some indication that verbal memory images are particularly well suited to retaining information about the serial order of events. Paivio and Csapo (1969) presented words and pictures at a sufficiently fast rate that the pictures could not be recoded verbally and the words could not be recoded nonverbally. They employed four tasks, two of which (memory span and serial learning) required memory for the order of the items and two of which (recognition and free recall) did not. Their main finding was that the words were superior to the pictures only when order information was required.

In this chapter, we have relied on the association as the mechanism of secondary perception. But associations serve other functions, as well. The time has come to consider associations more generally.

Associative Memory

chapter 4

Associative processes add a dimension of meaning to the analogue model.

By binding percepts together with one another and with more abstract mental states, associative organization establishes a layer of meaning beneath the surface appearances. We are not born knowing that the sound "chair" represents a certain visual–tactual stimulus, or that the appropriate responses to that visual–tactual stimulus include sitting, or that the referent of the sound "furniture" is related to the referent of the sound "chair." We learn these relations. Most of our knowledge about what leads to what in the world is accumulated in our memories as a consequence of experience. In this chapter, we will consider the fundamental nature of the way in which such knowledge is represented.

The key concept in this chapter will be the association. Our memory, as we shall argue, seems to be at base associative. Yet this chapter on associative memory will end with the tale only half told. For associative memory is used by the executive system, and the executive system employs conceptual, logical, and syntactic plans for retrieving information from associative memory. Many properties that are ordinarily thought of as characterizing associative memory, most notably, conceptual, logical, and syntactic relations among elements, seem to be better understood as characteristics that depend heavily on executive processes. They will be discussed in a later chapter.

The same associative mechanism seems to be involved in both secondary perception and associative memory proper. But secondary perception seems to constitute a special case in which the elements associated are sufficiently primitive to involve the appearance of things (Hebb, 1968) and in which the mechanism of association is supplemented by mechanisms of primary perception (Asch, 1968). Associative memory proper, on the other hand, seems to involve both perceptual elements and more abstract elements, and these seem to be bound together only by associations.

An experiment by Saltz (1971) nicely illustrates the distinction between associative activation of elements and executive activation of elements by way of associations. It shows that, while immediate associations seem to be automatic, mediated associations seem to be subject to voluntary control.

Practice on the pairs "chien–dog" and "fleur–flower" will facilitate later practice on the same pairs and interfere with later practice on "chien–flower" and "fleur–dog" (see Figure 61). The interference effect in the second case is a very strong effect; it seems to be due to automatic associations, for the learner cannot inhibit them, even though they are causing him great difficulty. It is this kind of associative activity with which we shall be concerned in this chapter.

On the other hand, let us say that a subject first learns "chien–dog" and "fleur–flower" and then learns "dog–hund" and "flower–blume," establishing the chains: "chien–dog–hund" and "fleur–flower–blume" (see Figure 61). This learning will facilitate later learning of "chien–hund" and "fleur–blume" but, and this is the important point, will not interfere with later learning of "chien–blume" and "fleur–hund." Here, it appears that associations are subject to voluntary control, being used when they help and ignored when they would hinder. It is this use of associative information which we will take up later, when we come to the executive system.

William James (1890) wrote of the "flights and perchings" of thought. The "flights" seem to be executive movements through memory, and the "perchings" seem to be points where the execu-

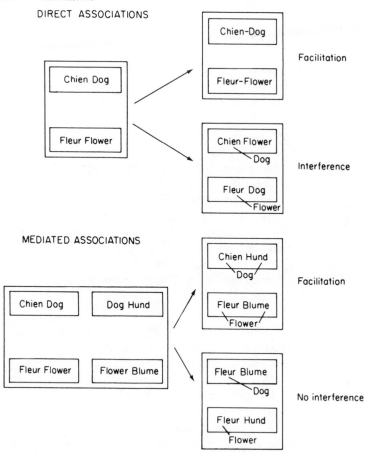

FIGURE 61.   *Direct and mediated associations.*

tive pauses to "get its bearings," by permitting the automatic activation of an associative context that will direct it on its next "flight." To extend another of James's metaphors, the "stream of consciousness" seems to follow an unconscious bed of automatic associations. In this chapter, we shall be concerned with the "perchings" and the activation of the unconscious bed of associations.

We shall begin this chapter by attempting to establish four characteristics of associations. Following that, we shall consider the notion of a schema, verbal and nonverbal associative memory, and the role of associative memory in thought, particularly in language, logical reasoning, and problem solving.

Associations

Associations seem to be graded in strength, to be contentless, to be activated automatically, and to be activated in parallel. Let us examine the evidence for each of these four assertions.

Strength

There is by no means complete agreement as to whether associations differ in strength, so let us look into the matter. Traditionally, two kinds of laws describe the formation of associations. Primary laws, the most important of which is the law of contiguity, state the conditions that determine what will be associated with what, and secondary laws state the factors that determine the strength of the association. It is the secondary laws with which we are concerned here. The most important of these are frequency, recency, and arousal.

Frequency. The law of frequency asserts that the more frequently an association is activated, the stronger it becomes. This would seem to be adaptive in that it would make associative memory more veridical by drawing the more trustworthy features of the world more boldly. A law of frequency would assure that degree of covariation was represented.

There is no question that, in most cases, covariation between stimulus and response, or between one idea and another, increases with practice, following the familiar learning curve. The more one rides a bicycle or performs an analysis of variance, the better one gets at it. There is no disagreement here, and, from the point of view of adaptation, this would seem to be all that matters.

Disagreement arises in connection with what occurs at the level of individual associations. The incremental learning view (Hull, 1952; Underwood & Keppel, 1962) asserts that associations that connect stimuli with correct responses are gradually being increased in strength as a function of trials. The one-trial learning view (Bower, 1967; Estes, 1964; Guthrie, 1952) asserts that any association is changed from zero strength to full strength in a single trial and that what practice does is increase the number of associations that connect stimuli with correct responses.

Several studies (Bower, 1961; Polson, Restle, & Polson, 1965; Rock, 1957; Suppes & Ginsberg, 1962, 1963) have attempted to isolate single associations in verbal paired-associate learning tasks and have shown that the strength of these associations crosses the threshold from responding correctly at the chance level to responding correctly 100% of the time in a single trial. Underwood and Keppel (1962) have pointed out, however, that this does not mean that associative strength changes from 0 to 100% in a single trial. It is quite possible that changes in strength occurred before the threshold for correct responding was crossed and that changes continue to occur after this threshold has been crossed. One must be careful to distinguish learning from performance (see page 304).

Indeed, evidence exists to indicate that changes do continue to occur after the threshold for correct responding has been crossed. Even after the subject is responding at the 100% level, latencies continue to decline gradually (Millward, 1964; Suppes, Groen, & Schlag-Rey, 1966) as does the galvanic skin response (Kintsch, 1965). Taken together, these data suggest a sudden, conscious change at the level of the executive system, followed by a gradual change as control is turned over to lower, associative mechanisms. We shall examine this transition in detail in the next chapter. For now, we would argue simply that these results are perfectly consistent with the notion that practice can produce continuous changes in associative strength.

Recency. The law of recency asserts that the more recently an association has been activated, the stronger it is. Although judgments of recency are apparently based, at least in part, on factors other than strength (Underwood, 1969), there is no question but that covariation between stimulus and response, or between one idea and another, tends to decline with time, following the familiar forgetting curve. The adaptive significance of a law of recency would seem to be to update our memories and keep them abreast of a changing world.

Disagreement occurs at the level of interpretation. The two dominant explanations of forgetting are decay in the strength of the association in question and interference from competing associations. According to decay theory, an association A–B will spontaneously become weaker with time. According to interference theory, A–B will not change as a function of time, but will be interfered with by learning A–C; thus, it is learning a new home phone number that causes the old one to be forgotten.

Decay and interference mechanisms are not incompatible. Actually, interference theory is a retrieval theory, and interference effects do not seem to be found where retrieval is not required, in recognition tests (Bower & Bostrum, 1968; Postman & Stark, 1969; Wickelgren, 1967). Interference theory is, therefore, more appropriately considered later, in connection with plans for information retrieval. This leaves us, then, with the question of whether information in the representational system decays or not.

Where there is no specific task to interfere with prior learning, rate of forgetting appears to be a constant. Lists varying in meaningfulness and similarity, though learned at different rates, are all forgotten at the same rate (Underwood, 1964). And lists learned under different instructions, though learned at different rates, do not differ in rate of forgetting, even up to 15 weeks (Delin, 1969). Moreover, individual differences in rate of forgetting are negligible (Underwood, 1964). Such constancy suggests a process, like decay, that is determined more by physiological than information-processing factors. The fact that rate of forgetting in goldfish depends on the temperature of the water during the retention interval (Gleitman, 1970) is consistent with this view.

Arousal. The law of arousal is a refinement of the old law of vividness (Brown, 1854). It asserts that the more aroused the learner is during or shortly after learning, the greater the increment in associative strength. Arousal is indicated by pupillary dilation, changes in heart rate and blood pressure, and lowered skin resistance (Kahneman, 1973; Sokolov, 1964). A positive effect of arousal on associative strength would seem to be adaptive in that it would make associative memory more relevant to the needs of the system. A law of arousal would ensure that relevance was represented.

Consider the evidence. Traumatic childhood events tend to be well remembered (Freud, 1949). Emotionally charged words are remembered better than neutral words after 24 hours (Corteen, 1969; Kleinsmith & Kaplan, 1963, 1964; Walker & Tarte, 1963). Bursts of noise during the learning period produce better learning (Berlyne, Borsa, Craw, Gelman, & Mandell, 1965; Berlyne, Borsa, Hamacher, & Koenig, 1966; Berlyne & Carey, 1968). Anxious people acquire classically conditioned responses more rapidly than do nonanxious people (Taylor, 1951, 1956). Moderate amounts of handgrip tension facilitate verbal learning (Courts, 1939). Increased amounts of reinforcement lead to increased associative strength (Collier & Marx, 1959). Damage to the amygdala eliminates arousal and prevents learning (Pribram, 1971).

In all of these cases, it is not clear whether the effects of arousal are on attention during learning (Kahneman, 1973) or on the process of memory consolidation following learning (McGaugh, 1969). Yet we would like to know which, for it is the process of memory consolidation that seems to provide particularly strong evidence for the notion of associative strength.

Consolidation is the process of transferring information from STM or ITM into LTM; and the evidence is that this process takes considerable time: If the process is allowed to run to completion, the increment in associative strength induced by a repetition will be greater than if the process is interrupted. There are several treatments that will interrupt the consolidation process: electroconvulsive shock, anesthetics, convulsant drugs, and antibiotics (Agranoff, 1968; Barondes, 1968; Cherkin, 1969; Duncan, 1949). If such treatments are administered immediately after a learning trial, there is no evidence of learning on a later test, because consolidation was not allowed even to begin. If, on the other hand, they are administered some hours after a learning trial, there is no evidence of disruption, because consolidation was allowed to run to completion. At intermediate intervals, the effects are intermediate, as shown in Figure 62 (Harlow, McGaugh, & Thompson, 1971).

A second trial may also constitute an interruption of the consolidation process. If this is so, then the fact of consolidation would account for the fact that it is often more efficient to space repetitions out in time, rather than to mass them together (Muller & Pilzecker, 1900), spacing allowing the consolidation induced by each trial to run to completion before the next trial is begun (McGaugh & Hostetter, 1971).

Evidence on the possible function of dreaming is consistent with these findings and is of considerable interest in its own right. There is evidence that experiments with high arousal tend to be included in dreams (Breger, 1969) and that dream deprivation (waking subjects during periods of rapid eye movements, which is when dreaming usually occurs) disrupts consolidation of memories of events that preceded the period of sleep (Harlow, McGaugh, & Thompson, 1971).

Manipulations that disrupt consolidation may be subject to the

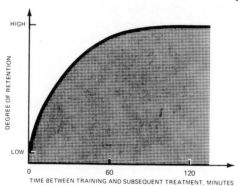

FIGURE 62. *Associative strength as a function of consolidation time.* [Taken, with permission, from H. F. Harlow, J. L. McGaugh, and R. F. Thompson, Psychology (San Francisco: Albion, 1971), p. 321.]

interpretation that they are punishing and produce their effects by inhibiting performance rather than disrupting learning (Lewis, 1969; Lewis & Maher, 1965). Yet manipulations that facilitate consolidation do not seem to be open to such alternative interpretations. Increasing arousal is such a manipulation. Furthermore, any effects of arousal-increasing manipulations that are performed after learning has taken place would seem to be clearly interpretable as effects on the consolidation process, rather than on the learning process. Such manipulations include chemical stimulants (Krivanek & McGaugh, 1968; McGaugh & Krivanek, 1970) and electrical stimulation of the reticular formation (Denti, McGaugh, Landfield, & Shinkman, 1970). Administered shortly after learning, these treatments facilitate performance on a subsequent test.

The fact that degree of consolidation varies continuously as a function of time (see Figure 62) would seem to provide strong evidence for continuous gradations in associative strength. This fact cannot be accounted for by the assumption that what changes is, not the strengths of a fixed number of associations, but the number of *different* associations of a fixed strength. Guthrie (1952), Estes (1964), and Bower (1967) have made such an assumption, where the associations are conceived of as differing with respect to the particular stimulus elements involved. Anderson and Bower (1973) have also made such an assumption, but where the associations are conceived of as differing with respect to the particular relations established between the same elements. In either case, it is difficult to see how different associations could be added after the learning period.

On the other hand, the fact that degree of consolidation varies continuously as a function of time could be accounted for by the assumption that what changes is the number of *identical* associations of a fixed strength. It is not difficult to imagine a process that would form multiple copies of new traces simply as a function of time (Bernbach, 1970). However, the difference between this version of the one-trial learning view and the incremental learning view would seem to be minor, and a choice between these views would seem to have no bearing on any statements made elsewhere in this book.

Lack of Content

To say that associations are contentless is to say that they differ from one another only in degree, in terms of strength. In this, they are to be contrasted with relations, which differ from one another in terms of content: part–whole, subject–predicate, coordination–superordination, antecedent–consequent, cause–effect, means–end, and a very large number of others. The association (Hebb, 1949; Osgood, 1968; Postman, 1968; Voss, 1972) and the relation (Asch, 1968; Chomsky, 1965; Mandler, 1967) are the two most important ways of thinking about the way covariation is represented in LTM. Whereas associations are strong or weak, relations are true or false. "Salt" is strongly associated with "pepper," but, although the relation, "Salt is a coordinate of pepper," is true, the relation, "Salt is a part of pepper," is false. Strength and truth are quite different matters.

It is a simple matter to demonstrate that both strength information and relational information are represented in LTM. As just one example, when people attempt to think of uses for a brick, the responses tend both (*a*) to bear the specified relation to brick, rather than to be simply free associations to the word, and (*b*) to occur in an order and with a latency that is related to their frequency of occurrence in free association.

The position we shall take here is that relational information, as well as strength information, is represented in the form of associations. Thus, instead of "salt" and "pepper" being connected by means of a special "coordination" link (see Figure 63a), they are presumed to be connected by means of associations, but by way of an element that is associated to a "coordination" element (see Figure 63b).

Though labeled and unlabeled connections are logically equiva-

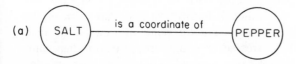

(*a*) SALT — is a coordinate of — PEPPER

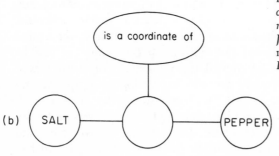

(*b*) SALT — is a coordinate of — PEPPER

FIGURE 63. *Two ways relations could be represented in associative memory.* [*Taken, with permission, from J. R. Anderson and G. H. Bower, Human associative memory (Washington, D.C.: Winston, 1973), p. 89.*]

lent (Norman & Rumelhart, cited in Anderson & Bower, 1973, p. 88), unlabeled associations possess certain advantages. One is explanatory economy. Treating relations as elements adds only a small number of elements to a store of elements that must be vast, to begin with, instead of adding a large number of kinds of connections to what would otherwise be presumed to be a single kind of connection. Another advantage of unlabeled associations is greater explanatory power. Selection of items on the basis of unlabeled associations can be either relation specific (for example, if both the "salt" element and the "coordination" element are activated) or not (if only the "salt" element is activated). As we shall see, both types of selection seem to take place. While labeled and unlabeled connections would seem to be equally efficient in a parallel system (see Anderson & Bower, 1973, p. 90), which associative memory is presumed to be, labeled connections would seem to be more efficient in a serial system, which the executive system seems to be; and the executive system, as we shall see, does appear to make extensive use of relations.

To say that associative memory, while representing relations, is not essentially relational is to say that it is possible to activate an element of associative memory without relational properties becoming manifest. To say that associative memory is essentially associative is to say that it is not possible to activate a relation without strength properties becoming manifest. We shall consider evidence for each of these assertions.

First, what evidence suggests that it is possible to activate an element in associative memory without relational properties becoming manifest? A number of findings suggest that connections that are quite heterogeneous from the point of view of the relations involved may be treated as equivalent; strengths may sum without regard to the relations involved to determine a response or to determine what will enter consciousness.

To begin with an anecdotal example, the condensation in dreams observed by Freud (1955) provides an illustration of heterogeneous associations cooperating to elicit a common response. For example, in a dream Freud once had, a dried flower figured prominently. It turns out that not one, but a number of associations seem to have determined the symbol of the dried flower, which represented Freud's concern over having given up love and life for an academic career. The flower was cyclamen, his wife's favorite; he seldom remembered to bring his wife flowers, or to give her the attention that he should. The flower, a symbol of life and love, was dried for study, in much the same way that Freud had transformed sex for scientific study, rather than lived it. The flower resembled cocaine; Freud had carried out extensive studies on cocaine, and these studies, in a number of ways, symbolized his ambition.

A study by Deese (1959) provides an experimental demonstration of heterogeneous associations cooperating to elicit a common response. Deese was able to predict the frequency of occurrence of particular intrusions in free recall on the basis of the frequency with which each intrusion occurred as a free associate to the words on the stimulus list. As an example, read the following list quickly once, turn the book over, and then attempt to write down all the words on the list:

TABLE
SEAT
SIT
ROCKER
COMFORT
WOODEN
REST
STOOL

The chances are fairly good that you wrote down the word "chair," which is associated with all the words on the list. When Deese presented the 12 most common associates to "chair" to his subjects for recall, 36% erroneously recalled "chair." The percentages in his study ranged from 0% intruding "butterfly" in attempting to recall its 12 most common associates to 44% intruding "sleep" in attempting to recall its 12 most common associates. Deese's principal finding was that these frequencies of intrusion can be predicted quite well ($r = .87$; see Figure 64) on the basis of overall associative strength. Whereas "butterfly" occurs close to 0% of the time when subjects are asked to write down the first word that each of its 12 most common associates brings to mind, "sleep" occurs over 30% of the time when subjects are asked to write down the first word that each of its 12 most common associates brings to mind. The important point, in the present context, is that overall associative strength predicts frequency of intrusion quite well, despite the fact that, in computing overall associative strength, one sums over relations that are not at all homogeoneous. In the example, "table" and "chair" are coordinates; "sit" and "chair" are verb and object; "rocker" and "chair" are part and whole; and so forth.

Finally, strength can be summed over relations to predict semantic similarity. Intuitive grouping of stimuli by subjects asked to put all the names together that go together can be predicted by

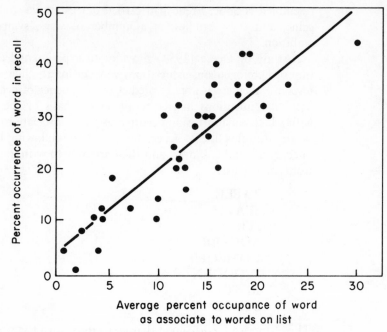

FIGURE 64. *Deese's data on the frequency of occurrence of particular intrusions.* [From J. E. Deese, "On the occurrence of particular intrusions in immediate free recall," Journal of Experimental Psychology, 1959, **58,** 17–22. *Copyright 1959 by the American Psychological Association. Reprinted by permission.*]

means of associative overlap (Weingartner, cited in Deese, 1965). Associative overlap counts words that have more associations in common as more similar than words that have fewer associations in common, without taking any account of the relation the associates bear to the stimulus word. An example of an intuitive grouping predicted by means of associative overlap is, "bird, wing, bees, fly, nature," versus "moth, butterfly, insect, bug, cocoon." Notice that the relations within and between these groups are quite heterogeneous; the groups are intuitive, not rational. These three lines of evidence, then, suggest that associative strength often operates without respect to the relations involved.

Second, what evidence suggests that it is not possible to activate a relation without strength properties becoming manifest? A number of findings suggest that connections that are homogeneous, from the point of view of the relations involved, are not necessarily treated as equivalent.

For one thing, relational symmetry is no guarantee of associative symmetry. The relation between "black" and "white" is the same as that between "white" and "black"; they are coordinates or op-posites. Yet "black" yields "white" in free association considerably more often than "white" yields "black" (Miller, G. A., 1969). Also, judgments of class membership and class inclusion are strongly af-fected by associative relations. Collins and Quillian (1969) showed that reaction time was faster to the question, *Is a canary yellow?* than to the question, *Can a canary fly?* and faster to this question than to the question, *Does a canary have skin?* They explained these differences in terms of the fact that the class of canaries is included in the class of birds and the class of birds is included in the class of animals and in terms of the assumption that property of being yellow is attached directly to canary, the property of flying is at-tached directly to bird, and the property of having skin is attached directly to animal. Their explanation was, thus, in terms of the conceptual relations involved. We shall consider this explanation in greater detail when we come to the executive system and the discussion of conceptual relations. Our present concern is with an alternative explanation of such patterns of reaction times in terms of associative strengths. Such an explanation assumes, for example, that "yellow," "fly," and "skin" are all associated directly with "canary," but at different strengths. There is evidence to support such an explanation. Conrad (1972) and Rips, Shoben, and Smith (1973) have shown that such reaction times are predicted more accurately by association norms than by one's intuitions about the highest level in the conceptual hierarchy at which a given property would be attached. For example, whereas dogs are mammals and mammals are animals, "animal" is a more frequent response to "dog" than is "mammal," and reaction time is faster to the ques-tion, *Is a dog an animal?* than to the question, *Is a dog a mammal?*

Automatic Activation

The experiment by Saltz (1971) described at the beginning of this chapter suggests that immediate associations are automatic and not subject to voluntary control. Several other findings point to the same conclusion.

Underwood (1965) found that, when a continuous list of words is presented and the subject is asked to indicate for each word whether it is old (that is, was presented earlier in the list) or new, subjects frequently report as old words that are associates to words presented earlier in the list. For example, if "dog" is presented, the subject may, on encountering "cat" later in the list, believe that "cat" had been presented earlier. In a sense, "cat" had been pre-sented earlier, for when "dog" was presented it automatically and unconsciously elicited the associative response "cat" (and presumably many others as well).

Keele (1972) presented color names, control words, and nonsense forms printed in different color inks. The subject's task was to report the color of the ink in which a word or nonsense form was printed and to do so as quickly as possible. Each color name was printed in a color other than the one it named; thus, "red" might be printed in green ink, "green" in blue ink, and "blue" in red ink. Keele's main finding was that color-naming reaction time for the semantically relevant words (the color names) was much slower than for the other two conditions.

The fact that meaning makes a difference indicates that processing is carried to the semantic level for both semantically relevant and semantically irrelevant words. The fact that reaction time for the semantically irrelevant words is the same as that for the nonsense forms indicates that this semantic processing does not require central processing (see pages 152–154). Thus, it would seem that both perception and activation of a meaning response, not only can be accomplished automatically, but, as in Saltz's (1971) study, cannot be voluntarily inhibited, even when they are causing great difficulty.

A study similar to Keele's has been performed by Winkelman and Schmidt (in press), using an arithmetic task. True–false reaction times were obtained for equations involving addition. Reaction time was greater where the incorrect answer was a product of the two numbers $(4 + 3 = 12)$ than where it was not $(4 + 3 = 10)$. Apparently, a stimulus like "4 + 3" automatically elicits such responses as "7" and "12."

Lewis (1970) obtained a congruent result in a dichotic stimulation study. In dichotic stimulation, two different messages are presented simultaneously, one to each ear. Apparently, we can attend to only one ear at a time (Broadbent, 1958). If the subject is required to shadow the message coming in one ear, that is, to repeat each word as soon as he hears it, and to do this as rapidly as he can, the message to the unattended ear seems not to be processed voluntarily or consciously. Indeed, shadowing reaction time is ordinarily unaffected by the message to the unattended ear. There is an exception, however, and the exception can be anticipated from the results of Keele's experiment: When the word presented to the unattended ear is associatively related to the word being shadowed, shadowing reaction time is increased. It seems that all the words to the unattended ear are being processed automatically up to the semantic level.

A particularly impressive kind of evidence for the automatic activation of associations comes from a series of experiments by Posner and Boies (1971), employing the sensitive probe reaction time technique. The experimental task was to indicate as rapidly as possible whether two successively presented letters had the same name (for example, the letters **A** and **a**) or different names (for example, the letters **A** and **b**). First, the time it takes to generate the name of the letter associatively was estimated by determining the point at which increasing the interval between the first and second letters had no further facilitating effect on reaction time to the second letter. This point was around .5 second. Next, the involvement of central processing (defined in the next chapter) in this process was determined by inserting a probe task (depressing a key in response to a tone) at various points in the main task and measuring the effect of the main task on reaction

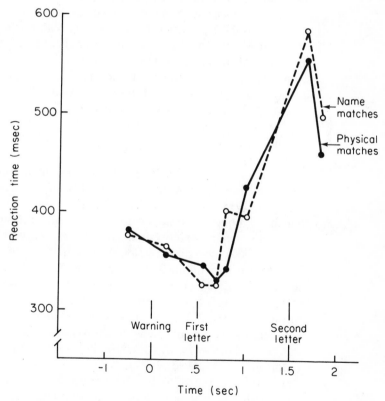

FIGURE 65.   *Probe reaction time evidence for automatic processes.* [*Taken, with permission, from M. I. Posner,* Cognition: An Introduction (*Glenview, Ill.: Scott, Foresman, 1973*), *p. 134. An adaptation from M. I. Posner and S. W. Boies,* "*Components of attention,*" Psychological Review, *1971,* **78,** *391–408.*]

time in the probe task. The idea is that the probe task, which involves central processing, will be affected by those stages in the main task that also involve central processing (are voluntary) but will be unaffected by those stages that do not involve central processing (are automatic). The results are shown in Figure 65. During the .5 second required for associatively generating the name of the first letter, there is no effect on probe reaction time, indicating that this process is quite automatic. It is only after the name has been obtained that central processing is required.

Parallel Activation

Although all of the preceding studies are consistent with the notion of parallel activation of associations, none seems actually to require such a notion. Stronger evidence comes from an experiment by Leeper and from the choice reaction time literature.

Leeper (1935) presented his subjects with stimuli such as those shown in Figure 66. What he found was that verbal cues like, "It is a musical instrument," were powerful aids to recognition. Presumably, this same cue would also facilitate recognition of fragmented pictures of a violin from a variety of different angles and fragmented pictures of a variety of different musical instruments. Such a result is more suggestive of parallel, than serial activation of the various representations associated with "musical instrument."

The strongest evidence for parallel processing, however, is necessarily based on reaction times, for parallel means parallel in time. Hyman (1953), for example, varied the number of stimuli to which a unique response had to be made and measured reaction time. His major finding (similar to the top curve of Figure 67; Posner, 1966) was that reaction time is a linear function of the logarithm of the number of alternatives. Thus, it takes longer to select 1 out of 8 responses than 1 out of 4 responses and longer to select 1 out of 4 responses than 1 out of 2 responses, and, furthermore, the difference between the 2- and 4-alternative cases is equal to the difference between the 4- and 8-alternative cases.

A parallel model for this situation has been proposed by Morton (Morton, 1970; Keele, 1973). When a stimulus is presented, strength is presumed to be simultaneously built up in all idea units with which it has an association. When one idea unit becomes sufficiently stronger than the others, it is activated. Presumably, each idea unit is in a one-to-one relation with a particular response in this experimental situation. The greater the number

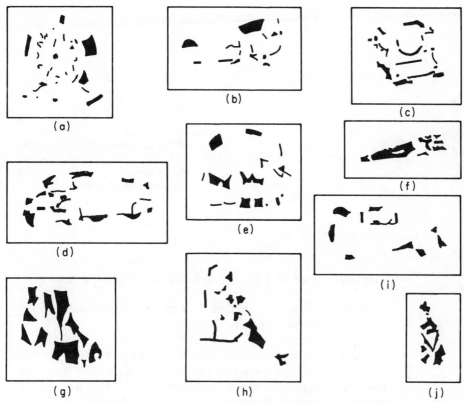

FIGURE 66. *Fragmented figures used by Leeper. (a) alarm clock, (b) airplane, (c)typewriter, (d) bus, truck, (e) elephant, (f) saw, (g) shoe, (h) boy and dog, (i) automobile, (j) violin. [Taken, with permission, from R. Leeper, "A Study of a neglected portion of the field of learning—the development of sensory organization," Journal of Genetic Psychology, 1935, **46**, 41–75.]*

of responses that are being considered, the longer it takes for one idea unit to become sufficiently stronger than the others to be activated. This model predicts that reaction time will be logarithmically related to number of alternatives. (See also Egeth, 1966; Sternberg, 1966.)

Though the mathematics of the argument are beyond the scope of this treatment, it may be helpful to compare the choice reaction time situation with a one-way analysis of variance. The following correspondences would be established, then:

Number of levels on the independent variable = Number of alternative responses

Significance level = Decision criterion

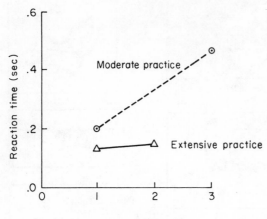

FIGURE 67. *Reaction time as a function of number of alternative responses and reaction time. [Adapted, with permission, from M. I. Posner, "Components of skilled performance," Science, 1966, **152**, 1712–1718. Copyright 1966 by the American Association for the Advancement of Science.]*

Subject = unit of time during which information is sampled

Number of subjects required to reach the significance level = Time required to reach a decision

In the analysis of variance, so long as each subject takes all conditions (processing is parallel), the number of subjects (reaction time) is an approximately linear function of the logarithm of the number of levels on the independent variable. On the other hand, if each subject takes only one condition (processing is serial), the function relating number of subjects to the logarithm of the number of levels on the independent variable is nowhere near linear.

Several studies have confirmed Hyman's basic finding and shown, in addition, that the slope of the function decreases with practice (see Figure 67). In the analysis of variance model, this effect of practice corresponds to increasing the size of the experimental effect; in terms of associative memory, it would correspond to increasing associative strength.

Morton's parallel model can also account for an additional finding of Hyman's, which is of particular interest. Consider a set of four stimuli, A, B, C, and D, each occurring with a probability of .25. We have seen that Hyman compared reaction time in such a situation to reaction time where, say, only stimuli A and B are used. We might say that, in this second situation, A and B occur with probabilities of .50 and that C and D occur with probabilities of zero. Hyman's additional finding pertains to intermediate cases, such as the case where A and B each occur with probabilities of

.40 and C and D each occur with probabilities of .10. "Partially eliminating" alternatives in this manner yields reaction times which are intermediate to those obtained where the alternatives are fully equiprobable with the other alternatives and to those obtained where the alternatives are fully eliminated. These results strongly suggest a parallel, analogue mechanism.

Other researchers have, like Hyman, varied the number of alternative responses against which a stimulus has to be compared and found similar effects on reaction time. Two of these relate to an experiment by Sternberg (1966), in which he presented a number of digits to be held in STM, presented a test digit, and asked whether the test digit was among those in STM. Reaction time, in this case, was a linear function of the number of items in STM. Sternberg's results, unlike Hyman's, suggest a strictly serial process. They will be discussed later, in connection with the executive system.

Hunt and Love (1972) performed the same experiment on a gifted memorizer, however, and found reaction time to be unrelated to the number of items in STM, a result suggestive of parallel processing. An experiment by Morin, DeRosa, and Stultz (1967) provides some information about the mechanisms that might underly parallel processing in this situation. The items they presented to be held in STM corresponded to a structure in LTM, for example, the digits 3, 4, 5, 6. In such cases, test digits that are near the boundaries of the set in memory (like 2 or 7) are responded to slowly, and those that are far away (like 10 or 17) are responded to rapidly. This suggests an analogue representation of the digits in terms of something like an "intensity code" and a judgment that is almost perceptual in nature. In such a model, it is not the number of digits, but the distribution of their "intensities," that would affect reaction time.

A similar result has been obtained in judgments of which of two letters comes first in the alphabet. Anderson and Bower (1973, p. 409) have developed a serial model for representing the ordinal position of items and have predicted, on the basis of this model, that reaction time to verify the true statement, **X** *is to the left of* **Y**, will increase with the ordinal distance between **X** and **Y**. Precisely the opposite result has been obtained, however. Reaction time for judging whether two letters are in forward or reverse alphabetical order is faster the farther apart the letters are in the alphabet (Pollack, 1967). Again, ordinal position seems to be represented by a kind of "intensity tag," and judgments seem to be much like perceptual judgments.

Schematic Organization

The notion of a schema was first introduced by the neurologist Head (1920), who wrote:

> Every recognizable change enters consciousness already charged with its relation to something that has gone before, just as on a taximeter the distance is presented to us already transformed into shillings and pence.

Bartlett (1932) extended Head's notion to memory in general, and Piaget (1952a), Hebb (1949), Lashley (1951), Woodworth (1938), and Neisser (1967) appear to have held similar views.

A particularly interesting case is the generalized reality orientation described by Shor (1959):

> I had been asleep for a number of hours. My level of body tonus was fairly high and my mind clear of dream-images so that I believe I was not asleep but rather in some kind of trance-like state. At that time I was neither conscious of my personal identity, nor of prior experiences, nor of the external world. It was just that out of nowhere I was aware of my own thought processes. I did not know, however, that they were thought processes or who I was, or even that I was an *I* [p. 586].

This is an infrequent experience, but probably one most of us have had at one time or another. A similar experience may be the feeling of the uncanny, when we confront a stimulus that, for the moment, at least, we simply do not know how to interpret. It is only in those rare moments when they are not functioning that we become aware of the normally smooth and silent operation of our schemas.

The schema that is active at one moment provides us with expectations about what is likely to happen in the next moment. When a variety of different objects, for example, different apples, lead to similar expectations, they are, in effect, classified together. Thus, associative schemas add to primary and secondary perception a third mechanism for classification. Whereas things classified together perceptually look alike, things classified together schematically do not necessarily look alike; they just seem to go together. Although they have overlapping properties, these properties may be either perceptual or abstract. Wittgenstein's (1953) description of "family resemblances" refers to such schematic classification. Here, he is arguing with Russell, who believed that all classification was conceptual.

Consider for example the proceedings that we call "games." I mean board games, card games, ball games, Olympic games, and so on. What is common to them all?—Don't say: "There *must* be something common, or they would not be called 'games' "—but *look and see* whether there is anything common to all. —For if you look at them you will not see something that is common to *all*, but similarities, relationships, and a whole series of them at that. To repeat: don't think, but look! —Look for example at board games, with their multifarious relationships.

Now pass to card games; here you find many correspondences with the first group, but many common features drop out, and others appear. When we pass next to ball games, much that is common is retained, but much is lost. —Are they all "amusing"? Compare chess with noughts and crosses. Or is there always winning and losing, or competition between players? Think of patience. In ball games there is winning and losing; but when a child throws his ball at the wall and catches it again, this feature has disappeared. Look at the parts played by skill and luck; and at the difference between skill in chess and skill in tennis. Think now of games like ring-a-ring-a-roses; here is the element of amusement, but how many other characteristic features have disappeared! And we can go through the many, many other groups of games in the same way; can see how similarities crop up and disappear.

And the result of this examination is: we see a complicated network of similarities overlapping and criss-crossing: sometimes overall similarities, sometimes similarities of detail.

I can think of no better expression to characterize these similarities than "family resemblances"; for the various resemblances between members of a family: build, features, color of eyes, gait, temperament, etc. etc. overlap and criss-cross in the same way. —And I shall say: "games" form a family [Wittgenstein, 1953, pp. 31f.]

Galton and, later, Woodworth (1938) suggested that the recording of experience in the form of schemas is much like the process of forming a composite photograph by printing photographs of different faces on top of one another. In both composite photographs and schemas, presumably, the constant features are drawn in heavily, and the variable features are washed out. All that would seem to be required to produce schematic representations in the variable world of Heraclitus is the law of frequency operating in a parallel associative memory. Because the most frequently repeated associations will be stronger than the others, both the average pattern and the degree of variation about the average will be represented. Because the most frequently repeated associations do not represent all the features in any stimulus, the schema will be, as its name implies, a rough sketch.

A particularly interesting fact about schemas is that, because no single stimulus is likely to have all the features represented by the most frequently repeated associations, the schema will be a kind of supernormal representation, supernormal, however, in the sense that it possesses more of the frequent features than any single stimulus, rather than in the sense that it exaggerates these features. Bransford and Franks (1971), using both geometric figures and sentences, found that subjects were actually more likely to report having previously seen a stimulus that contained all of the common features but that they had not seen before than a stimulus that contained only some of the common features but that they had seen before.

Their results with sentences are particularly interesting. Here, atomic propositions are regarded as the repeated elements, and molecular propositions incorporating varying numbers of the atomic propositions are the stimuli. For example, the molecular proposition, *The rock which rolled down the mountain crushed the tiny hut beside the woods,* can be considered to contain the following four atomic propositions: 1. *The rock rolled down the mountain.* 2. *The rock crushed the hut.* 3. *The hut was tiny.* 4. *The hut was beside the woods.* Subjects were more confident that a sentence had been presented, the greater the number of previously presented atomic propositions it contained. Thus, subjects would be most confident of having seen the full molecular proposition (the schema), even though it had not been shown before. In addition to the notion of a supernormal representation, the Bradford and Franks experiment also points to another interesting fact about classification on the basis of schemas, as opposed to classification on the basis of concepts. It is meaningful to talk about the degree to which a fruit looks like an apple or the degree to which a term paper deserves an "A," whereas it is not meaningful to talk about the degree to which a number is odd or the degree to which an assertion is self-contradictory. Once again, the representational system is seen to have the characteristics of an analogue system.

Not all associative classification is schematic, however. While schematic classification is based on the number of features, perceptual or abstract, that objects have in common, items can be classified together associatively on a basis that is quite arbitrary and unrelated to their features. For example, numbers activate one associative unit, and letters another (Brand, 1971; Posner, 1970). Here, classification is not based on the number of common features, for numbers are not like one another any more than they are like letters. Here, also, classification is quite discrete; it is not possible to say that a particular nonsense form is any more like a number than like a letter (though, of course, it is possible to say that it is more like a particular number than a particular letter).

Of special interest is the relation of schemas to consciousness.

There seems to be a paradox here. What fits in with the schema enters consciousness, and what does not fit in with the schema also enters consciousness, although by a different route.

Herbart (Boring, 1929, pp. 256ff) said that of all those ideas below the limen of consciousness, only those that fit in with the unity of consciousness find so little resistance that they can rise above. Treisman (1960) has obtained support for this notion. She presented a different message to each ear and instructed subjects to shadow the message coming in one ear and to ignore the message coming in the other ear. The message to be ignored was a string of unrelated words, while the message to be shadowed was a meaningful message. Suddenly, she switched each message to the opposite ear. The subjects' reaction was to continue following the original message for several words before they became aware that it was now coming in the other ear. Thus, what fits in with the schema enters consciousness readily, even though it comes from an unexpected direction.

But what does not fit in with the schema also enters consciousness. The pertinent data here have to do with the orienting reaction (Pavlov, 1927; Sokolov, 1963, 1965). The orienting reaction is a response to novel stimuli that is characterized by vasoconstriction in the limbs and vasodilation in the head.

One important fact about the orienting reaction is that it habituates to repeated or continued stimuli. When the airplane engine starts up, you orient to it, but after a while you pay no further attention to it. Learning is involved here. A "neuronal model" (Sokolov, 1963) of the world is formed, and what fits the model is processed unconsciously. Repetition or continuation of a stimulus is not actually necessary; any definite expectation seems to be sufficient. Unger (1964) found an orderly disappearance of the orienting response to successive numbers presented in ascending order.

A second important fact about the orienting reaction is that it reappears if expectations fail to be confirmed. Sokolov (1969) has shown that when a single flash of light is omitted from a regular series, a major orienting reaction occurs soon after the time at which the omitted light was due, and Unger (1964) found an orienting response to a number presented out of sequence. This shows that the unattended stimuli are still processed, though at some lower level. It would seem that the neuronal model must routinely process a great many features of the environment in parallel. What fits in with this neuronal model does not enter consciousness, but what does not fit activates the orienting reaction and thereby gains entrance to consciousness.

How, then, do we resolve the paradox? The function of the schema seems to be to process the redundant aspects of experience and to present the informative aspects to consciousness. [Consistent with this interpretation is the fact that especially significant stimuli do not habituate. For example, Biryikov (described in Razran, 1971, p. 118) found that fox cubs who had eaten mice did not habituate to their squeaks, whereas those who had not eaten mice did.] When the flow of events is in accord with the expectations of the schema, this processing of the redundant aspects of experience is accomplished successfully at an unconscious level, and the informative aspects of experience enter consciousness without an orienting reaction. When, on the other hand, the flow of events violates the expectations of the schema, they can no longer be handled by unconscious, automatic processes, and higher processes are then called upon by means of the orienting reaction. In both cases, however, attention is called to the informative aspects of experience, and, in both cases, information enters consciousness charged, as Head (1920) said, with its relation to what has gone before.

It is interesting and important to note that the neuronal model and the subject's conscious expectations do not always coincide. Maltzman, Harris, Ingram, and Wolff (1971) exposed subjects to a constant level of illumination for 10 minutes. The illumination was then changed, then restored, in a series of regular alternations. Although the subjects surely realized the repetitive pattern of events, they continued to show larger orienting reactions when the illumination was changed from the initial adapting level than when it was restored to that level. Also, Furedy and Scull (1971) presented subjects with a random sequence of two events and noted that change from the preceding event caused a larger orienting reaction than did repetition of the preceding event, despite the fact that the verbally reported expectations of subjects in such situations favor change over repetition.

Woodworth (1938) said that, in responding to experience, we do more than simply activate the closest-fitting schema; we tend to represent experience in terms of a schema-plus-exception. The schema handles those features that an item shares with other members of its class, and the exception serves to distinguish it from them (see also Collins & Quillian, 1972). Thus, we speak of a pale light, a brass key, a honey-suckle-covered fence. This is the way the schema normally operates, coding the redundant features of the environment in an economical fashion and calling the non-redundant features to our attention. It thus serves the functions of both assimilation and accommodation.

In Hebb's (1949) view, activity in the schema (which he called a cell assembly) corresponds to consciousness. Pribram's (1971) view, however, seems more consistent with the foregoing considerations. In Pribram's terms, activity in the schema would handle the redundant aspects of experience by means of action potentials and, hence, would be outside of consciousness. It is what does not fit the schema that builds up graded potentials and generates awareness. This view seems to provide physiological substance for Freud's metaphor of consciousness as the tip of an iceberg.

Verbal and Nonverbal Associative Memory

The representational system, as we have noted, seems to be divided into a verbal and a nonverbal hemisphere. This suggests the possibility that verbal and nonverbal associations may be organized differently.

Hockett (1960) has suggested a basis for such a difference: One of the significant properties of language is its arbitrariness of reference. There is no intrinsic relationship between a word and its referent, such as the relation of similarity, or isomorphism, that holds between an image and its referent. Because words are arbitrary and images are not, it is reasonable to expect that they might be organized differently. Words are free to put things together on a functional or conceptual basis—boats, cars, trains, and planes; copper, iron, nickel, and silver—even though they do not occur together or look alike. It may be that it is contiguity in experience that forms the basis of organization in nonverbal associative memory and contiguity in thought, brought about by the executive system, that forms the basis of organization in verbal associative memory. Verbal associative memory may be the scratchpad of the executive system. Let us look at the little evidence that is presently available.

Karwoski, Gramlich, and Arnott (1944) obtained word associations to both pictorial and verbal stimuli and found differences. Whereas a picture of a fork leads predominately to the response "eat," the word "fork" leads predominately to "knife." And, whereas a picture of a comb leads predominately to "hair," the word "comb" leads equally often to "brush" and "hair."

An experiment by Codelia (1973) suggests a related difference. A number of items are spread out before a subject, and he is asked to group them into piles, putting together those that belong together. He can use as many or as few piles as he wishes, and the piles need not be uniform in size. When the items are pictures, subjects tend to group them into many small piles; when they are names of the pictured objects, subjects tend to group them into a few large piles. Verbal associative memory seems to be organized into broader categories than is nonverbal associative memory.

The distinction between verbal and nonverbal associative memory seems to capture part of Tulving's (1972) distinction between semantic memory and episodic memory. As Tulving put it,

> Episodic memory receives and stores information about temporally dated episodes and events, and temporal–spatial relations among these events. . . . Semantic memory is the memory necessary for the use of language. It is a mental thesaurus, organized knowledge a person possesses about words and other verbal symbols, their meaning and referents, about relations among them, and about rules, formulas, and algorithms for the manipulation of these symbols, concepts, and relations [p. 385f].

But Tulving goes on to say that semantic memory is distinguished from episodic memory by the greater variety of relations stored in it and by the fact that inference is possible in it. This is consistent with the notion that relations and inference require executive activity and that verbal associative memory is the scratchpad of the executive system.

The Role of Associative Memory in Thought

We shall be turning shortly from the representational system to the executive system. But before we leave the representational system, it should be noted that there has been a tendency to overplay the role of executive processes, and the result has been an unbalanced picture of cognitive functioning. Much as people tend to anthropomorphize in describing the behavior of animals, so also does it seem that the executive system, which is the system most heavily involved in scientific thinking, tends to "executomorphize" in attempting to produce scientific descriptions of cognitive behavior. Yet representational processes, as we have already seen in the case of perception, continue to play an important role in the higher mental processes. We turn now to a consideration of the ways in which associative memory is involved in language, logical reasoning, and problem solving.

Language

There has been a tendency (Anderson & Bower, 1973; Chomsky, 1965) to deal, not only with the surface structure of sentences, but also with their deep structure, or meaning, in terms of explicit syntactic rules. The tendency is to employ rules, but not associations, and to analyze syntax, but not semantics.

Chomsky (1957) sought to demonstrate the independence of syntax and semantics with the now-famous sentence, *Colorless green ideas sleep furiously*. This sentence is perfectly grammatical, yet the semantic constraints are certainly minimal: One does not ordinarily think of colorless green things, or of green ideas, and so forth. However, while computer simulations of syntactic theories of language regularly produce such strings, people ordinarily do not (see Osgood, 1968). People, as a general rule, say things that make sense—and yet that are often quite ungrammatical. Semantics takes precedence over syntax. Chomsky's sentence establishes the reality of syntax, but not its importance.

Often, it seems that syntactic analysis depends on semantic analysis, rather than the other way around. Consider the following sentences (Anderson & Bower, 1973):

He hit the boy with the long hair.

He hit the boy with the monkey wrench.

In order to understand the syntactic relation of "long hair" and "monkey wrench" to the rest of the sentence, one must know something about the meaning of these terms.

Yuille and Paivo (1969) obtained an experimental result which also suggests that syntax depends on semantics. They presented sentences that differed in both concreteness and grammaticality, for two recall trials. Concreteness refers to the ease with which the words in a sentence call forth imagery, and grammaticality refers to whether a sentence is in syntactical order or in a scrambled order. What they found was that grammaticality was effective only with concrete sentences.

It seems to be a peculiarity of syntactic rules that they can be readily extended beyond their normal range of usage to produce sentences that are grammatically correct but nearly incomprehensible. Miller (1967) has made the point delightfully well:

> . . . It is a feature of natural languages that sentences can be inserted inside of sentences. For example, "The king who said, 'My kingdom for a horse,' is dead" contains the sentence, "My kingdom for a horse," embedded in the middle of another sentence, "The king is dead. . . ."
>
> The question, of course, is whether we can do this more than once, that is to say, recursively. Let us try: "The person who cited, 'The king who said, "My kingdom for a horse," is dead,' as an example is a psychologist." Most people find this just on the borderline of intelligibility: if I had not prepared you for it, you probably

would not have understood. Let us go one step more: "The audience who just heard, 'The person who cited, "The king who said, 'My kingdom for a horse,' is dead," as an example is a psychologist,' is very patient." By now you should be ready to give up. If not, of course, I could go on this way indefinitely [p. 113].

Syntax would seem perfectly capable of handling one level of embedding, but additional levels seem normally to be handled at the semantic level. This conclusion is also suggested by the results of an experiment by Stolz (1967). Subjects were first given practice in decomposing self-embedded sentences into their component clauses. The sentences were of two types, exemplified by, "The vase that the maid that the agency hired dropped broke on the floor," and, "The dog that the cat that the bird fought scolded approached the colt." In the first case, syntactic structure is supported by semantic structure in that only the correct noun–verb pairs make sense (for example, vase—broke is acceptable, but not vase—hired). In the second case, syntactic structure stands alone in that any of the noun–verb pairs makes sense (for example, both dog—approached and dog—scolded are acceptable). Some subjects were given practice on sentences of one type, and others were given practice on sentences of the other type. When tested on sentences having just syntactic structure, only subjects who had practiced on sentences having just syntactic structure showed any evidence of having benefited from the practice. Apparently, when semantic constraints are available, subjects do not ordinarily employ syntactic rules in understanding sentences.

Schank (1971; Schank, Tesler, & Weber, 1970) has suggested that the most efficient course is to use syntax to comprehend a sentence only when all semantic means have failed, that syntax is important in sentence generation, but not in sentence comprehension. The fact that the speech area, like the verbal hemisphere, in general, seems to be divided into a representational portion and an executive portion also suggests that representational processes might be more important in the understanding of sentences and executive processes in their production.

Logical Reasoning

In the study of logical reasoning, there does not seem to have been any tendency (except, perhaps, in the work of Piaget) to stress executive processes. There seems always to have existed some doubt that the laws of logic are the laws of thought. Earlier, we showed that relations that are conceptually equivalent may differ in associative strength and that these differences in associative strength affect the answering of simple questions about conceptual relations. Those findings are pertinent here, as well, but we shall add to them some that were not pertinent to the earlier discussion.

Meyer (1970), Schaeffer and Wallace (1970), and Collins and Quillian (1972) found that the time required to respond "false" to statements of the form, *All A are B,* is less when A and B are semantically remote (*All typhoons are wheat*) than when they are semantically similar (*All mothers are writers*). The fact that the difference seems to vary about a single value, 100 milliseconds, suggests that an additional executive operation that is independent of semantic similarity is required in the latter case. Both Meyer (1970) and Schaeffer and Wallace (1970) hypothesize that a semantic test is performed initially and that this is followed, when necessary, by some further test. Work by Smith, Shoben, and Rips (1974) suggests that the semantic test is applied in parallel to both defining and nondefining features, whereas the later test is applied only to defining features.

Wason and Johnson-Laird (1972) point to important differences between syllogistic reasoning with concrete and with abstract materials. A syllogism is an argument of the following form:

All men are mortals.

Socrates is a man.

Therefore, Socrates is a mortal.

Syllogisms may be presented in a concrete form, as above, or in an abstract form, as follows:

All A are B.

C is A.

Therefore, C is B.

Using syllogisms stated in abstract terms, Woodworth and Sells (1935) reported what they called an "atmosphere effect." Subjects tend to accept universal, affirmative conclusions (*All A are B*) when both premises are universal and affirmative; to accept universal, negative conclusions (*No A are B*) when both premises are universal and negative; to accept particular, affirmative conclusions (*Some A are B*) when both premises are particular and affirmative; and to accept particular, negative conclusions (*Some A are not B*) when both premises are particular and negative. In addition, if either premise is negative or particular, subjects tend to accept negative or particular conclusions, respectively.

Earlier, Wilkins (1928) had found that syllogisms stated in concrete terms did not produce such an effect. Wason and Johnson-Laird (1972, p. 152) suggest that the normal way we reason about syllogisms is (1) to construct a first approximation to an answer on a formal basis, using rules of thumb, like, A *negative premise requires a negative conclusion*; then (2) to test this approximation against a semantic representation. The first step, by itself, would tend to produce atmosphere errors. With abstract material, it is difficult to perform the second step, and so the atmosphere errors tend to go uncorrected. With concrete material, it is easy to perform the second step and to correct the tendency to make atmosphere errors. Here, as in the experiments of Meyer (1970), Schaeffer and Wallace (1970), and Collins and Quillian (1972), a semantic test is performed; here, however, the effect of associative factors (the concreteness or meaningfulness of the terms) on the ease of performing the test is clearer.*

Perhaps an even clearer demonstration of the role of associative memory in syllogistic reasoning is the effect of prior beliefs on the conclusions we tend to draw. Whereas a syllogism requires us to perform logical operations on the premises in order to determine whether or not the conclusion follows, it seems that, instead, we often content ourselves with simply performing operations on the conclusion to determine whether or not it matches associative memory, that is, whether it is true or false. We thus are often inclined to accept or reject conclusions more on the basis of their factual truth or falsity than on the basis of the logical validity or invalidity of the arguments leading to them. To illustrate these two concepts, truth and validity have been made orthogonal in the

	TRUE	FALSE
VALID	All men are mortal. Socrates is a man. Therefore, Socrates is a mortal.	All heavenly bodies are made of green cheese. The moon is a heavenly body. Therefore, the moon is made of green cheese.
INVALID	All mammals have backbones. All dogs have backbones. Therefore, all dogs are mammals.	All triangles are plane figures. All circles are plane figures. Therefore, all triangles are circles.

FIGURE 68.   *Truth and validity in syllogistic reasoning.*

* See also the recent and very important work of Kahneman and Tversky (1973) and Tversky and Kahneman (1973).

set of syllogisms in Figure 68. The syllogism in the upper left, for example, is both valid and leads to a true conclusion. Using similar syllogisms, Janis and Frick (1943) found a preponderance of errors that involved accepting invalid–true syllogisms and rejecting valid–false ones. Sluggishness at the executive level permits associative memory to exert a conservative influence on thought, biasing the mind against novel conclusions.

A finding that supplements this nicely is that syllogisms with false premises require more time and are evaluated more accurately (Parrott, 1967). Apparently, when the premises are true, it is easy for subjects to slip into the error of evaluating the conclusion on the basis of what they believe to be true about the world. When the premises are false, however (that is when the subject is asked to assume to be true statements that he knows to be false), it is relatively clear that his beliefs about the world are irrelevant and that logical relations must be attended to.

Problem Solving

In problem solving, as well as in psycholinguistics, there has been a tendency to account for information processing in terms of explicit rules processed in a serial fashion (Newell, Shaw, & Simon, 1958, 1962; Newell & Simon, 1972) and to avoid anything so amorphous as the parallel activity of associative schemas. Such models of problem solving, however, seem to deal only with well-defined problems (Minsky, 1961; Reitman, 1965), that is, problems that provide explicit criteria for deciding whether a solution is acceptable. Problems in logic, chess, and cryptarithmetic provide examples.

Work on such problems is of great importance and will be considered later, yet ill-defined problems seem to be more common (Reitman, 1965) and in many ways more interesting. An example of an ill-defined problem is to write a good term paper (Reitman, 1965). Explicit criteria, as students so often complain, are not provided for deciding whether a given paper is good or not. Another example (Dill, Hilton, & Reitman, 1962) is to look into the possible opportunities operations-research techniques might offer a particular company. Another (Reitman, 1965) is to compose a fugue. In each of these cases, only the vaguest criteria for deciding on the acceptability of the solution are provided; the problem solver must provide the rest.

An ill-defined problem is an ambiguous problem, and the problem solver must resolve the ambiguities on the basis of his general knowledge. The process is similar to that involved in understanding an advertisement for a bank that shows open cans of red, yellow, and blue paint and reads, *We will supply the green* (Reitman, 1965). **Green** is ambiguous in that it could refer to either paint or money. The ambiguity is resolved, not by means of any grammatical or other formal rules, but by means of the knowledge that banks supply money and not paint.

Both Reitman and Reich (see Reitman, 1965) have developed computer simulations of problem solving that rely heavily on representational processes, as well as executive processes. Both have parallel associative memories.

Associative processes are important, not only in defining the problem, but also in generating solutions. This is particularly easy to demonstrate in the case of anagram problems. An anagram is a collection of letters (for example, **hecba**) which, when arranged in the proper order, forms a word (**beach**). Data on word frequency are readily available (Thorndike & Lorge, 1944). Johnson and Van Mondfrans (1965), using anagrams that had three solutions each, found that the solutions written first had the highest frequency, those written second had the next highest frequency, and those written last had the lowest frequency.

In all of the examples we have considered of the influence of associative factors on language, reasoning, and problem solving, associative memory can be seen as a source of resistance to change, of conservatism. James (1890) had this conservative influence of associations in mind when he wrote that habit is the great flywheel of society. Associations keep us doing what we have done before.

This conservative influence of associative memory can keep us from error (Brunswik, 1951). When the solution to an arithmetic problem does not "make sense"—the cake weighs 104 pounds; the man is −3 inches tall—we use an intuitive judgment based on associative memory to correct the results of a rational, executive process. This is useful so long as we do not content ourselves with the intuitive judgment. The value of such an intuitive judgment is in getting us to check our facts and our reasoning, for reason must be the final arbiter. After all, the notion that the world is round was, at one time, counterintuitive.

Although a good case can be made for associative memory providing resistance to change, an equally good case can be made for its serving as an important source of change. Campbell (1960) and others have pointed out that truly original thought cannot be achieved by entirely rational means. Because reason always operates within a system of assumptions, some extrarational organization is needed to move outside these assumptions and conceive new ones. What is required is an intuitive leap.

Automatic associative processes are reported by such diverse creative thinkers as Shelley, Ernst, Spencer, Gaus, Hadamard, and Poincaré, working in the arts, philosophy, mathematics, and science (Ghiselin, 1952). Often these processes appear to have the autonomy and creativity of the dream process. According to Ghiselin (1952), creative production by a process of purely conscious calculation seems never to occur.

Apparently, even among ordinary subjects, the more creative are more inclined to make use of associative processes when they are helpful. Wallach & Kogan (1965) presented children with sets of objects, such as a comb, a watch, a pocketbook, and a door, and asked them to put together what seemed to belong together. The interesting comparison had to do with the use of conceptual groupings (here, "hard objects") and associative groupings (here, "getting ready to go out"). While the subjects of high intelligence and low creativity tended to use only conceptual groupings, the highly creative subjects made use of both associative and conceptual groupings.

Perhaps the purest case of extrarational associative thought is incubation. Amy Lowell, the poet (in Ghiselin, 1952), describes the process well:

> I registered the horses as a good subject for a poem; and, having so registered them, I consciously thought no more about the matter. But what I had really done was to drop my subject into the subconscious, much as one drops a letter into a mail-box. Six months later, the words of the poem began to come into my head, the poem—to use my private language—was "there" [p. 110].

We shall return to the associative generation of original ideas, and to incubation, in particular, later, in the discussion of problem-solving strategies that operate on representational processes.

As to the inevitable question of what determines when associative influences will resist change and when they will stimulate change, little seems to be known. It may have to do in part with motivation: Those who are motivated to seek certainty can find strong associations to rely on; and those who are motivated to seek diversity can find weak associations to explore.

An experiment described by Mednick (1962) suggests that this is the case. Subjects were given a series of noun–nonnoun pairs. If the subject chose the noun, a low-frequency associate to the stimulus word was presented as a reinforcer (for example, "father–eggbeater"); if the subject chose a nonnoun, a high-frequency associate to the stimulus word was presented as a reinforcer (e.g., "white–black"). Subjects divided into two groups. Some learned to choose the nouns because that got them the "right" answer, and others learned to choose the nonnouns for the same reason, because that got them the "right" answer. We shall look more closely at such differences when we discuss motivation in creative and authoritarian personalities.

We turn now to Part III and the executive system. Yet we have already become somewhat familiar with the executive system. We have seen something of how it uses information combined by perception and displayed in consciousness. We have seen something of how it activates associations and explores perceptual and associative memory. We have seen something of how it participates in the formation of new associations and thus writes in the representational system. We have seen something of how it cooperates with the representational system in language, reasoning, and problem solving. And we have seen something of how it chooses on the basis of values. We now turn to a closer examination of these matters.

THE EXECUTIVE SYSTEM

part III

General Characteristics
of the Executive System

chapter 5

The executive system directs thought and behavior on the basis of both information in the representational system and its own goals.

Although the representational system can do much—organizing and interpreting information about the state of the environment —the executive system is necessary for directing sequences of responses and for guiding the flow of thought. It is the executive system that accounts for goal-directed behavior. We begin with the important concept of direction.

Direction

It is important at the outset to distinguish between directed and undirected thought. Undirected thought consists simply of the idle wanderings of the mind, as in dreams and daydreams. Directed thought tends toward a particular end, a goal, as in problem solving. It is directed thought that most clearly engages the executive system and that, in its most advanced form, constitutes Level III intelligence.

Perhaps the simplest example of undirected thought is free association, and the simplest example of directed thought is controlled association. In a free association test, a person is given a list of words and asked to write down next to each the first word that it brings to mind. Thus, to "table," most people respond, "chair"; to "salt," "pepper," and to "mountain," "hill." An item on a free association test may be considered to be a miniature daydream.

In a controlled association test, a person is asked to give for each of several words a word that stands in a particular relation to it. Thus, he might be asked to give the opposite of each word (up–down, hot–cold, right–left) or to name the superordinate category to which each word belongs (dog–animal, peach–fruit, shirt–clothing) or to give a novel use for each of several objects (brick–paperweight, coathanger–beam balance, eraser–spring). An item on a controlled association test may be considered to be a miniature problem-solving task.

Whereas British associationists, such as Hobbes, Locke, and the Mills, sought to account for both directed and undirected thought in terms of associations, psychologists at Wurzburg, such as Selz, showed that directed thought requires additional, executive mechanisms (see Humphrey, 1951). Let us begin, however, by considering some data that can be accounted for in terms of associations alone.

Free association tasks, of course, present no problem to associationists. Free associations to each of three stimuli, obtained from 70 subjects, are presented below. The reason for including the rather unusual stimulus "opposite of" will become clear shortly.

Cold	35% **Hot**, 6% **Winter**, 6% **Sick**, 4% **Warm**
Ebony	58% **Black**, 8% **Wood**, 6% **Magazine**, 4% **Ivory**, 4% **White**
Opposite of	14% **Black**, 6% **Truth**, 6% **Right**, 4% **Up**, 4% **Hot**, 1% **White**

Such frequencies are assumed to reflect associative strength (Marbe, 1901). As we have seen, associative strength can be used to predict behavior in a variety of situations.

Now, consider the following controlled association task:

The opposite of cold is   91% **Hot**

Here, the response can be predicted on the basis of associative responses to the individual stimuli. **Opposite of** leads to **hot** 4% of the time, and **cold** leads to **hot** 35% of the time. The total associative strength for **hot** (4% + 35% = 39%) is greater than that for any other response. (We would be hard-pressed to justify percentages as the best measure of associative strength or adding as the best way to combine these measures. These procedures should be regarded only as illustrative. The same point could have been made just as well by using any of a variety of alternative procedures.) Because **hot** is the response most frequently given, it would appear that no new principles are needed to account for directed thought. It would appear, in other words, that directed thought is merely a special case of associative thought, specifically, associative thought in response to a compound stimulus. This idea is at least as old as the British associationists and at least as recent as Hebb (1949).

Whereas some examples of directed thinking can be explained in terms of associations, others cannot, and therefore the explanation does not seem to be correct. Only one counterexample is necessary to make the point.

The opposite of ebony is   74% White, 10% Ivory

The response with the highest total associative strength is neither **white** nor **ivory**. "White" occurs 1% of the time to **opposite of** and 4% of the time to **ebony** (1% + 4% = 5%). And **ivory** occurs 0% of the time to **opposite of** and 4% of the time to **ebony** (0% + 4% = 4%). The response with the highest total associative strength is **black,** which occurs 14% of the time to **opposite of** and 58% of the time to **ebony** (14% + 58% = 72%). Thus, the response that, by an overwhelming margin, has the highest total associative strength is never given. The reason is that it does not fulfill the requirement of being the opposite of **ebony.** Such a requirement, or direction, supplements associations in directed thinking.

Directions do supplement, rather than replace, associations in directed thinking. In the last example, the direction restricted the acceptable responses to those which would in some sense be considered to be the opposite of **ebony,** but this still permitted two responses (as opposite of **right** would permit either **left** or **wrong**). Other directions, such as coordinate of **dog** or uses for a **brick,** permit a much greater number of responses. Among the set of responses that fulfill the requirements of the direction, relative frequency of occurrence is determined by associative strength (Osgood, 1968). The free-association strength of **white** is somewhat higher than that of **ivory** (the difference in this example is so small that it should be considered only illustrative), and, indeed, **white** occurs more frequently in the controlled association task. Both direction and association act as selecting mechanisms (Maier, 1970) in directed thinking.

A further consideration (Johnson, 1955) indicates that direction functions, not only as an editor, but also as a stimulus, helping to activate by means of associations the items that it will later screen. If direction were just an editor, applied after ideas had been generated by free association, then it would be just as efficient (*a*) to ask a person to produce free associations to **brick** and then later to ask him to indicate which of these associates represent uses for a brick, as (*b*) to ask him to produce **uses for a brick**, in the first place. The fact that it is far more efficient to specify the direction indicates that direction does have stimulus properties, that it activates associated ideas, as well as screens them. This is consistent with the notion, presented earlier, that relations are elements in associative memory, just like other elements. These two functions of direction seem distinct, however, for ideas are frequently activated that are rejected at the screening stage. Activation precedes editing.

To generate ideas that will meet certain standards, then, it would seem that those standards should be kept well in mind during production so they can serve as stimuli. Several techniques for developing creativity have been based on the contrary notion that standards should be temporarily set aside so as not to hinder imaginative thought. These techniques seem to have been uniformly not very successful. One of these techniques is called brainstorming (Osborn, 1953). It attempts to separate production of ideas from judgment of ideas, to divide problem solving into a preliminary stage of relatively undirected thought and a later stage of directed thought. The idea is that undirected thought functions better when left alone. The value of brainstorming is questionable (Dunnette, Campbell, & Jaastad, 1963; Taylor, Berry, & Block, 1957), and, more specifically, suspending judgment during the production of ideas has been found actually to impede creative thought (Manske & Davis, 1968). Directed thought seems to be more effective than undirected thought.

Originality training represents another attempt to enhance creativity (Maltzman, 1960; Maltzman, Belloni, & Fishbein, 1964). In originality training, people are given practice in generating unusual ideas. Such practice is effective in increasing the number of original ideas produced; however, it has no effect on the number of creative ideas produced (Manske & Davis, 1968).

The distinction between originality and creativity is an important one. An original idea is simply a novel idea, one that no one has come up with before. Creative people produce original ideas, but so do mental patients. A creative idea is an idea that is original and that meets certain standards. If it is an invention, it must work; if it is a theory, it must account for data; if it is a work of art, it must communicate. Representational processes, as we saw earlier, can play an important role in the generation of original ideas. Executive processes, however, are essential if the ideas are to have any value, to be creative. Creativity requires direction.

At least two techniques for developing creativity are consistent with the notion that direction should be changed, rather than suspended, during problem solving, and both have proved effective. Maier (1933) simply told his subjects that they should look in new directions for the solution to the problem, particularly when a direction they were following had gotten them stuck for awhile. Hyman (1964) improved on this technique by having his subjects either positively evaluate the creativity of others' ideas or negatively evaluate their own. Maier's technique and both of Hyman's techniques were found to facilitate problem solution.

The way in which direction shifts during problem solving and the way it elicits a number of related solutions before shifting is illustrated in Duncker's classic representation of the course of solution of the tumor problem. The tumor problem is to discover how you can destroy a tumor in a person's stomach (see Figure 69) by means of X rays, but without damaging the surrounding healthy tissue. The most complete exploration of the solution space that Duncker observed is represented in Figure 70.

Direction also seems to be important in inductive reasoning. This is indicated in an experiment by Wason (1960) on generating and testing hypotheses. Subjects were told that the three numbers, 2, 4, 6, conformed to a simple rule and that their task was to try to discover the rule by generating successive triads of numbers, which the experimenter would then identify as either correct or incorrect. The rule was: numbers in increasing order of magnitude. A very general rule was chosen so that positive instances of it would also tend to be positive instances of the more

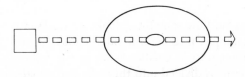

FIGURE 69. *Duncker's tumor problem.* [*Adapted from K. Duncker, "On problem-solving,"* Psychological Monographs, 1945, **58** (*Whole No. 5*). *Copyright 1945 by the American Psychological Association. Reprinted by permission.*]

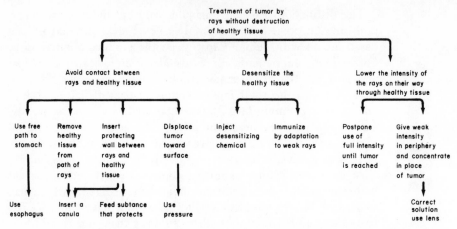

FIGURE 70. *Hierarchy of directions generated in working on Duncker's tumor problem. The representation here is called a solution space. [Adapted from K. Duncker, "On problem-solving," Psychological Monographs, 1945, 58 (Whole No. 5). Copyright 1945 by the American Psychological Association. Reprinted by permission.]*

restricted hypotheses which would be likely to occur first to the subjects.

One finding was that subjects tended to generate only instances that conformed to their current hypotheses. Thus, if a subject was entertaining the hypothesis of successive even numbers, he might test: 4, 6, 8; 20, 22, 24; and 100, 102, 104 (and learn nothing); before thinking of the hypothesis of successive alternative numbers and testing 1, 3, 5 (and finally learning that his previous hypothesis was incorrect). This finding seems to provide some support for Kuhn's (1962) notion that scientists relinquish a theory only when an alternative theory is available. It apparently takes a new theory, a new direction, to enable a scientist to look for data that might be inconsistent with an old theory. Ways to vary one's direction will be considered in the chapter on plans for productive information retrieval.

The data we have considered so far are quite objective, dealing with kinds and sequences of attempted solutions. The Wurzburg psychologists (see Humphrey, 1951) also obtained some introspective data that seem to bear on the distinction between representational and executive processes; some thoughts are accompanied by images and some are not.

If we are trying to imagine how something looks or works, we tend to see images. For example, imagine a wooden cube, painted black on the outside and cut into 27 smaller cubes in the following manner: the original cube is divided into thirds by two equally spaced vertical cuts in the front–back direction; then it is divided into thirds again by two equally spaced vertical cuts in the left–right direction; and, finally, it is divided into thirds once again by two equally spaced horizontal cuts. The problem is to say how many of the 27 smaller cubes thus formed are black on 3 sides, how many are black on 2 sides, how many are black on 1 side, and how many are black on no side. In solving this problem, people seem invariably to report "seeing" the blocks in their mind's eye.

However, some thoughts appear not to be accompanied by imagery. These appear to be the "turning points" in thought. In executing a plan, we often have identifiable experiences of choice or lack of choice, and these do not appear to be accompanied by imagery. Consider the task of multiplying the numbers within each set of parentheses by one another (so that, in the first case, $12 \times 3 = 36$):

$$(12, 3) \ (41, 8) \ (16, 9) \ (31, 6) \ (274).$$

The plan cannot be applied in the last case. This probably produces a mild feeling of surprise, puzzlement, or consternation, but no particular imagery. Or consider the problem: Why are all numbers of the form 117, 117; 407, 407; and 823, 823 divisible by 13? Initially, you probably have a feeling of being without a plan. If it is pointed out that all of these numbers are divisible by 1001, however, you probably get a feeling of definiteness, of having some way to proceed. In neither case, though, do we seem to have any specific imagery associated with these feelings.

Although the trend in recent years seems to be to dismiss the imageless thought findings without giving them a real hearing, Binet, Pratt, and Humphrey (see Humphrey, 1951) have all concluded that the Wurzburgers were correct in reporting imageless thought. Indeed, the distinction between imageful and imageless thought seems to correspond to the distinction made by Locke (1959), a very keen observer of his own mind, between ideas that come through the senses and those that come from reflection on the operations of the mind.

More recent experiments on both STM and LTM search continue to indicate the importance of executive processes. In the "missing scan" version of the STM test (Buschke, 1963a,b), for example, the subject is presented with a sequence of digits like, 4, 5, 6, 7, 9, and asked to indicate which digit was missing. A notion of associative strength alone would have to predict high response strengths for 4, 5, 6, 7, and 9, and a low response strength for 8; yet 8 is the answer given. It gains "strength," apparently, only after the incoming information has been edited (in this case, compared with the sequence, 4, 5, 6, 7, 8, 9) to determine where the discrepancy lies.

Both associative and editing stages show up in LTM experiments. Peterson (1967) found that, when additional time is given to respond in a paired-associates task, subjects are more likely to give correct responses. Apparently, what happens is this. Early in learning, subjects learn to identify the correct response, so that they know whether a given response they have generated is correct or not. This corresponds to the editing function. At this stage, however, the associative strength of the correct response is low, so that it cannot yet be generated rapidly and may not even be generated until after one or two incorrect responses have been generated and then rejected by the editor. Later in learning, when associative strength is high, the first response generated is simply passed on by the editor, and so we are not even aware of the editing function. Peterson has obtained evidence that learning to recognize a correct response may occur on a single trial, while learning to generate it quickly takes place over several trials.

Physiologically, the frontal cortex (see Figure 13, page 38) seems to be important in maintaining direction. Patients with lesions in the frontal cortex lack initiative, planning ability, and foresight (Hebb & Penfield, 1940). They have difficulty in planning and following a route through a stylus maze (Milner, 1965) and in changing from one plan to another, for example, from one way of sorting cards to another (Milner, 1963).

More precisely, the frontal cortex seems to be required for imposing new organization on that provided by perception or associative memory, for directed thinking. Patients with gunshot wounds in the frontal cortex are deficient in the rod-and-frame test (Teuber & Mishkin, 1954). The rod-and-frame test requires a subject in a dark room to adjust a luminous rod, located within a nonadjustable tilted luminous frame, to true vertical. This test appears to assess the capacity to impose new organization on the visual organization provided by the frame (Witkin, 1959). Similarly, monkeys with damage to the frontal cortex fail on a double alternation task (go twice to the right, then twice to the left), unless the intervals between responses to different sides are made longer than the intervals between responses to the same side, so that the organization can be handled at the perceptual level (Pribram & Tubbs, 1967).

It is well known that damage to the frontal cortex interferes with STM in lower mammals. Short-term memory in animals is assessed by means of the delayed-reaction test, in which (*a*) food is placed before the animal; (*b*) a cover is placed over the food, and an identical cover is placed beside the first; and (*c*) the animal is allowed, after a variable delay, to choose and look under one of the covers. There are large phylogenetic differences in the ability to perform this task. The maximum delay that can be tolerated before responding is reduced to the chance level is seconds in rats (Hunter, 1913; Honzik, 1931), hours in cats (Adams, 1929), and one or two days in chimpanzees (Yerkes & Yerkes, 1928). In adult humans, the maximum delay is indefinitely long. If you saw a check for a million dollars put under one of two identical cups and were told that it would be yours if you remembered where it was, there is no doubt but that, if necessary, you could choose correctly after decades. The delayed-reaction task may be taken to be the simplest task that involves directed thinking—simply maintaining a representation.

Damage to the frontal cortex reduces the maximum delay in this task, at least in animals other than man. A revealing additional finding is that animals with damage to the frontal cortex perform as well as normal animals if the lights are turned off during the delay interval (Malmo, 1942). This is consistent with the notion that the frontal cortex is important in imposing a new organization on that provided by perception; turning off the lights reduces the competition from perception and thus reduces the need for organization in the frontal cortex.

Damage to the frontal cortex does not affect STM in man, as measured by the number of digits that can be reported back immediately. However, a different kind of test suggests that the same general ability is involved. Same–different judgments for stimuli separated by 1 minute are impaired by damage to the frontal cortex if the stimuli are repeated from trial to trial but not if new stimuli are used on each trial (Prisko, cited in Milner, 1964). Apparently, using the same stimuli from trial to trial builds up associative interference, and patients with damage to the frontal cortex are not able to impose a new organization on the organization in associative memory.

There is reason to believe that the association nuclei of the thalamus and the limbic system (see Figure 12, page 37) cooperate with the frontal cortex in carrying out executive functions. The association nuclei of the thalamus are anatomically closely connected with the frontal cortex, and, in species where the frontal cortex is well developed, the association nuclei are also well developed (Smith, 1965). Presumably, the association nuclei cooperate with the frontal cortex, perhaps in maintaining contact with the posterior association cortex. However, no evidence seems to be available on their exact function.

The limbic system is also intimately connected with the frontal cortex (Miller, Galanter, & Pribram, 1960) and presumably co-operates with it. Although the function of the limbic system is not well understood, its closed-loop connectivity suggests that it might serve a holding (Pribram, 1971) or amplifying (Milner, 1970) function. It is thought to be important in emotion (MacLean, 1958; Papez, 1937), and emotion does seem both to sustain and to intensify behavior. It is also thought to be important in sequential behavior (Pribram, 1969), and this may be because sequential behavior requires maintenance of a context in order to keep track of one's place in the sequence.

The hippocampus, a portion of the limbic system, seems to be important in learning. In rats, damage to the hippocampus produces learning difficulties, particularly in learning complex mazes and in extinguishing old habits (Kimble, 1963). The effect seems to be similar in man. People with hippocampal damage seem unable to learn (Milner & Teuber, 1968), even unable to learn the instructions for an experiment designed to test their capacity for learning (Lindsay & Norman, 1972). This statement does not seem to apply to motor skill learning, however. A patient with bilateral hippocampal damage was found to learn a mirror-drawing task at a normal rate, though he did not remember having performed the task before (DeJong, Itabashi, & Olson, 1968). The hippocampus appears to be important, not only for information storage, but also for information retrieval. Electrical stimulation of the hippocampus has been found to call forth images, feelings, and concepts (Penfield, 1969).

Organization of the Executive System

What we have, to this point, been loosely calling "the executive system" is organized on at least two levels: what we might call a superordinate executive system and one or more subordinate executive systems. As we shall see, the superordinate executive system seems to be the locus of conscious intention, will, or effort; it seems to employ goals; and it seems to involve central serial processing. A serial process, we have noted, is a process in which only one thing is done at a time. A process is said to be central when, like the ticket booth at a fair, its participation is required to keep a number of other processes going. Processes are said to be peripheral when, like the various rides at a fair, they do not directly influence one another. The subordinate systems seem to be automatic and to involve processing that is peripheral, in that more than one such system can operate in parallel. For example, we can sing while we play the guitar.

The Superordinate Executive System

At the control center of the executive system is a system that is often referred to as the central processor (CP). Under certain conditions, at least, the capacity of CP seems to be a single item; that is, CP appears to be capable of doing only one thing at a time, to be strictly serial.

An experiment by Sternberg (1966) makes the point nicely. Sternberg presented a set of digits to be held in STM, followed by a probe digit. The subject's task was to indicate as quickly as possible whether the probe digit was or was not included in the set. When the number of digits in STM was varied, reaction time turned out to be a simple linear function of the number of items in STM that the subject had to check. This means, of course, that, when the probe digit was not included in the set, reaction time was a simple linear function of the number of items in the set (see Figure 71), since the entire set had to be searched. Items were processed at the very rapid rate of 26 per second.

However, reaction time was also a simple linear function of the total number of items in the set when the probe digit was included

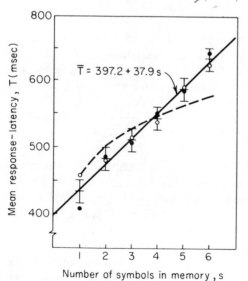

FIGURE 71. *Time to search items in STM. (Filled circles represent positive responses, and unfilled circles represent negative responses. Broken curve indicates upper bound for parallel processing.)* [*Taken, with permission, from S. Sternberg, "High speed scanning in human memory," Science, 1966,* **153**, *652–654. Copyright 1966 by the American Association for the Advancement of Science.*]

in the set (see Figure 71). This leads to the conclusion that search is exhaustive, rather than self-terminating. In other words, even when the subject encounters the target digit early in his search, he goes on to search the rest of the list before responding. This may seem inefficient, but Sternberg suggests that, at the very rapid rate of 26 symbols per second, it may be faster to search the entire list than to stop after each item to determine whether or not a match has been made.

The superordinate executive system, as we have said, seems to be the locus of intention, will, or effort. A variety of physiological measures have been employed to index effort. Dilation of the pupil appears to be the best single index (Kahneman, 1973). The pupil dilates during difficult pitch discriminations (Kahneman & Beatty, 1967), during the viewing of unpredictable random shapes (Pratt, 1970), and at the presentation of each successive digit in an STM task (Kahneman & Beatty, 1966). Frequency of eye movements and blinks and magnitude of galvanic skin response also provide useful information. For example, turning inward to think is associated with a dramatic increase in the rate of eye movements (Lorens & Darrow, 1962), and listening attentively is associated with an inhibition of eye movements (Gopher, 1971). The frequency of blinks follows similar rules.

There are at least two distinctively different states of effort: (*a*) a state of passive acceptance, where the increase in pupil size is accompanied by a decrease in heart rate, and (*b*) a state of active manipulation, where the increase in pupil size is accompanied by an increase in heart rate (Kahneman, 1973). The situations involving passive acceptance that have been studied include the interval between an alerting signal and the stimulus in a reaction-time experiment (Chase, Graham, & Graham, 1968; Lacey & Lacey, 1964, 1966; Webb & Obrist, 1970) and the interval between a neutral conditioned stimulus and an aversive unconditioned stimulus in a conditioning experiment (Jenks & Deane, 1963; Obrist, 1968). A decrease in heart rate is typically accompanied by a marked reduction of irrelevant movement (Obrist, Webb, & Sutterer, 1969; Webb & Obrist, 1970), which speeds reaction time (Obrist, Webb, Sutterer, & Howard, 1970). The situations involving active manipulation that have been studied include resisting painful or distracting stimulation (Lacey, 1967), adding digits (Tursky, Schwartz, & Crider, 1970), and solving problems (Lacey, Kagan, Lacey, & Moss, 1963).

Effort is determined in part by conscious intentions, but largely by the requirements of the task. Kahneman, Peavler, and Onuska (1968) asked subjects to perform an easy and a difficult task under varying conditions of monetary incentive and risk. The major determinant of effort, as measured by pupil diameter, was the difficulty of the task; incentive had only a marginal effect. The primary determinant of effort thus seems to be the rate at which mental activity is performed, which is perhaps best viewed as the number of TOTE's (see below) required per unit time (Kahneman, 1973). This seems to be why we make errors in easy tasks even though we are capable of putting forth greater effort when difficult tasks demand it (Kahneman, 1973).

Attention seems to be divisible at low levels of effort and more nearly unitary at high levels. It is this feature of the experience of attention that suggests the metaphors of "a beam of light of varied width" (Hernandez-Peon, 1964) or "a lens of variable power" (Eriksen & Rohrbaugh, 1970; Eriksen & Hoffman, 1972). For example, Lindsay (1970) found near-parallel processing at low levels of effort, but not at high levels of effort. The information conveyed by absolute judgments on a dimension did not decrease markedly as a function of the number of concurrent stimuli judged, but this was true only when the stimuli were highly discriminable.

Easterbrook (1959) has presented a theory along these lines to account for the fact that there is an optimal level of arousal for tasks and that this optimal level is lower for more complex tasks (the Yerkes–Dodson law). When arousal is low, irrelevant, as well as relevant, cues are processed. When arousal is optimal, only relevant cues are processed. And, when arousal is high, not all relevant cues are processed. Because complex tasks involve more relevant cues than do simple tasks, the optimal level is lower for complex tasks. When arousal is increased by means of incentives (Bahrick, Fitts, & Rankin, 1952), acoustic noise (Broadbent, 1971, p. 430), or drugs (Callaway & Stone, 1960), performance improves on a simple central task and deteriorates on a peripheral task, consistent with Easterbrook's theory. It is of particular interest that acoustic noise improves performance on the rod-and-frame test (Oltman, 1964) and on the Stroop test (Callaway & Stone, 1960; Houston, 1969), both of which are simple tasks in which the main difficulty is ignoring insistent irrelevant cues.

The organization of the superordinate executive system seems to be fairly well captured by the TOTE (Test–Operate–Test–Exit) representation (Miller, Galanter, & Pribram, 1960). Figure 72 represents hammering as a TOTE unit. The TOTE is entered, and a test is performed to determine whether the hammer is up. If that test fails, the hammer is raised, and the test is repeated. If the test succeeds this time, the TOTE is exited, and control is passed to the next TOTE in the plan.

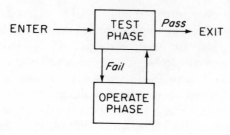

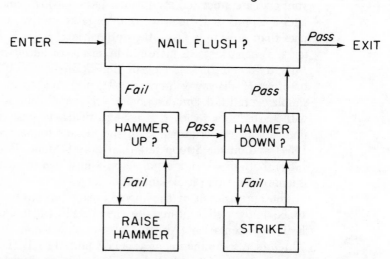

FIGURE 72. *A generalized TOTE unit and a TOTE unit for raising a hammer. [Adapted, with permission, from G. A. Miller, E. Galanter, and K. H. Pribram, Plans and the structure of behavior (New York: Holt, 1960), p. 34.]*

Actually, of course, there is more to hammering than this; raising a hammer will not drive in a nail. Another TOTE is needed for lowering the hammer, and these two TOTEs must be organized into a larger TOTE under the goal of making the nail flush. A TOTE with these two levels is shown in Figure 73.

FIGURE 73. *A TOTE unit for making a nail flush, with subordinate TOTE units for raising and lowering the hammer. [Adapted, with permission, from G. A. Miller, E. Galanter, and K. H. Pribram, Plans and the structure of behavior, (New York: Holt, 1960), p. 36.]*

Certainly, a CP with a capacity of one item cannot achieve such organizational complexity on its own. Otherwise, when it was in even the simplest operate phase it would forget its goal. For goal-directed behavior to be possible, CP must be supplemented by some memory system. This may be EM, STM, or LTM. External memory helps us keep track of where we are in a plan when, for example, a half-painted wall reminds us where to start in again after opening another can of paint (Miller, 1967) or when a notebook reminds us where we left off writing last night. While we sometimes dispense with EM, for example, by closing our eyes to think, we seem always to make use of STM in directed thought. Short-term memory, sometimes alone and sometimes along with EM, provides the workbench for CP. Short-term memory will be of particular interest here. Long-term memory is, of course, of enormous help in keeping track of behavior sequences, but that is a matter for the section on subordinate executive systems.

The process of decoding control items in STM in the execution of a plan has been elucidated in a series of experiments by Johnson (1970). Johnson had subjects learn paired associates in which the stimulus was a digit and the response was a grouped series of letters, for example: 1—SB JFQ LZ. He then counted the number of errors at each position within a response term. The assumption is that errors will increase as a function of CP/STM load. He found that errors are high on the transitions from the last item in one group to the first item in the next and that the number of errors varies directly with the number of items in the group that is about to be produced. This suggests that subjects make all the decoding decisions for a group before producing any item from the group. Johnson also found that errors are particularly high on the first item in the sequence, and that these errors vary directly with (*a*) the number of items in the first group and (*b*) the number of additional groups in the sequence (but not the number of items in these groups). Thus, it seems that subjects make all the gross decoding decisions for the sequence and all the fine decoding decisions for the first group before producing any item in the sequence. The sequence TOTE is expanded into a series of group TOTEs; the first group TOTE is expanded into a series of item TOTEs; then the first item TOTE is activated.

The central processor and STM work so closely together that, in many discussions, writers do not bother to distinguish between them; and, occasionally, we shall refer simply to CP/STM, as we did in the foregoing paragraph. Not only does STM serve as a workbench for CP, but CP periodically refreshes items in STM. Let us consider each of these functions.

The process of refreshing items in STM by reactivating them is called rehearsal. Rehearsal is what you are engaged in when you mumble a phone number over and over to yourself as you go from the phone book to the telephone. Because rehearsal can maintain items indefinitely in STM, it must be eliminated in any attempt to measure the decay rate of STM. Since rehearsal is accomplished by CP, it can be prevented simply by occupying CP with some other task between the time that the stimulus is presented and recall is attempted. A task that has been used frequently for this purpose is counting backward by threes. With this method of rehearsal control and with nonsense trigrams as stimuli, the duration of STM appears to be around 20 seconds (Peterson & Peterson, 1959; see Figure 74). Since CP can be time-shared among a number of tasks, however, rehearsal control is usually not absolute, but a matter of degree. Only fairly difficult tasks will reduce the amount of CP capacity left over for rehearsal to a negligible amount (Posner & Rossman, 1965). Most tasks permit a fair amount of rehearsal and, thus, permit a limited number of items to be maintained in STM until needed.

Short-term memory is of great importance as a workbench for CP. The central processor can operate on only the number of items that can be held in STM, and this limits the complexity of solutions that can be readily attained. For example, it is quite

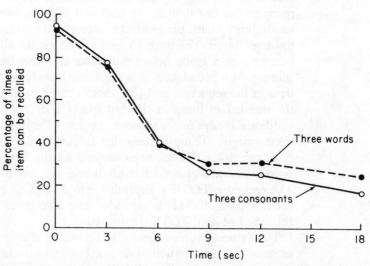

FIGURE 74. *The duration of STM.* [*Taken from B. B. Murdock, Jr., "The retention of individual items,"* Journal of Experimental Psychology, *1961,* 62, *618–625. Copyright 1961 by the American Psychological Association. Reprinted by permission.*]

easy to multiply 3×4 "in your head" when you have no other items in STM. It is somewhat more difficult to perform the same multiplication when it is part of the task of mentally multiplying 83×54, because you must also remember the digits 8 and 5. And it is considerably more difficult to multiply 3×4 when it is part of the task of mentally multiplying 38×45. This is, of course, because you must also remember the digits 1, 9, and 0 (the product of 5×38), the digit 2 (part of the product of 4×8), and the digit 3 (the part of the product of 4×8 that is carried over).

Quastler and Wulff (1959) examined STM and rate of information processing in a lightning calculator who could, for example, multiply two 8-digit numbers in 54 seconds. They found that his maximum rate of information processing, 24 binary decisions per second, was not extraordinary, being comparable to that of an expert pianist and to that of at least one person who happened to be working in their laboratory. It is also quite close to the 26 binary decisions per second observed by Sternberg (1966) in ordinary subjects. Quastler and Wulff found that the lightning calculator's STM capacity, on the other hand, was several times the normal span. They concluded that what makes a lightning calculator is an extraordinary STM capacity plus the ability to carry on in an orderly fashion for very long stretches. Thus, the difference is in STM, not in CP.

The capacity of the average person's STM is now believed to be about 5 items (Mandler, 1967; Murdock, 1965). But let us back up a little bit. Several years ago, Miller (1956; see also Muller & Schumann, 1894; Wundt, 1896) pointed to a "magic number 7," which appears, as we shall see, in the span of STM, the span of attention, and the span of absolute judgment, as well as in the seven wonders of the ancient world, the seven seas, the seven deadly sins, the seven notes of the musical scale, the seven colors of the spectrum, and the seven days of the week. Miller said he did not believe that there was a single explanation for all of these 7's, but let us look more closely at the matter.

In the first place, the magic number for STM is really more like 5 than 7. In the classic STM experiment, a number of items (usually digits) is read to the subject, and he recalls immediately as many as he can. The number he can repeat back is usually close to seven. But, on closer examination, the seven appears to be made up of two components: five digits from STM and two from VSTM. The two digits from VSTM, of course, are the last two read by the experimenter, and, so long as there is no restriction on the order of report, they are the first two given back by the subject. Murdock (1962) points to several differences between the two items in VSTM and the five in STM: Only the latter are affected by rate of presentation and list length, and only the former are affected by delayed recall. Rate of presentation affects coding into STM, but, once coded, such items are not affected by delay, because they can be rehearsed. Finally, serial position curves for visual and auditory material (see Figure 75) suggest a distinction between a fleeting visual VSTM, a somewhat more lasting auditory VSTM, and a common STM (Morton, 1970). Errors increase as a direct function of serial position for the early items, which are held in STM, but there is a sharp drop in errors for the last 2 to 3 items, which are reported directly out of VSTM. The decrease in errors is greater for auditorily presented items than for visually presented items, however, because, as we have seen, auditory VSTM decays more slowly than visual VSTM.

But why this restriction of five items in STM? Some findings on the importance of control processes in STM (Neisser, 1967) seem to point in the direction of an answer. Items in STM seem not so much to be associated with one another as to be located in a rhythmic pattern. A number of observations point to this conclusion. One is that it is quite common to forget an item in the middle of a sequence and yet to recall the items that followed it and even to be able to indicate the position of the forgotten item in

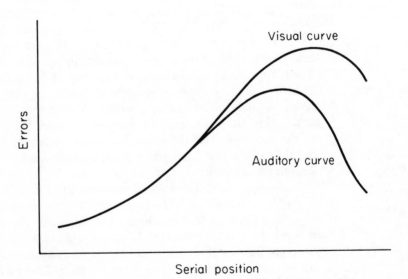

FIGURE 75. *Idealized serial position curves for visual and auditory material.* [*Taken, with permission, from J. Morton, "A functional model for memory," in D. A. Norman (Ed.), Models of human memory (New York: Academic Press, 1970), p. 220.*]

the sequence. Another is that errors in reporting items out of CP/STM are more likely to be based on similarity of position (193796 → 139796) than on similarity of the preceding item (193796 → 196793) (Conrad, 1959). Also, while repeating a sequence of items (193796, 193796) generally increases the number of items that can be reported, repeating the same sequence of items, but with a different rhythmic grouping (193 796, 19 37 96), does not (Bower & Winzenz, 1969).

Thus, the restriction of five items would seem to be a restriction on the number of positions possible in a rhythmic pattern. But, again, why this restriction? At present, we have no answer. It might be a space limitation, a restriction on the number of neural patterns that a particular structure can accommodate at one time. Or it might be a time limitation, a restriction on the number of patterns that CP can get around to and refresh before the first has decayed.

To return to our original question, "Is it the same mechanism that produces the limitation of approximately seven in the spans of STM, apprehension, and absolute judgment?" In the old span of apprehension experiments, to begin with them, subjects were to report the number of items (for example, dots) presented in a brief flash. The number of items correctly reported was found to increase linearly with increasing exposure time until, at about 100 msec, a total of eight items was reached (Woodworth, 1938). Subjects reported that all of the items were initially perfectly clear; it was just that they had trouble "remembering" them. Mackworth (1964) found that the number of digits, letters, colors, or shapes that could be reported from a brief exposure was directly related to the speed at which their names could be read aloud and, hence, presumably, at which they could be coded from VSTM into STM; and the linear relation reported by Woodworth also suggests just such a serial coding from VSTM into STM.

In order to avoid the artificial restriction of STM capacity, a sampling procedure can be used to measure the span of VSTM (Averbach & Sperling, 1961). A matrix of 12 letters, 3 rows of 4 letters each, is flashed. Then immediately after the stimulus has been terminated and while the image is still fresh in VSTM, one of three tones is presented: a high-frequency tone to indicate that it is the top row that should be reported; an intermediate-frequency tone to indicate that it is the middle row that should be reported; or a low-frequency tone to indicate that it is the bottom row that should be reported. Because the number of items to be reported, four, is now well within the capacity of STM, this capacity can no longer artificially restrict the number of items reported. If three of the four items in a randomly chosen row are reported, then it is reasonable to infer that $\frac{3}{4}$ of the items in the entire matrix, or nine, are available in VSTM at the time the tone is presented. Actually, as we have seen, the number is probably considerably higher than this. The span of apprehension, however, is strictly limited, and it seems to be simply the span of STM in a different guise. These two "magic numbers 7," then, are the same.

The span of absolute judgment, on the other hand, does not seem to be reducible to the span of STM. For one thing, whereas the span of STM seems to be a property of the superordinate executive system and to have a single value (see Morton, 1970), the span of absolute judgment seems to be a property of the representational system and to have different values for different modalities. While it is true that around five loudnesses (Garner, 1953) and six pitches (Pollack, 1953) can be discriminated, the number of absolute judgments that can be made along a single continuum ranges from three for curvature (Pollack; see Miller, 1956) to from 10 to 15 for positions on a line (Coonan and Klemmer, cited in Miller, 1956; Hake & Garner, 1951). Thus, it appears that Miller may have been right, after all, that the repetition of all these sevens is, in part, at least, "only a pernicious, Pythagorean coincidence."

We saw that STM may play an important role in keeping track of where in a plan we are by keeping goals in mind while we are working on subgoals. This enables us to embed TOTEs within TOTEs recursively, as the TOTEs for raising and lowering a hammer are embedded within the larger TOTE for making a nail flush. However, we might expect, from the fact that the capacity of STM is strictly limited, that the depth of recursion would likewise be strictly limited. This appears to be the case.

Miller (1967) has made the point for self-embedding sentences, as we saw earlier. It is quite easy to understand the sentence, "The king who said, 'My kingdom for a horse,' is dead," but it is extremely difficult to understand the sentence, "The audience who just heard, 'The person who cited, "The king who said, 'My kingdom for a horse,' is dead," as an example is a psychologist,' is very patient." Yet there are only two additional levels of embedding in the second sentence.

Yngve (1961) and Martin and Roberts (1966) have made this point for sentences more generally. The complexity of a sentence can be characterized by assigning to each word a number that represents its degree of embedding in the sentence structure and then averaging these numbers, called Yngve numbers, to obtain a mean for the sentence. The average depth of a sentence, measured in this way, is an important determinant of difficulty of retaining sentences in STM or in retrieving them from LTM.

Surely, however, our plans are frequently more complex than this. Even as I write, I make a stroke which is part of my plan for making a letter, which is part of my plan for making a word, which is part of my plan for writing a sentence, which is part of my plan for developing a thought, which is part of my plan for describing a cognitive system, which is part of my plan for describing cognition, generally. Though there would seem to be at least as many levels of embedding here as in Miller's last sentence, I felt considerably more cognitive strain in trying to comprehend Miller's last sentence. What is the difference? The difference is that the lower levels in my plan, making letters and words, are kept track of in LTM, and the higher levels, describing a cognitive system and describing cognition, generally, are kept track of in EM, in the form of an outline I have next to me. Thus, my STM is occupied only with making sentences to develop a thought. We have already considered EM, and we turn now to LTM. The automatic execution of lower levels in a plan by LTM is what we mean by a subordinate executive system.

The Subordinate Executive System

Suppes (1969) has shown deductively that anything that can be represented as a TOTE can also be represented in terms of associations, and Newell and Simon (1972) have shown inductively that complex human problem-solving can be described in detail in terms of productions, which seem to be equivalent to associations.

Despite this important structural similarity, however, there seem to be real differences between the superordinate and subordinate executive systems. We have already mentioned these, but let us review them. The superordinate system seems to operate by willing; the subordinate system seems to operate automatically. The superordinate system seems to be in consciousness; the subordinate system seems to be outside of consciousness. The superordinate system seems to be single and serial and thus able to do only one thing at a time; the subordinate system seems to be a parallel associative mechanism that is capable of doing more than one thing at a time. It seems a reasonable guess that the superordinate system involves the frontal cortex, as the site of conscious intention, and perhaps certain limbic structures, as the site of CP, and that the subordinate system in some way bypasses these. This speculation is supported by the finding that gross changes in brain wave patterns, such as desynchronization at the cortex and slow synchronous rhythms in the hippocampus, are commonly seen early in training but usually disappear with further training (McGaugh, 1973, p. 62).

The distinction between superordinate and subordinate levels corresponds to Miller, Galantar, and Pribram's (1960) distinction between strategies and tactics and seems to be what Newell and Simon (1972) had in mind in distinguishing between goal-directed behavior, which seems to require maintenance of a goal in STM, and behavior that is directed only in the sense of being a translation into associative terms of stimulus–response sequences that were originally components of goal-directed behavior.

Plans are formed in the superordinate system, and that is where they are executed during the early stages of practice. Later, after some practice, they become automatized, or mechanized, and turned over to subordinate systems. This process has been described both in the course of learning a single task and in the course of cognitive development.

Ach (1905) presented pairs of digits to his subjects. In some blocks of trials, the subjects were told to add the numbers, in others to subtract, and in others to multiply. The subjects at first had some conscious representation of each new task, but the consciousness of the task faded as the work on each series continued. Watt (1905–1906) obtained similar results using words as stimuli and such tasks as naming a part, naming a coordinate class, naming a subclass, or naming a superordinate class.

Fitts (1964) has identified three stages in skill learning: a cognitive stage, an associative stage, and an automatization stage. The cognitive stage seems to involve the superordinate executive system. It is during this stage that instructions and demonstrations are the most helpful; and, during this stage, the best performers seem to be those who are good at visualizing spatial relations (see Figure 76). The associative stage seems to be a transitional one, where the TOTE representation is being translated into an associative representation. The automatization stage seems to involve primarily the subordinate system. Here, errors are seldom made, and further practice serves mainly to make performance smoother and faster. Here, the best performers seem to be those with the fastest reaction times (see Figure 76).

Pew (1966) has provided a detailed picture of the process of automatization, in the case of what might be considered to be a miniature skill. Subjects had to control the horizontal movement of a continuously moving target by means of two switches, one of which moved the target to the left and the other of which moved it to the right. The highest level in the plan would pre-

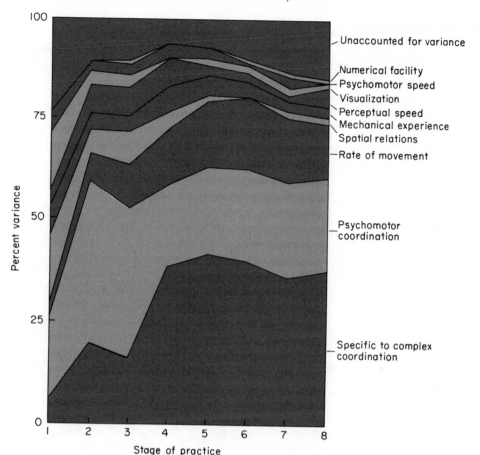

FIGURE 76. *Change in the factorial composition of a skill as a function of practice. This figure shows, for example, that spatial relations accounts for over 15% of the variance among individuals during the first stage of practice, but only about 2% during the last stage.* [Taken, with permission from E. A. Fleishman and W. E. Hempel, Jr., "Changes in factor structure of a complex psychomotor test as a function of practice," Psychometrika, 1954, **19**, 239–252.]

sumably be a test to determine whether the target is on center, analogous to the test, in the hammering plan, for seeing whether the nail is flush. Below this would be a TOTE for moving the target to the left and another for moving it to the right, analogous to the TOTEs for raising and lowering the hammer.

Three modes of operation were distinguished: closed loop, open loop, and modulation. The closed-loop pattern is the one described by Miller, Galanter, and Pribram (1960). Activating an operate phase, such as "push right switch," twice in succession requires

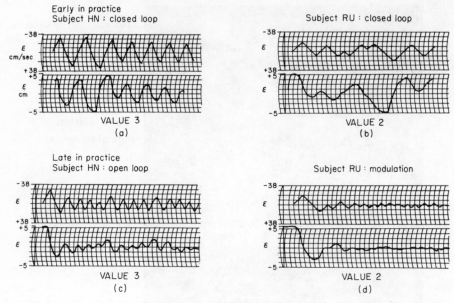

FIGURE 77. *Three degrees of automatization: closed-loop, open-loop, and modulation. (The lower record of each subject presents the displacement of the target with respect to the center of the cathode ray tube as a function of time; the upper record presents the instantaneous velocity of the target on a corresponding time scale.)* [*Taken from R. W. Pew, "Acquisition of hierarchical control over the temporal organization of a skill," Journal of Experimental Psychology, 1966, 71, 764–771. Copyright 1966 by the American Psychological Association. Reprinted by permission.*]

looping through the superordinate test. This results in long inter-response times (see Figure 77a,b). Closed-loop responding characterized all subjects early in learning.

Both the open-loop and the modulation patterns permit repeated activation of operate phases without intervention by the superordinate test phase. Thus, each involves a degree of automatization.

Automatization seems to be less complete in the open-loop pattern. While right–left–right–left (RLRL) alternations occur in bursts too rapid to permit testing between them (see Figure 77c), the bursts are separated by pauses, presumably to permit a superordinate test. Open-loop responding characterized the slow learners' final stage of performance.

Automatization seems more complete in the modulation pattern (see Figure 77d); RLRL alternations continue at a rate too high to permit interruption by the superordinate test, yet the relative durations of the Rs and Ls are varied so as to keep the target vacillating about the center. The operate phase is sufficiently automatized so as not to be disrupted at all by the superordinate test phase. Modulation characterized the fast learners' final stage of performance.

In some cases, automatization may be so complete that consciousness is completely bypassed in the selection of responses. Fehrer and Raab (1962) have reported that, whereas reaction time is inversely related to stimulus intensity, it is possible to decrease the conscious effect of a stimulus by following it immediately with a second, masking, stimulus (see p. 74), without having any effect on reaction time. Consistent with this, Kahneman (1968) has obtained suggestive evidence that the latency of conscious perception is about the same as that of overt responses in a simple reaction-time task. With practice, unconscious processes may bypass conscious processes in selecting routine responses.

Automatization has also been demonstrated in animals, in a shift from "place learning" to "response learning" as a function of practice. Place learning and response learning can be defined in terms of the maze in Figure 78. An animal is trained to go from S_1 to G_1 for food and then is tested by being placed at S_2. If it continues to go to G_1, the same place, it has demonstrated place learning; if it turns right, making the same response but going to a different place, it has demonstrated response learning. Rats tested early in training show place learning, and rats tested late in learning show response learning (Restle, 1957).

Automatization has been observed in the course of cognitive development, as well as in the course of learning a single task. Infants

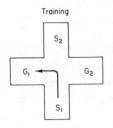

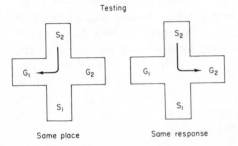

FIGURE 78.   *Place and response learning.*

seem to learn component TOTEs first, and, later, to integrate these into larger TOTEs. Piaget (1952a) has identified a developmental sequence that proceeds from primary circular reactions to secondary circular reactions to tertiary circular reactions to intentional behavior.

In a primary circular reaction, an infant makes a response, for example, releasing objects or making sounds, simply for the sake of making the response. It shows no interest, for example, in the fate of an object it has dropped, but seems to be concerned only with the mechanics of the response itself. Primary circular reactions are analogous to the TOTEs for raising and lowering the hammer in the hammering TOTE.

In a secondary circular reaction, the focus is on the object and the effect the response has on it. Now, the infant watches objects fall after releasing them. It is now learning something about the superordinate test phase, corresponding to making the nail flush.

In a tertiary circular reaction, the response is varied in active exploration. Objects may now be dropped in different ways and different effects observed. This adds control loops for varying the response in ways other than simply starting and stopping it, for example, changing the angle of the hammer if the nail starts to bend.

In intentional behavior, different TOTEs like those just described are organized hierarchically with respect to one another. One TOTE becomes the means and the other the end. Thus, an infant that has learned to move objects about and to drop objects may move an object, such as a pillow, that is blocking its way to another object that it wants to drop. Or one might drive a nail into a wall in order to hang something on it.

Thus, in the primary circular reactions, the infant learns about responses; in the secondary and tertiary circular reactions, about stimulus–response relations and about stimuli; and, in intentional behavior, about relationships among stimuli. Here, response learning precedes place learning.

Observations of children's behavior in searching for hidden objects (Piaget, 1952a) also point to the same conclusion—that response learning precedes place learning. In one test, an object is hidden behind a pillow. At first, the child will look for it only if he was in the process of reaching for it when it was hidden; later, he will look for it if he simply sees it hidden. In another test, an object is hidden behind the first pillow, taken out, and hidden behind a second pillow, all within full view of the child. At first, the child will look for the object only where he last found it; later, he will look for it where he last saw it go.

While the direction of change seems to be from place learning to response learning in the mature organism, it seems to be from response learning to place learning in the developing organism. Is this consistent?

In both cases, the direction is from processing in the superordinate executive system to processing in the subordinate executive system. What is in the superordinate system is new, and what is in the subordinate system is old and well learned. In the case of the infant, nothing is old and well learned. The infant is in a strange, complex world that is only occasionally comprehensible, in terms of sucking, grasping, or crying reflexes, and it is frequently groping in CP/STM with new patterns. Perhaps the infant begins with responses because the world of responses is simpler than the world of stimuli, and can be made even simpler by the circular reactions, in which the same response is repeated over and over again.

In the adult, responses, because of their simplicity and because of the great deal of early practice devoted to them, have become largely automatized. Thus, what tends to be in CP/STM are environmental goals: where in the maze the food is located, rather than what particular responses to make to get there. As a consequence of repeated practice, however, the behavior becomes automatized. Instead of being guided by a TOTE toward distant goals in EM or STM that require the attention of CP, large sequences of responses are now elicited by immediately preceding conditions, either in the environment or in the response system, itself (Guthrie, 1952; Keele, 1973). The practiced rat leaves the start box and initiates a sequence of responses that will, with very little further attention, take him to the correct goal box, thus leaving CP/STM free for, perhaps, happier thoughts about the food, itself.

Automatization frees CP/STM both to attend to additional tasks and to attend to strategic matters within a task. Automatization is what enables us to do more than one thing at a time, for example, to talk while driving, to sing while playing the guitar, or to think while shaving. In such cases, two subordinate systems are simultaneously performing serial tasks under the direction of the superordinate system, which is time-shared between them.

Automatization also frees CP/STM from having to deal with tactical matters and allows attention to strategy, to use Miller, Galanter, and Pribram's terms. Once we have learned the vocabulary and grammar of a language, we can begin to think in that language. Once we have learned the rudiments of architecture, we can begin to create buildings, or cities, that are functionally, structurally, and aesthetically sound. Once we have learned to execute a piece of music correctly, we can turn our attention to matters of expression.

As control of the details of short response sequences is turned over to the subordinate executive system, a process called "chunking," the superordinate executive system is freed to establish a higher-level organization among the commands for such sequences. Initially, thought and behavior are one, in that any intended action is automatically executed and in that the thought of one action cannot lead directly to the thought of another without the first action actually being performed. Thus, a novice chess player has to try out an intended move on the board to see what its consequences might be, and a rat has to run down an alley to see what is at the end. Overt trial-and-error is followed, with practice, by vicarious trial-and-error (VTE; Muenzinger, 1938). The chess player starts to move toward a piece and then withdraws, realizing in advance that he does not want to make that move. The rat hesitates at the choice point, looking to the right, then the left, before choosing. Vicarious trial-and-error in rats tends to be most frequent just before solution and more frequent in brighter animals (Meunzinger, 1938).

Symbolic responses in children seem first to involve overt imitation and then covert imitation (Piaget, 1952a). A child told to go get a hammer will sometimes be seen to move his arm up and down in a hammering motion. Piaget's (1952a) description of his daughter Lucienne solving a simple problem is particularly informative.

Piaget is playing with Lucienne, who is 1 year and 4 months old. He hides a watch chain inside an empty match box.

> I put the chain back into the box and reduce the opening to 3 mm. It is understood that Lucienne is not aware of the functioning of the opening and closing of the match box and has not seen me prepare the experiment. She only possesses two preceding schemes: turning the box over in order to empty it of its contents, and sliding her fingers into the slit to make the chain come out. It is of course this last procedure that she tries first: she puts her finger inside and gropes to reach the chain, but fails completely. A pause follows during which Lucienne manifests a very curious reaction. . . .
> She looks at the slit with great attention; then, several times in succession, she opens and shuts her mouth, at first slightly, then wider and wider.
> . . . [Then] Lucienne unhesitatingly puts her finger in the slit, and instead of trying as before to reach the chain, she pulls so as to enlarge the opening. She succeeds and grasps the chain [pp. 337–338].

In the adult, at least, neither overt nor covert muscular movements seem to be required for thought. A person who has been totally paralyzed by curare can apparently think perfectly clearly, as judged both from his subjective report after he was given an antidote and from the fact that he was able, after having been given the antidote, to give the answer to problems he solved while under the effects of curare (Smith, Brown, Toman, & Goodman, 1947).

> At intervals of a minute or less, during the period when communication with the subject was impossible, various statements were made, questions asked, stimuli presented, objects placed in the line of gaze and so forth, on which the subject was requested to report when speech returned. In each instance, the report was accurate in all details and properly oriented as to temporal sequence [p. 8].

Furthermore, the EEG was normal throughout, including disruption of the resting state in response to novel stimuli.

The intention to respond, on the other hand, may be necessary for thought. Subjects given training in deep and total relaxation of their muscles reported no imagery or thoughts (Jacobson, 1938; Max, 1937). This seems to be what is now called the alpha state. Apparently, it is the willing of responses, rather than their occurrence, that is critical to thought.

There seems to be a level of executive organization below what we have called the subordinate executive system. Whereas the organization that is in the subordinate system was once conscious and has become unconscious through automatization, organization in the deeper system seems never to have been accessible to consciousness. These systems have been revealed by studies of operant and hypnotic control of the smooth and cardiac muscles, the so-called "involuntary" systems. Miller and Banuazizi (1968) have trained rats to raise or lower their heart rates or their blood pressures by reinforcing changes in the desired direction with electrical stimulation of the reward center of the brain. Figure 79 shows their results. In what is his most striking demonstration of specificity of control over an "involuntary" system, Miller (1969) trained rats to blush in one ear and blanch in the other, by reinforcing differences in blood pressure between the two ears. It should be noted that these experiments were carried out on animals that had been paralyzed with curare to rule out the possibility that such effects might in any way be mediated by changes in the striated muscles of the "voluntary" response system.

Similar effects have been obtained under hypnosis. For example, Zimbardo (cited in Hilgard & Hilgard, 1972) has gotten hypnotized subjects to blush in one hand and blanch in the other on command. And, by means of what appears to be self-hypnosis,

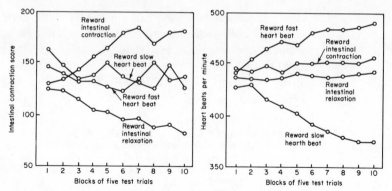

FIGURE 79.   *Control of automatic responses by reinforcement. [Taken from N. E. Miller and A. Banuazizi, "Instrumental learning by curarized rats of a specified visceral response, intestinal or cardiac,"* Journal of Comparative and Physiological Psychology, *1968,* **65,** *1–7. Copyright 1968 by the American Psychological Association. Reprinted by permission.]*

those practiced in transcendental meditation can apparently attain control over a variety of "involuntary" functions, including rate of metabolism (Wallace, 1970; Wallace & Benson, 1972).

Thus, there appear to be at least three levels in the executive system. The one that is most directly involved in thinking, however, and the one about which we shall have the most to say in subsequent chapters, is the superordinate executive system.

We conclude this section on the subordinate executive system by noting that part of the meaning of stimuli, their connotative meaning, seems to relate to the response system (Osgood, 1953). Connotative meaning has been most successfully measured by means of the semantic differential (Osgood, Suci, & Tannenbaum, 1957). In the application of this technique, a variety of stimuli are each rated on up to 76 pipolar scales whose ends are labeled by contrasting adjectives, such as "good–bad," "optimistic–pessimistic," "savory–unsavory," "warm–cold," and "honest–dishonest." It is easy to see how connotative, or metaphoric, meaning would be involved in, for example, rating a stimulus like "rock" on the "honest–dishonest" scale. The principal finding in studies using the semantic differential is that the scales tend to fall into three large groups, within each of which all scales tend to rate stimuli in the same manner. For example, any stimulus that is rated toward the "good" end of the "good–bad" scale tends also to be rated toward the "optimistic" end of the "optimistic–pessimistic" scale.

These groups, which seem to constitute the principal dimensions of connotative meaning, have been labeled Evaluative (good–

bad), Potency (strong–weak), and Activity (active–passive). (See also Wundt, 1896, and Schlosberg, 1952, for similar findings.) They may conveniently be represented as dimensions in a three-dimensional "semantic space." Figure 80 shows the semantic spaces for two subsystems in a multiple personality. The most important of these dimensions is the good–bad dimension. In terms of the response system, this may correspond to the difference between approach and avoidance responses. Subjects pull "good" words toward themselves and push "bad" words away more quickly than they are able to pull "bad" words toward themselves and push "good" words away (Solarz, 1960). Of lesser and about equal importance are the strong–weak and active–passive dimensions, which may correspond to vigor and speed of response, respectively. The fact that these same dimensions appear with a variety of stimuli (for example, pictures, words, and even sonar signals) and with a variety of subjects (for example, Americans, Mexicans, and Japanese; normals and schizophrenics) suggests that they reflect something more fundamental than the contiguity structure of experience, something more like a common response system.

Pollio (1966) has distinguished between the production of ideas on the basis of proximity in semantic space and the production of ideas on the basis of proximity in an associative network. Several findings suggest that, when subjects are asked to produce ideas in a category, the first few ideas seem to be based on associations, and the remainder seem to be based on relations in semantic space. The first few ideas are emitted more rapidly than the remainder, too rapidly to fit the mathematical function that describes the relationship between number of ideas produced and time (Bousfield & Sedgewick, 1944). Also, the first few ideas, unlike the remainder, tend to come from divergent portions of semantic space (Pollio, 1964). The clearest examples are the highly associated pairs, "good–bad," "strong–weak," and "active–passive," which, of course, are located at the far ends of semantic space. In children, all associations tend to come from neighboring regions of semantic space (Pollio, 1964). Indeed, children's earliest definitions seem to be in terms of responses: "a hole is to dig."

Thus, there seem to be two systems for representing meaning: an associative memory, which contains relational information that can be retrieved by the executive system, and a "space" of responses. The former is where denotative meaning, or dictionary meaning, would be located, and the latter is where connotative meaning, the meaning on which metaphors are based, would be located.

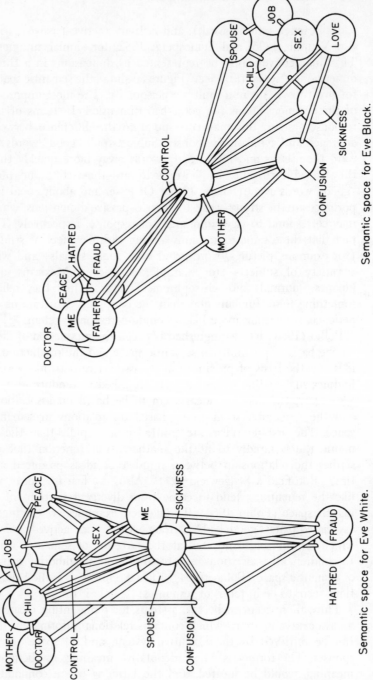

Semantic space for Eve White.

Semantic space for Eve Black.

FIGURE 80. Semantic spaces for two subsystems in a multiple personality. Each item is located in semantic space by taking its good–bad rating as its location on the x axis, its strong–weak rating as its location on the y axis, and its active–passive rating as its location on the z axis. [Taken, with permission, from C. E. Osgood, G. J. Suci, and P. H. Tannenbaum, The measurement of meaning (Urbana, Ill.: Univ. of Illinois Press, 1957), pp. 262, 266.]

The Verbal Executive System

The executive system, like the representational system, seems to be divided into verbal and nonverbal subsystems. It is important to be clear about the fact that the representational–executive and verbal–nonverbal distinctions seem to cut across one another. It does not seem to be the case either that the executive system is entirely verbal or that the representational system is entirely nonverbal. What evidence we have comes primarily from physiological studies.

In the first place, it has long been known that the speech area, located in the left hemisphere, is divided into a representational portion and an executive portion. The posterior portion of the speech area is concerned with the perception and understanding of speech; damage to this area produces what is called receptive aphasia, difficulty in understanding language (Geschwind, 1972). The frontal portion of the speech area is concerned with the generation of speech; damage to this area produces what is called expressive aphasia, difficulty in producing language (Geschwind, 1972).

Furthermore, a study by Corsi (see Milner, 1971) suggests that the left and right temporal lobes are involved in representing verbal and nonverbal events, respectively, and that the left and right frontal lobes are involved in imposing organization on verbal and nonverbal representation, respectively. In this study, a series of items was presented on cards. At intervals, test cards asked which of two items had been seen more recently. The tests measured two kinds of performance: recency discrimination, in which both of the items were old, and recognition, in which one of the items was old and the other had never been presented before. In a verbal form of the test, the items were words; in a nonverbal form, they were reproductions of abstract art. One finding was that temporal damage affected recognition and frontal damage affected recency discrimination. (Recall that frontal damage produces interference among repeated items, see page 151.) The other finding was that, in each case, damage to the left side affected performance on the verbal task, and damage to the right side affected performance on the nonverbal task.

These findings suggest that the left–right differentiation of function does not correspond in any way to the distinction between representational and executive processes. They seem to support the distinction between a posterior representational system and a frontal executive system and to suggest, furthermore, that each of these systems has been subdivided in man, one half for the non-verbal world that he shares with other creatures and one half for the verbal world that seems to be uniquely his.

When we get to the controllability of the verbal executive system, however, we shall see that things are not quite so simple. While it is apparently true that the verbal executive system is not *the* executive system, it does seem to be the most important locus of control. Because considerably more is known about the verbal than the nonverbal executive system, the following section will be devoted almost entirely to the former.

We have already considered the representational face of language. In the chapter on secondary perception, we saw that, while visual images seem to be organized spatially, verbal images seem to be organized nonspatially. And, in the chapter on associative memory, we saw that, while nonverbal associations seem to be organized on the basis of contiguity in experience, verbal associations seem to be organized on the basis of contiguity in thought. The picture that is emerging is of a verbal system that is well suited for achieving abstraction and independence from the environment.

Executive processes are, apparently, involved in both understanding and generating sentences. Although, as we have seen, words, and perhaps phrases, activate their meanings automatically, some executive activity seems to be necessary in order to put the pieces together to form a sentence. This is indicated in an experiment by Foss (1969), using the probe-reaction-time technique. The main task was to listen to sentences and either repeat each or make up a sentence to follow each. The probe task was to press a button when a word in the sentence began with a "b." Probe reaction time was longer when the "b" followed a low frequency or difficult word and when it occurred early in the sentence.

Yet executive processes seem to be more heavily involved in generating sentences. In concluding the first part of this book, we observed that the fact that we can understand far more sentences than we can produce is at least consistent with the notion that something is involved in generating sentences that is not involved in understanding them. And the facts that it is more difficult to understand written material while reading it aloud than while reading it silently and that bilinguals have difficulty in reading mixed-language texts when reading them aloud but not when reading them silently (Kolers, 1968) provide stronger support for this notion. The extra ingredient that seems to be involved in generating sentences would seem to be executive in nature. Reproduction of any material, as we shall see in the next chapter, seems to require plans for information retrieval, which are not required for recognition of the same material.

Language appears to be a complex interworking of vocalization, grammar, and symbolization. Phylogenetically, it appears that vocalization and symbolization emerged independently. Certain lower animals, notably songbirds, mynahs, and parrots, vocalize well but symbolize poorly. Chimps, on the other hand, vocalize poorly but symbolize well and can even construct sentences by using the sign language for the deaf (Gardner & Gardner, 1969). Mattingly (1972) has proposed that grammar evolved after vocalization and symbolization, as an interface between them. In support of this notion, Liberman, Mattingly, and Turvey (1972) point out that written language bears a simpler relationship to thought than does spoken language. It has not been difficult to design computer programs to understand written language, but it has so far been impossible to design one that can understand spoken language. Yet children find the complex speech code quite natural; they learn to understand the spoken word far earlier and with far less difficulty than the written word. Apparently, children, unlike computers, have an innate mechanism for interfacing vocalization and symbolization.

Speech certainly does not seem to be necessary for thought. There is abundant evidence that animals can solve problems of considerable complexity. And, among humans, there is no clear evidence of any difference between the congenitally deaf and the hearing on any of a large variety of symbolic tasks, aside from strictly verbal concept tasks. Such differences as do exist fall far short of the clear and unmistakable difference one would expect if speech were actually a requirement for symbolic behavior (Furth, 1966; Oleron, 1957; Oleron, Gumusyan, & Moulinou, 1966). Indeed, overt responses, in general, as we have seen, do not seem to be necessary for thought. It is apparently something more like the willing of responses, rather than their occurrence, that is critical. If grammar is innate, of course, the congenitally deaf may well have access to these mechanisms even though they have never heard speech sounds.

Yet Piaget has suggested that speech does contribute indirectly to the development of thought, in that it provides a means for communicating with others and, most importantly, for disagreeing with them. Disagreement often confronts us with contradictions in our thought, and becoming aware of contradictions in our thought, as we shall see shortly, is an extremely important mechanism in the development of operational thought. First we argue with others, and then we argue with ourselves. The result is the "little voice" that we often hear when thinking and that we imply is drowned out when we say that it is so noisy that we "can't hear ourselves think." An experiment by Murray (1965) suggests that the "little voice" may be more than a metaphor; he found that vocal rehearsal is not advantageous when there is a level of acoustic noise in the environment sufficient to drown out the subject's voice.

An experiment by Murray (1972) and one by Zajonc (1960) suggest that thought is closely related to communication, if not to speech. Murray showed that group discussion facilitates the acquisition of conservation in children, for example, the understanding that the amount of water is unchanged when water is poured from a short, wide beaker into a tall, narrow one. Attempts to accelerate the natural course of conservation have met only occasionally with success (Smedslund, 1961a,b), and then sometimes only after a great deal of training (Gelman, 1967). However, Murray produced rapid, striking facilitative effects on a posttest by means of a group-training procedure in which the group did not receive a score on a problem until all members of the group agreed on a response, a technique which required members of the group to discuss the problem and to explain their views to each other.

Zajonc (1960) showed an effect of communication variables on information retrieval. Subjects read a job application letter; then half were told they would have to transmit this information to someone else, and half were told they would receive additional information about the person who wrote the letter. All were then asked to write down what they could recall from the letter. Those intending to transmit information scored higher than those intending simply to receive information on measures of differentiation and organization. Perhaps this is why it is said that you never really learn until you have to teach.

The verbal executive system seems to have two important properties that distinguish it from the nonverbal executive system: It is more controllable, and it is propositional.

Controllability

The controllability of language can be illustrated in a number of ways. One line of evidence has to do with hemispheric differentiation. The left hemisphere, as we have seen, seems to be the "natural" hemisphere for processing verbal information. It is this hemisphere that processes verbal information in the vast majority of people. The fact that is pertinent here is that, where the left hemisphere is the one that processes verbal information, it is the left hemisphere's hand that is the better controlled. This, of course, is the right hand. Thus, the fact that most people are left brained and right handed constitutes indirect evidence for the controllability of the verbal executive system.

The strongest evidence comes from the research of Luria (1961). In studying the process by which children gain control over their responses, Luria has shown both that language is more controllable than gross motor responses and that it can be used to control gross motor responses. Children were asked to perform a response when a light came on and to refrain from performing it otherwise. The response was either the verbal response of saying "go" or the gross motor response of squeezing a rubber bulb. The rubber bulb was connected to a pen which made recordings like those in Figures 81 and 82. For children around 2, both verbal and motor responses were erratic, sometimes occurring when the light was on and sometimes occurring when it was off (Figure 81a). For children around 3, verbal responses were well controlled, but gross motor responses remained erratic. At this age, however, verbal responses could be used to control gross motor responses. By having the child say "go" every time the light came on, and then squeeze, the squeezing responses were brought under control (see Figure 81b). If the

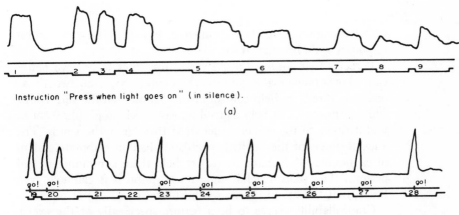

Instruction "Press when light goes on" (in silence).

(a)

Do accompanied by reactions to speech impulses .

Valya S.   3 yrs.

(b)

FIGURE 81. *The control of nonverbal responses by verbal responses. Depressions of the bottom line indicate on-time for the light stimulus; each onset is numbered. Elevations of the top line indicate bulb-squeezing responses.* [Taken, with permission, from A. R. Luria, The role of speech in the regulation of normal and abnormal behavior (New York: Liveright, 1961).]

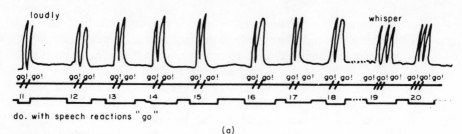

do. with speech reactions "go"

(a)

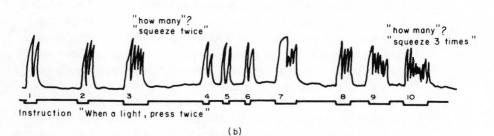

Instruction "When a light, press twice"

(b)

FIGURE 82. *The lack of control of nonverbal responses by the semantic aspect of verbal responses. Depressions of the bottom line indicate on-time for the light stimulus; each onset is numbered. Elevations of the top line indicate bulb-squeezing responses.* [Taken, with permission, from A. R. Luria, The role of speech in the regulation of normal and abnormal behavior (*New York: Liveright, 1961*).]

verbal responses were then eliminated, however, the gross motor responses again became erratic.

It seems that adults also use verbal responses to achieve better control over nonverbal responses. The dancer says, "one–two–three, one–two–three," to help control his steps, and even the singer says, "do, re, mi, . . ." to help control his voice. Many people seem to find it easier to remember a melody if they know the words. The ancient pipers of the Scottish Highlands had an elaborate system of canntaireachd (singing music) to help them communicate and perform their piobaireachd (pipe music), and it is claimed, even today, that the use of canntaireachd makes one a better piper.

Controllability seems to be a feature specifically of the executive component of language. The representational component does not seem to be essential. Luria (1961) found that it is the occurrence of words, and not their meaning, that controls the behavior of the 3-year-old child. Saying "go go" every time the light came on enabled the child to squeeze twice each time (see Figure 82a), but saying "press twice" did not (see Figure 82b). Moreover, saying "go" when the light was on and nothing when the light was off proved to be far more effective than saying "go" when the light was on and "don't go" when it was off. Similarly, adults, in giving themselves directions, as for opening a combination lock, will sometimes incorrectly say, "left, right, left," and yet correctly turn right, left, right. Apparently, in such cases, the superordinate executive system is controlling timing, through language, and the subordinate executive system is selecting responses on the basis of the context of preceding stimuli.

The initial weakness of the semantic function is probably why telling a child to stop taking his shoes off may induce him to take them off more quickly. It is not that he is being disobedient, but simply that he is responding to the occurrence of words, rather than to their meaning. This is probably also why children find the game "Simon Says" a great challenge; it is difficult to inhibit responding to commands that are not preceded by "Simon says. . . ."

Once again, it is important to note that it is what underlies language that seems to be important and not simply the words of the language. Persons with frontal damage can remember verbal instructions perfectly well, and yet these instructions do not control their behavior (Luria & Homskaya, 1964).

Miller, Galanter, and Pribram (1960) have suggested that the controllability of language is related to the phenomenon of hypnosis. In hypnosis, the hypnotist's language exerts the same imperative control over the subject's behavior that the subject's language ordinarily does. Three facts suggest that the relationship between hypnosis and language is a particularly close one: the voice of the hypnotist (rather than his personality, as is often believed) dominates the conscious experience of the hypnotized subject (Hilgard, 1968); hypnotized subjects are reluctant to talk (Miller, Galanter, & Pribram, 1960); and, when hypnotized subjects do talk, they frequently come out of hypnosis (Miller, Galanter, & Pribram, 1960).

The fact that the most effective procedure for inducing a hypnotic trance involves the suggestion to sleep leads one to look for similarities between hypnosis and sleep, and the fact that verbal learning cannot occur during sleep, while nonverbal learning can, suggests that in sleep, as in hypnosis, the verbal executive is shut down. Beh and Barratt (1965) produced classical conditioning during sleep by pairing one of two tones with shock. After several trials, the tone that had been paired with the shock elicited a characteristic EEG response. Weinberg (1966) produced instrumental conditioning during sleep, by having his subjects close a switch in response to a signal in order to avoid being awakened and in order to obtain a small monetary reward in the morning.

By marked contrast, not even the simplest kinds of verbal learning seem to take place in sleep. Simon and Emmons (1956) presented 10 different words as many as 82 times, and yet in the morning there was no evidence, even on a recognition test, that any of the words had been learned. Studies that claim to have obtained learning of verbal materials during sleep usually have not taken the care to confirm with EEG recordings that the subjects actually were asleep (Keele, 1973).

The controllability that language provides seems to be important for reactivating items in both STM and LTM. We shall discuss the activation of items in STM here and the activation of items in LTM in the next chapter, when we consider plans for reproductive information retrieval. Activation of items in STM is called rehearsal. Brown and Lenneberg (1954) have shown that language is important in this process. First, they measured the speed and reliability with which various colors could be named. Then, on each of several trials, they presented the subject with five color patches, had him wait for 30 seconds, and then asked him to pick out as many of the five colors as he could from a larger array of color patches. The objective finding was that the more readily named colors were the more accurately identified, and the introspective reports of the subjects were consistent with this, indicating that they were, indeed, repeating the names over and over to themselves to help them remember the colors.

It is at least consistent with this view to find that visually presented letters and digits, which, of course, have well-learned names, are confused in STM on the basis of acoustic or articulatory similarity, rather than on the basis of visual similarity (Conrad, 1964; Wickelgren, 1965, 1966). The letter "E," for example, is stored as the sound "ee" and confused with the sound "dee," rather than stored as the shape "E" and confused with the shape "F."

Recent thinking in psycholinguistics is consistent with the evidence we have considered on the close relationship between the executive component of language and the control of mental processes and overt behavior. The verb, which would seem to be especially close to action, appears to be emerging as the key to syntactic organization. Fillmore (1968) has noted that within a simple proposition there is usually one item, namely, the relation or the verb, that has the power to determine what other elements should appear in the proposition: "go" requires a direction, "hit" an object, "give" a recipient, etc. (See also Miller, 1972.) Rumelhart, Lindsay, and Norman (1972) have developed a psycholinguistic model in which the central concepts are (*a*) the event, an action-based scenario with its associated actors and objects, and (*b*) the episode, a series of events. The episode structure permits the model to encode procedures that it can later evoke to operate on the world or on its own memory structure. For instance, a cooking recipe could be stored in memory as a string of commands: *Add 1 cup of flour, then add an egg, while gently stirring, then. . . .* Winograd's (1972) and Anderson and Bower's (1973) models also express syntactic knowledge as procedures.

Thus, language seems to afford us a great deal of control over other processes; it provides us with "handles" for manipulating thought and behavior. We shall encounter more evidence to support this point in the next chapter, when we consider the role of language in the retrieval of information from LTM. Let us look now, however, at some evidence for the propositional nature of language.

Propositional Nature

When we consider the propositional nature of language, we encounter its real power. Language consists of sentences, or propositions, ranging in profundity from, *Bobby hit me!* to, *The ratio of the circumference of a circle to its diameter is not a simple integer.* It has been said that one good picture is worth a thousand words, and this is, indeed, often the case. Yet it is also true that one good sentence can be worth infinitely more than a thousand pictures. How would you say $E = mc^2$ with pictures?

What is a proposition? In its most primitive and concrete form, at least, it would seem to be a special kind of pattern of relationships among classes (subject, predicate, time, place, etc.) and their referents in the verbal system that is intended to correspond to some pattern in the nonverbal system. If it does so correspond, it is said to be true; if it does not, it is said to be false.

Developmentally, the discovery that the verbal and nonverbal worlds are intended to correspond may be rather sudden (Stern, 1928; Vygotsky, 1962). In the latter part of the second year of life, children begin asking questions about the names of things, and the growth of vocabulary shows a sharp increase. In the case of the deaf and blind Helen Keller, the discovery of the correspondence between the verbal and nonverbal worlds was particularly dramatic and seemed to occur in a single great insight.

The structure of the nonverbal world seems to be represented in the form classes, nouns representing things, prepositions representing static relations in time and space, verbs representing changes in time and space, and the modifier–modified relationship representing the exception–schema relationship. These seem to be linguistic universals (Greenberg, 1962). The verb–object relation-ship seems to be the first two-word utterance learned in at least English (Brown & Bellugi, 1964), Japanese (McNeill, 1966), and Russian (Slobin, 1966; Vygotsky, 1962). Modification seems to be learned later. The structure of the nonverbal world seems also to be represented in the subject–object order. As cause always pre-cedes effect in the nonverbal world, it seems that subject always precedes object in the simplest sentences of languages everywhere (Greenberg, 1962).

The basic structure of the executive system can also be seen in the structure of a sentence, for the plans for generating and com-prehending sentences, like all plans, are hierarchically organized. The structure of a sentence is revealed in what linguists call a phrase-structure analysis (Chomsky, 1957, 1965). Thus, the sen-tence, *The boy caught a fish*, can be analyzed into a subject, *the boy*, and a predicate, *caught a fish*. The predicate, in turn, can be analyzed into a verb, *caught*, and an object, *a fish*. This phrase-structure analysis is shown in Figure 83. Figure 84 shows a TOTE representation of sentences having the general form of this sen-tence.

This particular phrase-structure analysis seems to possess psycho-logical reality. There are several converging lines of evidence. Pauses in speech are much more likely following the first word of a phrase unit, yet such pauses are less likely to be reported by listeners than shorter pauses elsewhere in the sentence (Boomer, 1965). In recalling sentences, subjects often recall parts of sen-tences, and sentences are most likely to fragment at major phrase boundaries (Johnson, 1965). Finally, clicks sounded during the acoustic presentation of a sentence tend to be heard as if they occurred at major phrase boundaries (Garret, Bever, & Fodor, 1966). In this last study, acoustic variables, such as pauses and in-

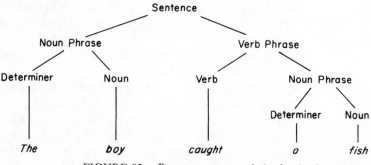

FIGURE 83.   *Phrase-structure analysis of a simple sentence.*

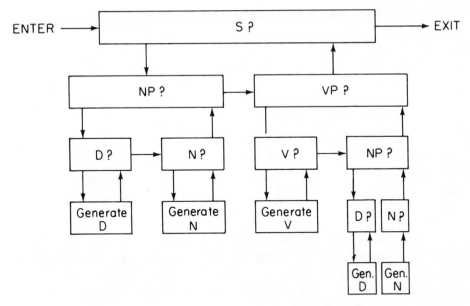

FIGURE 84.   A TOTE *representation of a simple sentence.* S = *sentence;*
NP = *noun phrase;* VP = *verb phrase;* D = *determiner;* N = *noun;* V = *verb.*

tonation, were carefully controlled by taping word strings and
splicing them together in different contexts to produce different
phrase-structure analyses. For example, there is a major break between *marrying* and *Anna* in, *In her hope of marrying Anna was*
surely impractical, but not in, *Your hope of marrying Anna was*
surely impractical. Clicks tended to be heard between *marrying*
and *Anna* in the first sentence, but not in the second.

A proposition, often represented simply by P, can, itself, become an object of thought. When the executive system operates
upon propositions, it operates on itself, and, in doing so, opens up
the whole world of logic and mathematics. The logician is concerned only with the truth value of propositions, not their particular meaning. This is why it is often said in jest that logicians,
along with mathematicians, are people who do not know what
they are talking about.

Operations can be performed on single propositions, on pairs of
propositions, and on operations on pairs of propositions (see Figure 85). Operations on single propositions are the transformations
(Chomsky, 1957, 1965), for example, the negative (*The boy did*
not catch a fish), the interrogative (*Did the boy catch a fish?*),
and the passive. (*A fish was caught by the boy*). The interrogative

Proposition	P			
Operation on proposition	$-P$			
Operations on pairs of prepositions	P and Q	$P \lor Q$	$P \rightarrow Q$	$P \leftrightarrow Q$
Reasoning	$P \rightarrow Q$ P therefore Q		$P \rightarrow Q$ $-Q$ therefore $-P$	

FIGURE 85. *Propositions and operations on propositions.*

and passive transformations seem to serve essentially communicative, rather than truth–value, functions. As such, they are of no concern to the logician. Negation, on the other hand, reverses the truth value of a proposition and is essential to logic. It is indicated by the negation symbol, as in $-P$.

It is interesting to note, incidentally, that children first indicate the negative transformation in much the same way that a logician does, by simply affixing a marker to the positive statement. Thus, *No wipe finger, Not fit,* and, *No drop mitten,* precede such forms as, *I didn't wipe my finger, That doesn't fit,* and, *Don't drop the mitten* (Bellugi, cited in Miller & McNeill, 1969).

There is also some indication that children learn to negate constituents of sentences before learning to negate entire sentences. In Japanese, if you ask, *Is your daddy gone?* a child could use *nai* as an adjective to indicate that his father is not present, or he could use it as an auxiliary to indicate that the statement is not true, that it is not the case that his daddy is gone. The one child on whom data have been obtained (McNeill & McNeill, cited in Miller & McNeill, 1969) learned the former well before learning the latter. This difference appears to persist in adulthood, negations of sentences being more difficult to process than negations of constituents of sentences (Clark, 1972). For example, Waddington (in Wason & Johnson-Laird, 1972) found that it took adults longer to understand sentences of the form, *Not all X are Y,* than to understand sentences of the form, *Some X are not Y.*

It takes longer to understand a negative proposition than an affirmative one. Wason (1961) obtained true–false reaction times for four types of statements: true affirmative (*34 is an even number*), false affirmative (*34 is an odd number*), true negative (*34 is not an odd number*), and false negative (*34 is not an even num-*

ber.) The negatives took longer than the affirmatives, and the falses took longer than the trues; moreover, the difference between the negatives and the affirmatives was greater than that between the falses and the trues.

If negatives are difficult to understand because they require an extra mental operation, then double negatives should be all the more difficult to understand, since they require two extra operations. Indeed, this seems to be the case (Wason & Johnson-Laird, 1972, p. 47). This is the depth of recursion problem again. Perhaps this is why double negatives, such as, *I ain't gonna do nothin'*, are so often misintended and misunderstood as single negatives. Repetition of the negative seems to have the effect of simply intensifying the negation, which suggests processing in the representational, rather than the executive, system.

We have considered propositions (for example, P) and their negations (here, $-P$). The conjunction of a proposition and its negation ($P \& -P$) is a contradiction. The verbal executive system, at least, appears to abhor contradictions. Indeed, one of the most effective ways to correct a person's reasoning seems to be to confront him with the contradictions inherent in his thinking. This was a favorite technique of Socrates, and it has been employed successfully in a number of experiments.

Smedslund (1961a,b) employed contradiction to teach conservation of substance. Young children do not realize that rolling a ball of plasticine out into a sausage shape leaves the amount of plasticine unchanged (or conserved). They believe there is more because it is longer. They also believe, however, that taking away some of the plasticine reduces the amount, as, of course, it does. Rather than simply rolling the ball of plasticine out into a sausage shape, as is usually done in such studies, Smedslund also removed a piece. Thus, the child was led to believe, on one basis, that there would be more plasticine and, on another basis, that there would be less. Introducing conflict in this manner facilitated acquisition of conservation.

Wason (1964) gave subjects problems of the following sort. Determine the correct figure in this statement, *Any employee aged 34 years, or more, will receive a salary of at least _____ a year*, on the basis of the following statements: one employee aged 24 receives a salary of £1800; another employee aged 37 receives a salary of £1600; etc. These last two statements are so arranged that the second contradicts an incorrect inference that subjects are likely to make on the basis of the first. On the basis of the first statement, that an employee aged 24 receives a salary of £1800, it is tempting to infer that any employee aged 34 years, or more, will receive a salary of at least £1800; yet the very next statement says that an employee aged 37 receives a salary of £1600, which is less. Wason presented such pairs consecutively in one experimental condition and separated by several sentences in another. The result was that subjects in the former condition were more likely to correct such erroneous inferences and not to repeat them than subjects in the latter. (See also Wason, 1969; Wason & Johnson-Laird, 1970.)

The notion that we learn from errors has a long history in the philosophy of science, from Mill's (1930) law of elimination to Platt's (1964) principle of strong inference. Laboratory studies of concept learning support this notion (Bower & Trabasso, 1964; Hanfman & Kasanin, 1942; Levine, 1970; Podell, 1958; Restle, 1962). A study by Podell (1958) is particularly interesting.

Podell studied contradiction by examining the effect of variety of experience on learning. Variety seems to have quite different effects on the representational and executive systems. For example, it interferes with learning in animals and facilitates learning in adult humans (see Podell, 1958). Podell demonstrated both effects in adult humans by instructing one group in a way that encouraged reliance on representational processes and another group in a way that encouraged reliance on executive processes. Subjects were presented either two (low variety) or twelve (high variety) stimuli. Half the subjects in each of the variety conditions were asked to rate the stimuli for aesthetic appeal, presumably primarily a perceptual judgment; and half were asked to determine which features the stimuli had in common. They were later asked to describe the stimuli from memory and were scored on the number of features recalled.

Those subjects who were instructed to rate the stimuli on aesthetic appeal recalled more common features (and also more variable ones) in the low-variety condition, whereas those who were instructed to look for common features recalled more common features (and fewer variable ones) in the high-variety condition. Subjects with the aesthetic set were apparently responding to isolated stimuli, and the more time they had to spend on each, the better they learned both the common and variable features of that stimulus. Subjects with the concept-learning set were apparently testing hypotheses as to what features characterized the entire set of stimuli, and the more different stimuli they were able to examine, the greater the opportunity to reject erroneous hypotheses about constant features on the basis of contradictory information. Podell concluded that the mechanism involved in the aesthetic subjects was summation, or schema-formation, and that, in the concept-learning subjects, contradiction was the important mechanism. [Similarly, Bregman and Charness (1970) found low variability to be better early in training and high variability to be better later.]

A corollary of this notion is that learning will occur only on error trials, that no learning will occur on trials on which the stimulus is classified correctly by the subject's current hypothesis. This appears to be the case, at least when the subject is testing only a single hypothesis at a time. To hold an adult human to a single hypothesis at a time, however, it is necessary to use complex stimuli and to present them at a fast rate. When stimuli are simple and plenty of time is available, subjects also learn on "correct" trials (Levine, 1970). This seems to be because they are testing more than one hypothesis at a time and stimuli on "correct" trials can also lead to learning by contradicting and leading to rejection of hypotheses other than the one on which the subject based his overt classification of the stimulus.

There is an interesting paradox connected with this. While it seems clear enough from the foregoing that contradiction is the best way to learn, people do not always seek contradictions. Wason (1960) showed, in the 2–4–6 experiment described earlier, that subjects tend to seek confirming, rather than disconfirming, information, at least when they have to generate their own instances. It is apparently difficult to conceive of the importance of contradiction.

Operations can be performed on pairs of propositions (see Figure 85), as well as on single propositions. Such operations are represented by the various binary connectives, for example, the conjunction (P & Q, read "P and Q"), the disjunction (P v Q, read "P or Q"), and the implication ($P \rightarrow Q$, read "If P, then Q").

It is important to note that the conditional, $P \rightarrow Q$, is not used in ordinary language in the same way in which logicians use it. To the logician, the statement, *If circles are square, one equals two,* is a true statement. It is true because the antecedant proposition, *circles are square,* is false, and whenever the antecedant of a conditional is false, the conditional as a whole is true. To the ordinary person, however, this strange statement is neither true nor false; it simply has no application (Johnson-Laird & Tagart, 1969). The statement is seen as applying only if circles actually are square, and, since circles are not square, no assertion is believed to have been made. Ordinary people seem more concerned with factual truth than logical truth; they seem interested not so much in the form of the sentences as in the underlying pattern of causal relationships to which they refer.

Johnson-Laird and Shapiro (cited in Wason & Johnson-Laird, 1972, pp. 73f) studied sentences that were logically identical but that had different causal implications. For example, the statement, *If prices increase, the firm goes bankrupt,* and the statement, *Prices increase only if the firm goes bankrupt,* are logically identical, but the first suggests that the price change causes bankruptcy, and the second suggests that bankruptcy causes the price change. Johnson-Laird and Shapiro found that subjects tend to reason from cause to effect in such sentences. When the first sentence is embedded in a reasoning problem, subjects tend to begin by assuming that prices increase, which leads to the conclusion that the firm goes bankrupt; however, when the second sentence is embedded in the same reasoning problem, they tend to begin by assuming that the firm goes bankrupt, which leads nowhere.

Finally, operations can also be performed on operations on pairs of propositions (see Figure 85). This is what we do in logical reasoning. Thus, if we represented, *The boy caught a fish,* by P and, *The boy must have pleased the gods,* by Q, and if we believed that catching fish is a sign that one has pleased the gods, we might reason:

$P \rightarrow Q$ *If the boy caught a fish, then the boy must have pleased the gods.*

P *The boy caught a fish.*

$\therefore Q$ *Therefore, the boy must have pleased the gods.*

Another line of reasoning might go as follows, where P represents, *They are dumping pollutants into the lake,* and Q represents, *There are fish in the lake:*

$P \rightarrow -Q$ *If they are dumping pollutants into the lake, then it is not the case that there are fish in the lake.*

Q *There are fish in the lake.*

$\therefore -P$ *Therefore, it is not the case that they are dumping pollutants into the lake.*

There are two interesting things to note about this second line of reasoning. One is that the conclusion is a negative proposition. It is an assertion about what will not be observed. As such, it may, quite unlike secondary perception and associative memory, lead to an expectation of something that has never before been experienced by the individual in question, for example, colorless and odorless effluents pouring into this lake. A system that can do this is most decidedly at Level III.

In the following dialogue, Sir Arthur Conan Doyle (1968) dramatizes the importance to logical thought of what is not observed:

> "Is there any other point to which you would wish to draw my attention?"
> "To the curious incident of the dog in the night-time."
> "The dog did nothing in the night-time."
> "That was the curious incident," remarked Sherlock Holmes.

A second interesting feature of the argument about the fish in the lake is that contradiction is involved. Q contradicts $-Q$ and thereby leads to rejection of P. We have already commented on the importance of contradiction in logical thought.

We have been talking to this point about the verbal executive system, but what about the nonverbal executive system? Can we say anything directly about it, beyond simply inferring that, in one respect or another, it is unlike the verbal executive system? It appears not. Of obvious relevance are the processes of artistic imagination. Nonverbal executive processes are surely involved, if anywhere, in the creation of novel visual, musical, and sculptural patterns. Yet we know virtually nothing about these processes. There is a clear need for work in this area, to complement the great amount of ongoing research in verbal behavior.

Of possible relevance is the puzzling case of idiot savants. Idiot savants, while generally quite deficient intellectually, possess extraordinary capacities in a limited area, such as calendar calculation. For example, one studied by Horwitz, Kestenbaum, Person, and Jarvik (1965) could tell almost instantaneously the day of the week for any date within a period of 6000 years and could also give the day of the month for the first Monday, second Friday, etc., in any month of any year within this period. The fact that he could only say, when asked how he did this, "It's in my head," suggests that the process is nonverbal. Two facts suggest that analogue mechanisms are heavily involved: one is the fact that this person was unable to add, subtract, multiply, or divide even single digits; the other, of course, is the great speed with which the calculations were performed.

The best we can do, it seems, is to close with a statement by Einstein (1952), which must be taken quite seriously and which attests to the importance of activity that seems to be at once both executive and nonverbal.

(a) The words of the language, as they are written or spoken, do not seem to play any role in my mechanism of thought. The psychical entities which seem to serve as elements in thought are cer-

tain signs and more or less clear images which can be "voluntarily" reproduced and combined. . . .

(b) The above mentioned elements are, in my case, of visual and
some of muscular type. Conventional words or other signs have
to be sought for laboriously only in a secondary stage, when the
mentioned associative play is sufficiently established and can be
reproduced at will . . . [p. 43].

The Adaptability of the Executive System

Several viewpoints suggest that the executive system is simple
and highly adaptive, that whatever complexity it may appear to
possess may be just the complexity of its surroundings showing
through. Simon (1969) makes the point well.

> We watch an ant make his laborious way across a wind- and wave-
> molded beach. He moves ahead, angles to the right to ease his climb
> up a steep dunelet, detours around a pebble, stops for a moment to
> exchange information with a compatriot. Thus he makes his weaving,
> halting way back to his home. So as not to anthropomorphize about
> his purposes, I sketch the path on a piece of paper. It is a sequence
> of irregular, angular segments—not quite a random walk, for it has
> an underlying sense of direction, of aiming towards a goal.
>
>   I show the unlabeled sketch to a friend. Whose path is it? An ex-
> pert skier, perhaps, slaloming down a steep and somewhat rocky slope.
> Or a sloop, beating upwind in a channel dotted with islands or
> shoals. Perhaps it is a path in a more abstract space: the course of
> search of a student seeking the proof of a theorem in geometry. . . .
>
>   Viewed as a geometric figure, the ant's path is irregular, complex,
> hard to describe. But its complexity is really a complexity in the sur-
> face of the beach, not a complexity in the ant [pp. 23–24].*

Or, as he says elsewhere (Simon, 1965), speaking specifically of
plans for problem solving, "the secret of problem solving is that
there is no secret."

Bandura (1969) seems to be making a similar point in arguing
against the basic assumption of trait theories that certain behavior
patterns, such as friendliness, honesty, and aggressiveness, are
characteristic of individuals and thus highly consistent across situations. Bandura (1960) and Bandura and Walters (1959) found,
for example, that aggressive responses in preadolescent and adolescent boys are highly discriminated, varying considerably as a function of the persons with whom they are interacting. Other studies
have shown leadership and honesty similarly to vary from situation
to situation. Mischel (1968) in a comprehensive review of the lit-

---

* Reprinted from *The Sciences of the artificial* by H. A. Simon, by permission of The M.I.T. Press, Cambridge, Massachusetts. © 1969, The M.I.T.
Press.

erature, found low correlations between measures of the same trait in different situations and also between different measures of the same trait in the same situation. Bandura (1969) concludes that "a high degree of behavioral flexibility is required if a person is to meet the complexities of ever changing environmental demands."

Similarly, Piaget (see Flavell, 1963) considers intelligence based on systems of executive operations to be the most highly adaptive, an intelligence in which both assimilation and accommodation are in equilibrium.

Thus, as we turn now to consider sets of plans for reproductive and productive information retrieval, we should expect these plans to reflect to a considerable extent the structure, as represented in perception and associative memory, of the problems they have been developed to handle.

Plans for Reproductive Information Retrieval

chapter **6**

Plans for forming both associative and inferential structures enable the executive system to retrieve stored knowledge.

In both this chapter and the next, we shall be concerned with plans for information retrieval, means by which the executive system gains access to knowledge stored in LTM. The difference is that in this chapter we shall be concerned with reproductive information retrieval, reproducing something in much the same form in which it was originally stored, whereas in the next chapter we shall be concerned with productive information retrieval, assembling something new out of fragments of information acquired in different contexts. Here we shall be concerned with recovery; there, with discovery.

Plans for reproductive information retrieval are often called plans for information storage. This is because they can be, and usually are, constructed during original learning of the material. Such plans, as we shall see, contain much that is specific to the material to be retrieved.

Plans for productive information retrieval are often called strategies for problem solving. They cannot be constructed during original learning of the material, for the material they bring together was originally learned for a variety of purposes and on a variety of different occasions. Such plans must be constructed during the solving of problems, during information retrieval, itself.

The reality of plans for reproductive information retrieval is amply demonstrated by differences between stimulated and unstimulated information retrieval.

Stimulated and Unstimulated Information Retrieval

A brain-damaged patient who can find his way through the complex maze of hospital corridors without difficulty cannot describe any of the routes he takes (Goldstein & Scheerer, 1941). Similarly, a child who can easily find his way about his neighborhood cannot draw a map of the neighborhood (Piaget & Szeminska, cited in Piaget, 1962).

The difference between going somewhere and telling someone how to get there seems to be one of stimulated recall versus unstimulated recall. In stimulated recall, information is retrieved on the basis of association to an external stimulus. The patient sees a corridor and recalls that it leads to the canteen, that it leads to the garden, or that he does not know where it leads. The child sees a street corner and recalls that it leads around to his friend's house. Stimulated recall is what is involved in a fill-in examination or a vocabulary test.

In unstimulated recall, information is retrieved on the basis of internal activity, with little or no support from external stimuli. Describing a route, drawing a map, and taking an essay examination all require that information be retrieved on the basis of internal activity.

In unstimulated recall, it seems that the executive system is operating on LTM, rather than upon the world. The mind, to use Bartlett's (1932) phrase, "turns 'round upon" itself to generate its own stimuli. This apparently first occurs in a rudimentary form during the second year of life (Piaget, 1952a; Stern, 1914). It appears first in deferred imitation, in which the child plays roles that he saw enacted on an earlier occasion (Piaget, 1952a). It is noteworthy that brain-damaged patients are frequently unable to take on roles in this fashion, in the absence of support from external stimuli. A patient might be able to drink water from a glass containing water, for example, but not be able to use an empty glass to show how to drink water. And he might be able to comb his hair when he has a comb in his hand and yet not be able to show how to comb his hair when he has no comb. A similar distinction can be made between recognition and stimulated recall. Indeed, recognition, stimulated recall, and unstimulated recall seem to be points along the same dimension. In recognition, a stimulus is presented, and the subject has only to indicate whether it is familiar or unfamiliar, as in a true–false or multiple-choice examination. In stimulated recall, as we have seen, a stimulus is presented, and the subject must recall a response. And, in unstimulated recall, the subject must recall a response for which there is no stimulus. The dimension is one of decreasing reliance on representational processes and increasing reliance on executive processes.

Some interesting differences have been found between recognition and recall. One such difference has to do with the importance of intention to learn. In what is called an incidental learning experiment, material is presented under two conditions: subjects in the intentional learning condition are told to learn the material, and subjects in the incidental learning condition are told to do something else with the material (read it to subjects in the intentional learning condition, rate it on humorousness, etc.). Subjects tend to learn in both conditions. When recognition is all that is required, there is little difference between the conditions; but, when recall is required, a substantial difference appears in favor of the intentional learning condition (Postman, 1964). Apparently, intention to learn is not necessary for changes to take place in associative memory; contiguity seems to be sufficient. The importance of intention seems to have to do with constructing plans for information retrieval.

Plans for reproductive information retrieval must (*a*) locate the material to be recovered and (*b*) reassemble its components. The material is located on the basis of some external or internal stimulus. We shall consider the nature of this stimulus when we discuss plans for memorizing. The material is reassembled on the basis of some form of internal organization. Organization can take two forms. If it is specific to the material at hand, we say that the material has been memorized. If it is applicable quite generally to other materials, as well, we say that the material has been understood. We shall consider the former kind of organization in the section on plans for memorizing and the latter in the section on plans for comprehension. First, however, let us look more closely at the difference between memorizing and understanding.

FIGURE 86. *Guthrie and Horton's puzzle box.*
[*From Psychology, by Norman L. Munn. Houghton Mifflin Company, 1961. Reprinted by permission. (After Guthrie, E. R., and Horton,
G. P.)*]

Memorizing and Understanding

The difference between memorizing and understanding was the
point at issue in the old trial-and-error (Guthrie, 1952; Thorndike,
1911) versus insight (Katona, 1940; Kohler, 1925) controversy.
For example, Guthrie and Horton (1946) found that cats that
had learned to push a stick to open a cage door (see Figure 86)
had difficulty in learning, in a transfer test, that the same stick in
a different position would also open the door. By marked contrast, Kohler (1925) found that chimps that had learned to use
a stick to rake in food from outside their cage (see Figure 87)
showed considerable ingenuity in devising stick substitutes when
no stick was even available, using a piece of cloth to whip in the
food or even making up a stick by bundling straw together.

The difference here seems to be one of generality of representation. We have encountered the notion of generality before, in discussing the value of information reduction. Kohler's chimps had,

FIGURE 87. *Kohler's stick problem.* [*Taken, with permission, from
D. Krech, R. S. Crutchfield, and N. Livson, Elements of psychology, 2d ed.
(New York: Knopf, 1969), p. 430.*]

apparently, in some way abstracted the essential notion of an extension of one's reach, for they were able to see a variety of objects as being equivalent, in this sense, to a stick. Guthrie and Horton's cats, on the other hand, seem to have had difficulty in abstracting the notion of moving the stick from irrelevant information about its location, for they had difficulty in responding in the same way even to the same stick in a new location.

Another indication of generality of representation is the shape of the learning curve. Not only did Guthrie and Horton's cats have difficulty in transferring to a somewhat different problem, but they even had difficulty in transferring from one trial to another of the same problem. Thus, their learning curves were gradual, as idealized in Figure 88. The learning curves displayed by Kohler's chimps, by contrast, were sudden, as idealized in Figure 88. Once they had solved the problem and raked in the food with the stick, they understood the solution in a very general way and thus transferred well both to subsequent trials and to subsequent problems.

Generality of knowledge, by itself, is no evidence for executive involvement, however, for as we have seen, mechanisms for selecting the relevant and rejecting the irrelevant, and thus for assimilating particular stimuli to somewhat generalized representations, are found at all three levels of knowing.

At Level I, in the mechanisms of primary perception, constant stimulation is suppressed and change in stimulation given emphasis. Here, as we saw, seem to be the innate mechanisms responsible for the transposition of relations that attracted the interest of such gestalt psychologists as Wertheimer (1959) and Kohler (1925).

At Level II, associative changes in secondary perception and

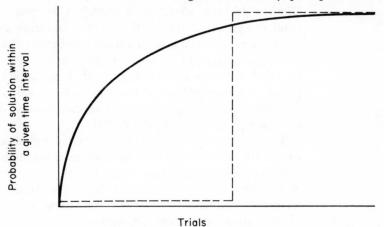

Trials

FIGURE 88. *Gradual (–) and sudden (– –) learning curves.*

associative memory emphasize repeated contingencies, thus giving rise to somewhat generalized associative schemas. These seem to account for many of the gestalt properties that Bartlett (1932) had in mind.

At Level III, the mechanism of selection is directed attention. As long ago as 1905, Ach distinguished between Level II and Level III abstraction, what he called associative and determined abstraction. For example, in the identification of a new species of bird, the ornithologist first looks for birds with long bills (determined abstraction), then notices that they have a particular song, habitat, and so forth (associative abstraction). Finally, the name "longbill" becomes a palpable sign for the impalpable knowing that members of this species have a curved bill, etc. Bruner, Goodnow, and Austin (1962) seem to have had the same process in mind when they described the process of learning to recognize *corpus lutea* (see page 3).

Directed attention, or analysis of a percept into attributes, seems to be part of what is involved in conceptual classification. Concepts are considerably more general than either percepts or associative schemas. To be classified together perceptually, objects must bear some overall resemblance to one another, as various leaves do, or various hands, or various works by deBussy. To be classified together associatively, objects must have been experienced before and must have been experienced in contiguity with the same response (thus it is that we can identify letters of the alphabet or Presidents of the United States), or significant features of those objects must have been experienced before in contiguity with the same response (thus, we can say *That's the way Bill Cosby would have told it,* or, *That's the kind of observation Sherlock Holmes would have made*). Concepts, on the other hand, can go well beyond both overall resemblance and contiguity in experience. On the basis of a small number of precisely specified defining characteristics, a concept can permit a new animal to be classified as a mammal, a new heavenly body to be classified as a planet, or a new problem in topology to be classified as insoluble. It is this capacity to go so far beyond the confines of past experience that places concepts at Level III.

A consequence of the fact that perceptual and associative mechanisms for classification tend to produce representations that are limited in their generality is that, when they err, they tend to err in the direction of overdiscrimination. We considered evidence for overdiscrimination in the representational system at the end of the chapter on secondary perception.

Similarly, a consequence of the fact that conceptual mechanisms for classification tend to produce representations that are quite general is that when they err, they tend to err in the direction of overgeneralization (Dawes, 1966). It is a commonplace that intellectuals, particularly inexperienced ones, tend to generalize too readily, for example, from historical cases to the present or from the laboratory to the natural world. The history of experimental psychology, alone, is filled with cases of early thinkers believing that all learning was learning by contiguity (Guthrie) or that all learning was learning by reinforcement (Hull), that all learning required such mechanisms as awareness (Erickson) or attention (Lashley) or that no learning required such mechanisms (Guthrie, Hull). The tendency to overgeneralize is nicely captured in the old tale of the blind men and the elephant: The one who felt the leg thought that an elephant was like a tree; the one who felt the tail thought that an elephant was like a rope; and so forth.

There is more to understanding, however, than generality in the way information from the stimulus is selected and combined. Understanding also involves going beyond the information given, relating what is present to what is not present. Even the simple mechanism of a wire screen classifies objects into those small enough to pass through it and those too large to pass through it. Yet it tells us nothing else about the objects. We have encountered the notion of going beyond the information given before, both in secondary perception and in associative memory. Hence, going beyond the information given, like generality of knowledge, is, by itself, no indication of executive involvement.

Representational and executive mechanisms for going beyond the information given, are quite different from one another, however. The following example will illustrate:

> Fordney glanced curiously at the interior of the sedan with its blood-soaked rear seat and followed the stretcher into the morgue of the small northern town.
> As the corpse, blasted by a shotgun charge, was lifted to a table, McHugh said, "I found this man on the old logging road about fifteen miles north of Oakdale. I was driving from my cottage on Black Ghost Lake to town when my headlights picked him out. I examined him, saw he was dead, and brought him here."
> "Don't you know that you are not supposed to move a dead body?" roared Police Chief Swanson.
> "Certainly!" snapped McHugh, "but the nearest phone is twelve miles. Did you expect me to leave him to the animals?"
> "You're lying," Fordney said [Adapted from Ripley, 1949].

Unless you have heard this story or a very similar one before, no associations to the story would indicate that McHugh was lying. To solve the mystery, you have to engage in reasoning. What you have to do is consider McHugh's story as an hypothesis and check to see how it squares with the facts that are mentioned. The correct line of reasoning goes somewhat as follows:

> *If the man was dead all the time that he was in the back seat (as McHugh claims), then his heart would not have been beating, and he would have bled little, if at all.*
>
> *It is not the case that he bled little, if at all. (The rear seat was soaked with blood.)*
>
> *Therefore, it is not the case that the man was dead all the time that he was in the back seat.*

Though we have seen that some measure of understanding exists in both the representational and the executive systems, it is the concepts and organized systems of concepts in the executive system that provide the highest level of understanding. This can be seen most clearly, of course, in logic, mathematics, and the sciences. Because plans for memorizing are, essentially, plans for writing in the representational system by activating and organizing images and associations, they achieve little in the way of understanding. It is plans for comprehension that make possible understanding at the level of explanation, rather than mere anticipation, that is, by relating concrete information to abstract conceptual systems.

We turn now to a consideration of factors that determine whether knowledge will be memorized or understood. Most of the research to be cited is concerned only with generality of knowledge, and not with the mechanism by which generality is achieved. However, we have tried to include only research for which we are able to argue that the effects are effects specifically on the executive system.

Factors That Determine Whether Knowledge Will Be Memorized or Understood

Understanding requires a certain capacity in the superordinate executive system. Intelligence establishes the limits of this capacity. Practice increases this capacity by turning routine chores over to the subordinate executive system. Moderate motivation keeps excessively high arousal from restricting this capacity. And intention to understand puts this capacity to use. Let us look, then, at the factors of intelligence, practice, moderate motivation, and intention to understand. It will be most convenient to begin with practice.

Practice

A difference in amount of prior experience relevant to the problem is undoubtedly one of the factors that accounts for the fact that Guthrie and Horton's cats showed narrow transfer, whereas Kohler's chimps showed broad transfer. Guthrie and Horton's cats had had no previous experience in activating stick levers for any purpose, but Kohler's chimps had grown up in the wild and presumably had had experience using sticks to extend their reach. Birch (1945) tested this notion by raising some chimps in captivity and keeping them from having any contact with sticks. When given Kohler's stick problem, only two out of six of them solved it in a 30-minute test period. (Actually, 1 of these 2 had had considerable experience with sticks, and the other solved the problem in a way that indicated lack of understanding.) Sticks were then left in their cages for 3 days, during which time they used them frequently for poking things and hitting each other. When retested, all of them solved the problem within 20 seconds. Unfortunately, it is not possible to say, on the basis of these data, whether the effect of practice is on the representational or the executive system. The data to be considered in what follows will speak more clearly to this point.

One of the clearest cases of the emergence of a plan has been provided by Harlow (1949). Harlow has shown that, after solving about 300 discrimination problems, monkeys learn the principle involved and can then solve subsequent problems in a single trial (see Figure 89).

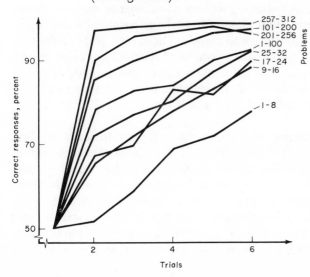

FIGURE 89.   *Nonspecific transfer as a function of practice.* [Taken, with permission, from H. F. Harlow, "The formation of learning sets," Psychological Review, 1949, **56,** 51–56.]

On a discrimination problem, the animal has to learn which of two stimuli has food under it. On each trial, both stimuli, say, a circle and a cross, are presented to the animal, and it is allowed to move one. The positions of the stimuli are varied randomly from trial to trial, but the food is always under the same stimulus. Learning on the first such problem shows the gradual learning curve reported by Guthrie and Horton (1946).

On the next discrimination problem, the stimuli would be different, say a triangle and a star, but the rules of the game would be the same: During a given problem, food is always under the same object. After around 300 such problems, the learning curves look like the one reported by Kohler (1925). The animal solves the problem on the first trial. If food is under the first object chosen, the animal continues to choose that object. If there is no food under the first object chosen, it switches to the other object and consistently chooses it.

Some ability to impose a new organization on that provided by the representational system seems to be involved here, for at the end of training, the animals show no tendency to choose a stimulus that was a positive stimulus a few problems back in preference to a neutral stimulus. The mechanism that has emerged seems to be an executive one, a plan, and it seems to be one that possesses considerable generality.

Whereas this experiment provides us with a fairly clear picture of the product of practice, others are more illuminating with respect to the mechanism by which this product is arrived at. We have said that practice increases the capacity of the superordinate executive system by turning routine chores over to the subordinate executive system. This appears to make it possible for the superordinate executive system to consider the various parts of the task simultaneously and, where a pattern of relationships exists among the parts, to apprehend these and achieve some measure of understanding. Let us see how this takes place in serial learning and free-recall learning and then, on a much larger scale, in cognitive development.

In serial learning, one might ask a subject to learn the list: DAX, MIB, DUT, CEF, VOR, XIL. DAX would be presented, and MIB would have to be recalled; then MIB would be presented, and DUT would have to be recalled; and so forth. Here, it is possible to recall items on the basis of an external stimulus, the immediately preceding item, and that is what appears to take place early in learning. Early in learning, the items in the list seem to be bound together by pairwise associations, as represented below:

DAX–MIB–DUT–CEF–VOR–XIL.

The reality of these associations has been demonstrated (Ebbinghaus, 1913; Youssef, 1967) by showing that such learning facilitates learning of a list that preserves some of these pairings (for example, ____ ____ ____ MIB DUT ____, where the blanks represent new nonsense syllables) more than learning of a list that preserves none of them (for example, ____ MIB ____ ____ VOR ____).

Later in serial learning, however, the items appear to be located within some overall pattern, rather than bound to one another. Now the effective stimulus for each item seems to be its position in the list, rather than the preceding item. This is represented as follows.

The reality of this organization has been demonstrated (Young, 1962; Youssef, 1967) by showing that, late in learning, transfer is greater to a list that preserves some of the positions (for example, ____ MIB ____ ____ VOR ____) than to a list that preserves some of the pairings (for example, ____ ____ ____ MIB DUT ____).

Practice seems to result in greater executive control in this example but not in comprehension, for there is no pattern among the elements in the sequence. In the experiment to be described, a patterned sequence is used, and comprehension does result. Bruner, Mandler, O'Dowd, and Wallach (1958) had rats learn to run right–left–right–left for food, that is, to turn right at the first choice point in a maze, to turn left at the second, and so on. They then transferred the rats to a left–right–left–right sequence, a sequence that was quite unlike the original in terms of which particular responses were made to which particular stimuli, but which involved the same general pattern of alternation. Groups that had barely learned the first problem showed negative transfer on the second, actually performing less well than animals that had not learned the first problem. Groups that had been given 20 trials beyond those required to reach criterion, however, showed, not greater negative transfer, but positive transfer, performing better than animals that had not learned the first problem. This may appear to be simply a shift from place-learning to response-learning with extended practice, but there is more to it than just this, as we shall see when we consider this experiment again under moderate motivation.

Apparently, with greater practice some notion of the general pattern of alternation was acquired. Mandler has reported that, when adult humans learn a finger maze, their knowledge of the maze seems to them to be fragmentary at first but later to involve an appreciation of the overall pattern of the maze that is in some sense simultaneous.

Experiments in free-recall learning also help to delineate the role of executive control processes in memorizing and understanding. In free-recall learning, one might present a list like,

**SEASON AVERAGE PENCIL TREE MARGIN
CLOUD   ISLAND   TEMPERATURE   BUCKET
STONE CARBON PAINT MUSIC BOOK HORSE**

and ask the subject to recall it immediately, in any order he wishes. Here, it is not possible to recall items on the basis of an external stimulus. From the outset, the subject must provide his own stimuli for recall. Because these stimuli must be held in STM, their number cannot exceed five. Thus, about five words will be recalled.

If the list is repeated several times, however, a larger number of words will be recalled, and, with sufficient practice, the entire list will be recalled. What practice seems to accomplish is the automatization of short sequences of items, a process known as "chunking" (Miller, 1956), so that each control element in STM can call upon several items, a "chunk."

Tulving and Patkau (1962) have demonstrated this process quite clearly, by measuring chunks in the recall of sequences on which subjects had had, in effect, increasing amounts of practice. (The sequences represented increasing orders of approximation to the sequences of words found in ordinary English.) They scored each attempt at recall in two ways: by counting the number of words recalled correctly and by counting the number of "unbroken strings" in recall. An "unbroken string" is defined as follows. Assume that the list presented earlier is recalled as follows:

**CLOUD   ISLAND   TEMPERATURE   SEASON
AVERAGE   TREE   STONE   MUSIC   BOOK**

In the context of the original list, this represents five sets of words that were reproduced in their original sequence:

**_SEASON_ _AVERAGE_ PENCIL _TREE_ MARGIN
CLOUD   _ISLAND_   _TEMPERATURE_   BUCKET
STONE CARBON PAINT _MUSIC_ _BOOK_ HORSE**

These are called unbroken strings. Thus, the number of words recalled was nine, and the number of unbroken strings was five. What Tulving and Patkau found is that, while the number of words recalled increases with practice, the number of unbroken strings remains constant at around five. The effect of practice is, apparently, simply to increase the size of the chunks. Chunking seems to be an executive process for, while it enhances recall, it has no effect on recognition (Kintsch, 1970).

Practice seems to result in greater executive control in this example. To the extent that there is a pattern among the elements in the sequence, it also results in greater comprehension. With continued practice in free recall, conceptual relations are noted among items, and conceptually related items are increasingly likely to be clustered together in recall (Bousfield, 1953; Bousfield, Cohen, & Whitmarsh, 1958). This appears to be what Descartes had in mind when he wrote, in *Rules for the Direction of the Mind*:

> If I have first found out by separate mental operations what the relation is between magnitudes A and B, then that between B and C, between C and D, and finally between D and E, that does not entail my seeing what the relation is between A and E, nor can the truths previously learned give a precise knowledge of it unless I recall them all. To remedy this, I would run them over from time to time, keeping the imagination moving continuously in such a way that while it is intuitively perceiving each fact it simultaneously passes on to the next; and this I would do until I had learned to pass from the first to the last so quickly that no stage in the process was left to the care of memory, but I seemed to have the whole in intuition before me at the same time. This method will relieve the memory, diminish sluggishness of our thinking and definitely enlarge our mental capacity [Descartes, *Rules for the Direction of the Mind*, Rule XI].

The great experiment is life, and the most profound effects of practice are seen in cognitive development. Infants seem to learn component plans first and, later, to integrate these into larger plans, the scope of inclusion becoming increasingly greater. Piaget (1952a), as we have noted in the last chapter, has identified a developmental sequence that proceeds from primary circular reactions to secondary circular reactions to tertiary circular reactions to intentional behavior and, finally, to operational thought. Here, we simply recall the earlier discussion and note its relevance to the current discussion of the role of practice in increasing understanding.

Intelligence

The capacity for understanding varies as a function of general intelligence. The most dramatic differences in intelligence, of

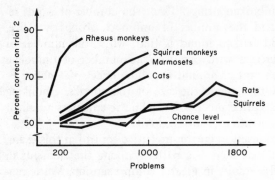

FIGURE 90. *Nonspecific transfer as a function of phylogenetic level. [Taken, with permission, from J. M. Warren, "Primate learning in comparative perspective," in A. M. Schrier, H. F. Harlow, and F. Stoll-nitz (Eds.),* Behavior of nonhuman primates, *Vol. 1 (New York: Academic Press, 1965).]*

course, are interspecies differences. The fact that chimps are more intelligent than cats undoubtedly provides an additional reason why Kohler's chimps showed more understanding than Guthrie's cats.

Substantial interspecies differences have been found in the ability to acquire learning sets. Rats and squirrels are clearly inferior to cats, racoons, and pigeons, which are clearly inferior to marmosets, which, in turn, are clearly inferior to rhesus monkeys (see Figure 90; Warren, 1965).

Kohler (1925) has related an amusing incident which shows that at least one component of general intelligence is the capacity to organize or integrate information. A bright and a dull chimp first observed a third chimp solve a problem. The solution involved sliding a box under a banana that was suspended out of reach from the ceiling, climbing on the box, and, finally, reaching the banana. After watching the demonstration, the bright chimp was able promptly to repeat the solution he had observed. The dull chimp, however, performed quite differently. He jumped up on the box, without first sliding it under the banana, and then ran over to the banana and reached for it! He had all the parts but could not put them together. Similarly, children, in imitating actions or in drawing pictures, and students, in writing answers to essay questions, frequently get the right parts but in the wrong order.

Moderate Motivation

It is a well-established fact in psychology that moderate levels of motivation facilitate productive information retrieval, or problem solving. This is expressed in the Yerkes–Dodson law, which we considered in the last chapter (page 155). The following experiment suggests that this law applies equally to understanding in reproductive information retrieval.

In the Bruner, Mandler, O'Dowd, and Wallach (1958) study described earlier, in which rats learned a right–left–right–left pattern through a maze, some conditions were run at a moderate level of motivation, 12 hours of food deprivation, and some were run at a high level of motivation, 36 hours of food deprivation. There were four groups, depending on whether motivation was moderate or high during original learning and whether motivation was moderate or high during the transfer test: MM, MH, HM, and HH.

The MM group showed positive transfer, and the HH group showed negative transfer. This is consistent with the Yerkes–Dodson law, but it does not tell us whether the effect was on information storage or information retrieval. A comparison of the MH and HM groups provides us with that information.

The MH and HM groups were equal to one another and to the MM group. What this indicates is that, during the transfer test, the MH group was using plans for reproductive information retrieval, and the HM group was using plans for productive information retrieval. While the MH group had achieved a generalized representation during original learning, when its motivation was moderate, the HM group could not do so until its motivation was reduced for the transfer test, at which time it constructed a generalized representation by a problem-solving process. It is particularly interesting that the HM group spent more time and vicarious trial-and-error (VTE) at the beginning of the test maze, suggesting that it was, indeed, solving a problem, while the MH group distributed their time and VTE more evenly over the maze.

Intention to Understand

We shall consider two factors here: intention to understand and verbalization. Intention to understand puts the capacity for understanding to work, and verbalization achieves the control and propositional generality characteristic of the verbal executive system. It is especially significant that these two factors seem to affect comprehension, for intention is at the very heart of the superordinate executive system, and verbalization is most intimately related to it. Their contribution to understanding adds further support to the notion that it is plans for comprehending that are involved in understanding.

Katona (1940) appears to have been the first to examine intention to understand, using card tricks and match tricks as stimulus materials. In one card trick, the experimenter would deal cards alternately from the top and the bottom of a deck that had been so arranged that dealing in this manner resulted in a red–red–

black–black sequence. One group of subjects was instructed to memorize the arrangement that would give this result, and another was instructed to discover how to arrange the deck so as to produce this result. One way to produce such an arrangement is to make a column of blanks, with one blank for each card in the deck, and then to write "red" in the top blank, "red" in the bottom, "black" in the second from the top, "black" in the second from the bottom, and so on, following the order of dealing.

The finding that is particularly relevant here is that subjects who had been instructed to understand could generalize their knowledge far better to different, but related, problems, such as arranging the deck so that dealing twice from the top, twice from the bottom, twice from the top, twice from the bottom would result in this same sequence.

It is also of interest that knowledge that was understood was retained better. This appears to be a general finding. The first careful work comparing forgetting of what seem to be representational and executive factors is that of Bunch (1936; Bunch & McCraven, 1938; Bunch & Lang, 1939). In a typical experiment, Bunch had subjects learn a list of paired associates. He then tested some subjects later by having them relearn the original list and other subjects by having them learn a different list. Those who relearned the original list could presumably profit from both information in representational memory about the specific nonsense syllables and information in executive memory about the general strategy for learning paired-associate lists. Those who learned a new list, with different nonsense syllables, could presumably profit only from information in executive memory. The results were that memory for specific information was quickly forgotten, following Ebbinghaus' (1913) forgetting curve (dropping from 100% to below 60%; see Figure 91), but that memory for plans for memorizing showed no loss (fluctuating about 40%; see Figure 91) over a period of three months. (See also Tresselt & Leeds, 1953; Anderson & Johnson, 1966a.)

Podell's (1958) study, described in the last chapter, is also relevant to intention to understand. Subjects who were given instructions to understand showed a greater potential for transfer than those who were given instructions simply to make aesthetic judgments, for the former recalled more common features and fewer variable ones.

The best-controlled and most conclusive study yet performed on the effects of verbalization on understanding seems to be that of Gagne and Smith (1962), yet it leaves much to be desired. They used the disk transfer problem (see Figure 116), in which a pile of

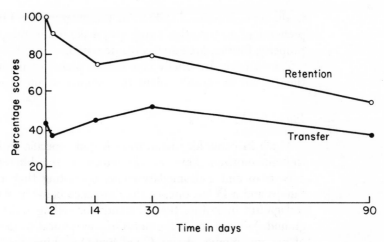

FIGURE 91. *Specific and nonspecific transfer as a function of retention interval. [Taken, with permission, from M. E. Bunch, "The amount of transfer in rational learning as a function of time,"* Journal of Comparative Psychology, *1936,* **22**, *325–337.]*

graduated disks must be moved from post A to post C by moving one disk at a time and never placing a larger disk on a smaller one. Subjects in a verbalization condition, where they were required to state a reason for each move, both made fewer unnecessary moves in solving the problem and were better able to state the principle at the end.

The problem here is that instructions to verbalize may also have induced a greater intention to understand, so we cannot be certain that verbalization, itself, had an effect. There seems to be no study, unconfounded by intention to understand, that demonstrates a facilitating effect of verbalization.

To recapitulate to this point, when information must be retrieved, rather than merely recognized, executive activity is required. Plans for reproductive information retrieval are involved when material is retrieved in much the same form in which it was originally stored, and plans for productive information retrieval are involved when material is put together in a new arrangement to fulfill a novel purpose. Plans for reproductive information retrieval are of two kinds: plans for memorizing and plans for comprehending. Several factors affect whether knowledge will be memorized or understood; these seem to have to do with the capacity of the superordinate executive system and the use to which it is put.

We noted earlier that man's verbal executive system is distinctively controllable and propositional. Plans for memorizing seem to make use primarily of the controllability property, activating items in the representational system for various purposes. Plans for comprehension, on the other hand, also make use of the propositional property, for they are essentially inferential.

Let us begin by briefly considering plans for memorizing and then go on to consider plans for comprehension at some length.

Plans for Memorizing

Much in plans for memorizing is quite specific to the material to be memorized. Thus, we can remember the difference between a bactrian and a dromedary camel by noting that a **B** has two humps and a **D** has one, or the difference between stalactites and stalagmites by noting that **C** stands for ceiling and **G** stands for ground. We can recall the notes of the musical scale with the aid of two mnemonics: Every Good Boy Does Fine, for the notes on the lines; and **FACE**, for the notes between the lines. Or, using a system with a somewhat broader range of application, we can employ the digit-to-consonant coding scheme below to make long numbers into words or phrases for easier recall (see Loisette, 1896):

1	t, l	(one stroke)
2	n	(two strokes)
3	m	(three strokes)
4	r	("four" ends in "r")
5	v	(Roman numeral for "5")
6	b, d	(physical resemblance)
7	k	(calligraphic "k" resembles "7")
8	f	(script "f" resembles "8")
9	g, p, q	(physical resemblance)
0	z, s, sh	("z" for "zero"; "s" and "sh" sound like "z")

Thus, the base of the natural logarithms, $e = 2.71828$, can be recoded as, Naturally, Knowing Logarithms Furthers Numerical Facility. It may seem a dubious economy to recode 6 digits as 43 letters; however, remember that it is not the number of items, but the number of chunks, that counts. In terms of items, techniques for making material easier to remember usually add to the amount of material to be remembered. In doing so, however, they usually reduce the number of chunks. Several such systems have been summarized in a *Dictionary of Mnemonics* (1972).

Detailed descriptions of specific plans for memorizing, while often of practical use, are of limited general interest. Fortunately, something can be said about general characteristics of plans for

Stimulus Figures

Word list 1		Word list 2

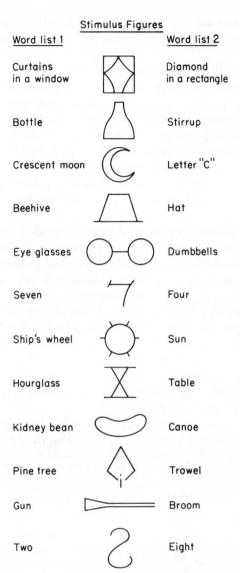

Curtains in a window	Diamond in a rectangle
Bottle	Stirrup
Crescent moon	Letter "c"
Beehive	Hat
Eye glasses	Dumbbells
Seven	Four
Ship's wheel	Sun
Hourglass	Table
Kidney bean	Canoe
Pine tree	Trowel
Gun	Broom
Two	Eight

FIGURE 92. *Stimuli and verbal labels used by Carmichael, Hogan, and Walter.* [*Taken, with permission, from L. Carmichael, H. P. Hogan, and A. Walter, "An experimental study of the effect of language on the reproduction of visually perceived form,"* Journal of Experimental Psychology, 1932, **15**, 73–86.]

is particularly interesting. Subjects went into a waiting room in which there was a poster on the wall. They were then taken into another room and asked either to describe the poster in as much detail as possible or to perform a control task that had nothing to do with the poster. All subjects were later shown the original poster and asked whether it was the one they had seen before. Subjects who had attempted to recall the poster were more likely to say erroneously that it was not the one they had seen before.

The reasons they gave had to do with its failure to match, in one way or another, the somewhat distorted descriptions that they had produced in recall.

Allport and Postman (1945) have studied this effect in a more socially significant situation. Subjects viewed a complex streetcar scene which contained, among other things, a black man and a white man obviously arguing. The white man had a razor in his hand. Many distortions were produced in recall, despite the fact that subjects knew that they were being tested for accuracy of recall. The most socially significant distortion can, perhaps, be anticipated: some subjects remembered the razor as having been in the black man's hand. The implications for the trustworthiness of legal testimony are obvious.

While coding the unfamiliar in terms of familiar words helps recall, going one step further and coding words into sentences seems to help even more (Martin, Boersma, & Cox, 1965). As we have seen earlier, the production of both multiple-link associations and sentences appears to require executive processes.

New information can also be interpreted, as we have already seen, in terms of images, which can then be combined by integrating them into compound images. The effectiveness of this technique is attested to by the fact that it seems to be used by nearly all stage memory experts (Hunter, 1957; but see Hunt & Love, 1972, for an exception). Manipulation of images, as we have seen, seems to require executive processes.

An interesting plan for using imagery in this fashion has been described by Miller, Galanter, and Pribram (1960). You have first to learn:

> *One is a bun.*
> *Two is a shoe.*
> *Three is a tree.*
> *Four is a door.*
> *Five is a hive.*
> *Six is sticks.*
> *Seven is heaven.*
> *Eight is a gate.*
> *Nine is a line.*
> *Ten is a hen.*

Learning this scheme is made easy by the fact that the paired terms rhyme and by the fact that you probably already know half of the paired terms from the nursery rhyme that begins, *One, two, buckle my shoe; three, four, open the door.* . . . (This much of the plan, incidentally, illustrates the use of familiar word associations to facilitate information retrieval.)

With this scheme in mind, you can now easily commit to memory a list of ten items. Let us consider the words *moon* and *eyeglasses* as though they were the first two items on such a list. *Moon* is the first item, so an image of a moon has to be integrated into the same image with an image of a bun. You could imagine a full moon sandwiched between two halves of a bun, perhaps with a hungry astronaut cracking his teeth on it.

This is certainly a bizarre image, but this may be all to the good. It has frequently been claimed (see, for example, Miller, Galanter, & Pribram, 1960; Norman, 1969) that bizarre images are superior to mundane ones as information retrieval mechanisms. Though there seems to be no direct evidence to support this conclusion, it is certainly consistent with the findings we considered previously on the importance of having a stimulus that accesses a unique location in memory.

The next item is *eyeglasses,* and the next position in the plan is, *Two is a shoe.* A pair of eyeglasses and a shoe must be integrated in the same image. Perhaps a wise-looking old wrinkled shoe with gold-rimmed spectacles will do the job, or a high-heeled shoe with curvaceous glasses, or a tennis shoe with sunglasses, or a military boot with a monacle. Coding the same thing in many ways greatly increases the probability that at least one of the retrieval mechanisms will succeed.

Once you have coded a list in this fashion—and it is surprisingly easy to do—you can then read off all the items backward or forward, or, if you really want to impress your friends, you can read off the odd numbered items in forward order and the even numbered items in reverse order.

Though this one-is-a-bun scheme makes a nice stage demonstration, it would not seem to be very useful for, for example, studying for a psychology examination. A better way to apply the power of imagery to the task of learning meaningful materials would seem to be to organize the materials as much as possible around graphs and diagrams.

There is more to be said about organization, however, than that it involves use of familiar words and word associations and the integrating power of imagery. Organization is hierarchical (Mandler, 1967). This is necessarily the case, because information retrieval involves the executive system, and the executive system is hierarchically organized. Hierarchical organization in the executive system seems to be a consequence of the limited capacity of STM (Mandler, 1967). We can apparently think of only five topics at a time, though we can subsequently turn our attention to any of these and think of five subtopics under it. It would seem that plans for information storage that explicitly take into account this feature of the executive system would be more efficient. Organizing material into an outline form is such a plan.

Miller has observed that hierarchical organization is apparent even in copying a picture, say, of a face. First, the general shape is drawn in. Then the eyes, nose, mouth, and ears are roughly sketched in. These would correspond to the Roman numerals in an outline. Then, details may be added to the eyes, corresponding to capital letters A, B, and C under Roman numeral I; and to the nose, corresponding to A and B under II; and so on.

The phenomenon of scalloping (Bousfield & Sedgewick, 1944; Bousfield & Barclay, 1950) and the phenomenon of clustering (Bousfield, 1953) both reveal the limited focus of the executive system in recall. If you have someone recall items, such as names of states, from memory, you will find that the items are recalled in bursts. If you plot number of items recalled against time, the curve will not be smooth but will show scallops. Apparently, what one does is search for items of a particular type, like Western states, exhaust that category, then search for items of another type, like Great Lakes states, exhaust that category, and so forth. The mechanism that produces scalloping in reproductive information retrieval is undoubtedly the same mechanism that, as we saw earlier, produces a hierarchy of solution attempts in productive information retrieval. This mechanism is direction, which, moreover, is limited in its capacity.

Clustering is a closely related phenomenon. We have already mentioned it in passing. If the list,

**IRON   CARROTS   LAWYER   TOMATO   LEAD
DOCTOR   ZINC   SQUASH   TEACHER**

is presented to be recalled immediately, in any order, the words tend to be rearranged. Words belonging to the same conceptual category or associative cluster tend to be recalled together, for example,

**IRON   LEAD   ZINC   CARROT   TOMATO   SQUASH
DOCTOR   LAWYER   TEACHER**

Moreover, not only clusters, but also subclusters within these, can be demonstrated in recall. Cohen and Bousfield (1956) compared three 40-item lists, one organized into four categories, one organized into eight categories, and one organized hierarchically into four categories, each of which was further divided into two categories. The last list, for example, might contain the names of ten animals, five canine and five feline; ten countries, five European and five South American; ten personal names, five masculine and five feminine; and ten weapons, five shooting and five cutting. The fact that this list yielded the highest clustering and recall scores suggests that both levels of the hierarchy were effective.

Kintsch (1970) has also obtained evidence for hierarchical organization in clustering, as well as evidence for the fact that the existence of clusters affects only recall and not recognition.

The phenomena of scalloping and clustering suggest that the basic organization of LTM retrieval systems is in terms of lists and lists of lists. List structure has proven to be a powerful and widely applicable basis of LTM organization in computer models of cognitive processes (Newell, 1961; Newell & Simon, 1972).

Plans for memorizing include repetition as well as organization, accommodation as well as assimilation. Two things can be noted briefly about repetition in memorizing: It is beneficial to practice active recall, and it is frequently beneficial to distribute practice. Students often study by simply rereading material in their texts, and yet it has long been known (Gates, 1917) that practice "with the book closed" can be more valuable. Some studies have shown that it is beneficial to spend up to 80% of the time trying actively to recall material, as opposed to simply rereading it. Recall involves a plan for information retrieval, and such plans seem to be formed most effectively by actually attempting to use them.

Distribution of practice refers to increasing the time between practice periods. Distribution of practice is most likely to be efficient where there is a large component of rote learning (Underwood, 1961), hence its inclusion in this section on plans for memorizing. The explanation for the efficiency of distributed practice is, as we saw earlier, still uncertain (Melton, 1970).

Plans for Comprehending

Plans for comprehending are concepts and systems of concepts. We have said that understanding involves a high level of generality and a capacity to go well beyond the information given. And we have already seen that concepts achieve a higher level of generality than any other equivalence category and have at least hinted at the fact that the operations of inference by which concepts are related to one another greatly enlarge the capacity to go beyond the information given.

Let us expand on this second point. Consider the difference between memorizing the following sentences and recoding them in terms of a system of comprehension, or inferential memory.

> *Nikki is brighter than Gail.*
> *Gail is brighter than Susan.*

Two relationships are expressed, one between Nikki and Gail and one between Gail and Susan.

In memorizing, these statements would be recorded fairly directly, in much the same way that a tape recorder might record them. Thus, if a rote learner were asked whether Nikki is brighter than Susan, he would have to reply that he was not given that information. A rote learner has little capacity for going beyond the information given.

In comprehension, these statements would be recoded in terms of some system of concepts. Here, an ordering would be used. Ordering may be very briefly characterized (we shall consider it at length later) as involving the assumption that, if A is greater than B, and B is greater than C, then A must be greater than C. An ordering can thus be represented as

$$A > B > C$$

plus the rule that, of any two items, the one on the left is greater than the one on the right. Our two sentences then become coded as

Nikki > Gail > Susan.

There are two values to an inferential memory: simplification and ability to go beyond the information given. They are but different sides of the same coin. Simplification comes from the fact that, in such a memory, information that can be inferred is not explicitly stored. If we had been told that Nikki is brighter than Susan, that information would not have been explicitly stored, and the overall representation would have been no different from the preceding one. In an inferential memory, only the essential, non-redundant statements are stored. It is just such statements that we are likely to underline in reading a text.

Ability to go beyond the information given comes from the fact that, in an inferential memory, information that is not explicitly stored can be inferred. This is the other side of the coin. In the example, we were not told that Nikki is brighter than Susan, yet, if asked, we would readily say that she is. Moreover, we could not even say, unless we had also stored the sentence by rote, whether we had been specifically told this or were simply inferring it.

There is a large class of inferences based simply on substituting equivalent terms for one another. For example, from the fact that George Washington was Martha Washington's husband and the fact that George Washington lived at Mt. Vernon, we can infer that Martha Washington's husband lived at Mt. Vernon. Or, from the fact that John kicked Bill and the fact that to kick means to move one's foot forcefully against something, we can infer that John moved his foot. (See Anderson & Bower, 1973.) We shall not be concerned with inferences of this sort, but shall direct our discussion to the more interesting case of inferences based on classes and systems of classes.

The ability to think in terms of classes and systems of classes represents a major step forward in cognitive development. The principal dimension along which cognitive development seems to proceed is one of increasing abstraction, an increasing ability to take into account a variety of points of view; and thinking in terms of classes and systems of classes, executive or operational thought, increases considerably our ability to take into account a variety of points of view.

An experiment by Piaget illustrates the difference. A child is shown a table with three distinctive mountains on it and four dolls seated around it, one on each side. The child is then shown four pictures of the table, one from the point of view of each of the dolls. When he is asked to indicate which picture shows the table as the doll nearest him sees it, he has no difficulty in selecting the correct picture. However, when asked to indicate which picture shows the table as any of the other dolls sees it, the preoperational child continues to choose the picture that shows the table from his own point of view.

Adults, as well, sometimes have difficulty in seeing situations from another's point of view. Legal systems are addressed to this problem and, in principle, represent human relationships in a way that is invariant from different points of view: *All are equal before the law.* The Golden Rule, *Do unto others as you would have others do unto you,* is a moral precept that would seem to require a capacity to see situations from the point of view of the other. The following epitaph from an old Scottish tombstone suggests that God do likewise:

> *Here lies I, Martin Elginbrodde,*
> *Have mercy on my soul, Lord God,*
> *As I would do were I Lord God,*
> *And Ye were Martin Elginbrodde.*

For Piaget (see Flavell, 1963), it is the appearance of conservation that marks the beginning of operational thought. Piaget has

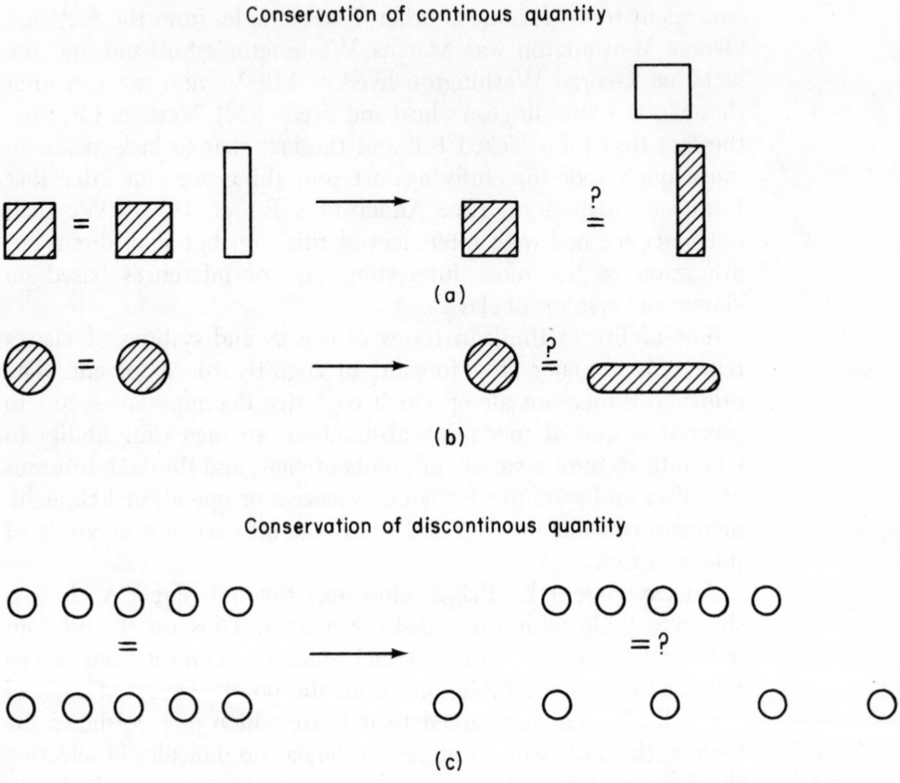

Conservation of continous quantity

(a)

(b)

Conservation of discontinous quantity

(c)

FIGURE 93.   *Tests for conservation.*

studied the conservation of both continuous and discontinuous quantities. In one kind of conservation of continuous quantity experiment (see Figure 93a), water is poured from a short, wide beaker into a tall, narrow one, and the child is asked whether the quantity of the water is more, less, or the same as before. In another kind of conservation of continuous quantity experiment (see Figure 93b), a round ball of clay is rolled out into a sausage shape, and the child is asked whether the amount of clay is more, less, or the same as before. In a conservation of discontinuous quantity, or conservation of number, experiment (see Figure 93c), a row of objects is spread out, and the child is asked whether the number of objects is more, less, or the same as before.

In each case, conservation is indicated if the child says that the operation had no effect on the quantity. Before the age of operational thought, the child, as we have seen, makes perceptual judgments, saying that there is more water in the second beaker because it is taller (or less because it is narrower), that there is more clay in the second case because it is longer (or less because it is thinner), and that there are more objects in the second case because the line is longer (or fewer because it is less dense).

Conservation seems to represent another step away from the perceptual world of appearances. The conserver seems to focus on the operations involved. He knows what is changed by a particular operation and what is not, and perceptual judgments are, in a sense at least, not even relevant.

An experiment by Bruner, Olver, Greenfield *et al.* (1966) shows that imposing a new organization on that provided by perception is at least part of what is involved in conservation. We considered this experiment earlier in discussing perception and thought, but it is equally appropriate to consider it in the present context. The principal finding, you will recall, was that screening the beakers from view facilitated conservation. Children who could see the pouring operation but could not see the beakers when they made their judgments conserved, where previously they had failed to. Moreover, many of them continued to conserve even after the screen was removed. This screening technique seems to work in the same way as turning off the lights in the delayed-reaction experiment: By reducing competition from the representational system, it permits the executive system to function more effectively. Once a child has acquired conservation, he is able to resist misleading perceptual influences on his own.

An experiment by Smedslund (1961b) shows that perceptual judgments are, in some cases, actually irrelevant for the mature conserver. In a conservation of weight experiment, he secretly removed a piece of clay as he rolled it out into a long, thin shape. When the conserver said the amount was the same, Smedslund weighed the clay to show that it was lighter. The conserver's response was to question the trustworthiness of this perceptual information by saying that there must be some trick and sticking to his assertion that changing the shape of the clay leaves its mass unchanged.

The reasons conservers and nonconservers give for their judgments point even more specifically to conservation as involving a shift from perceptual to operational thought. Bruner, Olver, Greenfield *et al.* (1966), in a conservation of volume experiment, found that, whereas all nonconservers referred to the size or shape of the beaker or the appearance of the liquid, almost none of the conservers did. The conservers, instead, made statements like: *It's the same water; You just poured it; If it were still in the first glass, there wouldn't be anything different;* or *You haven't added or subtracted any from the water.*

The child seems to have learned what various operations change and what they leave unchanged. The emphasis, in the conservation experiment, on operations that leave essential features unchanged would seem appropriate for introducing plans for comprehension, for it seems to be just such operations that are involved in the various conceptual schemes that we shall be discussing. If you wish to make sense out of the mess on your desk, for example, you rearrange the papers, not burn them. That is, you make responses that leave the integrity of what you seek to understand intact. The various operations of mentally combining, dividing, and rearranging may, as Piaget believes, actually be derived from the executive components involved in carrying out comparable overt responses.

These mental operations are organized into a number of very general conceptual systems. In all, we shall consider five: classes, dichotomies, orderings, nested classifications, and cross-classifications (see Figure 94). Let us preview them briefly before taking each up in detail.

The simple class is the building block of conceptual systems. It consists of a single set. A set is simply a collection of objects.

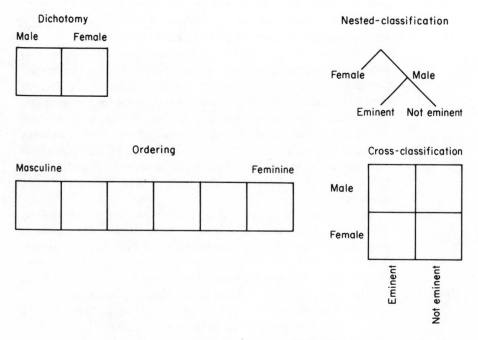

FIGURE 94.   *Conceptual systems.*

Dichotomies and orderings consist of sets of sets. Specifically, they are variables; that is, they consist of nonoverlapping sets. To say that sets do not overlap is to say that a given object can be a member of one or the other but not both. Dichotomies, such as sex, are bivalent variables, the two values in this case being male and female. Orderings, such as social class, are multivalent variables, the values here most commonly being upper class, middle class, and lower class. To say that the sets in each variable do not overlap is to say that the same person cannot be both male and female, in the one case, and cannot be in more than one social class, in the other. As we shall see, there is actually more to be said about orderings than simply that they are multivalent variables.

Nested classifications and cross-classifications consist of sets of sets of sets. They are multivariate systems. Specifically, they consist of sets of overlapping variables. To say that variables overlap is to say that sets from one overlap sets from the other. In nested classifications, such as the biological classification system, overlapping is partial in that not all pairs of sets from different variables overlap. The distinction between mammals and marsupials, for example, applies to vertebrates but not to invertebrates. Thus, a given animal can be a vertebrate and a marsupial or a vertebrate and a mammal, but not an invertebrate and a marsupial or an invertebrate and a mammal. Similarly, in the minds of all too many people, the distinction between eminent and noneminent persons is seen as applying to men but not to women, as in "American Men of Science" (see Figure 94).

In cross-classifications, such as basic institution (government, religion, family, etc.) by culture (Hopi, Winnebago, Roman, English, etc.) overlapping is complete, and we say that the variables are crossed. Each of the basic institutions is found in all cultures; each culture has all of the basic institutions.

These five plans fall into three hierarchically organized levels: Nested classifications and cross-classifications are formed from dichotomies or orderings, and these in turn are formed from classes. Classes and dichotomies appear to be formed in early childhood (Atwood, 1964; Vygotsky, 1962), orderings in middle childhood (Piaget, 1952a), nested classifications somewhat later, and cross-classifications at the end of childhood (Inhelder & Piaget, 1958; Piaget, 1964). The sequence that seems logically inevitable appears to occur, although it has not yet been observed in a single study.

In the following discussion, particular attention will be paid to classes and to cross-classifications. This is because each introduces a new level of thought. Classes introduce inferential, or operational, thought; and cross-classifications mark the transition from concrete operations to formal operations (see Flavell, 1963).

Classes

Representation of a simple class seems to involve (*a*) representation of an attribute (its intension), and (*b*) representation of a set of objects (its extension). Let us begin with attributes.

Attributes

Perception represents the appearance of the world in unanalyzed units. Associative memory gets at some of the reality behind appearances by joining perceptual units together. For a deeper penetration into reality, however, it seems to be better to break the perceptual units down into their elements and start afresh. This breaking down is what is meant by the term "analytic thought," and, as we shall see, it requires executive activity.

Dealing with attributes at the level of the executive system is quite a different matter from dealing with features at the level of secondary perception. When two things are classified together perceptually, it is because differences between them are not taken into account; when things are classified together conceptually, it is because differences between them are actively disregarded. There is an important difference between these two mechanisms for information selection, failing to take a difference into account and disregarding a difference. The child who calls both a dog and a cow "doggy" seems to have failed to see the difference (Brown, 1958). The adult who calls them both "mammal" sees the difference but is able, for present purposes, to disregard these differences and focus on those respects in which dogs and cows are alike. Whereas the child has an inadequate percept, the adult is able to analyze his percepts. As Aristotle put it, *Genius is the capacity to perceive similarity in dissimilars.*

Several lines of evidence support this analysis. Duncker (1945) pointed to visual fixedness as a barrier to thinking; a cork in a bottle, matches in a box, a branch on a tree are difficult to see as separable from their contexts and usable in others. The embedded figures test (Gottschaldt, 1938; see Figure 95) assesses the capacity to analyze a percept into its constituents, as does the rod-and-frame test (Witkin, Lewis, Hertzman, Machover, Meissner, & Wapner, 1954). Performance on both the embedded figures test and the

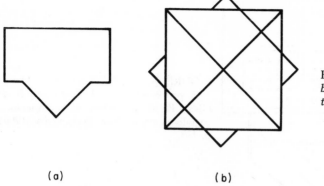

FIGURE 95. *An embedded figure.* (A *is contained in* B.)

(a)   (b)

rod-and-frame test is positively correlated with age and, within age, with problem-solving performance. Finally, object concepts (for example, articles of clothing) are discovered more readily than concepts based on spatial, color, or number attributes (Grant & Curran, 1952; Heidbreder, Bensley, & Ivy, 1948).

The value of representing attributes, rather than things, is perhaps nowhere more clearly illustrated than in the Bruner, Olver, Greenfield *et al.* (1966) Twenty Questions and bulb-board tasks. In the game of Twenty Questions, if you told an adult that a person's car went off the road and crashed and asked him to find out why in 20 or fewer questions, he would begin with a series of constraint-locating questions: Was it due to mechanical failure; if so, was the failure in the brake system? Asking questions about aspects of the situation, he would gradually build up a description of the correct answer. This is the most efficient way to proceed (Taylor & Faust, 1952).

The child, however, asks questions differently. He describes complete situations: Did the driver happen to leave the window open, and was it in the summer, and did a bee fly in the window and sting him and make him go off the road? The child is unable to build up a description, one feature at a time. It is as though he thinks in terms of intact, unanalyzed images.

This is revealed also in the bulb-board experiment. In the bulb-board experiment, the subject is shown three boards with light bulbs on them, like those in Figure 96. The top two boards have patterns lit up on them, here a "T" and a "—." All the bulbs on the bottom board are initially unlit. The bottom board is wired with one of the displayed patterns, so that on-pattern bulbs will light up when pressed and off-pattern bulbs will not. The child's task is to determine which of the displayed patterns is wired into the test board and to do so with as few presses as possible. An

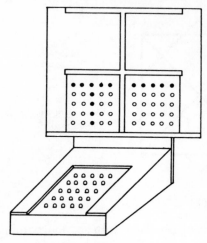

FIGURE 96. *Olson's bulb board. [Taken, with permission, from J. S. Bruner, R. R. Olvar, P. M. Greenfield et al., Studies in cognitive growth (New York: Wiley, 1966), p. 138.]*

adult could solve this problem with one press, pressing any of the bulbs which are part of one pattern and not the other. This requires an ability to analyze a stimulus into attributes, however; and, as we have seen, young children do not have this ability. What children do is copy entire stimuli to see whether they can be reproduced on the test board. Thus, a child might start by pressing all the on-pattern bulbs for the "T." Even after the vertical line has been completed, he will go on to complete the horizontal line before deciding that it is the "T," rather than the "—" that has been wired into the test board.

In this section, then, we have seen that thinking in terms of attributes is not only an achievement but one that possesses great potential for increasing intellectual power.

Sets

Attributes, alone, do not make a class, however. Attributes are used in plans for memorizing, as well as in plans for comprehension. Attributes provide only the defining characteristics, the intensive meaning, of a class. A class must also have an extensive meaning. It must refer to a collection, or set, of objects. Attributes are seen to characterize objects before they are seen to characterize sets of objects.

This transition is revealed most clearly in studies of complexes by Vygotsky (1962) and Bruner, Olver, Greenfield *et al.* (1966). Vygotsky asked children to select blocks that resembled a target block and to indicate why they selected each. Bruner and his co-workers asked children to tell in what way members of a set of objects were like one another and different from specified others outside the set. Both investigators reported two basic patterns:

thematic groupings and complexes. We shall add a third: pseudo-concepts.

In thematic groupings, objects are related to objects, not on the basis of shared attributes, but on the basis of a shared context. An example which relates the stimuli, *bananas, peaches,* and *potatoes,* is: *The little boy was eating a banana on the way to the store to buy some peaches and potatoes.* The objects are simply put together in a theme or story. Mythological explanations tend to have this character.

In complexes, each object is related to the object considered just previously, on the basis of a shared attribute, but the linking attributes characteristically differ from object pair to object pair. An example is: *Banana and peach are both yellow, peach and potato are round, potato and meat are served together, meat and milk both come from cows.* As in a chain, there is no common bond linking all objects. It is in such a manner that the meanings of words drift through time. Thus, the Latin word *villa* meant a large home, with all its attendant buildings; then it was changed to mean a village; then a villager; then a person of low status; and, finally, to the modern word *villain.* Though each step in the chain is reasonable, there is no reasonable connection that links *villain* directly to *villa.* Similarly, the course of discussion at meetings tends to drift from topic to topic, until it is so far from the topic at hand that someone wonders, *How did we ever get off on this?*

In pseudoconcepts, all objects are related to one another on the basis of the very same attribute, yet a class concept is still not involved. An experiment by Hanfmann and Kasanin (1942; see also Vygotsky, 1962) distinguishes between concepts and pseudo-concepts. Consider a child trying to select objects that an experimenter has in mind. The experimenter is thinking of tall objects, but the child is selecting green objects. So far, all the objects he has selected have been both green and tall, so the experimenter has said, *That's right,* for each. At this point, because of the consistency among his choices, we can be reasonably confident that this child is able to represent attributes. However, we do not yet know whether he can represent classes. One way to tell would be to observe his response when he has selected an object that is green but not tall and the experimenter has said, *That's not right.* A child operating at the level of classes will reject the class of green things and try another. A child operating at the level of attributes and objects, on the other hand, will reject only the object and will go on to select other green objects. Thus, it is quite possible to represent an attribute without representing a class.

It would also seem quite possible to represent a set of objects without representing a class. We can consider the set, *Something old, something new, something borrowed, something blue,* or the set, *1, 7, spinnaker,* even though the items within each set seem to have no attribute in common. A set may seem closer to a class than does an attribute, for it at least deals with more than one object. Yet, because it lacks a defining attribute, it is not quite what we mean by a class. It is simply a list. It is like a container without a label. This difference is not a trivial one: While it is possible to determine, by examining some members of a class, what new objects will and will not be included in the class, this is not possible in the case of unlabeled sets. The defining attribute adds to the list a mechanism which makes inference possible.

We turn now to systems of classes, the simplest of which is the dichotomy, which consists of but two classes.

Dichotomies

We often tend to think in terms of a world that is partitioned into two mutually exclusive categories: men and women, young and old, bright and dull, black and white, rich and poor, capitalists and communists, doves and hawks, friends and foes. The statement, *If you're not for us, you're agin us,* illustrates this kind of thinking.

We can trace the phylogenetic and ontogenetic origins of dichotomous thinking by means of experiments on intradimensional and extradimensional transfer. Experiments on intradimensional and extradimensional transfer employ stimuli, like those in Figure 97, that differ on two dimensions, here, shape and brightness. In the simplest version of this kind of experiment, two groups of animals would be trained to discriminate, for example, WC and WS from BC and BS (where WC = white circle, WS = white square, BC = black circle, and BS = black square), with WC and WS positive and BC and BS negative. The figures might be placed on maze doors, and the animals would learn that, given a choice between WC and BC or between WC and BS, they should choose WC, and, given a choice between WS and BC or between WS and BS, they should choose WS. After this preliminary training, one group would be tested on intradimensional transfer and the other on extradimensional transfer.

In intradimensional transfer the originally relevant dimension (in this case, color) remains relevant. Thus, the intradimensional group would learn to approach BC and BS and to avoid WC and WS.

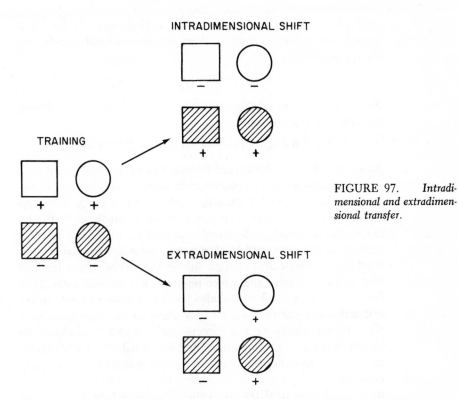

FIGURE 97.   *Intradimensional and extradimensional transfer.*

In extradimensional transfer, the originally relevant dimension becomes irrelevant, and a new dimension becomes relevant (in this case, shape). Thus, the extradimensional group would learn to approach WC and BC and to avoid WS and BS. (Actually, half would learn this and half would learn to approach WS and BS and to avoid WC and BC, and their scores would be averaged.)

The interesting question is whether the intradimensional group or the extradimensional group performs better on the transfer task. It turns out that this depends on both phylogenetic and ontogenetic level. Animals (Bitterman, 1960) and preverbal children (Kendler & Kendler, 1959, 1970) perform better on the extradimensional task; verbal children and adults perform better on the intradimensional task (Kendler & Kendler, 1959, 1970).

What does this tell us? The superiority of extradimensional transfer in primitive organisms can be explained if we assume that what primitive organisms do is respond to a unitary representation of each stimulus, which includes both relevant and irrelevant features. If each stimulus is given a unique identity in this way, we can represent this fact by referring to them by letters, A for white circle, B for white square, C for black circle, and D for black square. For immature animals, then, intradimensional transfer can be represented as:

$$(A+, B+, C-, D-) \rightarrow (A-, B-, C+, D+).$$

New responses must be learned for all four stimuli. Extradimensional transfer can be represented as:

$$(A+, B+, C-, D-) \rightarrow (A+, B-, C+, D-).$$

New responses must be learned for only two of the four stimuli.

The superiority of intradimensional transfer in advanced organisms can be explained if we assume that advanced organisms represent dimensions. Thus, two stages would be involved. In the example, these would be learning to attend to color, and learning that white is positive and black negative. Intradimensional transfer would involve making a change only in the second stage: learning that black is positive and white negative. Extradimensional transfer, on the other hand, would also involve making a change in the first stage: learning that shape is now the relevant dimension. Note that the superiority of intradimensional transfer is evidence for the representation of dimensions, not just attributes, for attributes are involved in either case. Rats learn discriminations on the basis of attributes quite readily (Lashley, 1942; Lawrence, 1963), yet find extradimensional transfer easier than intradimensional transfer.

If we change the stimuli in this example, changing the black stimuli to black people, the white stimuli to white people, the circles to warm, constructive people, and the squares to cold, destructive people, we come out with an interesting prediction. The prediction is that, in adult humans, when white racism proves invalid, black racism will be considered, and only when black racism is seen also to be invalid, will skin color be rejected as irrelevant and attention turned to characteristics of the person, himself.

Similarly, male chauvinism tends to be followed by female chauvinism, and blind obedience to authority in childhood tends to be followed by equally blind rejection of authority in adolescence. What we seem to have in such cases is a Hegelian dialectic: Thesis leads to antithesis before leading to a cognitively more difficult solution.

A dichotomy is a list, and a very short one; but it is more than simply a list. Like all inferential systems, a dichotomy involves a set of assumptions. These are that (*a*) like objects are similarly related to other objects and (*b*) unlike objects are dissimilarly related to other objects (Heider, 1958). Consider a world of good

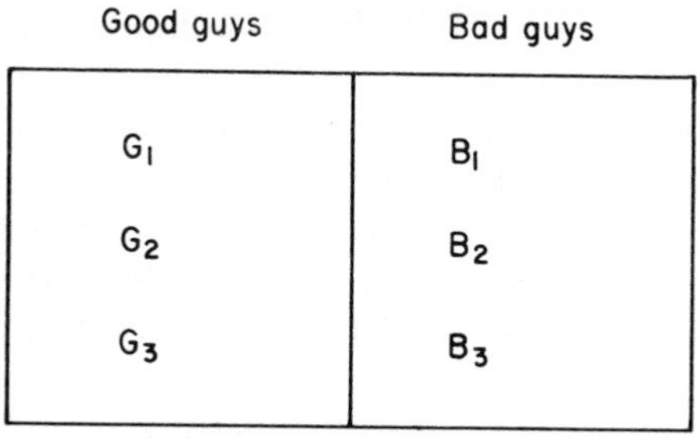

Good guys   Bad guys

G_1	B_1
G_2	B_2
G_3	B_3

FIGURE 98. A *dichotomy*.

guys and bad guys (see Figure 98): G_1, G_2, G_3, B_1, B_2, and B_3. To illustrate the first assumption, G_1 and G_2 are alike in that both are good guys; and they are both related in the same way to G_3 (they are both like him; *Any friend of yours is a friend of mine*) and to B_1 (they are both unlike him; *Anyone who hates dogs and children can't be all bad*). To illustrate the second assumption, G_1 and B_1 are unlike; and they are related in different ways to G_2 (G_1 is like him and B_1 is unlike him) and to B_2 (G_1 is unlike him and B_1 is like him). Thus, all those who oppose capitalism may be seen as communists.

The tendency to think dichotomously shows up in the effect of prestige suggestion on attitude change. Certain attitude change data can be accounted for by the assumption (Osgood & Tannenbaum, 1955) that, when a source delivers a message supporting a particular person, point of view, or product, the receiver's attitudes toward both the source and the object tend to move together, toward an intermediate position. Thus, a politician will have a greater impact on attitudes if he makes some statements supporting the receiver's regional, ethnic, or occupational biases (motherhood and apple pie) before launching into his message. The important point in the present context, however, is that this intermediate position is not simply an average of the attitude toward the source and the attitude toward the object, but a weighted average, with the more intense attitude being weighted the more heavily. Thus, if a highly valued politician supports an issue the receiver has only moderate feelings about, the receiver's attitude toward the issue will change more than his attitude toward the politician. As a consequence of this weighting of the extremes, attitudes tend to drift toward the extremes of positive or negative evaluation. The structure tends toward a dichotomy.

The tendency to think dichotomously also shows up in the perception of messages whose source is unspecified. There is a tendency either to assimilate such messages to your own attitude or to contrast them with your own attitude. Hovland, Harvey, and

Sherif (1957) presented a mildly antiprohibition message to various groups on different sides of a campaign to repeal prohibition in the state of Oklahoma. Those whose initial position was quite similar to that expressed in the message saw the message as being even more similar to their own view (assimilation), and those whose initial position was quite dissimilar from that expressed in the message saw the message as being even less like their own view (contrast).

Both dichotomies and orderings appear to be important in attitude organization. Since an attitude is a memory with an evaluative component, it is not difficult to see why attitudes would tend to become organized unidimensionally. Attitudes involve strong feelings, and feelings differ primarily along a positive–negative continuum (Osgood, Suci, & Tannenbaum, 1957; Schlosberg, 1952; Wundt, 1896).

While both this section and the next are particularly relevant to attitude organization, factors that tend to bring about attitude change are considered elsewhere: factors that operate on individual attitudes, in the chapter on associative memory, and factors that operate on systems of attitudes in the chapter on value and choice.

Orderings

Dichotomies and orderings are both variables, or partitions. Orderings, however, involve more than two classes. When the number of classes exceeds two, it becomes very important to consider the way in which the classes are related to one another.

The fundamental distinction is between symmetrical and asymmetrical relations. Examples of symmetrical relations are "is a sibling of," "=," and "≠." If A is a sibling of B, then B is a sibling of A, and if $A = B$, then $B = A$. Formally, a relation, r, is said to be symmetrical if the following condition holds: $Arb \leftrightarrow BrA$.

Examples of asymmetrical relations are "is an ancestor of," ">," and "<." If A is an ancestor of B, then it is not the case that B is an ancestor of A, and if $A > B$, then it is not the case that $B > A$. Formally, a relation, r, is said to be asymmetrical if the following condition holds: $ArB \leftrightarrow -(BrA)$.

An example of a partition in which the relations among the classes are symmetrical would be fruits. Consider the relation "are not the same as." If peaches are not the same as apples, then apples are not the same as peaches. An example of a partition in which the relations among the classes are asymmetrical would be cost. Consider the relation "is greater than." If the cost of peaches is greater than the cost of apples, then it is not the case that the cost of apples is greater than the cost of peaches.

Relations can hold between individuals as well as classes: Nikki is brighter than Gail, and Gail is brighter than Susan. Because we have already considered the nature of classes, we shall focus in this section on relations. What we shall have to say will apply equally to relations among individuals and to relations among classes, and we shall use examples of both. We shall be concerned here with asymmetrical relations only, that is, with orderings, for they seem to be the more interesting psychologically.

Formally, an ordering is a set of relations that possesses asymmetry, transitivity, and completeness (DeSoto, 1960, 1961). It is these properties that make an ordering more than simply a list of individuals or classes and that make inference possible. A consideration of these formal properties will enable us to understand better this pervasive cognitive structure.

A clear example of an ordering is military rank (see Figure 99). The relation expressed by the arrows in Figure 99 can be verbalized as "is a higher rank than." It is clearly an asymmetrical relation.

The relations in an ordering are also transitive. This is a very important property. Relations are said to be transitive if and only if the following condition holds: If A bears the relation to B and

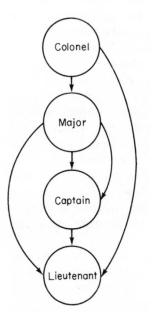

FIGURE 99. *An order-*
ing.

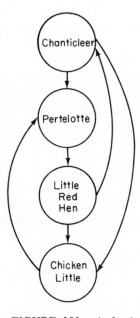

FIGURE 100. *A domi-*
nance structure.

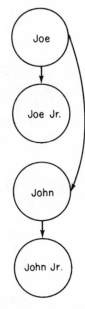

FIGURE 101. *A partial*
ordering.

B bears the relation to *C*, then *A* bears the relation to *C*. Formally, *ArB* & *BrC* → *ArC*. If colonel is a higher rank than major and major is a higher rank than captain, then colonel is a higher rank than captain. An example of an intransitive relation is "is a parent of," for, if *A* is a parent of *B* and *B* is a parent of *C*, then *A* is not a parent (but a grandparent) of *C*. Another example of an intransitive relation would be "lives next door to," for, if *A* lives next door to *B* and *B* lives next door to *C*, then *A* cannot live next door to *C*. The mathematical relations "=" and ">" are both transitive.

In addition to being asymmetric and transitive, the relations in an ordering are also complete. Completeness simply requires that, for any *A* and *B*, *A* bears the relation to *B*, or *B* bears the relation to *A*.

A set of relations that differs from an ordering in lacking transitivity (while possessing both asymmetry and completeness) is called a dominance structure. A classic example is pecking orders in lower animals (see Figure 100). Many species of animals establish pairwise pecking relations such that, when one member of a pair attacks, the other always retreats. These seem to exist as isolated pairwise relations, however, and to lack the higher structure that transitivity would impart. Cycles of intransitivity, such as Chanticleer dominating Pertelotte, Pertelotte dominating the Little Red Hen, and the Little Red Hen dominating Chanticleer, are common. Dominance structures also appear in the relations among large social groups and institutions. For example, the mayor may influence the police, and the police may influence the blacks, but the blacks may, nevertheless, influence the mayor (DeSoto & Albrecht, 1968).

For transitivity to exist among relations, those relations must be thought about together (DeSoto & Albrecht, 1968). Chickens are not bright enough to do this; and, in relations among large social groups, different members of a group may be involved in relations with different other groups, and thus the same people may not think about all the relations. The point here is that transitivity often reflects a simplifying assumption in the structure of inferential thought, rather than a characteristic of the structure of the world.

A set of relations that differs from an ordering in lacking completeness (while possessing both asymmetry and transitivity) is called a partial ordering (see Figure 101). Because all arrows are unidirectional ("is the ancestor of"), asymmetry is satisfied. Because, from, for example, Joe → John and John → John, Jr., you can conclude Joe → John, Jr., transitivity is satisfied. Yet the struc-

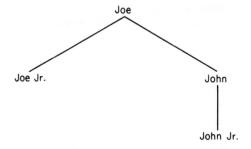

FIGURE 102. *The partial ordering in Figure 101 redrawn to reveal its family-tree structure.*

ture is incomplete, for two relationships are not specified, that between Joe, Jr., and John and that between Joe, Jr., and John, Jr.

Figure 101 was drawn to facilitate comparison with the diagrams of orderings and dominance structures, but the family tree pattern, which is a particular case of partial ordering, becomes more apparent if the diagram is rearranged, as in Figure 102.

To say that we tend to think in terms of orderings is to say that, when relations are asymmetrical, we tend to infer transitivity and completeness. DeSoto (1960) compared the importance of transitivity and completeness by comparing the ease with which subjects were able to learn orderings, partial orderings, and dominance structures. Subjects learned various structures by learning different arrangements of statements like, *Herb influences Dave; Dave influences Jerry; and Jerry influences Herb.* Orderings were learned more easily, and partial orderings were learned with only slightly more difficulty. Dominance structures, however, were by far the most difficult to learn, taking about three times as many trials as orderings. Transitivity, then, seems to be a more important property of an ordering than is completeness. This is undoubtedly because it is transitivity that permits inferences and thus makes for economy in information storage.

DeSoto has observed that the tendency to think in terms of orderings has led thinking men astray throughout history. We say, for example, that man descended from the apes. But this is not true. The structure is a partial ordering, not an ordering. Man and the apes are descended from a common ancestor. Aristotle's Great Chain of Being (Lovejoy, 1936) was an attempt to construe the evolutionary tree as an ordering. DeSoto's point is that, since transitivity and completeness are properties of inferential thought, they are likely to appear where people are thinking.

Orderings can be understood completely in terms of a single variable. Though each of the partial orderings and dominance structures described above was described in terms of only one kind of relationship, such as "dominates," their very complexity suggests that more than one variable is actually involved. For example, pecking is undoubtedly not a univariate matter; different chickens undoubtedly have somewhat different pecking styles and encounter one another under somewhat different circumstances. If we think multidimensionally, it is not difficult to see how A might win against B and B against C and yet, under a different set of circumstances, C win against A. The tendency to think in terms of both dichotomies and orderings can be characterized as a tendency to think unidimensionally.

It is this tendency to think unidimensionally that leads us to regard George Washington as "first in war, first in peace, first in the hearts of his countrymen," whereas he was more probably at a different level on each of these variables. What we have done is to collapse three variables into one. Indeed, the tendency to think unidimensionally would appear to be the mechanism responsible for the culturally universal tendency to think in terms of heroes and villains.

Unidimensional thinking also seems to be what is involved in the halo effect (Asch, 1946), which appears in such tasks as rating job applicants and grading exams. If an applicant is particularly attractive, for example, he will tend to be rated as more intelligent, friendly, and so forth. If the first question on an essay exam is answered well, ambiguities in answers to subsequent questions will tend to be interpreted in the student's favor. (A way the student can often capitalize on the halo effect is to write his best answers first, but a way the teacher can avoid the halo effect is to grade the first questions of all exams, then the second questions of all exams, and so forth.)

Unidimensional thinking is involved when one believes that academic performance can be adequately represented in terms of a unidimensional grading system, or that intellectual ability can be adequately represented in terms of a unidimensional scale of test scores, or that social relations can be adequately represented in terms of a unidimensional arrangement of social classes. It is well established, for example, that intelligence, as the complexity of this book might suggest, differs on a number of dimensions (Guilford, 1967; Spearman & Jones, 1950; Thurstone, 1947). And social organization seems to be more adequately represented as a complex structure of overlapping groups.

Granted that there exists a powerful tendency to think in terms of orderings, it then becomes important to ask how, precisely, we make inferences when thinking in terms of orderings. This question has received a great deal of attention (Clark, 1969a, 1969b;

DeSoto, London, & Handel, 1965; Hunter, 1957; Huttenlocher, 1968). We shall attempt to summarize the research on this topic by considering just two questions, one having to do with the comprehension of statements about individual relations and one having to do with the combining of such statements.

Our first question will be: Is it easier to understand the statement, A *is greater than* B, or the statement, B *is less than* A? To answer this question, we give subjects, A *is greater than* B, and, B *is greater than* C, and ask them, *Is* A *greater than* C? We also give them, C *is less than* B, and, B *is less than* A, and ask them, *Is* C *less than* A? Finally, the reaction times for answering these two questions are compared. The fact that the former is faster suggests that it is easier to understand, A *is greater than* B, than, B *is less than* A. The question is, why?

DeSoto, London, and Handel (1965) have presented an image theory. They hypothesize that people think of orderings in terms of images and that, when thinking in terms of images, it is easier to work from top to bottom than from botton to top and from left to right than from right to left. Thus, in comprehending, A *is greater than* B, we would locate A and then locate B below it, working from the top down. This accounts for the data we have considered, yet it does not always work. It is faster to understand, A *is deeper than* B, than to understand, B *is shallower than* A (Clark, 1969a). This is true despite the fact that, in translating, A *is deeper than* B, into an image, we would locate A and then locate B above it, working from bottom to top.

Clark (1969a) has presented an alternative theory, in terms of linguistic principles. The linguistic principle that applies to this particular case is that of lexical marking. One of the ways of expressing the relationship (for example, *greater than, deeper than*) is called unmarked and is presumed to be fundamental; the other (here, *less than, shallower than*) is called marked and is presumed to be derived from the unmarked form (see Clark, 1969a,b).

In support of this distinction are the findings that children can understand the unmarked forms at an earlier age than the marked forms (Donaldson & Wales, 1970) and that adults are better able to remember the unmarked forms (Clark & Card, 1969). Also, the unmarked form can be used either to name a position on the scale or, in a neutral sense, to name the scale as a whole, whereas the marked form can be used only to name a position on the scale. Thus, if you ask, *How tall is he?* he could be either tall or short, but, if you ask, *How short is he?* you are implying that he is short.

The strongest evidence for the principle of lexical marking comes from sentences called negative equatives. It is easier to understand,

A *isn't as good as* B, than to understand, B *isn't as bad as* A (Clark, 1969a,b). This, of course, is because *good* is unmarked and *bad* is marked. Yet, in terms of the image theory, the reverse should be true; for, in translating these sentences into images, we would work from the bottom up in the first case and from the top down in the second.

But the principle of lexical marking does not always work either, for left and right are both marked, and yet, A *is to the right of* B, is, in fact, easier to understand than, B *is to the left of* A, in accord with the image theory (DeSoto *et al.*, 1965). Shortly, we shall consider a possible resolution of this inconsistency.

Let us turn now to the problem of combining statements. Our second question is whether it is easier to combine, A *is greater than* B, and, B *is greater than* C, in that order or in the reverse order, B *is greater than* C, followed by, A *is greater than* B. De-Soto, London, and Handel (1965) and Hunter (1957) predict that the former will be easier, Hunter on the basis of an assumed natural order and DeSoto *et al.* on the basis of the assumption that it is better to begin with one of the end terms. Their data support this prediction.

Clark (1969a,b) and Huttenlocher (1968), however, make the opposite prediction, that, B *is greater than* C, A *is greater than* B, will be easier. Their predictions are based on linguistic considerations, though different ones. Huttenlocher's prediction is based on the mobility of the subject of a sentence. The principle of mobility states that it is easier to move a term that is in the subject of a sentence than to move a term that is in the predicate. Thus, it is easier for children to add a third block, C, to a pattern of two blocks, A and B, when they are told, C *is below* A, or, C *is above* B, than when they are told, A *is above* C, or, B *is below* A (Huttenlocher, 1968). Because the second sentence in our example adds the third term to the pattern, it should be easier to understand if the third term is in the subject.

Clark's prediction is based on the principle of primacy of functional relations. Stated briefly, this principle assumes that, A *is greater than* B, is sometimes remembered simply as, A *is greater*. If, B *is greater than* C, is presented first and is recalled only as, B *is greater*, then, when, A *is greater than* B, is presented, the subject can reason that it could have been only C that B was greater than and thus reconstruct the original information. On the other hand, if, A *is greater than* B, is presented first and is recalled only as, A *is greater*, then when, B *is greater than* C, is presented, the subject will have no basis for inferring whether it was

B or *C* that *A* was greater than. Huttenlocher's and Clark's data support their predictions.

Thus, both theories and data are discrepant. Wason and Johnson-Laird (1972) have suggested a possible resolution. They suggest that something like images are used early in practice, when the subject is trying to get an overall understanding of the problem, but that, later, when he knows exactly what is required in the situation, the process becomes automatized in terms of something like a shorthand linguistic representation. One fact that supports this interpretation is that DeSoto's subjects, judging by the number of errors they made, seem to have been less practiced than Clark's.

An experiment by Wood (1969) also supports this interpretation. The image theory assumes that the two premises are combined into a unified representation of the three terms, and the linguistic theory assumes that information about the items is stored separately. What Wood showed is that unified representations are employed early in practice, and piecemeal representations, later. He used series problems involving several terms. After a variable number of practice problems in which an, *Is A greater than B?* type of question was always asked, he would give a test problem that asked for information that was not required by the kind of question to which the subject had become accustomed. Early in practice, these questions were answered well, suggesting that a unified representation was being formed at that time; very quickly, however, subjects began to fail on these questions, indicating that they had adopted a more abbreviated representation. Although Wason and Johnson-Laird's proposed resolution is an attractive one, it is clear that a great deal more work will have to be done before we can claim to understand how people make inferences when thinking unidimensionally.

Number. The most sophisticated and precise rendering of a single dimension is in terms of number. The acquisition of number represents a major step toward mathematical thought. There seem to be two major steps in this acquisition: learning to count and learning to conserve number. The following experiment by Piaget (1952b) shows how a child who can count but not conserve thinks. Six vases are placed in a row before the child, and six flowers are arranged above them, one above each vase. The child is asked whether there are more flowers or more vases, and he indicates that they are the same. Next, the flowers are spread out into a longer line, and the child is questioned again. This time he says that there are more flowers, because the line is longer (or sometimes, that there are more vases, because that line is denser). When asked to count the flowers, he counts to six, and when asked to count the vases, he again counts to six. Yet he insists that they differ in number.

According to Piaget (1952b), number involves both classes and relations. A child who can count but who has not acquired number classes will count the number of objects in a set without realizing that the last number counted represents the number in the set. If he is asked to count the number in a set and then, as soon as he has finished, asked how many items there are in the set, he will say, *I don't know,* or count them again, or do something other than simply answer with the last number counted. If, after he has counted the objects, you hide them and ask him how many there are, he cannot tell you. When he eventually becomes capable of performing successfully on these tasks, he is able to let a number represent a set of objects, that is, to think in terms of number classes.

But number also involves relations: The number class "5" is greater than the number class "4." Children learn to think in terms of number classes before they can think in terms of relations among them. This is consistent with the present analysis of plans for comprehension. If two closed fists are held out to a child who is between these stages and he is told, *There are 4 candies in this hand and 5 candies in this hand. Which hand do you want?* he will choose randomly.

Number makes measurement possible, by enabling us to apply units repeatedly and count the number of times we have applied them. And measurement, in turn, enables us to correct many errors in sensation and perception, such as the curvilinear relationship between physical intensity and psychological magnitude, or the effects of adaptation level.

The tissue paper problem provides a dramatic illustration of the way in which mathematics can correct intuitive judgments. Imagine doubling a piece of tissue paper twice, by folding it in half and then folding it in half again, so that it is now four layers thick. And imagine that this procedure is continued until the paper has been doubled 50 times, in all. (Assume that this is possible.) How thick will the folded paper be if a single sheet is .001 inch thick?

The mathematics goes as follows. After one doubling, it is $2(.001)$ inch thick; after two doublings, it is $2 \times 2(.001)$ inch thick, or $2^2(.001)$ inch thick; and after 50 doublings, it is $2^{50}(.001)$ inch thick. This works out to be around 200,000,000 miles, or a little longer than the distance from the Earth to the sun! Sometimes our intuitive judgments are badly in need of correction.

A very practical illustration of this same principle is the growth of populations. Consider one family with 4 children. If all of these children follow their parents' example and this is continued for 10 generations, this one family will number 1,048,576 individuals, the population of a rather large city. We cannot trust simple intuition in making judgments about such matters.

Dichotomies and orderings are unidimensional, but the world is not. The large number of variables that are included in most mathematical equations reflects the fact that, even in the simplest of natural situations, many dimensions are important.

Before we turn to multidimensional plans for comprehension, however, we must consider an important case that seems to represent a transition between unidimensional and multidimensional thinking: the case where more than one dimension is considered serially but no two dimensions are considered simultaneously. This pattern appears quite commonly when people assign stimuli to response classes on the basis of information on a number of dimensions (Anderson, 1962; Goldberg, 1968; Hammond & Summers, 1965; Hoffman, 1960).

Consider a member of a graduate admissions committee rating applicants on probable success in graduate school. He begins by estimating probable success on the basis of the dimension he considers most important, let us say grade point average (GPA). Then he estimates probable success on the basis of the dimension he considers next most impotant, perhaps the verbal score on the Graduate Record Examination (GRE). And, finally, he combines these two estimates by means of something like a weighted average. In combining information in this way, he is not considering the possibility that a high-GPA–low-GRE person and a low-GPA–high-GRE person may be quite different kinds of people from the point of view of probable success in graduate school. He processes the two dimensions separately and does not consider the ways they might relate to one another, or interact. Clinical psychologists (Goldberg, 1965), radiologists (Hoffman, Slovic, & Rorer, 1968), and stock brockers (Slovic, 1969) have all been found to combine information in an approximately additive fashion in reducing multidimensionality to unidimensionality.

Exceptions to additivity have been reported, but these may be attributable to effects in the representational, rather than the executive, system. The most thoroughly studied exception is the primacy effect: First impressions are more important than later ones. One explanation for this effect is a nonadditive one, that early information affects the interpretation of later information (Asch, 1946). Thus, in our example, one would interpret a low GRE differently for a person with a high GPA (perhaps as reflecting low motivation) than for a person with a low GPA (as a direct reflection of ability) and not simply compute the same value into an average in both cases. Asch showed that, in forming impressions of others from lists of adjectives, subjects define a word like *witty* differently when it follows *warm* than when it follows *cold*. This would seem to be an effect on associative memory.

The other explanation for the primacy effect is an additive one, that later information is simply less likely to be attended to. Two findings support this interpretation. One is that subjects are less likely to recall the later items, and the other is that, when told they will be tested for recall, they recall both early and late items and show no primacy effect (Anderson & Hubert, 1963). A limited capacity for attention is exactly what we would expect of executive processes. The finding that even highly trained judges rarely use information from more than two or three dimensions (Hoffman, Slovic, & Rorer, 1968) also points to the conclusion that an extremely limited capacity is involved in classification tasks of this sort.

Another exception to additivity is an inconsistency effect: When two items of information are inconsistent, one tends to be rejected (Anderson & Jacobson, 1965; Slovic, 1966). Thus, in our example, if GPA were high and GRE low, one might reject GRE as invalid (perhaps the applicant had a bad day when he took the test) and not compute it into the average at all. Reitman (1965) has suggested that inconsistencies are signaled to the executive by associative memory. If this is so, one would expect inconsistencies to have effects on tasks of this kind only if the inconsistencies are at the level of percepts or direct associations.

Though we seem to combine information from different dimensions without taking their interrelationships into account in such cases, we employ more sophisticated plans for comprehension in others. The two most important multidimensional plans for comprehension seem to be nested classifications and cross-classifications. To these we now turn.

Nested Classification

To think in terms of nested classification and cross-classification, we must be able to think in terms of set inclusion, to be able to think of one set as included within another (Dawes, 1966; Ger-

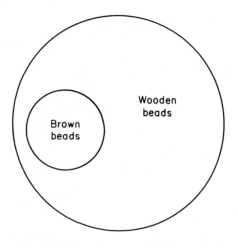

FIGURE 103.   *Set inclusion.*

gonne, 1817). Experiments by both Piaget and Bruner illustrate set inclusion and indicate that it is an intellectual achievement.

Piaget (1964) found that a child who could identify the brown beads, the white beads, and the wooden beads in a collection of 10 brown wooden beads and 5 white wooden beads (see Figure 103) could not necessarily answer correctly questions like, *Are there more brown beads or more wooden beads?* This is true even though they could say that there were more brown beads than white beads. Among young children, the most frequent answer to this question is that there are more brown beads. The difficulty with this question is that it requires the child to think on two different levels, to compare a subset (A) with a set that includes it. But the child, able to think on only one level, compares A with its complement, −A, and answers that there are more brown beads (than white beads). He is thinking in terms of a single, binary dimension.

Similarly, Bruner, Olver, Greenfield *et al.* (1966) found, in both the Twenty Questions and bulb-board experiments that children just beginning to employ constraint-locating questions (classes) would ask just one such question and then revert to describing specific objects or events. They could not narrow in on the answer by subdividing classes: *Is it a plant? If so, is it a food? If so, is it a vegetable?* Instead, their questioning went more like: *Is it something to eat? If so, is it ice cream?*

Miller, Teller, and Rubenstein (1966–1967) have provided a detailed description of a particular nested classification in adult subjects. Their procedure was to present people with 48 nouns and to ask each to classify the nouns in any way that seemed appropriate to them. Miller *et al.* then arranged the nouns into cate-

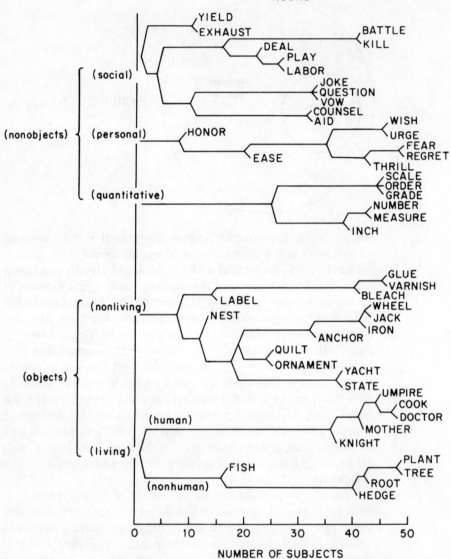

NOUNS

FIGURE 104. *A nested classification. (The terms in parentheses are suggested names for the clusters.)* [*Taken, with permission, from G. A. Miller, V. Teller, and H. Rubinstein, Seventh Annual Report, The Center for Cognitive Studies, Harvard University, 1966–1967, pp. 19–25.*]

246

gories and subcategories (see Figure 104), by putting into the same category nouns that were frequently classified together and into the same subcategory nouns that were even more frequently classified together. The major distinction turned out to be between objects and nonobjects. Objects were divided, in turn, into living and nonliving; but, as is to be expected in a nested classification, nonobjects were divided differently, into social, personal, and quantitative. Furthermore, living objects were divided into human and nonhuman, and this distinction was not applied elsewhere.

Another example of a rather complex nested classification is the British Commonwealth. The British Commonwealth is divided into the United Kingdom, the Republic of Ireland, Canada, etc. The United Kingdom is divided, in turn, into Great Britain and Northern Ireland. And, finally, Great Britain is further divided into England, Scotland, and Wales.

Collins and Quillian (1969) obtained evidence for a nested classification in terms of the time it takes to answer various questions. They obtained reaction times for answering the following questions and others like them: *Can a canary sing? Can a canary fly? Does a canary have skin?* The results are shown in Figure 105, along with the times for indicating whether a canary is a canary, whether a canary is a bird, and whether a canary is an animal.

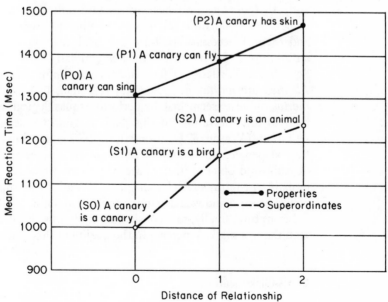

FIGURE 105. *Another nested classification.* [*Taken, with permission, from A. M. Collins and M. R. Quillian, "Retrieval time from semantic memory," Journal of Verbal Learning and Verbal Behavior, 1969, 8, 240–247.*]

The results suggest that the properties of flying and having skin are not associated directly with canary but with the names of the superordinate classes of which canary is a member (see also Johnson-Laird & Gibbs, in Wason & Johnson-Laird, 1972).

We saw earlier that, as a general rule, direct associations seem to be quite important in such situations (Conrad, 1972; Rips *et al.*, 1973). If you were asked whether a human has hair, you would not have to reason that a human is a mammal, that mammals have hair, and that, therefore, a human must have hair. You would know this directly. However, there are certainly other situations where inference would be required, for example, if you were asked whether Spinoza had hair (Anderson & Bower, 1973).

When we took a close look at reasoning in orderings, we saw that the process was not as "logical" as we might have expected. Subordinate mechanisms involved in generating images and producing sentences seemed to play important roles. The criteria for evaluating responses seems to be logical enough. But the mechanisms for generating them seem to have more of a "whatever works" quality about them, and there seem to be alternative routes to the same end. We get the same impression when we look more closely at reasoning in nested classifications.

In dealing with single statements, like, *All mothers are writers*, and, *All typhoons are wheat*, as we saw earlier, people seem first to perform a semantic test to see whether the sets overlap at all and then, if necessary, perform a logical analysis, which requires an additional 100 msec (Collins & Quillian, 1972; Meyer, 1970; Schaeffer & Wallace, 1970). And, in combining statements, like, *All men are mortal*, and, *Socrates is a man*, to yield, *Socrates is mortal*, subjects seem first to perform a quasi-logical analysis and then to test the results of this analysis against a semantic representation (Wason & Johnson-Laird, 1972). In the case of untrained people, this semantic representation is probably in terms of real-world objects; in the case of persons trained in logic, it is probably in terms of Euler diagrams. Clearly, reasoning is an involved process, and we have much to learn about it.

Let us turn, finally, to a consideration of cross-classifications and, with them, a marked increase in the quality of thought.

Cross-Classification

In classes, different percepts are related by features; and, in dichotomies and orderings, different features are related by variables. In cross-classifications (though not yet in nested classifications), different variables are related by relationships. All of these systems of operations establish connections among isolated events (percepts, features, variables) and thus make possible a coordination of points of view (Piaget, see Flavell, 1963). As we proceed from classes, to orderings, to cross-classifications, the scope of inclusion becomes increasingly greater.

Scientific method involves thinking in terms of cross-classifications, most notably those used to represent relationships and factorial designs (see Anderson, 1971). Scientific description and explanation, on the other hand, make use of whatever inferential scheme seems most appropriate to the task at hand. For example, nested classification seems quite appropriate for describing the similarities and differences among living things. And it seems to be orderings and nested classifications that are involved in the two kinds of scientific explanation, explanation in terms of an intermediate mechanism and explanation in terms of a superordinate principle (Anderson, 1971).

We shall see, as we examine formal operations, that there is a continuing tendency to think in terms of the concrete. People at the level of formal operations are capable of thinking formally, but they by no means always do. Indeed, one might formulate a general principle to the effect that we tend to deal with situations at the lowest possible cognitive level. We have already seen that what can be handled unconsciously does not seem to enter consciousness and that what can be thought about unidimensionally tends not to be thought about multidimensionally. It seems also that what can be comprehended at lower levels tends not to be thought of in terms of cross-classification.

There are two aspects to thinking in terms of cross-classification: generation of possibilities and elimination of possibilities. It is characteristic of thinking at this stage to begin with a consideration of all that is possible and then to locate the actual within this framework. Indeed, it was in this spirit that the first chapter of this book was written.

Generating Possibilities

Generating possibilities in the form of a cross-classification involves set disjunction, rather than simply set inclusion, to be able to think of one set as partially included within another (Dawes, 1966; Gergonne, 1817). The biological classification system, for example, involves only set inclusion. A given class can be seen as being included only in the class above it; mammals can be only vertebrates, not invertebrates. Set disjunction enables us at least to

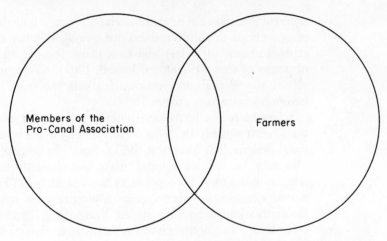

FIGURE 106.   *Set disjunction.*

entertain the possibility of such things as invertebrates with mammary glands. This is what is involved in thinking in terms of cross-classifications.

Dawes (1966) obtained evidence that set disjunction is more difficult than set inclusion. Dawes presented his subjects with a description of political relations on a fictitious island. The description included statements like those diagrammed in Figure 106. Statements like, *Some members of the Pro-Canal Association are farmers,* involved set disjunction, while others, like, *All senators are ranchers,* involved set inclusion. What Dawes found is that subjects make more errors on the disjunctions, tending to recall them as inclusions. Thus, they might tend to remember incorrectly that all members of the Pro-Canal Association are farmers.

Generation of a cross-classification requires what Piaget calls formal operations. Formal operations seem sufficiently different from what Piaget has called concrete operations to justify speaking of the two as different levels of knowing. Perhaps we might call them Levels IIIa and IIIb. Both concrete and formal operations are capable of operating on memory. Concrete operations seem to operate only on representational processes, however, on specific content. Formal operations, on the other hand, seem to operate on executive processes. They seem to be operations on operations, themselves, and thus able to deal with the form of an argument, independent of its content. Whereas concrete operations deal with the actual; formal operations deal with the possible (Piaget, see Flavell, 1963). The fact that formal operations are applied to form alone is what gives rise to the facetious comment that logicians and mathematicians, who clearly operate at the level of formal operations, are people who do not know what they are talking about. This is true of formal operations generally, and it is what gives them their power.

Either concrete operations or formal operations can be applied to classes, dichotomies, orderings, and nested classifications, but only formal operations can be applied to cross-classifications (Inhelder & Piaget, 1958). The reason may be that generation of a cross-classification requires crossing of variables, which often involves the generation of empty cells, that is, cells with no known empirical content. Form must be considered in advance of content. Filling in such empty cells is what chemists have done in looking for new elements to fill in the periodic table or what physicists have done in looking for new subatomic particles to fill in the cross-classification formed by multiplying the variable matter–antimatter by type of particle (proton, electron, positron, etc.).

It is because the structure of concrete operations is content dependent that conservation is achieved for different contents at different ages (Flavell, 1963). Conservation of continuous and discontinuous quantity are achieved around the age of 6 to 7 years. Conservation of weight and volume, however, are not achieved until 9–10 and 11–12 years, respectively. (The child has conserved weight when he realizes that two originally identical balls of clay will still weigh the same when one is rolled into a different shape, and he has achieved conservation of volume when he realizes that they will still displace the same amount of water.)

Because the structure of formal operations, on the other hand, is content free, an ability to think multidimensionally makes its appearance in a number of contexts at about the same time, for example, double reference, proportion, probability, and hydrostatic equilibrium (Inhelder & Piaget, 1958). Double reference involves predicting the net rate of movement of an object that is moving along a support that is, itself, moving. Two dimensions must be taken into account simultaneously. Similarly, both proportion and probability involve taking simultaneous account of a numerator and a denominator. And hydrostatic equilibrium requires taking simultaneous account of force and distance. All of these tasks require taking account of two dimensions at the same time, and success in dealing with all of them is achieved at about the same age, at around 11–12.

An ability to think multidimensionally, according to Piaget, involves an understanding of both compensation and negation. When we understand that both length and thickness affect, in a compensatory fashion, the ease with which a rod can be bent, we can figure out how to increase the length of a rod without also increasing the ease with which it can be bent. And the child understands the trick in the statement, *Heads I win, tails you lose,* when he sees that the change in the verb compensates for the change in the subject, with the result that there is no real difference between heads and tails. We can also imagine the negation of factors. It is by imagining the negation of all factors that produce friction that one is able to conceive of frictionless motion. Similarly, we can conceive of an ideal gas or an ideal society.

An experiment by Inhelder and Piaget (1958) illustrates the difference between concrete and formal operations in a problem that requires the generation of possibilities (see Figure 107). Subjects are shown four identical flasks of colorless liquids (1, 2, 3,

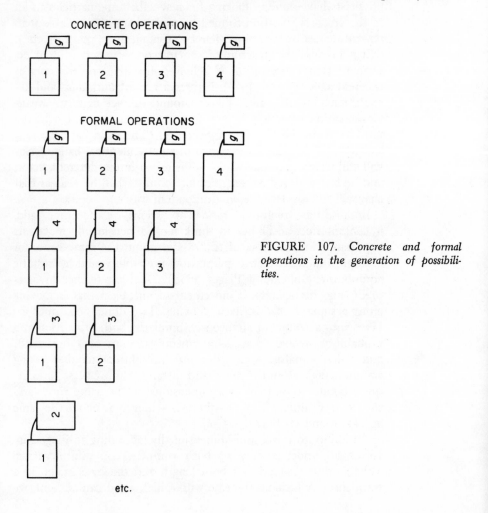

FIGURE 107. *Concrete and formal operations in the generation of possibilities.*

etc.

and 4) and a small dropper bottle of colorless liquid (g). They are then shown a glass which contains some combination of the liquids in the flasks and which turns yellow when g is added. The problem is to find which combination of liquids produces a yellow solution when g is added.

A subject at the level of concrete operations adds g to 1, then to 2, then to 3, then to 4, and says, *I think I did everything. I tried them all.* When it is pointed out to him that he took each of the flasks separately and he is asked what else he could have done, he says, *Take two bottles at the same time.* But what he does is combine 1 + 4 + g and 2 + 3 + g, establishing two sets of flasks between which he never makes combinations, a nested classification.

An older subject immediately tries out all combinations of two flasks with g, quickly finding that 1 + 3 + g yields the yellow color. He then goes a step further, combining first 2 and then 4 with the yellow solution, and finds out that, while 2 makes no difference, 4 cancels the effect.

Formal operations is the age at which the adolescent becomes aware of larger social and philosophical concerns. He begins to see social reality as but one among a set of possibilities. Concrete operations accept what is in representational memory, that is, content; they are directed only toward understanding what is given. To illustrate, a person thinking at this level might be inclined to take human aggression as a given and to learn to live with it. Formal operations, on the other hand, begin with organization in the executive system, which, at the very outset, generates a set of possibilities for consideration. To continue the illustration, a person thinking at this level would be more capable of seeing human aggression as but one among a set of possible behaviors, generated by various combinations of environmental and genetic factors; and, hence, he would be more capable of seeing that one might alter the status quo.

Eliminating Possibilities

Generation of all possibilities provides a framework for thinking; however, for this to result in knowledge of the world, we must reduce these possibilities to those that correspond to actuality (Attneave, 1959; Garner, 1962). We shall consider two cases: the case where we are concerned with only a single causal variable and the case where we are concerned with many causal variables.

Single Causal Variable. Let us say that the causal variable we are interested in is vitamin C intake and that we are interested in the effect this variable might have on the number of cold-free days within a given period of time. To examine the relationship between two variables, we must consider all the possibilities represented by the cross-classification formed by their product.

The simplest such cross-classification is the one shown in Figure 108, in which each variable is a dichotomy, here, 0 mg versus 1000 mg of vitamin C supplement and low versus high incidence of cold-free days.

Each of the patterns in Figure 108 has the status of an assertion about the actual state of affairs. Note, however, that each is a statement of relationship between two variables, not an assertion about which value of either variable obtains in any particular situation. Thus, $A \rightarrow B$, for example, asserts that, if one takes 1000 mg daily supplements of vitamin C, one will enjoy a high incidence of cold-free days, yet it makes no assertion as to whether any particular individual actually takes such supplements. As statements of relationship, then, these patterns represent rather abstract assertions about the actual state of affairs. Piaget refers to such assertions as propositions and to manipulation of them by symbolic logic as propositional thinking. Russell's (1926) term molecular proposition seems preferable, however, for it recognizes both the similarities and differences between them and the atomic propositions of which they are composed. Before any data are gathered, these molecular propositions have the status of hypotheses.

To determine which relationship obtains, we must determine which of the cells are filled and which are empty. Notice that, in order to determine which hypothesis is correct, all four cells of the cross-classification must be examined. In concrete operations, the cross-classification is not generated in advance and, hence, is not considered as a whole. Rather, those portions of the table that we happen to have encountered are all that are taken into account. This can lead to a number of kinds of errors (Anderson, 1971).

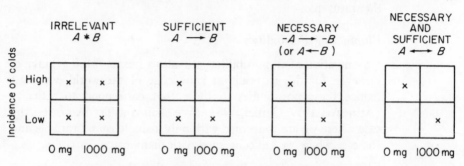

FIGURE 108. *Possible patterns of relationship between an independent variable and a dependent variable.*

Sometimes we focus on only a single cell, as in advertisements which boast, *We have many reports from satisfied users.* What we would like to know, in this case, is whether users are more satisfied with the product in question than with some competing product—that is, whether there is a relationship between product, on the one hand, and user satisfaction, on the other. We need data for both values of the product variable, call them Brand I and Brand II, and both values of the user satisfaction variable, satisfied and dissatisfied. Yet all that we have been told is that a large number of cases fall in the Brand I/Satisfied cell. The man who concludes from the fact that he has worked hard and is successful that hard work is a sufficient condition for success is also making this error, as is the person who counts just those times that he has had "precognitive" hunches and been correct.

Much more frequently, we focus on a single column. This is the error we make when we fail to obtain data in a control condition. A classic example is superstitious thinking. It is characteristic of both superstitious laboratory animals (Skinner, 1953) and superstitious people that they obtain data in situations where they have followed their superstitious practices but, because they do not think to abandon these practices, or are afraid to abandon them, obtain little or no data in situations where they have not followed them.

Consider horoscopes. It is not uncommon for a person to read his horoscope regularly, find that it usually fits his case, and then conclude on this basis that there is something to horoscopes. Such a conclusion is not warranted. To say that there is something to horoscopes is to say that there is a relationship between what stars people are born under and what happens to them; the reason people take the trouble to look up their own horoscopes is that they believe that what they say is more applicable to their own particular cases than what other horoscopes might say. The relevant cross-classification is formed from the variables: my horoscope versus other horoscopes, and satisfactory predictions versus unsatisfactory predictions. All four cells in this cross-classification must be examined. If a person wishes to determine whether there is anything to horoscopes, he should not only look at his own horoscope and keep track of the number of satisfactory and unsatisfactory predictions; he should also obtain control data by looking at other horoscopes and keeping track of the number of satisfactory and unsatisfactory predictions they make. (He should also do this "blindly." That is, he should read horoscopes and rate their degree of satisfactoriness before he looks to find out which are his own. If he does not, his ratings might be influenced more by whether or not the horoscope is his own than by what it says.)

An experiment by Wason (1968) is pertinent. The subject was shown four cards, each with one of the symbols, *E*, *K*, *4*, or *7* on its face, and was told that each card had a letter on one side and a number on the other. His task was to name those cards, and only those cards, which would have to be turned over to determine whether the following rule was true or false: If a card has a vowel on one side, then it has an even number on the other side.

In terms of Figure 108, this rule is of the form: vowel → even. It asserts that having a vowel on one side is a sufficient condition for having an even number on the other. Applying the general cross-classification to this particular problem yields the cross-classification in Figure 109. Each card actually belongs in a particular cell, but, since we have information only about one side of any card, we can indicate only which row or column it belongs in. The informative cards are the 7 and the *E*, for, if the rule is to hold, the 7 must fall in the odd–consonant cell, and the *E* must fall in the even–vowel cell. The *4* and the *K* are not informative, because the rule permits the *4* to fall in either the even–consonant or the even–vowel cell and the *K* to fall in either the odd–consonant or the even–consonant cell. The answer to the problem is, therefore, that the 7 and the *E*, and only those cards, must be turned over to test the rule.

This seems clear enough when we are thinking in terms of the appropriate cross-classification; however, it is ordinarily quite difficult to see. The vast majority of subjects say either, "*E*," which is single column thinking, or, "*E* and *4*," which seems to be a compound single-column thinking. Apparently, when we have a rule to test, it is difficult for us to see the relevance of terms not specifically mentioned in the rule, here, the odd number, 7.

The fact that subjects have great difficulty in seeing the relevance of the odd number, 7, has an interesting practical implica-

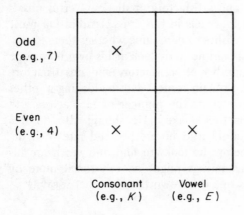

FIGURE 109.   *Cross-classification analysis of Wason's four-card problem.*

tion. In order to be able to appreciate the relevance of this card, one has to be able to understand the following line of reasoning:

> *If there is a vowel on one side, then there must be an even number on the other.*
> *There is not an even number on this side. (There is a 7.)*
> *Therefore, there must not be a vowel on the other.*

It is important to check the 7 to make sure that there is not a vowel on the other side. But this is the same pattern of reasoning (denying the consequent) that is involved in statistical inference.

> *If the null hypothesis is true, then the obtained results are such as would be expected to occur .05 of the time or less.*
> *It is not likely that the obtained results are such as would be expected to occur .05 of the time or less.*
> *Therefore, it is not likely that the null hypothesis is true.*

Like Wason's subjects, students of statistics have considerable difficulty with this pattern of reasoning.

For some reason that is not yet understood, the presence of a familiar context greatly facilitates performance on the vowel–even problem. Johnson-Laird, Legrenzi, and Legrenzi (1972) couched the problem in terms of sealed and unsealed envelopes with 4¢ stamps and 5¢ stamps on the other side, in a concrete condition, and in terms of envelopes with Ds and Cs on one side and 4s and 5s on the other, in an abstract condition. The number of subjects solving the problem correctly was 21 out of 24 in the concrete condition and 2 out of 24 in the abstract condition, and there was no transfer from one condition to the other. Once again, logical thought does not seem to be perfectly "logical," even at the level of formal operations.

Ward and Jenkins (1965; Jenkins & Ward, 1965) have shown that even subjects who use the information in all four cells rarely reason correctly about relationships. Consider the cross-classification in Figure 110, which represents the predictions of an Oregon weather man. There is no relationship between his predictions and the weather, because the chances that it will rain are the same, 90% whether he predicts rain (81/90) or no rain (9/10). We tend to see such a pattern as representing a high degree of relationship, however, for instead of comparing these two percentages, we tend to compute an overall percentage of accuracy. In this case, the weatherman is accurate 82% of the time. It is easy to be this accurate in Oregon, or in the Mohave Desert, where there is not much variation to predict.

Other studies support Jenkins and Ward's findings for cross-classifications formed from bivalent variables (Peterson & Beach, 1967). However, it is surprising to find that subjects are quite

OUTCOME	PREDICTION: No Rain	PREDICTION: Rain
Rain	9	81
No Rain	1	9

FIGURE 110. *The percentage of accuracy fallacy.*

accurate in estimating correlations from cross-classifications formed from multivalent variables (Peterson & Beach, 1967). Perhaps it is that these cross-classifications are too complex to be processed as such in CP/STM and that part of the job must be turned over to analogue perceptual processes, which would seem well suited to such a task. It seems consistent with such an interpretation that subjects are also better able to combine information from several predictors than from few predictors (Peterson & Beach, 1967).

Many Causal Variables. In the real world, there are always many possibly relevant variables. Although the preceding considerations are always applicable, because we always eventually get down to pairwise relationships, additional considerations, having to do with both information selection and information combination, are involved in dealing with the possibility of multiple causality.

At the level of concrete operations, the concern is more with producing a strong perceptual effect than with untangling causal possibilities. Thus, a child who has decided that long rods bend more than short ones might demonstrate this by comparing a long, thin rod and a short, thick one "so you can see the difference better" (Inhelder & Piaget, 1958). This is what experimental scientists call confounding variables, and it is clearly an unsound practice if one is interested in explanation. The concrete operations child cannot focus on more than one variable at a time. He cannot see that the presence of a second variable complicates inferences about the first.

The formal operations child acquires the ability to deal with more than one variable at a time. This enables him, as we have seen, to deal with problems in proportion, probability, double reference, and hydrostatic equilibrium. It also enables him to design adequate experiments.

There seem to be three stages in learning to design adequate experiments: the controlled experiment, the coordinated series of controlled experiments, and the factorial experiment. In the follow-

Uncontrolled Experiment		Controlled Experiment		Factorial Experiment	
A_1	A_2	A_1	A_1	A_1	A_1
B_1	B_2	B_1	B_1	B_1	B_1
B_2	B_2	B_1	B_1	B_1	B_1
B_1	B_1	B_1	B_1	B_1	B_1
B_1	B_2	B_1	B_1	B_2	B_2
B_1	B_1	B_1	B_1	B_2	B_2
B_1	B_1	B_1	B_1	B_2	B_2

FIGURE 111. *Uncontrolled, controlled, and factorial experiments. A_1 and A_2 represent different experimental conditions; that is, different values on the independent variable. B_1 and B_2 represent different values on a potentially confounding variable.*

ing discussion, we shall use A to represent the variable of interest and B to represent some other variable that must be taken into account in evaluating A.

In a controlled experiment (see Figure 111), A is manipulated, while other variables are held constant. The isolated controlled experiment is adequate for only a restricted class of problems. In the pendulum problem (Inhelder & Piaget, 1958), for example, the subject is to find out which of the following four factors affects the rate of oscillation of a pendulum: the length of the string, the weight of the object on the end of the string, the height from which the pendulum is released, or the force with which the pendulum is released. An uncoordinated series of controlled experiments will lead to the correct conclusion in this case, that variation in the length of the string is a necessary and sufficient condition for variation in the rate of oscillation and that all of the other factors are irrelevant.

While use of the controlled experiment shows an appreciation of the possibility that variables other than A might affect the phenomenon of interest, it shows an appreciation only of the simple effect of B and not of the possibility that it might interact with A. The controlled experiment seems to be another manifestation of that transition between unidimensional and multidimensional thinking that we considered earlier, where more than one dimension is considered serially but no two dimensions are considered simultaneously. Here again, thinking is multidimensional in terms of main effects but unidimensional in terms of interactions.

Interactions may be crucial. Figure 112 illustrates the basic patterns of interaction between two independent variables. In order to determine which pattern holds in a particular case, all four cells

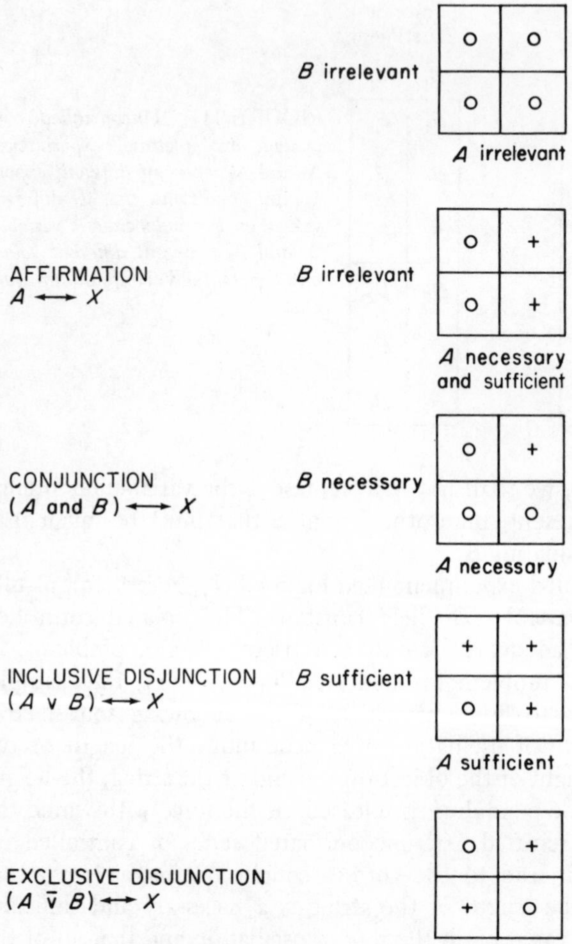

B irrelevant

A irrelevant

AFFIRMATION
A ⟷ X

B irrelevant

A necessary
and sufficient

CONJUNCTION
(A and B) ⟷ X

B necessary

A necessary

FIGURE 112. *Possible patterns of interaction between two independent variables.*

INCLUSIVE DISJUNCTION
(A v B) ⟷ X

B sufficient

A sufficient

EXCLUSIVE DISJUNCTION
(A v̄ B) ⟷ X

of the table must be examined. Note that the four cells in this table are defined by the values on two independent variables, not by the values on one independent and one dependent variable, as in the case we considered earlier. The same principle applies, though: The full cross-classification must be examined. This can be accomplished by means of either a coordinated series of controlled experiments or a factorial experiment.

The second stage in learning to design adequate experiments is the coordinated series of controlled experiments. In coordinated series of experiments, some account is taken of the possibility of different patterns of interaction, because experiments are no longer interpreted in isolation.

Positive focusing (Bruner, Goodnow, & Austin, 1962), the simplest of these, takes account of the possibility that more than one variable may constitute a necessary condition; that is, it takes account of the possibility of conjunctive patterns. In positive focusing, you begin with the first positive instance, say a description of the plane that won the distance event in the *Scientific American* International Airplane Contest. Let us say that this description consists of the attributes: leading edges of wings at a 30° angle to one another, surface of wings at a 10° angle to the base of the plane, wing surfaces flat, waterproof bond paper used. Let us call these variables L, S, W, and P, respectively. This collection of attributes is called the positive focus. In the positive focusing strategy, you vary one of these features at a time to determine whether it is relevant; that is, you conduct a series of controlled experiments. Thus, you might begin by varying L. If it affects the distance flown, you leave it in the focus; if not, you drop it from the focus. It is the maintenance of a focus in this way that provides the coordination among the experiments. Once each feature has been checked in this way, the problem is solved, assuming that the concept is a conjunctive one.

Conditional focusing (Hunt, 1962) is a more sophisticated strategy. It takes account of all of the possible patterns of interaction illustrated in Figure 113. Let us see how this strategy would be applied to the learning of an inclusive disjunction, say white or triangle, where each variable provides a sufficient condition for the occurrence of the effect. The first step is to look for an attribute, say white, that tends to characterize positive instances and not negative instances and then to classify the stimuli on this basis (see Figure 113a). The second step is to examine all the stimuli that possess this feature to see whether they are all positive instances. They are, and so these stimuli need not be considered further. The third step is to examine all the stimuli that do not possess this feature to see whether they are all negative instances. They are not; some are positive, and some are negative. These must be processed further.

The fourth step is to apply the strategy recursively to just these stimuli, that is, to look for an attribute, say triangularity, that tends to characterize positive instances and not negative instances in this subset and then to classify the stimuli on this basis (see Figure 113b). The fifth, and final, step is to examine each of these subsets, to see whether the one consists entirely of positive instances and the other consists entirely of negative instances. Because they do, the classification tree thus formed is adequate to classify stimuli according to the rule: white or triangle.

If the pattern had been an exclusive disjunction, $A \veebar B$ (read "A

CONCEPT : WHITE OR TRIANGLE

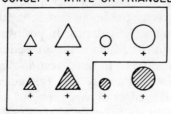

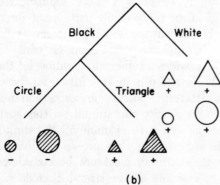

FIGURE 113. *Learning an inclusive disjunction by means of conditional focusing.*

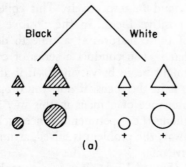

or B but not both), an additional test would have been added, as in Figure 114. But, because the distinction between B and −B is nested separately within A and −A, we have a representation of the classification rule that is not fully at the level of formal operations.

Neisser and Weene (1962) and Haygood and Bourne (1965) obtained evidence that adults employ conditional focusing. Neisser and Weene, for example, examined all possible ways of classifying stimuli into a positive set and a negative set on the basis of two dichotomous variables. On the basis of the relative number of trials required to learn each classification, they were able to order the classifications into three groups. Group I, the easiest, consisted of

CONCEPT : (WHITE AND TRIANGLE) OR (BLACK AND CIRCLE)

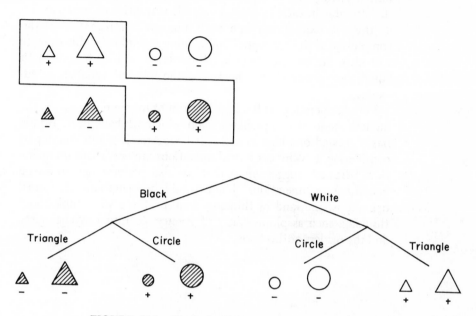

FIGURE 114. *Final classification tree for an exclusive disjunction learned by means of conditional focusing.*

simple concepts $(A, -A, B,$ and $-B)$. Group II consisted of both conjunctions $(A \& B, -A \& B, A \& -B,$ and $-A \& -B)$ and inclusive disjunctions $(A \vee B, -A \vee B, A \vee -B,$ and $-A \vee -B)$. Group Group III, the most difficult, consisted of exclusive disjunctions $(A \bar{\vee} B$ and $A \bar{\vee} -B)$. This ordering would be predicted from the fact that the conditional focusing strategy would form classification trees with one test for all concepts in Group I, with two tests for all concepts in Group II, and with three tests for all concepts in Group III.

The third stage in learning to design adequate experiments is the more elegant factorial experiment. This can be seen in the use of the truth-table strategy (Guy, 1969). The cross-classifications in Figure 106 are all equivalent to the truth tables used by logicians to define statements in logic, hence the name of the strategy. Let us say that the relevant variables are $A/-A$ and $B/-B$. The first thing a subject using this strategy does is to generate an empty cross-classification, a truth table, from these variables, yielding the four cells: $A \& B, A \& -B, -A \& B,$ and $-A \& -B$. Instead of focussing on a particular subset of stimuli, on what is given, he begins by representing all possibilities in advance, as is characteristic of formal operations. The next step is simply to determine whether the stimulus in each of these four cells is positive or negative. To do this will require only four trials, one per cell, regardless of the complexity of the concept. Thus, a subject employing this strategy will learn Neisser and Weene's three levels of classification with equal ease, provided that he knows the relevant variables in advance.

Formal operations is the highest form of inferential memory, the highest mode of comprehension on which we have data. Bruner has suggested one higher, and it is fitting to close this chapter by considering it. Whereas formal operations are operations on operations, Bruner's suggestion is that we also perform operations on operations on operations. These would be operations on formal operations, the kind of thinking done by those who think about thinking, such as philosophers of science, cognitive psychologists, and the readers of this book.

Plans for Productive Information Retrieval

chapter 7

Plans for both reducing steps and increasing variability increase the efficiency with which the executive system can construct new knowledge.

In this chapter, as in the last, our concern is with plans for information retrieval. Here, however, our concern is specifically with productive information retrieval, the construction of something new out of components of information acquired at different times, in different contexts. Here, we are concerned with problem solving.

Christensen, Guilford, and Wilson (1957) have obtained some data which point to interesting differences in the temporal course of productive and reproductive information retrieval. Ideas seem to be produced at a decreasing rate in reproductive tasks, such as naming cities, quadruped mammals, or birds (see Figure 115) but at a constant rate in productive tasks, such as naming impossibilities or clever plot titles. Though the explanation for this difference is not yet clear, the difference, itself, is intriguing.

Productive thought is not essentially inferential, or logical, but moves across logical gaps by "intuitive leaps." Intuition has an "unscientific" sound to it, but it is interesting that it is in precisely

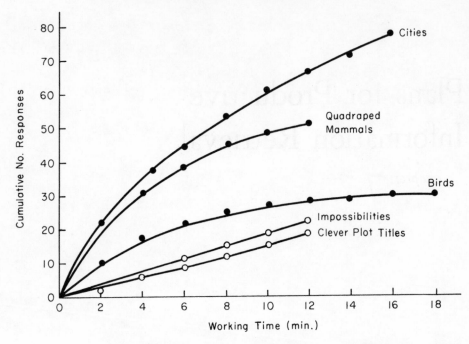

FIGURE 115.   *Rates of reproductive* (●) *and productive* (○) *information retrieval.* [*Adapted from P. R. Christensen, J. P. Guilford, and R. C. Wilson, "Relations of creative responses to working time and instructions," Journal of Experimental Psychology, 1957, 53, 82–88. Copyright 1957 by the American Psychological Association. Used with permission.*]

those areas where inferential systems are the most highly developed, mathematics and physics, that we seem to hear the most about the importance of intuition (Bruner, 1960). Perhaps intuitive processes stand out with special clarity against a background of such rigor.

To understand productive thought, we must begin with the notion of randomness. Whereas inferential thought enables us to discover unrealized possibilities that are implicit in a system, only thought that involves some randomness or extrainferential organization can enable us to get outside of the current system and discover a new one (Campbell, 1960). Sometimes randomness seems to be generated externally, by a "happy accident," what is called serendipity. It was by accident that Curie left some radium in the same drawer with a photographic plate and thus discovered X rays, and it was by accident that Land knocked over one of his three primary-color projectors and literally stumbled on the observation that two primary colors are sufficient to project a scene in full color. Such cases have occurred with some frequency in the history of creative thought.

But chance alone is not likely to lead to many creative ideas in a lifetime. The classic illustration of the futility of unconstrained random search is trying to produce a great book by having monkeys bang away at typewriters for millions of years (Newell & Simon, 1972). Though it is possible to write a great book in this way (whereas it is not possible to do so with inferential thought alone), it would certainly not be practical.

So we must impose some constraints on random search. Reasonable constraints on random search are what we call problem-solving strategies, or heuristics. Heuristics are procedures that increase the probability of finding a solution within an acceptable period of time. They do this by confining our search to regions where the solution is likely to be found. Consider, as an example, the heuristic of looking for likely letter combinations in solving anagrams. If we were to search in an unconstrained manner for the sequence of the letters **EHT** that constitute a word, we would be searching through a "space" of six possibilities: **EHT, ETH, HET, HTE, TEH,** and **THE.** If we were to begin by looking for likely letter combinations, we might decide to keep the **T** and the **H** together. This would reduce the search space to just two possibilities: **E(TH)** and **(TH)E.** In the first case, the probability of obtaining a solution on, for example, the first attempt is 1/6; in the second case, it is 1/2. Application of the heuristic of looking for likely letter combinations has thus increased the probability of finding a solution quickly. The gain is not large in this example, which is intended to be only illustrative, but in more complex problems it may be enormous.

Heuristics, by their very nature, sometimes fail. Indeed, what we mean by a tricky problem is one for which trusted heuristics do not work. When applied to the anagram **OHT,** for example, the heuristic of looking for likely letter combinations will reduce the search space to **O(TH)** and **(TH)O,** neither of which is a word.

Heuristics seem to be of two general kinds: those that reduce the number of steps in executive processing—what we shall call the heuristics of simplification; and those that activate potentially relevant items in representational memory—what we shall call the heuristics of stimulus variation. The former have been emphasized by those working on computer models of problem solving (Newell & Simon, 1972), models which have relied heavily on executive processes (Reitman, 1965). The latter have been emphasized by those concerned with perceptual (Duncker, 1945; Kohler, 1925) and associative (Saugstad, 1957) processes in problem solving. Even though the heuristics of stimulus variation have their effects on representational memory, they are, nonetheless, plans for productive information retrieval carried out by executive processes and are, thus, appropriately considered at this point.

The Heuristics of Simplification

There are several ways to achieve simplification and, hence, to reduce the probable number of steps that must be taken by the executive system. All are clear examples of information reduction. They seem to have their effects by reducing the number of paths considered, average path length, or both. The first such heuristic to be considered, eliminating elements, reduces both number of paths and path length.

Eliminating Elements

A problem may be simplified by eliminating elements. This can be shown most clearly in the case of the disk transfer problem (see Figure 116). The problem, as you will recall, is to move all the disks to either of the other posts, moving only one disk at a time and never placing a larger disk on a smaller one. The original problem was presented in terms of 21 disks, which would require over a million moves. The number of moves can be reduced to seven by reducing the number of disks to three. This heuristic has been called the planning heuristic (Newell, Shaw, & Simon, 1962), because the principle discovered with the simplified version of the problem forms a plan for solving the larger problem.

The disk transfer problem is atypical in that the elements, the disks, are of equal importance. In most problems, the elements differ in importance, and it is the less important ones that are selectively eliminated. Thus, in anagram problems, the vowels tend to be ignored, and thinking takes place primarily in terms of the consonants; and, in chess, the pawns tend to be disregarded

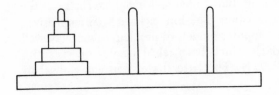

FIGURE 116.   *The disk-transfer problem.*

and the heavy pieces attended to. Similarly, maps, diagrams, and models represent important elements selectively.

Eliminating Relationships

A problem may be simplified by eliminating relationships among the elements, without necessarily eliminating any elements. Usually, as might be expected, relationships differ in importance, and it is the less important ones that are eliminated. This can be accomplished by analyzing the problem into relatively independent subproblems. What we have here is hierarchical organization again. Hierarchical organization is useful in the construction of solutions, as it useful in construction generally.

Analysis into subproblems is an important heuristic in architecture (Alexander, 1964). Consider the problem of selecting a floor plan and a style for a house. Assume that, by eliminating elements, we have reduced the number of floor plans we wish to consider further to five (**A, B, C, D,** and **E**) and the number of styles we wish to consider further also to five (**a, b, c, d,** and **e.**) If we treat this as a single problem, there are $5 \times 5 = 25$ possibilities in the search space (**Aa, Ab, Ac, Ad, Ae, Ba, Bb,** etc.) Suppose, however, that the problem is first analyzed into relatively independent subproblems. Suppose that we treat selecting a floor plan as one subproblem and selecting a style as another, on the assumption that whatever floor plan and style we happen to decide upon can be made to go together. There will then be 5 possibilities in the search space for each subproblem and $5 + 5 = 10$ for the entire problem, instead of the 25 we started out with. In real life, the simplification achieved is usually much greater. The trick, is to discover subproblems that are relatively independent.

Analysis into subproblems is the heuristic psychologists use when they think in terms of intervening variables. Instead of examining all $m \times n$ possible relationships between m stimulus variables, such as amount of practice and amount of reinforcement, and n response variables, such as probability of a correct response and response latency, they examine the m relationships between each of the stimulus variables and an intervening variable, such as associative strength, and the n relationships between the intervening variable and each of the response variables, for a total of only $m + n$ relationships (MacCorquodale & Meehl, 1948). Theory simplifies.

Difference reduction (see Newell, Shaw, & Simon, 1962) is a special case of this kind of heuristic. A simple example of difference reduction is the child's game Button, Button, Where's the Button?

In this game, one person hides a button somewhere in a room, and a second person looks for it. In addition, the first person provides cues to guide the second person's search, saying "warmer" or "colder" after every few steps the searcher takes to indicate whether the searcher is getting closer to, or farther from, the button.

Difference reduction involves analysis into subproblems plus testing of the environment to determine when each subproblem has been solved. This is information resampling again. In Button, Button, Where's the Button?, the subproblems consist of getting just a few steps closer to where the goal might be, and the testing involves listening for the "warmer" and "colder" signals. The alternative would be going all the way to one place and looking there for the button, going all the way to another place and looking there for the button, and so on. In anagram solving, difference reduction takes the form of looking for likely letter combinations. The first subproblem is to try different arrangements of pairs of letters, and subsequent problems are to try different arrangements of larger numbers of letters. The test, in each case, is an intuitive judgment as to whether a particular arrangement constitutes a likely letter sequence in English. Duncker's (1945) hierarchy of solution attempts and the Bruner, Olver, Greenfield *et al.* (1966) Twenty Questions and bulb board tasks also provide relevant examples.

In chess, difference reduction takes the form of trying to improve one's position on the board. Chess is far too complex to enable a player to deal with a game as a single problem, that is, to make his opening move with a particular checkmate pattern in mind. He must divide the problem into subproblems, first trying to achieve a good opening position, then a good middle-game position, and finally a good end-game position and checkmate. Moreover, he continually performs various tests to evaluate the strength of his position relative to that of his opponent. A good chess player considers number and strength of pieces, in terms of a scoring system which assigns a different point value to each piece; mobility, in terms of the number of squares each piece attacks; center control; king safety; and other factors.

Difference reduction is sometimes called "hill climbing." The analogy is to a person climbing a hill in a fog. Since he cannot see the peak, he cannot deal with the problem as a whole, but must look up the hill a short way, walk to that point, look up again, walk to that point, and so forth, gradually reducing the difference in elevation between his present position and the peak. This analogy suggests a danger in difference reduction. Our climber could easily wind up on a false peak. It would seem that the process of theory construction is full of false peaks. Because our knowledge is strictly limited, we develop theories to account for what we know, not for all that might be known. Our progress, like that of the climber in the fog, is guided by what limited vision we have. Thus, we frequently ascend to a heliocentric theory, a phlogiston theory, or one of the many monistic theories that have appeared in psychology.

A final example of difference reduction, Newell, Shaw, and Simon's (1962) safe-cracking example, will give some idea of the power of this heuristic. Assume that there are 10 digits on the dial of a safe and that a 4-digit sequence is required to open the lock. If you attempt to open the safe by dialing a 4-digit sequence, trying the door, dialing another 4-digit sequence, trying the door again, and so forth, you will be searching in a space of $10 \times 10 \times 10 \times 10 = 10,000$ possibilities. There are 10 possible initial digits, and each of these can be followed by any of 10 digits, so there are $10 \times 10 = 100$ possible two-digit starting sequences. Each of these sequences, in turn, can be followed by any of 10 digits, which yields $100 \times 10 = 1000$ possible three-digit starting sequences; and so forth (see Figure 117a for a more simplified example).

If the lock is not too well made, you can divide this problem into subproblems by listening for clicks. The first subproblem is determining the first digit in the sequence. You turn the dial until it clicks, and then you have solved that subproblem. This required searching a space of 10 possibilities, but, because you have solved this subproblem, you need to consider only one of these possibilities further, the one that produced the click. The next subproblem is determining the second digit in the sequence. Again, you turn the dial until it clicks, and you have solved that subproblem. And, again, you need not consider any further the space you have already searched. The total number of possibilities in the entire problem then becomes $10 + 10 + 10 + 10 = 40$, a considerable reduction from 10,000 (see Figure 117b; Newell, Shaw, & Simon, 1962).

In some of the examples we have given, such as Button, Button, Where's the Button?, a step is taken, and then a test is applied to determine whether that step reduced the difference between the present position and the goal. In others, such as chess, the difference between the present position and the goal is determined first, and then some means for reducing this difference is sought in memory. At this point additional plans for reproductive and

COMPLETE SEARCH   2 × 2 × 2 × 2 = 16 possibilities

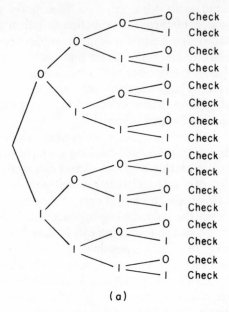

(a)

DIFFERENCE REDUCTION   2 + 2 + 2 + 2 = 8 possibilities

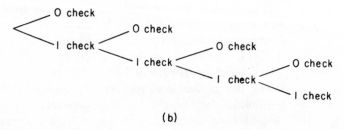

(b)

FIGURE 117.   *A simplified example of the safe-cracking problem: four dials, with only the digits 0 and 1 on each dial.*

productive information retrieval may be brought into play. Determining the difference between the present position and the goal and then seeking ways to reduce this difference is what Newell and Simon (1972) call means–end analysis.

> I want to take my son to nursery school. What's the difference between what I have and what I want? One of distance. What changes distance? My automobile. My automobile won't work. What is needed to make it work? A new battery. What has new batteries? An auto repair shop . . . [Newell & Simon, 1972, p. 416].

Choosing a Less Connected Start

If you went to the *Psychological Abstracts* to look up an article by Miller and Isard, you would be well advised to look under "Isard," rather than "Miller," for there are far fewer Isards than Millers. Another way of saying this is to say that "Isard" provides a less-connected start; it is connected to fewer paths, in this case, index entries.

An important example of choosing a less-connected start is working backward. Ordinarily, in solving a problem, we proceed in a forward direction, from what is given to what is required. This is an efficient way to proceed where the givens are less connected than the goal, where, as in Figure 118a, fewer paths lead out from the givens than lead to the goal.

Practical problems usually conform to this pattern (Polya, 1957). For example, consider the following problem: How can a scout who has been sent to check an area upstream send a message back to his troops, indicating whether they should follow him or not, in such a way that the message will be difficult to intercept? In this problem, the goal allows many possibilities, for there are many ways to send a simple message so that it will be difficult to intercept. The givens permit far fewer possibilities, for all that is explicitly given is that the sender will be upstream from the receiver. Analysis of the materials (Duncker, 1945) is thus more

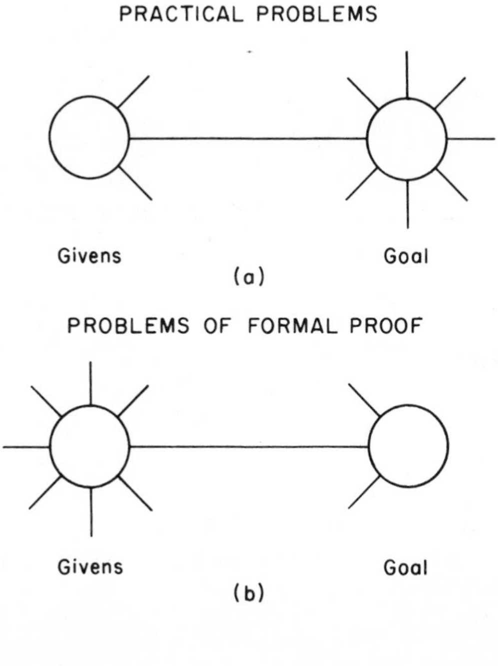

PRACTICAL PROBLEMS

Givens   Goal
              (a)

PROBLEMS OF FORMAL PROOF

Givens   Goal
              (b)

FIGURE 118.   *The structure of practical problems and problems of formal proof.*

likely to be helpful here than analysis of the goal (Duncker, 1945). (The solution is to dye the stream one color for "go" and another for "no go.")

Another way to solve a problem is to work backward (Duncker, 1945; Polya, 1957) from the goal to the givens. This is an efficient way to proceed where the goal is less connected than the givens, where, as in Figure 118b, fewer paths lead to the goal than lead out from the givens.

Problems in formal proof usually conform to this pattern (Polya, 1957). Let us consider an elementary proof in geometry as an example. Figure 119 depicts an isosceles triangle, that is, a triangle in which two sides (here, sides *AC* and *BC*) are equal. The problem is to prove that angle *CAD* equals angle *CBD*. The proof begins with construction of the line *CD*. If we were to try to solve the problem in a forward direction, this is where we would begin, by considering various possible constructions and where they would lead us. This is a highly connected start, however; for there are many possible lines we could draw, and each could lead us in any of a variety of directions.

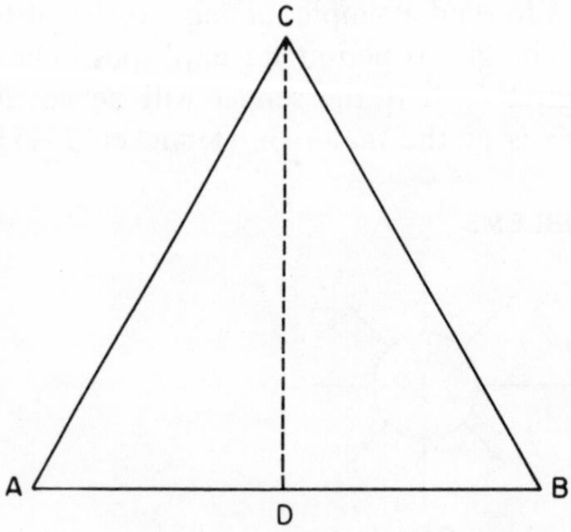

FIGURE 119. *A problem of formal proof.*

Given: *AC = BC*

To Prove: ∠*CAD* = ∠*CBD*

Proof:

AC = BC	Given
CD = CD	Identity
∠*ACD* = ∠*BCD*	Construction
△*ACD* = △*BCD*	Angle-side-angle = angle-side-angle
∠*CAD* = ∠*CBD*	Corresponding parts of equal triangles are equal

Q.E.D.

Let us, instead, start with what we are to prove, that angle CAD equals angle CBD, and try to work backward from there. You may recall from high-school geometry that the usual way to show that two angles are equal is to show that they are corresponding parts of congruent triangles (that is, triangles that can be superimposed so that they will coincide exactly at all points). We seem to have little choice here. If we need two triangles, then we will have to construct a line. So we construct CD, and let us construct it so that is bisects angle ACB, because that will make it easier to prove that the two resulting triangles are equal. Again, we seem to have little choice. By working backward, we have obtained a reasonable construction. What remains to be seen is whether it will do the job.

One way to prove that two triangles are equal is to show that two corresponding sides and the included angle are equal. We know that side AC equals side CB, because that is given in the definition of an isosceles triangle. And we know that line CD in one triangle equals line CD in the other, because it is the same line. Finally, we know that the included angles ACD and BCD are equal, because we constructed CD so that it would bisect angle C. Thus, triangle ACD is congruent with triangle BCD, and angle CAD equals angle CBD.

What would have been difficult to accomplish by working forward was achieved in a fairly direct manner by working backward from the less-connected goal. Newell, Shaw, and Simon's (1958) Logic Theorist program routinely employs the working backward heuristic in constructing proofs in formal logic and has demonstrated its prowess by constructing proofs for three-fourths of the theorems in Chapter 2 of Whitehead and Russell's *Principia Mathematica*, even discovering one proof that is shorter and more elegant than the one published by Whitehead and Russell, themselves.

Two other kinds of problems that would seem often to be solved by working backward are poetry writing and joke writing. The least connected place to begin writing a line of poetry is with the final word, for it must rhyme. And the least connected place to begin writing many kinds of jokes is with the punch line. The following joke seems to be a very good example of this kind of joke, though it is not a very good example of a joke.

> *One day, the zoo attendant noticed that the porpoises were engaged in love making. Afraid that this might embarrass some people, he went to get some seagulls to feed them. On his way back with the gulls, he encountered a*

*lion sleeping in his path. As he was stepping gingerly over
the lion, a policeman arrested him.
The question is, What was the charge?
The answer: Carrying gulls across a staid lion for immoral
porpoises.*

Such a joke is most likely to have been written by working backward from the punch line.

Starting with the Shortest Path

If there is no reason to believe that one path is any more likely
than another to lead to solution, then it is reasonable to try the
shortest path first. Thus, the radio repairman makes sure that the
set is plugged in before he performs any more complex tests, and
the physician questions his patient and takes his temperature before having any laboratory tests performed. Similarly, Newell,
Shaw, and Simon (1958) programmed their Logic Theorist not
to consider paths that led to complex expressions.

Starting with the Previously Most Successful Path

Trying paths in order of past success will reduce the probable
number of paths that must be tried, although it will occasionally
lead to einstellung effects. Einstellung (Luchins, 1942) is the application of a previously successful plan in a situation in which it
is no longer optimal. Einstellung has most frequently been studied
by means of water-measuring problems. For example, the same
plan provides the simplest solution to each of the following problems.

with these jars	*measure out this quantity*
1. 21, 127, & 3 quarts	100 quarts
2. 14, 163, & 25 quarts	99 quarts
3. 13, 38, & 10 quarts	5 quarts

This plan is to fill the middle jar, then subtract one filling of the
first jar and two fillings of the third. Though this plan will also
work when given 28-, 59-, and 3-quart jars and asked to measure
out 25 quarts, a simpler plan is also possible, filling the 28-quart
jar and subtracting one filling of the 3-quart jar. Persistence in the
old, less efficient plan constitutes a demonstration of the ein-

stellung effect. The Logic Theorist was programmed to start with the previously most successful path, and, as would be expected, it occasionally did show einstellung effects. Despite occasional einstellung effects, however, this is a very valuable heuristic.

The Heuristics of Stimulus Variation

It is representational memory that provides the extrainferential organization required for creative thought, and the heuristics of stimulus variation increase the chances that this activity will lead to problem solution. These heuristics can conveniently be considered to be of three kinds: adding stimuli, removing stimuli, and rearranging stimuli.

We shall consider the possible effects of these heuristics on two stages that are frequently reported to occur in creative thought (Wallas, 1926). One of these is the stage of conscious effort to achieve the solution. This stage is often further analyzed into a stage of preparation and a stage of production of ideas, but we shall not do so because preparation and production are not clearly delineated from one another, there being much movement back and forth between them. The second, the stage of incubation, is a stage during which the thinker has given up conscious work on the problem but during which, according to his own report, progress is made on the problem (for example, Poincaré, Lowell, in Ghiselin, 1952). The end of the period of incubation is marked, often rather dramatically, by illumination, the "Eureka!" or "Aha!" experience, when the germ of the solution suddenly flashes into the thinker's conscious mind.

There is an experience that is familiar to all of us that may constitute a "miniature" example of incubation, suitable for laboratory analysis. This is the experience of trying to recall a word (the stage of production), giving up for a while (the stage of incubation), and then having the word suddenly come to mind (illumination; see Polya, 1957).

The fact that illumination frequently occurs when the conscious mind is directed, according to the thinker's report, toward something not at all related to the problem suggests that the occurrence of illumination is determined by unconscious factors, by the unconscious, parallel processes of representational memory. In examining the heuristics of stimulus variation, we shall encounter several hypotheses, not mutually exclusive, as to what some of these factors might be.

Adding Stimuli

New stimuli will produce new patterns of activity in the representational system, and these may provide the fresh point of view that is so often required for problem solution (Duncker, 1945; Wertheimer, 1945). This heuristic is likely to be more effective, however, if some selection is exercised over the stimuli that are added. Techniques that selectively add stimuli that are in some way related to the problem are likely to be the most helpful. The techniques that we shall consider have this property.

One way to add stimuli selectively is to represent the problem in different terms. If you asked a beginning geometry student whether the hypoteneuse of a right triangle is longer or shorter than the sum of the two sides, he might very well be baffled. But, if you expressed the question in more concrete terms, asking him whether it would be shorter to take a path that cuts across a vacant lot or to take the sidewalk that goes around it, he would quickly give the correct answer. On the other hand, if the question were whether the areas on the two sides of the path are the same or different, it might be necessary for him to think of the path in more abstract terms, as simply the diagonal of a rectangle, before he could get the solution. Creative problem solvers often shift between concrete and abstract ways of representing the problem (Gordon, 1961).

Duncker's mountain-climbing problem can be used to illustrate how a change in representation can make a difficult problem suddenly easy. The problem is as follows (see Figure 120):

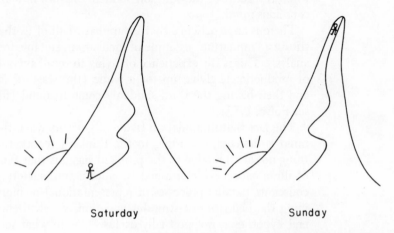

Saturday   Sunday

FIGURE 120.   *The mountain-climbing problem.*

> A man climbs a mountain on Saturday, leaving at day-
> break and arriving at the top near sundown. He spends
> the night at the top. The next day, Sunday, he leaves at
> daybreak and heads down the mountain, following the
> same path that he climbed the day before. The ques-
> tion is this: Will there be any time during the second
> day when he will be at exactly the same point on the
> mountain as he was at that time on the first day?

Note that the problem is not to determine what the time will be,
but simply to determine whether there will be such a time.

It can help to represent this problem in abstract terms, by plot-
ting the journeys on a graph (see Figure 121), with distance up the
mountain as the ordinate and time during the day as the abscissa.
The ascent will then be represented by a line that begins at the
lower left-hand corner of the graph and climbs slowly to the top
of the graph on the right-hand side. The descent will be represented by a line that begins at the upper left-hand corner of the
graph and goes more or less quickly to the bottom. It is obvious
that there is no way to draw this second line without it crossing
the first. The point of crossing, or course, is the point at which
time (on the abscissa) and place (on the ordinate) are the same
for both ascent and descent.

The use of graphs and diagrams, generally, provides a change of
representation which can facilitate solution. A special case is the
substitution of Euler diagrams for symbolic logic notation, a
change which led to new advances in logic.

Another way to add stimuli selectively is to think of an analogy.
Gordon (1961) has reported an amusing example. A problem-
solving group was trying to design a dripless catsup bottle. After
a period of futility, someone considered the remarkable anus of the
horse, which dispenses but never drips. The design feature that

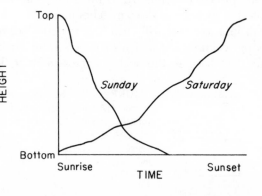

FIGURE 121. *An abstract representation of the mountain-climbing
problem.*

makes this possible is an outer opening that closes upon an inner one and serves as a cover for it. With this principle to work with, the problem was quickly solved. It appears that creative thinkers often use biological analogies in their thinking (Gordon, 1961; Mawardi, 1959).

Still another way to add stimuli selectively is to work on a related problem (Polya, 1957). If you cannot solve a problem in solid geometry it often helps to try the analogous problem in plane geometry. A variation of working on a related problem is reading related literature.

A final way to add stimuli selectively is to talk with someone about the problem you are working on. In simply asking questions, the other person will often provide stimuli that suggest novel ways of looking at the problem. Sometimes, in anticipating questions the other person might ask, you provide these stimuli for yourself. Thomas (Barber & Fox, 1958) worked on and off for eight years trying to determine why injection of the enzyme papain causes wilting of the ears in rabbits. He finally found the answer while lecturing on the problem. In attempting to explain the problem to students, he had to consider more closely an unlikely hypothesis that he had rejected at the outset, on the basis of insufficient data. In performing the experiment properly, he found that this hypothesis was the correct one.

The addition of stimuli provides one hypothesis of incubation, that incubation is simply a period of waiting until a stimulus occurs that suggests the solution to the problem. As legend would have it, at least, it was the additional stimuli of rising water in a bathtub and a falling apple that suggested solutions to the problems Archimedes and Newton had been pondering.

Szekely (1945) has shown experimentally how such a thing can happen. He gave subjects the following problem. Nine matches (see Figure 122) are placed, horizontally, in three rows and three columns. The subject is then given three matches and told to add them to the pattern in a way that will yield four matches per row and four matches per column. He had his subjects work on this problem until they had become thoroughly engrossed in it, but

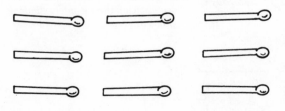

FIGURE 122. *Szelely's match problem.* [*Adapted, with permission, from L. Szekely, "Zur Psychologie des Geistigen Schaffens,"* Schweitzerische Zeitschrift für Psychologie und ihre Anwendungen, *1945,* **4,** *110–124.*]

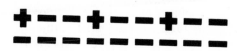

FIGURE 123. *Szekely's "control for rehearsal."* [Adapted, with permission, from L. Szekely, "Zur Psychologie des Geistigen Schaffens," Schweizerische Zeitschrift für Psychologie und ihre Anwendungen, 1945, *4*, 110–124.]

stopped them before they had solved it, telling them they would be able to work on it again in a later session.

Before the promised second session, however, the same subjects were used in a presumably unrelated experiment on rote learning. As a supposed "control for rehearsal" in this experiment, they had to cross out every third dash in a field of dashes, as in Figure 123. During this task, many subjects suddenly discovered the solution to the match problem, which is to lay the additional matches across those in one of the diagonals, as in Figure 124.

Szekely's study suggests that a problem can continue in the form of an unconscious readiness to respond to certain kinds of stimuli for at least as long as a day. This period could quite conceivably be much longer in the case of thinkers who are intensely committed to a problem and who have worked on it for months or years.

A study by Maier (1931a) indicates that stimuli can suggest the solution to a problem without the thinker's becoming aware of the connection. Maier asked subjects to tie together two strings that were suspended from the ceiling, but that were placed far enough apart to prevent a person from taking hold of one and then walking over and reaching the other. This is the two-string problem that we have encountered before. The solution, you will recall, was to tie a weight to the end of one of the strings and get it swinging, then to take hold of the other string and grasp the swinging string as it came near. The crucial insight was the notion of getting one string swinging.

Maier had his subjects work on the problem for a while. Then, as a hint, he walked across the room and "accidentally" brushed against the string so as to get it swinging. This hint suggested the

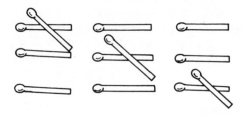

FIGURE 124. *Solution to Szekely's match problem.* [Adapted, with permission, from L. Szekely, "Zur Psychologie des Geistigen Schaffens," Schweizerische Zeitschrift für Psychologie und ihre Anwendungen, 1945, *4*, 110–124.]

solution to most subjects, but apparently by two different mechanisms. Some subjects solved the problem in a series of steps and were aware of the role of the hint. Both the sequential nature of the solution and the awareness suggest that executive mechanisms were involved in these cases. Other subjects, however, solved the problem in a single flash of insight, and, though the solution followed shortly after the hint, were not aware of the role of the hint. Both the immediacy and the lack of awareness suggest that representational mechanisms were involved in these cases, and sound very much like the illumination that has been reported to mark the end of incubation.

There are four features that seem to characterize incubation, and we shall be interested to see what each of the hypotheses has to say about them. First, the incubation period seems always to be preceded by a period of preparation. Creative thinkers have reported this (Ghiselin, 1952; Hadamard, 1945; Wallas, 1926), and Silviera (1971) has shown experimentally that, for an incubation period to be effective, a certain minimum preparation is required. We should ask of a theory of incubation whether it can tell us what is accomplished during the preparation period.

Second, the incubation period often seems to begin when the problem solver is stuck and able to make no further progress. This, also, is reported by creative thinkers (Ghiselin, 1952; Hadamard, 1945; Wallas, 1926) and gains some additional support from an unpublished study by Donald W. Taylor, in the Stanford series of problem-solving studies. Taylor had his subjects take breaks in solving a problem, under two conditions. Some subjects were interrupted at arbitrary times by the experimenter, while others were allowed to choose their own times for breaks. The principal finding was that subjects who chose their own times for breaks were more likely to solve the problem. Although these results are subject to other interpretations and cannot therefore be given much weight, they are consistent with the notion that subjects tend to take breaks when they are stuck and that it is such breaks that are the most beneficial. Silviera (1971) obtained incubation even though she interrupted her subjects herself, but this may have been because her subjects were stuck, or close to being stuck, anyway. She did not compare this condition with one in which subjects chose their own time for breaks. Although the necessity of being stuck certainly cannot be considered to be established, we should ask of a theory of incubation whether it has anything to say on this point.

Third, incubation takes time, which seems to be measured in

minutes or hours for laboratory subjects (Silviera, 1971) and in weeks or months for creative thinkers (Ghiselin, 1952; Hadamard, 1945). If the process is, indeed, the same in the two cases, then perhaps duration of incubation is related to some measure of problem difficulty. We shall want to see whether a theory of incubation has anything to say about this.

Fourth, and finally, the incubation period seems often to be terminated by a flash of insight. This is frequently reported by creative thinkers (Ghiselin, 1952; Hadamard, 1945; Wallas, 1926), though Silviera (1971) obtained incubation with very little evidence of sudden illumination. We shall want to see what a theory of incubation has to say on this point.

The notion that incubation is simply a period of waiting until an appropriate stimulus suggests the solution seems to predict only some of these characteristics. The preparation period would serve to activate relevant criteria, so that appropriate stimuli will be responded to. Incidentally, because secondary perception can be influenced by set, stimuli that are only superficially related to a problem might be misperceived in ways that would suggest its solution, a fact which makes it more probable that an adequate stimulus will be encountered. Getting stuck seems to have no interpretation in this hypothesis. The incubation period, itself, would be just a matter of waiting for a "happy stimulus" to occur and, as such, would seem to be affected more by external than internal conditions. Furthermore, incubation would not be a continuing process; nothing would be accomplished until the "happy stimulus" was encountered, at which point the problem would be solved. Sudden illumination would seem, on the basis of Maier's (1931d) results, to be predicted for all those cases where the problem solver felt the idea to come "out of the blue."

This hypothesis seems to have the most to say about preparation and illumination and little to say about the incubation period itself. Perhaps what we have looked at so far is the way the requirements for a solution are firmly established during the early stage of conscious effort and the way those requirements later respond to the germ of the solution and flash it into consciousness. Perhaps the germ of the solution, the "happy stimulus," sometimes comes from memory, rather than through the senses. If this is so, then this hypothesis and one or both of the other two hypotheses, which are hypotheses about changes that take place in memory, may actually be complementary, describing different aspects of the same process.

Removing Stimuli

Another way to change organization in the representational system during the stage of conscious effort is to remove irrelevant or misleading stimuli. That such stimuli can greatly hinder solution is well illustrated by the following two statements of the old St. Ives problem:

> **The original version:**
> *As I was going to St. Ives*
> *I met a man with seven wives.*
> *Each wife had seven sacks;*
> *Each sack had seven cats;*
> *Each cat had seven kits.*
> *Kits, cats, sacks, and wives,*
> *How many were going to St. Ives?*
>
> **A simplified version:**
> *I was going to St. Ives.*
> *How many were going to St. Ives?*

Similarly, it is more difficult to add up a column of numbers when they are preceded by dollar signs, and still more difficult when they are preceded by British pound signs.

Thus, irrelevant or misleading stimuli should be removed in some way. The trick, of course, is to decide which stimuli are irrelevant or misleading. Both Polya (1957) and Duncker (1945) have suggested that the problem solver ask himself exactly what the solution requires.

The removal of stimuli provides a second hypothesis of incubation, that incubation is simply a period of waiting until the effects of irrelevant stimulation are forgotten. Such a hypothesis, of course, must provide a mechanism for separating the relevant from the irrelevant. This mechanism may be differential forgetting (McGeoch & Irion, 1952). Weaker items are forgotten more rapidly than stronger ones, and, presumably incorrect items tend to be weaker than correct ones.

Adamson and Taylor (1954) have shown that functional fixedness decays in a matter of days. They established functional fixedness by having their subjects use either a switch or a relay to close an electrical circuit. They then gave them a choice between the relay or the switch to use to weight the end of the string in Maier's two-string problem. Initially, the irrelevant stimulation that resulted from using the critical object to close a circuit made it difficult to see it as useful for a weight. The effects of the irrelevant task soon decayed, however, following a typical forgetting curve and disappearing entirely by the end of one week. [It is interesting, incidentally, to compare this forgetting curve with one suggested by Wickelgren (1970) for ITM. Both last on the order of about a week.]

According to the forgetting hypothesis of incubation, the period of conscious preparation has negative effects, along with the positive, and the function of the incubation period is to allow the weaker, negative effects to be reversed. Thus, a period of preparation would be required for incubation to have any value. The forgetting hypothesis would seem to require longer incubation periods for more difficult problems, where problem difficulty is measured in terms of the associative strength of irrelevant items. As we have seen, there is some evidence that this may be the case.

Whereas the addition of stimuli hypothesis of incubation implied no change in representational memory during the incubation period, the removal of stimuli hypothesis implies at least a modest change: forgetting. The next hypothesis to be considered implies considerably more unconscious activity.

Rearranging Stimuli

A final way to change organization in the representational system during the stage of conscious effort is to rearrange stimuli. We tend to think differently about the same objects when we encounter them in different temporal or spatial arrangements.

The temporal orderings *on* and *no*, *boathouse* and *houseboat*, *dog bites man* and *man bites dog* are responded to quite differently. When asked to cross out the word that does not belong in the sequence *skyscraper, temple, cathedral, prayer*, people tend to cross out *prayer*; but, when asked to cross out the word that does not belong in the sequence, *prayer, temple, cathedral, skyscraper*, they tend to cross out *skyscraper* (Cofer, 1951).

Spatial arrangements also make a difference. The chess board looks quite different from your opponent's side. In Figure 125a, a rectangle is drawn inside a circle, with one corner on the circle and the diagonally opposite corner on the center of the circle. The other diagonal is drawn in with a dashed line and indicated to be 10 inches long. The problem is to find the area of the circle. This problem is easier to solve if it is the other diagonal that is drawn in, for here it is clear that this diagonal also equals the radius of the circle, and with the radius one can readily obtain the area.

Find the area of the circle, given
the diagonal of the rectangle

Find the area of the triangle, given
the two sides

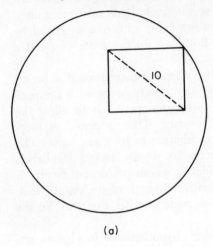

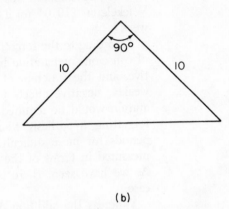

(a)

(b)

FIGURE 125.   *Two area problems.*

The problem in Figure 125b makes the same point. An isosceles triangle is shown in which the two equal sides are each 10 inches long and the enclosed, apical angle is equal to 90°. The problem is to find the area of the triangle. This problem is made easier if the triangle is rotated 135°, for then it is easier to see that the triangle is half of a square whose sides are 10 inches long.

Rearranging stimuli can reduce functional fixedness. As we have seen earlier, Duncker (1945) has shown that a cork in a bottle is more difficult to see as useful in solving a problem than a cork lying beside a bottle and, similarly, that a matchbox full of matches is more difficult to incorporate into a problem solution than an empty matchbox. Let us look at the matchbox problem. A subject is given a box of matches, birthday candles, and some thumbtacks (see Figure 126): His problem is to mount the candles on the wall in such a way that they can be lighted without burning the wall. Most subjects begin by trying to mount the candles on the wall with the thumbtacks, which will not work. The solution is to tack the drawer of the matchbox to the wall and mount the candles on it with candle drippings (see Figure 127). This solution is more readily attained by subjects who are initially presented with these materials in a different spatial arrangement, with an empty matchbox next to a pile of matches.

Rearrangement of stimuli provides a third hypothesis of incubation, that incubation is a period in which items in representational memory are activated in different combinations and permutations.

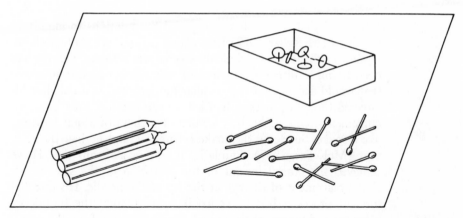

FIGURE 126.   *Duncker's match problem.*

Although there is no direct evidence for this hypothesis, it is the one to which most creative thinkers seem to subscribe (Ghiselin, 1952).

The facts that the mechanisms of dreaming produce fantastic rearrangements of recently activated items in memory (Breger,

FIGURE 127.   *Solution to Duncker's match problem.*

1969) and that dreams have suggested the solutions to important problems (McKellar, 1957) lend plausibility to such an hypothesis. It was in a dream that Kekule discovered the benzene ring. He had been trying to discover a molecular arrangement of carbon atoms that would account for the peculiar properties of benzene, but his directed thought processes had led him to consider only linear arrangements. One night, he dreamed of a chain of atoms writhing like a snake. Suddenly the snake bit its tail, and he had the solution (McKellar, 1957). Similarly, it was in a dream that Howe achieved the crucial insight in the invention of the sewing machine, placement of the eye at the tip of the needle. His directed thought processes had never led him to question the traditional placement of the eye at the end of the needle away from the point. The insight came from a dream in which he was being attacked by savages wielding spears—with holes in their tips (McKellar, 1957). One difficulty with dreaming as a model of incubation, however, is that, while it is true that dreaming does seem to be an excellent example of undirected thought, it takes place in consciousness, and incubation is presumed to be an unconscious process. Perhaps a more plausible mechanism is the continuous alteration of associative memory by the parallel activity of automatic associations to stimuli and conscious thoughts.

Poincaré (in Ghiselin, 1952) seems to have provided the best articulated statement of the rearrangement hypothesis of incubation.

> Permit me a rough comparison. Figure the future elements of our combinations as something like the hooked atoms of Epicurus. During the complete repose of the mind, these atoms are motionless, they are, so to speak, hooked to the wall; so this complete rest may be indefinitely prolonged without the atoms meeting, and consequently without any combination between them.
> On the other hand, during a period of apparent rest and unconscious work, certain of them are detached from the wall and put in motion. They flash in every direction through the space (I was about to say the room) where they are enclosed, as would, for example, a swarm of gnats or, if you prefer a more learned comparison, like the molecules of gas in the kinematic theory of gases. Then their mutual impacts may produce new combinations.
> What is the role of the preliminary conscious work? It is evidently to mobilize certain of these atoms, to unhook them from the wall and put them in swing. . . . The mobilized atoms are therefore not any atoms whatsoever; they are those from which we might reasonably expect the desired solution [p. 41].

In another part of the same work, Poincaré points out the following:

> The sterile combinations do not even present themselves to the mind
> of the inventor. Never in the field of his consciousness do combina-
> tions appear that are not really useful, except some that he rejects
> but which have to some extent the characteristics of useful combina-
> tions [p. 36].

Poincaré says a great deal in these few lines. He says something
about the role of the stage of conscious effort: Elements from
which we might reasonably expect the solution are activated. He
says something about the period of incubation, itself: The elements are rearranged over and over again. And he says something
about illumination: Some mechanism, presumably the one we considered in discussing the first hypothesis of incubation, that is
sensitive to the requirements of a solution responds to a likely
arrangement and enables it to enter consciousness. He says nothing about getting stuck. But, perhaps, as we suggested earlier, getting stuck is not essential to the process of incubation, itself;
perhaps getting stuck is important only in calling attention to the
phenomenon by making sudden illumination possible.

It is interesting to compare this hypothesis, the unconscious
work hypothesis, with the forgetting hypothesis. The forgetting
hypothesis is a negative hypothesis. It tells us what drops out of
memory, but it does not tell us how what is left in memory man-
ages to flash into consciousness during illumination. The unconscious work hypothesis says that what is in memory is active, and
it is not difficult to see how an active pattern might gain entry to
consciousness.

Some neurons in the central nervous system are known to fire
spontaneously (Milner, 1970). Reitman (1965) has suggested that
our unconscious memory is continuously active and has developed
a computer simulation of such a memory. And Neisser (1967) has
observed that those little out-of-place thoughts that occasionally
flit by the margins of our consciousness, without any apparent relation to what is currently occupying our attention, may actually
be evidence of such unconscious activity. These out-of-place
thoughts seem to be what May (1969) calls the "demonaic" elements of thought, the wellspring of creativity. It seems that, if
enough parallel associative influences converge on a thought, it
will enter consciousness even though it does not fit with anything
we are consciously thinking about at the time. If consciousness is
broad, the probability of such thoughts gaining entrance should
be increased. Perhaps this is why creative ideas are so often reported as occurring while walking, shaving, or passing from the
waking to the sleeping state.

Thus, we may someday find that we will be able to put all three hypotheses together. The complete story would then go something like this. During the period of conscious work, two things are accomplished: The requirements for a solution are fixed well in mind and relevant ideas are activated. During this period, problem solving is carried as far as it can be by conscious effort (at least in those cases where the incubation effect is sufficiently dramatic to be recognized as such) and the problem solver feels that he is stuck and can go no further. During the incubation period, itself, the activated elements are continuously combined and recombined, with the irrelevant elements gradually becoming less influential. Illumination occurs when a current pattern in either EM or LTM matches the requirements of a solution.

Thus, we end these two chapters on plans by seeing, once again, that thought is by no means entirely "upstream" from the representational system to the executive system (Bruner, 1970), but involves a good deal of interaction between the two. We will have occasion to make the same point again in the next, and final, chapter.

Value and Choice

chapter 8

The executive system chooses among courses of action on the basis of values, some of which pertain to the enhancement of its own functioning.

Plans for information retrieval enable us to generate alternative possibilities for action. These possibilities must then be evaluated and a choice made among them. Here we must be concerned with value.

Some environmental events are necessary for the continued existence of a system, and others threaten its continued existence. An adaptive system will tend to seek the former and avoid the latter. Those that it seeks are said to be positively valued, and those that it avoids are said to be negatively valued.

Whereas the representational system seems to be basically concerned with knowledge of covariation within the environment, the executive system seems to be basically concerned with knowledge of covariation between the environment and the system, with knowledge of the impact of the environment on the system and of the system on the environment. It is in the executive system that value seems to be represented, and it is here also that choice seems to take place, as values guide responses toward the beneficial and away from the harmful.

Value

A distinction can be made between events that are important for the individual system, itself, and events that are important for supraindividual systems of which it is a part. The needs for things like food, water, and air obviously relate to the first category, and the needs for sex and affiliation obviously relate to the second. Sex is important for the continuation of the species, and affiliation, which involves such feelings as love, loyalty, and trust (Harlow, 1958) is important for the maintenance of such supraindividual systems as the family, the tribe, and the nation. We shall be concerned here primarily with motivation directed toward events that are important for the individual system.

Even more specifically than this, we shall be concerned with cognitive motives. Within those motives that pertain to the individual, we may distinguish between those that relate to the body and those that relate to the mind, between such motives as hunger and thirst, on the one hand, and curiosity, on the other. In the language of computer science, we might say that the distinction is between motives that are concerned with maintaining the hardware and those that are concerned with maintaining the software, or programming. The latter, the cognitive motives, are the ones most directly relevant to our concern with knowing, learning, and thinking. They would seem to be found only in Level II and Level III systems.

The noncognitive motives seem to have a fairly precise anatomical locus. The hypothalamus contains receptors sensitive to such internal conditions as blood sugar level, salt concentration, and temperature. Stimulation of these receptors seems to have two effects. It activates automatic responses, such as the release of bodily stores of a needed substance (Olds, 1958). And it seems also to activate both innate consummatory responses, such as eating and drinking (Teitelbaum, 1967), and learned responses, such as bar pressing and maze running, which precede these consummatory responses and are presumably maintained by their reinforcing action (Glickman & Schiff, 1967; Olds, 1958). Such a reinforcing action seems to be indicated by the effects of electrical stimulation of the hypothalamus and related areas, stimulation at certain points acting like a reward and stimulation at others acting like a punishment (Olds & Olds, 1965). However, it should be noted that these effects are not free from other interpretations (Ball & Adams, 1965). Hypothalamic "reinforcement" is unlike reinforcement, in the usual sense, in that its effects extinguish very rapidly, and yet it is like it in that human subjects report hypothalamic stimulation to be satisfying, relaxing, or joyful (Heath & Mickle, 1960).

The cognitive motives have not been located anatomically with any certainty, but it is to be presumed that they are based on organization in the cortex or closely related structures, since such cognitive motives as curiosity seem to increase, across species, with increasing cortical development.

Conflict Optimization

The cognitive motives seem to be understandable in terms of tendencies to seek or avoid conflict, more specifically, to optimize conflict. The preference for an intermediate level of conflict is, in ordinary language, a preference for being interested—as opposed to being bored, on the one hand, and confused, on the other. Conflict has been defined by Berlyne (1965) as the product of importance and uncertainty:

$$\text{Conflict} = \text{Importance} \times \text{Uncertainty}.$$

Importance has to do with the difference in value between the anticipated consequences of an adaptive response and those of a maladaptive response. Thus, a choice between two paths might not produce much conflict in a person going for a walk, yet produce a great deal of conflict in a person trying to get out of a burning forest. Importance is higher in the second case, because the difference between one response and the other might be a matter of life or death. Similarly, importance is generally higher in a national election than in a school election.

It should be understood that the responses in question may be conceptual, as well as overt. Simply noticing that a path leads to a river or a lake prepares a person to make use of that path on a later occasion. And deciding that one candidate is better than the others prepares a person to work and vote for that candidate when the time comes. Conflict motivation refers, not just to conflict among overt responses, but also to conflict among symbolic responses.

Uncertainty is a measure of the extent to which a person is unsure of which response to make. Uncertainty increases as a function of two factors. One is the number of responses that are considered. Thus, uncertainty is greater if there are four paths than if there are two, and uncertainty is greater if there are four candidates than if there are two.

Uncertainty also increases with the degree to which the responses are equal in strength. Thus, uncertainty about two paths would be greater if they were entirely unfamiliar and nothing was known about either than if one was known to lead in the general direction of a lake and the other was known to lead away from the lake. And uncertainty about two candidates would be greater if they were closely matched than if one were clearly superior to the other.

These two aspects of uncertainty, number of alternative responses and equality of strength of alternative responses, are the same factors that, earlier, we saw to be important in determining the time required for the associative selection of responses by the subordinate executive system. Both are represented in the mathematical measure of information (Attneave, 1959; Garner, 1962; Shannon & Weaver, 1949), which is linearly related to reaction time and presumed to be linearly related to conflict motivation.

Importance seems to be a matter of activation or arousal, and uncertainty seems to be a matter of direction. The first seems to be emotional and the second motivational, as a poet once put it, "the sails and rudder of the ship of the soul." Schacter and Singer (1962) seem to have separated emotion and motivation experimentally. They manipulated emotion by injecting adrenaline in some subjects and a neutral control solution in others; and they manipulated motivation by varying the stimulus conditions, having a stooge, ostensibly injected with the same drug, act euphoric in one condition and angry in the other. The subjects injected with adrenaline were more affected than the control subjects, but in different directions, those with the euphoric stooge laughing more with or at him and those with the angry stooge expressing more anger with or toward him.

The notion of conflict optimization states that we seek an intermediate level of conflict. If conflict were low, say if a good candidate for school president were running against someone you knew could not handle the job, so that both importance and uncertainty were low, you would have little tendency to seek out information about the election. If conflict were moderate, say if two closely matched candidates who convincingly said quite different things about national goals were running for President of the United States, you would be likely to follow the election closely, reading the election articles in the newspaper before others, fore-going other activities to watch the candidates debate on television, and bringing the topic up in conversation. If conflict were quite high, say if you were one of the candidates, yourself, or a candidate's spouse, you might find the situation very trying, preferring other activities when there was a moment and looking forward to the day when the whole thing would be over.

Low Conflict. Let us first consider how we seek conflict and then consider how we reduce it. The tendency to seek conflict, to seek uncertainty about things of importance, has been called by White (1959) competency motivation. It is a yearning for adventure and challenge. It seems that our brain is designed to function, not to be idle, and is disrupted when it has nothing to work on. The concept of ego involvement is relevant here. People do not become ego involved in tasks that are very easy; they are not interested in performing such tasks, and performing them successfully gives them no feeling of success or accomplishment (Hoppe, 1930). A motive to seek situations that require a moderate rate of information processing would certainly seem adaptive, since it would keep the organism learning and thinking about its environment.

One way to increase conflict and relieve boredom is to increase importance. This is undoubtedly one reason why people bet: *Let's put a little money on it to make it more interesting.* Betting affects importance, but it does not affect the probabilities. Seeking thrills, directly or vicariously, seems also to fall in this category. Thus, the high-wire act is more exciting than the low-wire act, and is still more exciting if there is no net.

Another, more interesting way to increase conflict and relieve boredom is to increase uncertainty. Thus, a monkey that has been kept in an empty compartment will learn responses that open a window so he can look out (Butler, 1953, 1954). Though he will work to look into an empty room, he will work harder to look out at an electric train running around a track, and still harder to look out at other monkeys. Moreover, the longer he is kept in the compartment, the harder he will work to look out of it.

A related effect is observed under the more extreme conditions of sensory deprivation (Bexton, Heron, & Scott, 1954; Heron, 1957). A person who is put in a dark, soundproof room and immersed in body temperature water finds the situation quite uncomfortable, and many subjects find it difficult to remain in such a situation for more than an hour or so. Subjects in these experiments often do such things as wiggling their fingers to provide stimulation, or they may hallucinate. Similarly, Antrobus, Singer, Goldstein, and Fort-gang (1970) have obtained suggestive evidence that daydreaming occurs in response to low levels of task complexity.

Moderate Conflict. Once in a situation that induces conflict in the intermediate range, we think. Once we have "food for thought," we "consume" it (Flavell, 1963). We "stop and think" until we have obtained enough information to reduce uncertainty to the point where an appropriate response is clearly indicated (Berlyne, 1965). Conflict motivation keeps pressure on us until we are prepared to respond. This would seem adaptive; for, in nature, not to respond quickly is often not to survive.

While a variety of stimuli will suffice to awaken conflict and relieve boredom, only quite specific stimuli can reduce it and satisfy our curiosity. Whereas almost any magazine in a waiting room will serve to relieve boredom, there is often only a single book in the entire library that will provide the information required to reduce uncertainty about a particular question. To reduce uncertainty, stimuli must be informative with respect to the alternatives in question. Only particular stimuli or ideas can relieve conflict in the student of physics torn between the notion of light as a wave and light as a particle; in the theologian struggling with the notion that there is an all-good, all-powerful God and the notion that there is evil in the world; or in the youth simply wondering whether "absence makes the heart grow fonder" or "out of sight is out of mind."

People are more interested in acquiring additional information about unfamiliar animals than about familiar animals (Berlyne, 1954). And students are more interested in learning the name of the author of a book, the less certainty there seems to be among teachers as to who actually wrote it (Berlyne, 1962). Moreover, this is true both when uncertainty is increased by increasing the number of authors to whom teachers are supposed to have attributed the book and when uncertainty is increased by making the teachers' votes more evenly divided among the authors they have supposedly suggested (Berlyne, 1962). Finally, the discovery methods of education (Bruner, 1960; Covington & Crutchfield, 1965; Suchman, 1961; Smedslund, 1961a; Worthen, 1968) make use of conflict motivation, presenting the student with a problem to which the material is relevant and asking him to guess at the answer before presenting the material. Discovery methods seem to generate more interest on the student's part and to result in longer retention and better transfer.

High Conflict. It is important to note that we seek only moderate levels of conflict. High levels of conflict elicit not thought but withdrawal. For example, Hoppe (1930) found that subjects do not get ego involved in tasks that are very difficult; they are not interested in performing such tasks, and performing them unsuccessfully gives them no feeling of failure. As James (1890) wrote,

> I, who for the time have staked my all on being a Psychologist, am mortified if others know much more psychology than I. But I am content to wallow in the grossest ignorance of Greek [p. 310].

Apparently, where uncertainty is high, conflict can often be avoided by decreasing importance, by not becoming involved.

Where this option is not open to us, we seek other ways to reduce conflict. Thus, Allport and Postman (1945) found that rumors in World War II increased as a function of both the importance of the topic and the degree of uncertainty that surrounded it. Because the rumors reduced conflict, they were told, listened to, and retold with great interest, even though their accuracy was often questionable. Also, during times of threat, we tend to regard people about whose loyalty we are not absolutely certain as enemies, for it makes us uncomfortable to have someone around who arouses any feelings of uncertainty about matters of importance. Thus, Americans of Japanese descent were put in "relocation centers" during World War II, and a prominent United Nations negotiator once complained that, whenever he was trying to settle a dispute, each side tended to see him as favoring the other. We shall consider a variety of techniques for avoiding or reducing high conflict in a later section.

A particularly interesting response to high conflict is described by Kozielecki (1961). He told subjects in a concept-learning experiment that the information they were given about the correctness of their classifications would be false a certain proportion of the time. The way they responded was to regard information that confirmed their current hypothesis as true and information that disconfirmed it as false. As a consequence, data could increase their confidence in their current belief but not decrease it.

Our responses to low, moderate, and high levels of uncertainty can be seen in the comings and goings of fashions (see McClelland, Atkinson, Clark, & Lowell 1953). If a person listens repeatedly to a novel melody line, he at first finds it unpleasant because it is too discrepant from anything he is used to, too unpredictable, too productive of conflict. As he continues to listen to it, however, he begins to find it pleasant. With further exposure, it becomes unpleasant again, but this time because it is boring, rather than confusing (Skaife, 1967). One reason why styles are so short lived in modern times is undoubtedly that exposure is so concentrated by the mass media. Fads often come back, but only after sufficient time has passed to render them, once again, a change from what we have become accustomed to.

The adaptive significance of the preference for moderate uncertainty would seem to be that it has the effect of stimulating growth at the edges of knowledge. We engage situations that are slightly discrepant from what we are used to in order to keep life interesting. Then we learn about those situations, reduce conflict, and are ready to move on again in a never-ending quest for knowledge and mastery. As Tennyson (1906) had Ulysses say,

> Yet all experience is an arch where thro'
> Gleams that untravell'd world, whose margin fades
> Forever and forever when I move.

Individual Differences in Optimal Level of Conflict

There are important individual differences in what constitutes an optimal level of uncertainty. While Ulysses might wish "to sail beyond the baths of all the Western stars until I die," others of us are content simply to improve our bowling scores. We differ in adventuresomeness. In general, creative people seem to prefer a high level of uncertainty, and authoritarian people seem to prefer a low level of uncertainty.

The Creative Personality. Creative people prefer more complex, asymmetric designs (Barron, 1955; MacKinnon, 1962; see Figure 128). In making mosaic designs, they produce greater complexity and asymmetry and use more colors. While they appear to be, on a number of measures, more stable than noncreatives, and the men appear quite masculine, creatives nevertheless tend to score higher than noncreatives on all the abnormal scales of the MMPI, and the men score higher on the femininity scale. One possible resolution of this seeming paradox is that these people are better able to accept the complexity that is in all of us, that they do not need to deny aspects of their personality that conflict with their dominant self-image (MacKinnon, 1962). They seem comfortable with both external and internal complexity. Finally, creatives differ considerably from noncreatives in their liking for abstract thinking (Taylor & Barron, 1963) and in their greater interest in the

These drawings were preferred
by creative individuals

These drawings were preferred by
randomly chosen individuals

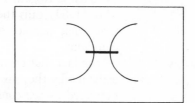

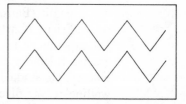

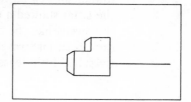

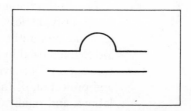

FIGURE 128. *Drawings preferred by creative and randomly chosen individuals.* [*Reproduced by special permission from* The Welsh Figure Preference Test *by George S. Welsh, Ph.D. Copyright 1949. Published by Consulting Psychologists Press, Inc.*]

significance of facts than in the facts themselves (MacKinnon, 1962a,b). Since interpretations of facts seem less certain than the facts they interpret, this could be, in part at least, another reflection of a general preference for uncertainty, a taste for conceptual adventure.

Earlier, we saw that the analogue nature of the representational system and its extralogical organization seem to be essential to creative thought, and here we find that creative individuals seem to be those who are sufficiently comfortable with complexity to be at home thinking in either predominately representational or predominately executive modes (Hanfman & Kasanin, 1937, 1942; Wallach & Kogan, 1965). They are not frightened by what Rollo May (1969) calls the demoniac, that primitive wellspring of creativity that peoples our dreams and the margins of our waking conscious.

The fact that creatives have a high sense of efficacy may help to explain why they are comfortable with high conflict. Creatives are described as self-confident (Wallach & Kogan, 1965), as having good opinions of themselves (MacKinnon, 1962a,b), as having high ego strength (Barron, 1965; Taylor & Barron, 1963), and as being self-sufficient (Cattell & Drevdahl, 1955; Taylor & Barron, 1963). An experiment by Guthrie (1966) suggests that people have a greater tolerance for conflict where they have a high sense of efficacy. He studied two classes of highly aroused subjects, people waiting to sky dive and people waiting to undergo surgery. The former showed an increased sensitivity to perceptual detail, while the latter showed a decreased sensitivity to perceptual detail. The sky divers, like the creatives, presumably had a high sense of efficacy; their fate was in their own hands. The patients, like noncreatives, had little sense of efficacy; their fate was in the hands of the surgeon.

The Authoritarian Personality. With regard to preferred level of uncertainty, at least, creative personalities seem to represent one extreme, and authoritarian personalities, the other. Authoritarians are characterized by concern with authority relationships, stress on conventional behavior, denial of one's own "immoral" impulses and projection of them onto others, depersonalization of social relations, and rigidity of thought processes (Adorno, Frenkel-Brunswik, Levinson, & Sanford, 1950; Brown, 1965). Of particular concern to us is their rigidity of thought processes and preference for low levels of uncertainty.

But let us start back a way. The dynamics of authoritarianism are thought to be set in motion when the authoritarian is punished arbitrarily and severely by his parents for his "faults" and also for being critical of any of theirs (Adorno *et al.*, 1950). The arbitrariness and the severity of the punishment seem to have somewhat different, though mutually enhancing, effects.

The arbitrariness of the punishment is a matter of emphasizing moralistic rules to which the child must simply submit, rather than principles that are explained to him and that he can understand. A consequence of arbitrary discipline is that the child learns that he cannot rely on internal guides to behavior, his own feelings and judgment, but must rely on the external structure of clear perceptions, dictates of authority figures, group opinions, and rules. This is presumably the origin of the preference for low levels of uncertainty. Because internal uncertainty is so high, external uncertainty must be especially low to yield an optimal level of total uncertainty (see Garner, 1962, p. 344).

A consequence of severe punishment is that the child tends to become anxious when he is aware of any of his own or his parents' faults; later, he comes to repress such awareness and to idealize both himself and his parents (Brown, 1965). Though intense negative feelings, particularly aggressive impulses, still occur in response to critical stimuli, the authoritarian can no longer recognize these in himself, for he has learned to avoid these anxiety-provoking cognitions. Instead, he sees the behavior of others as being responsible for arousing these feelings in him. *You can't play touch football when everyone else is playing tackle. One simply has to concern himself with the overemphasis on sex these days.* He sees his behavior as but the response of a decent person to an unpleasant situation.

This is what Freud called projection, and the mechanism is presumably much like that which led Schacter and Singer's (1962) normal subjects to perceive the effects of adrenaline as being effects of the context. The difference is that, whereas it was the experimenter who kept Schacter and Singer's subjects ignorant of the real cause of their feelings, it is repression that keeps authoritarians ignorant of the real causes of their feelings.

Adorno *et al.* (1950) found that white Anglo-Saxon Protestants who hate Jews are also likely to hate blacks, Russians, and other out-groups, a fact which suggests that the reason for the hatred has more to do with the personality of the hater than with any qualities of the targets of his hatred. Hartley (1946) even found that such people tend to dislike "Wallonians," "Danerians," and other fictitious groups. Sears (1936) found that some fraternity members who were rated extremely high on negative traits, such as stinginess, tended to rate themselves low on these traits and to rate others high on them. As Alexander Pope put it,

> *All is infected that the infected spy,*
> *As all is yellow to the jaundiced eye.*

The preference for low uncertainty shows up in a number of ways. First, authoritarians tend to have opinions about most things of concern to them. Frequency of "don't know" replies correlates negatively with dogmatism, as does delay in arriving at a decision (Long & Ziller, 1965). In the words of the poet, *It ain't the things we don't know that hurts us so; it's the things we know that ain't so.* Second, the opinions expressed by authoritarians tend to be simple. They tend to have dichotomous conceptualizations of sex roles, kinds of people, and values, and they are unlikely to see both positive and negative aspects of themselves or their parents or to express both love and hatred for the same person (Frenkel-Brunswik, 1954). This contrasts sharply with the MMPI data on creatives. Third, they are reluctant to change their opinions on the basis of perceptual data. This is what is meant by rigidity of thought processes. Kaplan and Singer (1963) found a correlation of −.61 between dogmatism and sensory acuity, and Klein, Gardner, and Schlesinger (1962) found that intolerant subjects less readily reverse figure and ground in ambiguous figures, less readily experience distortion when wearing distorting lenses, and less readily respond when asked to say what a Rorschach inkblot looks like. An experiment by Frenkel-Brunswik (1949) provides a particularly nice illustration of rigidity of thought processes in authoritarians. A picture of a dog is gradually changed into a picture of a cat, and the subject is asked to identify it at several steps along the way. All subjects start off saying that it is a dog, of course, and all subjects end up saying that it is a cat, but the authoritarians persist longer in calling it a dog.

In closing this discussion, let us consider an experiment by Atkinson and Litwin (1960) that would seem to be related to authoritarianism. Atkinson and Litwin examined motivation to achieve success (McClelland's achievement motivation) and motivation to avoid failure as predictors of preferred throwing distance in a ring-toss game. While most subjects preferred to throw from an intermediate distance, at which the subjective probability of success was about .50, those low in motivation to achieve success and high in motivation to avoid failure showed a pronounced tendency to throw from positions either nearer or farther from the target, that is, from positions where the probability of success was closer to 1.00 or 0. Because the point where the subjective probabilities are .50 is the point of greatest uncertainty, and hence the point of greatest conflict, it appears that persons more motivated to avoid failure than to achieve success prefer lower levels of conflict, which is also true of authoritarians. When they are close, they cannot miss, and when they are far, they can hardly be expected to make it, so a miss is not really a failure.

The importance of fear of failure, in the present case, and the fact that severe punishment is presumed to have been prevalent in the early life of authoritarians, suggests that this link is more than a superficial one. Another finding that suggests that punishment and fear of failure are the important causal factors is Raphelson's (1957) finding that motivation to achieve success correlates −.43 with both verbal and galvanic skin response measures of anxiety.

We have touched upon a number of values, both cognitive and noncognitive. Any of these is likely to get us into situations where we have to make choices, either to choose to satisfy one value rather than another or to choose among different means for satisfying the same value.

Choice

The real world imposes constraints on the satisfactions we can achieve and on the means that will enable us to achieve them. In our fantasy, we can have many lovers, but in the real world we ordinarily have just one mate. In our fantasy, we can accomplish all things, but in the real world, we ordinarily have just one vocation. Reality forces us to choose. Choice are of two types: choices among means and choices among ends.

Choice among Means

When we choose between two paths to a goal, we do so on the basis of what we know about the paths. Thus, in choice, knowing is translated into doing in order to achieve certain ends. The difference between knowing and doing is an important one, at least in higher organisms, where the coupling between the two is loose and motivational considerations determine whether knowledge will be expressed in action.

The distinction between knowing and doing appears in the study of perception as the distinction between perception and response. It is important in even so simple a task as judging whether a weak stimulus was or was not present, for the absolute threshold depends not only on stimulus intensity but also on the costs of saying the stimulus is present when it is not and of saying it is not present when it is (Swets, 1961). For example, a person is more likely to perceive slight noises in the woods if he is told there are bears about than if he is told there are rabbits about. This is quite likely what accounts for the negative correlation between dogmatism and acuity that we noted earlier (Kaplan & Singer, 1963). Dogmatic subjects might be as able to perceive differences as anyone else but, because they find change uncomfortable, be unwilling to take them into account.

The distinction between perception and response is of great importance in perceptual defense studies; in fact, many people (Zajonc, 1962) believe that what has been called perceptual defense is really just response suppression. The basic finding (McGinnies, 1949) is that emotionally negative stimuli, such as swear words, have to be flashed more often than emotionally neutral stimuli in order to be reported. The perceptual defense interpretation is that emotionally negative stimuli are less likely to be seen. The response suppression interpretation is that they are less likely to be reported, that the subject sees the negative stimuli as well as the neutral ones but wants to make very sure before guessing such words, because to guess such words erroneously would be quite embarrassing. Some very sophisticated attempts have been made to control response factors in perceptual defense experiments (Bootzin & Natsoulas, 1965; MacKinnon & Dukes, 1964). Although there seems to be a genuine perceptual component in the perceptual defense effect, as we saw earlier, it is clear that response factors account for the greater part of the effect.

The distinction between knowing and doing appears also in the study of learning, as the distinction between learning and performance. An animal that has learned the path through a maze to the goal box will not take that path unless it is hungry and expects food in the goal box (Thistlethwaite, 1951; Tolman, 1932). More recently, this analysis has been extended to the study of human memory (Murdock, 1965), and it has been argued (Waugh & Norman, 1965), for example, that the superiority of recognition over recall may, in some situations, at least, be a difference in doing rather than in knowing, that is, that the difference may be attributable to motivational factors. The same analysis that has been applied to perceptual defense (Freud's "primary repression") has also been applied to repression (Freud's "secondary repression") with similar results, at least for laboratory studies (MacKinnon & Dukes, 1964): Response factors are important, and perhaps all-important, in laboratory studies of repression.

The notion that both perceptual defense and repression effects are both essentially response effects is consistent with the notion that it is the executive system that tends to move toward the pleasant and away from the unpleasant. The representational system seems to take value into account only in the sense of degree, drawing in the important features of the world with greater emphasis (Tolman, 1932; Muenzinger, 1935). The executive system, on the other hand, distinguishes between positive and negative value. The tendency to seek positive percepts or images and to avoid negative ones is what Freud called *primary process thinking*. It is what seems to be involved in fantasy and in perceptual defense and repression. The tendency to defer gratification and to employ indirect means to obtain the positive objects, themselves, or to avoid the negative objects, themselves, is what Freud called *secondary process thinking*. It is interesting to note that there seems to be a tendency, in primary process thinking, for the executive system to respond toward representations of objects in much the same way that it responds toward the objects themselves (Osgood, 1953), to seek thoughts of positively valued things and to avoid thoughts of negatively valued things. This would seem to be a not altogether adaptive outgrowth of an essentially adaptive design feature. While it is adaptive to take steps to avoid negative things, it is not adaptive to avoid thoughts of negative things—for example, the possibility of a nuclear war—and "stick one's head in the sand." It is only in the case of secondary process thinking that reality constraints are taken into account in moving toward the pleasant and away from the unpleasant, and it is only here that one must choose among means.

The way in which values are combined with knowledge to yield a decision is fairly well represented by the maximization of expected utility model (Edwards, Lindman, & Phillips, 1965), though with some modifications. Let us first distinguish between riskless and risky choice.

If you are given a choice between a $1 bill and a $10 bill, that is riskless choice. If you choose the $10 bill, you will get the $10 bill for sure. No risk is involved. And, of course, the same is true if you choose the $1 bill. This is not a very interesting situation, because it is easy to predict what people will do. If you are given a choice between betting on a particular face of a die and getting $10 if that face comes up or betting against a particular face and getting $2 if that face does not come up, that is a risky choice. If you choose to bet on a particular face, you may get the $10 or you may get nothing, depending, of course, on whether or not that face comes up. The choice to bet against a particular face is also risky, though the risk is not as great.

Risky choice is more interesting, partly because it is more difficult to predict how a person will choose, partly because important real-life decisions (in a world in which there are usually more relevant variables than we are able to take into account) seem to be risky decisions, and partly because risky choice can be considered to be the more general case, with riskless choice being simply a special case where the probabilities are 0 and 1.00.

To illustrate the maximization of expected utility model for risky choice, let us consider a decision that clearly involves just a single basis of value, an investment decision. Here, the basis of

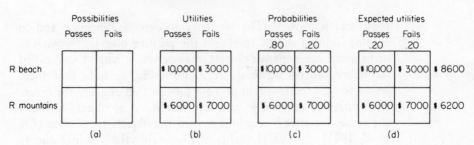

FIGURE 129.   *Choice among means to the same end, under conditions of uncertainty.*

value is money. Let us say that the choice is between buying land on the beach and buying land in the mountains. And let us say that which will be the better choice depends on some circumstances that are not entirely predictable: whether or not a bill to preserve the shoreline ecology passes. These possibilities can be represented in the cross-classification shown in Figure 129a, called a decision matrix.

Thus, there are four possibilities. We could buy land on the beach, and the bill could pass. We could buy land on the beach, and the bill could fail. We could buy land in the mountains, and the bill could pass. And we could buy land in the mountains, and the bill could fail.

Before we can make a decision, we must evaluate these possibilities. We must attach a value, or what in this context is usually called a utility, to each of these possible outcomes. This has been done in Figure 129b, in terms of the number of dollars we would expect to realize from our investment over a 10-year period. The utilities are thus, respectively, $10,000; $3000; $6000; and $7000.

We need one other item of information, however, before we will be ready to make our decision. We need to know what the chances are that the bill will pass. Thus, in addition to utilities, we need probabilities. Let us assume that the probability that the bill will pass is .80 and the probability that it will fail is .20, as shown in Figure 129c. The probabilities in a decision matrix must sum to 1.00, as they do here. These probabilities represent the residual uncertainty that remains after we have obtained as much information as we can about the situation. If we had no information, the probabilities would each be .50, the highest level of uncertainty possible with two alternatives. If we had perfect information, the probabilities would be 1.00 and 0, or 0 and 1.00, and the situation would be reduced to one of riskless choice.

But we do not have perfect information, and yet we must proceed. To make a decision rationally, we should compute the average, or expected, utility for each response and then choose the response with the highest expected utility (see Figure 129d). This is called maximizing expected utility. It would be simpler just to determine the utility of each response, but we cannot do that because it will be one value if one state of the world obtains (the bill passes) and another value of the other state of the world obtains (the bill fails). So we must compute what the average would be over all possible states. This is done as follows:

$$EU_1 = .80(\$10,000) + .20(\$3000)$$
$$= \$8000 + \$600$$
$$= \$8600.$$
$$EU_2 = .80(\$6000) + .20(\$7000)$$
$$= \$4800 + \$1400$$
$$= \$6200.$$

In order to maximize expected utility, then, we choose Response 1 (R_1), because its expected utility, $8600, is higher than that of Response 2 (R_2), $6200.

To see that this is like computing an average, imagine that this decision has to be made on 100 occasions. On 80 of these, we expect, the bill will be passed, and on 20 it will not. Thus, R_1, to consider just this example, will have a utility of $10,000 on 80 occasions and a utility of $6000 on 20 occasions. To take an average, we add up all the values and divide by the number of values, in this case, 100. This is represented in the following equation:

$$\text{average} = \frac{(80 \times \$10,000) + (20 \times \$6000)}{100}.$$

But this is equal to the following equation:

$$\text{average} = \left[\frac{80}{100} \times \$10,000\right] + \left[\frac{20}{100} \times \$6000\right].$$

And this, of course, equals the equation we used above:

$$\text{average} = .80(\$10,000) + .20(\$6000).$$

The general form of the equation for expected utility is:

$$EU = p_1u_1 + p_2u_2 + p_3u_3 + \cdots + p_ku_k.$$

With this equation, we can compute the expected utility for each of any number of alternative responses, taking into consideration any number of possible states of the world. The only restriction is that the probabilities for the various states of the world sum to 1.00.

This model turns out to be a good first step toward describing human decision making. This is not to say that people actually perform such calculations when they are deciding whether to carry an umbrella or whether to go to college, but that they do something which has much the same results. When overworked by repetitive decisions, subjects often adopt a unidimensional strategy, such as choosing the highest probability of winning or minimizing the maximum loss, but under good conditions they seem to take expected utility into account (Slovic, Lichtenstein, & Edwards, 1965).

The maximization of expected utility model needs to be modified in some respects, however, and supplemented in others. We need to say something more about the alternatives, the utilities, the probabilities, and also the notion that it is the mean, or expected, utility that is maximized.

Two things need to be said about alternatives. One is that we often neglect to consider many response alternatives because they do not occur to us. Often, the real difficulty is not in selecting the best among those alternatives that occur to us, but in conceiving of alternatives. This is a problem in reproductive or productive information retrieval.

The other is that we often leave many alternatives unexamined, because we have already come up with a satisfactory alternative and we do not consider it worthwhile to continue evaluating additional alternatives in the hope of finding a better one (Simon, 1957). This is called satisficing, rather than maximizing. When we choose a doctor, house, or car, we do not evaluate all the available doctors, houses, or cars, but stop when we have found one that is satisfactory.

One important thing needs to be said about utility, or subjective value, and that is how it is related to objective value. Winning $100 is, apparently, not as good as losing $100 is bad. This is easy to demonstrate to yourself by considering whether you would be willing to bet $100 on the toss of a coin. Although the expected objective value of such a bet would be $.50(\$100) + .50(-\$100) = \$0$, most people are not indifferent to such a bet; it actually has a negative subjective value, or utility, for them.

The relationship between utility and objective value is thought to be something like that represented in Figure 130 (Coombs, Dawes, & Tversky, 1970). From this, we can see that the utility of $+\$100$ is $\sqrt{100} = 10$ units, and the utility of $-\$100$ is $-(100^2) = -10,000$ units. The expected utility, then, of wagering $100 on the toss of a coin is $.50(+10) + .50(-10,000) = -4995$ units.

This may explain why people buy insurance. In terms of ex-

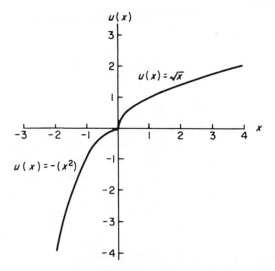

FIGURE 130. *A suggested relationship between subjective utility* $(u(x))$ *and objective value* (x). *[Taken, with permission, from C. H. Coombs, R. M. Dawes, and A. Tversky,* Mathematical psychology *(Englewood Cliffs, N.J.: Prentice-Hall, 1970), p. 120.]*

pected value, it does not make any sense to buy insurance. If it did, insurance companies would quickly go out of business. For example, it costs about $25 to insure a house for $20,000 for one year, and the probability that the house will burn down in that year is much less than 1/1000. If we buy insurance, we lose $25 per year, no matter what happens. If we do not buy insurance, the expected objective value is less than .001(−$20,000) + .999($0), or less than −$20 per year. Objectively, we should not buy insurance. If, instead, we use the utilities from Figure 124, the expected utilities are $-(25^2) = -625$ units if we buy insurance and $.001 \times -(20{,}000^2) + .99 \times -(0) = -400{,}000$ units if we do not. Subjectively, we must buy insurance. Thus, the reason people buy insurance may be that negative utilities increase at a faster rate than negative objective values.

With regard to the matter of probabilities, subjective probabilities differ from objective probabilities in at least two significant ways.

One, we tend to underestimate high probabilities and to overestimate low probabilities (Davidson, Suppes, & Siegel, 1957). It seems that we have too little confidence in our knowledge. This is particularly true when we must combine information obtained on different occasions in arriving at our estimate (Edwards, Lindman, & Phillips, 1965).

Two, when we take previous occurrences of an event into account, we tend to be subject to the "gambler's fallacy." After a long run of heads, the probability of getting heads on the next toss is still .50, but we tend to believe otherwise. We tend to believe that it is less, as though the tosses were not truly unrelated events. In general, however, we tend to estimate probabilities fairly well (Peterson & Beach, 1967).

The last piece of information we wish to add to the maximization of expected utility model has to do with utility variance. Utility variance, as well as the mean, or expected, utility, is of importance. Many people prefer to bet a dollar, rather than a penny, on the toss of a coin. This cannot be predicted on the basis of expected value, which is zero in both cases, or on the basis of expected utility, which is greater in the former case. It appears that, in addition to the noncognitive values that expected utility represents, the cognitive value of optimal level of conflict is also important. It is more interesting to bet a dollar than a penny. This is presumably at least one reason why people gamble. There seems to be no reason to doubt, however, that this value is weighed along with others according to an averaging model of the kind we have been considering.

We would like to conclude this section by considering a special, but important, case of choice among alternative means to the same end, the case where the alternatives are simply conceptual and the end is amount of information transmitted. Consider the problem of grading sheets of plywood. Let us say that you are given a large number of sheets of plywood and asked to classify them as "good," "average," or "poor."

If you are buying, you will tend to overuse the lower categories, because you want to get the most for your money, and, if you are selling, you will tend to overuse the higher categories, because you want to get a good price for your merchandise. On the other hand, if you are neither buying nor selling but simply sorting the sheets of plywood for your own use, so that you will be able to find the kind you want on some later occasion, you will tend to use all categories equally. Classifying all the sheets as "good," or classifying them all as "poor," would not do you any good at all. Parducci (1963, 1965) has shown, under conditions where information transmission is the important goal, that we tend (*a*) to adjust the range of our response categories to the range of stimulus categories and (*b*) to put the same number of stimuli in each category.

This range–frequency adjustment of response categories results in context effects. Consider five grades of lumber, **A, B, C, D,** and **F.** A person who has purchased grades **A, B,** and **C** will tend to call grade **B** "average," whereas a person who has purchased grades **B, C,** and **D** (or **A, B, C,** and **F**) will tend to call grade **C** "average." This is the second time we have encountered context effects. The first was in the discussion of adaptation level.

Adaptation level and the range–frequency adjustment of response categories would seem to be based on quite different mechanisms, one representational and the other executive. Adaptation level seems to affect the representation of the stimuli, themselves, and the range–frequency adjustment seems to affect the assignment of these stimuli to response categories. We can suggest a number of differences between these two mechanisms.

First, while adaptation level affects the appearance of things, range–frequency adjustment seems to operate even where the appearance of things is not altered, as in the judgment of numbers in the context of different distributions (Parducci, Calfee, Marshall, & Davidson, 1960). Second, while adaptation level may be different for the two sides of the body, one would expect range–frequency adjustment to be central. For example, one would expect inclusion of lumber grade **F** in the range of stimuli to have the same effect on the judgment of **A**, **B**, and **C**, even though **A**, **B**, and **C** were viewed with one eye and **F** with the other. And, third, while adaptation level does not seem to be affected by instructions, it would seem that the range–frequency adjustment would be.

So much for choice among means to the same end. Choice among incompatible ends seems to be a different matter altogether.

Choice among Ends

Choice among ends does not seem to have received as much attention in the literature, and so, most regrettably, we shall have less to say about it. The essential difference seems to be that choice among means is a unidimensional matter, and choice among ends, a multidimensional one. In the first case, response alternatives are evaluated primarily on the basis of their relative positions, in terms of expected utility, along a single continuum. In choosing among ends, however, the process is more complex, as the following description of a person trying to decide whether to buy a cast iron stove or a sheet metal stove to heat his summer cabin in Maine should make clear (DeRivera, 1968).

> Initially, the person decided on a cast iron stove because it looked more handsome and rugged, would hold the heat longer, and was not as hazardous as the sheet metal stove. However, when he tried to purchase a cast iron stove, he found that the price of new stoves was too high (about $50.00), and that the few second hand stoves available were the wrong shape or size. Thus, budgetary and aesthetic interests blocked the action. A friend then urged him to purchase a sheet metal stove; this could be done for only $5.00. The friend argued that such a stove was not dangerous in the summertime when

it would not be crammed with wood. Furthermore, the sheet metal stove was more useful in the summer since it would rapidly take the chill off the cabin and would not retain heat into midday. In spite of all the arguments for a sheet metal stove, the person could not bring himself to buy such a stove because of its poor looks. He associated the handsome ruggedness of a cast iron stove with the coast of Maine and the character of its people. He had a strong interest in having the stove "fit with its surroundings." Finally, however, he brought himself around to also liking the sheet metal stove. He accomplished this by stressing the fact that Maine lobstermen often used sheet metal stoves in their cabins on the offshore islands. Thus, the sheet metal stove came to represent the hardy ingenuity of the Maine lobstermen and took on an "it's not handsome but it sure works" quality where the ugliness of the stove actually added to its charm. The sheet metal stove was immediately purchased. Note that by changing the meaning of the looks of the stove, the interest in a handsome stove was bypassed so that a decision could be made [p. 117].

The choice here is not between two ways to get the same stove, but between two different stoves. Moreover, these stoves differ on a number of dimensions, among them cost, aesthetic value, utility, and safety.

Such a choice has been analyzed, in terms of the Lewinian framework, as a double approach–avoidance conflict (Dollard & Miller, 1950; see Figure 131). Our purchaser tends to approach the cast-iron stove because it is handsome but also to avoid it because it is expensive. Similarly, he tends to approach the sheet metal stove because it is cheap but also to avoid it because of its poor appearance.

Such conflicts tend to produce a great deal of vacillation. The reason is apparently that the avoidance gradient is steeper than the approach gradient (Dollard & Miller, 1950; see Figure 131). What the approach gradient, by itself, says is that the closer we get to a goal, the more motivated we are to attain it. This is probably why attempts to break out of prison are most frequent shortly before release time. What the avoidance gradient, by itself, says is that the closer we get to a feared situation, the more motivated we are to avoid it. Anyone who has gone to the dentist knows that there is some truth in this.

The fact that the avoidance gradient is steeper (Brown, 1948) leads to a prediction of vacillation in such situations. When we are far from the goal, the approach gradient is higher, and we tend to be attracted toward the goal: *That is a mighty fine looking stove.* As we get closer to the goal, either in action or in thought, its negative characteristics increase in potency at a faster rate than its positive ones until the predominant tendency is to be repelled from it: *Sure is expensive, though.* This is probably the mechanism

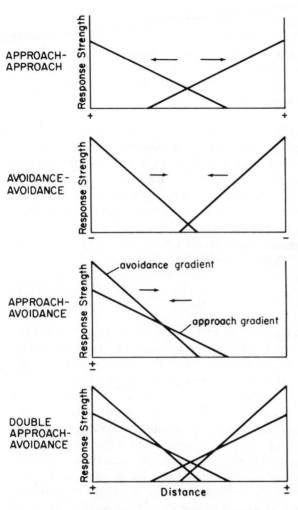

APPROACH-
APPROACH

AVOIDANCE-
AVOIDANCE

APPROACH-
AVOIDANCE

DOUBLE
APPROACH-
AVOIDANCE

FIGURE 131. *Patterns of conflict among ends. [Adapted, with
permission, from Neal E. Miller,
"Experimental studies of conflict,"* in Personality and the behavior disorders, *edited by J.
McV. Hunt. Copyright 1944.
Renewed © 1972, The Ronald
Press Company, New York.]*

that causes some couples to fight when they are together and pine
when they are apart and that causes students to look forward to
the end of the term until it is so close that the prospect of finals
looms large in their minds.

Approach–approach conflicts, on the other hand, should be resolved quickly, for the closer one gets to one of the goals, the more
inclined he should be to continue toward that goal. The only clear
case of an approach–approach conflict would seem to be a choice
among different means to the same end. Choices among different
ends would seem always to involve the double approach–avoidance pattern, because choosing one end always involves giving up
the positive qualities of the other. Dollard and Miller seem to be

correct in saying that vacillation indicates the existence of avoidance tendencies, but the existence of avoidance tendencies need not imply a negative stimulus, for they can be produced by the possibility of losing a positive one, as well. We vacillate even in choosing from a menu—indeed, it would seem that the more tantalizing the alternatives are, the longer it takes us to make up our minds.

DeRivera (1968) suggests that choosing among ends requires a reevaluation process. The purchaser brought himself around to liking the sheet metal stove well enough to buy it by emphasizing the fact that Maine lobstermen often use such stoves. He reevaluated its appearance. Such a reevaluation process would seem to be necessary in order to overcome the tendency to vacillate, by developing enough response strength for one alternative so that a choice can be made. We must often create an end that will satisfy many interests (DeRivera, 1968).

After the Choice

Once we have chosen an end that has both positive and negative qualities, a state of dissonance exists. The positive qualities are consistent with the choice, but the negative ones are not. Whereas before the choice we made unbiased attempts to reevaluate the positive and negative qualities of each alternative, now our efforts are biased; we seek to view the alternative we have chosen in as favorable a light as possible. To conflict among alternative courses of action, we respond with unbiased thought; to conflict among alternative courses of action plus responsibility for having chosen one of the alternatives, we respond with biased thought. For example, in choosing a car, we begin by evaluating the positive and negative features of each alternative in an unbiased fashion in order to make the best choice. Whatever car we choose, however, will undoubtedly have some negative features, and other cars will have some positive features. After the choice, we tend to emphasize the positive features of the car we have bought and the negative features of other cars in order to be able to live with the choice we have made. As Benjamin Franklin so succinctly put it, *Keep both eyes open before marriage and one eye closed after.*

The Ego and Dissonance

Here, we encounter an extremely important component of human intelligence: the ego. No cognitive psychology can be complete that does not have a place for the ego, for the ego is capable of applying distortions to the output of virtually every knowing mechanism we have considered to this point.

What the ego seems to be is a high-level component of the executive system. From one point of view, it seems to be an equivalence category that represents what is common to the various things a person has done. And, from another, it seems to be the apex of a hierarchically organized system of behavior dispositions, or attitudes, a system in which peripheral attitudes, that apply to rather specific situations, are justified in terms of central attitudes, that apply more broadly.

Moreover, the ego appears to be a subsystem that has distinct needs of its own. It seems to be important, in the first place, to maintain positive value in the ego. In order to be able to act effectively, it seems that we must believe, with little equivocation, that our efforts are to good ends. To be effective, we must believe that we are effective; we must have confidence in ourselves.

It also seems to be important to maintain consistency among the attitudes that constitute the ego. Identity seems to be a matter of consistency among behavior dispositions (Lecky, 1945), and the alternative seems to be role diffusion (Erikson, 1956). This seems to be captured in the current expression, "getting it all together."

In order to maintain positive value and consistency in the ego, we employ a variety of techniques, such as repression and rationalization, called defense mechanisms (Freud, 1937). We shall consider these in detail shortly, but first it will be most instructive to have a look at Bettelheim's (1943) description of ego defense and the formation of a new ego in the revealing, though harsh, light of living in a concentration camp.

During the first year or so, the typical prisoner attempted to maintain the integrity of his old ego, the organization of behavior dispositions that served him well on the outside, in the hope of returning to his former life.

> . . . If the author should be asked to sum up in one sentence what, all during the time he spent in the camp, was his main problem, he would say: to safeguard his ego in such a way that, if by any good luck he should regain liberty, he would be approximately the same person he was when deprived of liberty.
>
> He has no doubt that he was able to endure the transportation, and all that followed, because right from the beginning he became convinced that these horrible and degrading experiences somehow did not happen to "him" as a subject, but only to "him" as an object. The importance of this attitude was corroborated by many statements of other prisoners, although none would go so far as to state definitely that an attitude of this type was clearly developed already

during the time of the transportation. They couched their feelings usually in more general terms such as, "The main problem is to remain alive and unchanged," without specifying what they meant as unchanged. From additional remarks it became apparent that what should remain unchanged was individually different and roughly covered the person's general attitudes and values [p. 431].

Maintaining the integrity of the old ego was made difficult by the fact that old behaviors were severly punished and radically different behaviors reinforced, at least in the negative sense of not being punished. The initial mode of adjustment seems to have been to attempt to maintain two egos: a set of behavior dispositions and values appropriate for the camp and a set of behavior dispositions and values appropriate for the outside world. The distinction between "him" as an object and "him" as a subject thus quickly became elaborated into a distinction between "him" as a prisoner and "him" as he once was.

This separation of behavior patterns and schemes of values inside and outside of camp was so strong that it could hardly be touched on in conversation . . . [p. 432].

Prisoners who had been in the camp for on the order of three years or more (Bettelheim, himself, was not in this long) seemed finally to relinquish the old ego. Their main concern was no longer to maintain their former identity but to live as well as possible within the camp. The unreality of camp life had finally become reality to them. They accepted as their own the values of the guards and even imitated their manner and dress. Positive values appeared in connection with aspects of camp life, as though they had to convince themselves that what they were doing made sense. So nearly complete was the change (though in many respects it was never complete) that the old prisoners became apprehensive at the thought of returning to their former lives.

Bettelheim concludes by saying,

It seems that what happens in an extreme fashion to the prisoners who spend several years in the concentration camp happens in less exaggerated form to the inhabitants of the big concentration camp called greater Germany [p. 452].

We wish to suggest that Bettelheim's observations have still wider significance, that the same thing happens in less exaggerated form to all of us as we adjust to the natural and social constraints of the world at large: We develop an organization of central values and behavior dispositions, an ego, that enables us to function as effectively as we are able in the world we regard as reality, and, once established, this organization resists change.

When there is a conflict within the ego, we experience dissonance (Festinger, 1957), that is, when there is an inconsistency between an equivalence category for generating positively valued responses and a particular negatively valued response that we have
made freely and must accept responsibility for. If you believe that
it is desirable to make wise purchases, the discovery that a house
you bought is in a smog belt will tend to create a state of dissonance. Whereas, before you purchased the house, you would have
been most interested in hearing that it is in a smog belt, now
there is a tendency for you to avoid or distort such information.
The very same information that would have aroused conflict (curiosity) before now arouses conflict plus responsibility (dissonance.)

A variety of techniques for dealing with dissonance have been
identified, some of which are the ego-defense mechanisms described by Freud (1937). These techniques are generally considered to be irrational; however, the techniques, themselves, can be
employed either rationally or irrationally (Kroeber, 1963). It is the
end to which the techniques are put, the reduction of dissonance,
that is irrational. After the decision, as before, arousal of conflict
leads to efforts to reduce it. But now there is a difference. After
the decision, these efforts tend to be biased, and we tend to reduce
conflict in a way that justifies the decision and the ego values that
support it.

Techniques for dissonance reduction are thought to be learned
like any other behaviors. A technique is discovered, through trial-
and-error or imitation, to reduce dissonance and is repeated. With
continued use, the behavior becomes automatized and is eventually
carried out by the unconscious mechanisms of the subordinate
executive system. Different individuals come to rely on different
techniques because of their reinforcement histories, and these
differences contribute to differences in personality. In addition to
reinforcement history, there is an indication that intelligence may
also be a factor. As we shall see later, repression seems to require
less intelligence than does rationalization.

The techniques for dissonance reduction, or ego defense, may
be roughly divided into four categories: reducing responsibility, reducing importance, reducing uncertainty, and identification. Let
us take them up in that order.

Reducing Responsibility

Reducing responsibility is simply disowning the decision. This
seems to be a primitive mechanism, for it appears frequently in
young children, in the familiar, *Now look what you made me do!*

Perhaps this explains why people will carry out acts in obedience to authority that they would never carry out on their own responsibility, such as delivering what they believe to be dangerously intense shocks to fellow subjects (Milgram, 1963). As the Nazi Eichmann said at the Nuremberg trials, *I was only obeying orders.*

Saying that someone else was responsible is not the only way to reduce commitment; another is to invoke necessity, to say that there was really no choice. Thus, one person, asked why he did not wear colorful ties, answered that he did not own any. Going to fortune tellers for advice, throwing the "I Ching," and generating random art by various means may all be essentially techniques for avoiding responsibility for the consequences of one's actions.

Reducing Importance

Reducing importance is saying, in effect, that the choice did not really make any difference, that things would have been pretty much the same in either case. We see this in the child's, *I didn't want it, anyhow,* an extreme form of which seems to be general apathy. Apathy has been noted in prisoners in concentration camps (Bettelheim, 1943; Schein, 1956) and in persons suffering prolonged unemployment (Eisenberg & Lazarsfeld, 1938). Eisenberg and Lazarsfeld concluded that "the last stage of unemployment consists of a general narrowing of activities as well as of outlook on life. There is also a narrowing of wants and needs [p. 378]." Apathy seems to be the last of three stages in the reaction to loss: protest, depression, and apathy (Robertson, 1953).

Another way of reducing importance is intellectualization. Instead of, or in addition to, denying importance, intellectualization seems to involve an excessive concern with the uncertainty part of the Importance × Uncertainty formula, that is, with contingencies and the estimation of probabilities. This is what a psychotherapy patient does when he learns to talk about his problems without coming to grips with the feelings involved. It is also what military strategists seem to do in employing such euphemisms as "deterrent," "defoliation," "antipersonnel devices," and "enemy." It is less disturbing to think about "increasing the body count" than to think about killing mothers, fathers, and children.

Reducing Uncertainty

Whereas, before the decision, attempts to reduce uncertainty are unbiased, directed toward finding out which alternative really is the best, now they are biased in favor of strengthening the alternative chosen or of weakening competing alternatives. There are two broad techniques for accomplishing this: not thinking and biased thinking.

The techniques of not thinking include (*a*) not thinking about the dissonant information, (*b*) not believing the dissonant information, and (*c*) not thinking about the relationship between the items of information that are dissonant.

Not thinking about the dissonant information at all seems to be a commonly used technique. Most of us think only rarely about the poor, the sick, the insane, the old, or the imprisoned. The expression, *Don't confuse me with facts; my mind's made up*, is used to make light of this technique.

This technique is the closest to simple repression, and several lines of evidence suggest that it is a primitive technique. Witkin (1965) has found both repression and denial to be characteristic of less analytic minds. Also, when subjects are given a variety of tasks to perform, some of which they are able to complete in the allotted time and some of which they are not, subjects with low ego strength tend to forget the tasks they failed on, while subjects with high ego strength tend to remember these tasks well (Rosenzweig, 1952, 1962; Zeigarnik, 1927). The fact that people seem selectively to expose themselves to consonant information and to avoid dissonant information in the real world but not in the laboratory (McGuire, 1968) might be at least partly attributable to the fact that laboratory subjects are usually college students and, as such, are adults of above average intelligence and ego strength. Though there is some indication that intellectuals tend to employ repression in preference to other mechanisms (Taylor & Barron, 1963), this is not necessarily inconsistent with the above analysis; intellectuals may simply be too well trained in reasoning to be able to fool themselves any longer with biased thinking. The function may be U-shaped.

There seems to be little to say about not believing the dissonant information. Obviously, one can, without really looking into the matter, doubt that our Government is supporting dictatorships, that police beat blacks, that the warnings of ecologists are anything more than "scare tactics," and so on. As one case in point, Jews who had made a decision to "sit tight" and hope for the best, following the German occupation of Hungary, refused to believe eyewitness accounts from respected community members of the slaughter and mass deportation of Jews in neighboring communities.

Not thinking about the relationship among dissonant items of information is what is called compartmentalization. One example is thinking about such items at different times, thinking one way on Sundays and another way on weekdays. Another example is thinking one way about someone else's behavior and another way about your own. A governor of a large state complained of those who "live off the state" by drawing welfare, yet through legalistic manipulations he managed to pay no state income tax at all. The following letter illustrates the mechanism beautifully (Masserman, 1946):

> I am surprised that anyone as well educated as you must be . . . would stoop to such a depth as to torture helpless little cats in the pursuit of a cure for alcoholics. . . . Instead why not torture the drunks . . . if such people are weaklings the world is better off without them. . . . My greatest wish is that you have brought home to you a torture that will be a thousand fold greater than what you are doing to the little animals. . . . I'm glad I am just an ordinary human being . . . with a clear conscience, knowing I have not hurt any living creature [p. 38].

In all such cases, one must avoid seeing the logical implications that one item of information has for another, as the child fails to see the inconsistency in the sentence, *There was once a man whose feet were so long he had to put his pants on over his head*. We saw an extreme form of compartmentalization in Bettelheim's account of the way prisoners maintained separate egos for inside and outside the concentration camp. Such extreme forms also occur in cases of multiple personalities, such as the one described in *The Three Faces of Eve* (Thigpen & Cleckley, 1957).

Biased thinking, or rationalization, seems to require more intelligence than not thinking. All the mechanisms available for unbiased thinking seem to be available for biased thinking. The only difference is that in unbiased thinking the conclusion follows from the premises, whereas in biased thinking the conclusion, that the course of action you have taken is the best course, is given in advance, and thought is used simply to give the appearance of rationality to this conclusion. There seem to be three kinds of biased thinking: (*a*) sweet lemon thinking, that is, increasing the attractiveness of the alternative to which you are committed; (*b*) sour grapes thinking, that is, decreasing the attractiveness of other alternatives; and (*c*) differentiation, or distinguishing between the present situation, in which the alternative to which you are committed is seen as appropriate, and other situations, in which other alternatives may be more appropriate.

Sweet lemon thinking may take the form of emphasizing the positive aspects of your position. Festinger and Carlsmith (1959) offered subjects who had just completed a boring experiment either

$1 or $20 to tell incoming subjects that the experiment was interesting and enjoyable. After the subjects had lied in this manner, the experimenters then asked them how interesting and enjoyable they thought the experiment actually was. Those in the $1 condition rated the experiment as more interesting and enjoyable than did those in the $20 condition. Whereas those in the $20 condition could justify the unattractive alternative of lying in terms of the money they were to receive, those in the $1 condition could justify it only by increasing the actual attractiveness of the experiment in their own minds. Similarly, people who were persuaded to eat grasshoppers by a person they disliked subsequently showed less aversion to grasshoppers than those persuaded by a person they liked (Smith, 1961; Zimbardo, Weisenberg, Firestone, & Levy, 1965).

Sweet lemon thinking may also take the form of active efforts to deemphasize the negative aspects of your position. One way to accomplish this is by thinking of other alternatives with negative aspects so as to lower the adaptation level and thus make the negative aspects of your position seem less negative, a technique called swamping. Thus, the smoker concerned about lung cancer may become interested in automobile accident statistics (Festinger, 1957), and a person with love problems may enjoy hearing about the love problems of others. Misery loves company.

Finally, sweet lemon thinking may take the form of seeking social support. Festinger, Riecken, and Schachter (1956) found that failure of end-of-the-world prophecies to materialize sometimes leads to increased efforts to gain converts.

Sour grapes thinking is the opposite side of the coin from sweet lemon thinking. It is directed towards the alternative not chosen, to emphasize its negative aspects or to deemphasize its positive ones. The fox in Aesop's fable declared that the grapes he could not reach were probably sour, anyhow; a lover we fail with is seen as a snob; and a course we do poorly in is seen as badly taught. Children who refrained from playing with certain toys in order to avoid mild punishment showed a less favorable evaluation of the toys than children who refrained from playing with them in order to avoid severe punishment (Aronson & Carlsmith, 1963; Freedman, 1965; Turner & Wright, 1965), and they refrained from playing with the previously forbidden toys weeks later, in the absence of any prohibition (Freedman, 1965).

Swamping is applicable here, as well as in sweet lemon thinking. A psychologist once commented of a considerably more productive colleague that there were a lot of people in his area doing more important work than he.

A consequence of sweet lemon and sour grapes thinking is that greater attitude change may be produced under conditions of insufficient external justification. When a choice is made to gain a small reward, to avoid a small punishment, or to satisfy a person of low prestige, a good deal of biased thinking is necessary to increase the attractiveness of the chosen alternative sufficiently to provide an internal justification for the choice. A further consequence of sweet lemon and sour grapes thinking is that greater attitude change is likely to occur when the course of action chosen involves some emotional cost. Thus, fraternity members undergoing a severe initiation would be expected to value the fraternity more highly afterwards than would fraternity members undergoing a mild initiation. Various studies have confirmed this general expectation (Gerard & Mathewson, 1966; Zimbardo, 1965). Similarly, diminished amounts of reinforcement and intermittent reinforcement lead to greater resistance to extinction (Lawrence & Festinger, 1962): "When the going gets tough, the tough get going."

Differentiation is a matter of distinguishing between situations in which the alternative you have chosen is appropriate and situations in which the dissonant information is relevant. Sometimes we lie, but lying is bad. This produces a state of dissonance. The dissonance can be reduced by distinguishing between "white lies," which are the kind we tell, and "black lies," which are the kind that are bad. Similarly, we might distinguish between figurative and literal interpretations of the Bible, believing in the first and accepting the fact that the second conflicts with science.

It is most interesting to listen to mountain climbers discussing a climbing accident. Not only are they very much concerned to determine exactly what the unfortunate climber did wrong, which is rational enough, in itself, but their hypotheses suggest that they are motivated to find something that he did that they would never have done, rather than something that he did that they also do and should therefore correct. When they find something that differentiates them from him, the search stops, and the relief is audible.

A number of the mechanisms we have been considering seem to form the basis of certain philosophies of life. Man, alone among the creatures of the earth, chooses to be or not to be, and awareness of this fact brings dissonance with it. Some seem to respond with repression. They are those who "don't think about such things" as their own existence and bury their minds in the details of living. Some seem to respond by reducing importance. They are those who think about their existence only in terms of some abstract system, philosophical, religious, or scientific, and thus avoid confronting its personal significance. Some seem to respond by differentiating between this life and an afterlife. They are able to accept the negative aspects of this life by regarding the afterlife as their real choice.

Others seem to respond with what seems to be the swamping mechanism of sweet lemon thinking. They consider their existence against a background of nonexistence. The starting point of many philosophical, religious, and literary attempts to convey a sense of the value of life seems to be a consideration of nonexistence. What if nothing existed at all? Where did everything come from? Why is it all here? The effect, in some ways at least, seems comparable to that of going out into the sunshine after being in the dark. The contrast enables one, at least briefly, to see and wonder at the brilliance, the richness, the very reality of existence. What we seem to have here is an attempt on the part of the executive system to correct an "error" introduced by a mechanism in the representational system, adaptation to the many constant positive features of life. The correction seems to be brought about by introducing another "stimulus," nonexistence, though it is not at all clear exactly how this works. It would be interesting to know whether it is possible to predict a person's general approach to a philosophy of life from a knowledge of the defense mechanisms that he tends to favor in more limited contexts.

Identification

A final mechanism for enhancing the ego is identification. Identification, with a person, institution, object, idea, or course of action, seems to be a mechanism for enhancing the value of one's ego by emphasizing the features that it has in common with some positively valued entity. Thus, the campaign worker increases his sense of worth by seeing himself as having some of the positive moral and personal attributes of the person he is working for, and the automobile enthusiast increases his sense of worth by thinking about the powerful car he owns as his car.

Identification seems to be more general than the other mechanisms for enhancing the ego. Whereas the mechanisms we have just been considering seem to address themselves to specific sources of dissonance, identification seems to address itself to the ego as a whole. We choose people we identify with on the basis of such general features as physical attractiveness, as well as on the basis of the adaptive value of specific decisions they have made. And we liken ourselves to them, not only on dimensions relevant to major choices, but on irrelevant dimensions, as well, tending to copy even their manner of speech and dress.

Several lines of evidence suggest that identification is often more important than specific conflict reduction in changing people's attitudes (McGuire, 1968). For one thing, the perceived competence of the source of a message is more important than his perceived trustworthiness. That is, his general prestige seems to be more important than the validity of the statements he makes to increase or decrease conflict. For another, awareness of the source's bias often actually facilitates attitude change in the direction of the bias, apparently by making it clear to the receiver what attitudes he must adopt in order to identify with him. Finally, the spoken word, which has more emotional appeal, is more effective than the written word, which yields better comprehension. These three findings suggest that the needs of the ego are often more important than rational considerations in determining the response of the system as a whole. It is important to note, however, that, among the more intelligent and the more successful, specific arguments are more important than an opportunity for identification in changing attitudes (McGuire, 1968).

The mechanism of identification would seem to be, basically, an adaptive one, a mechanism for the transmission of successful learned behavior patterns, much as genetic copying is a mechanism for the transmission of successful unlearned behavior patterns. Moreover, to the extent that it applies, among adults, primarily to the less intelligent and less successful, it may also be an adaptive mechanism for social organization, directing the less able in the footsteps of the more able. But to pursue such matters further would quickly lead us into questions about personality, society, and culture, and so here we must stop.

It is fitting that we should end our examination of knowing, learning, and thinking by considering the ego. For the ego is an important control center in man's cognitive system, particularly in the cognitive system of civilized man, whose physiological needs tend to be satisfied. It is the ego that often determines to what ends the rest of man's cognitive apparatus will be directed.

The ego seems to have needs of its own. Like curiosity, these are "software" needs. What is striking about these needs is that they are not always compatible with the needs of the larger system. The ego seems to be a kind of adaptive system that has evolved within an adaptive system, a subsystem that tends to act so as to nullify changes that would disrupt its own organization. As such, the ego seems to be a source of some of the best and some of the worst in man. It leads man to create. But it also leads him to create beyond the point of usefulness, and it leads him to destroy. All along, we have emphasized the adaptive qualities of various components of the human cognitive system, but we must question the adaptive value of the ego for the system as a whole; for the ego, in order to preserve its integrity, can lead us to deny our senses, to deny our memory, and to distort our thinking. The ego, like a corrupt government, seems often to neglect the needs of the larger system in favor of its own.

It would seem that, if man is to continue to flower, rather than to bring his brief story to an untimely end, his intelligence must be governed by reason, not pride. Hopefully, a greater understanding of the mechanisms of reason and the mechanisms of pride will further that end.

References

Ach, N. *Uber die Willenstatigheit und das Denken.* Gottingen: Vanderhoeck & Ruptecht, 1905. [Partial transl. in J. M. Mandler & G. Mandler (Eds.), *Thinking: From association to Gestalt.* New York: Wiley, 1964.]

Adams, D. K. Experimental studies of adaptive behavior in cats. *Comparative Psychology Monographs,* 1929, **6,** No. 27.

Adams, G. K. An experimental study of memory color and related phenomena. *American Journal of Psychology,* 1923, **34,** 359–407.

Adams, R. An account of a peculiar optical phenomenon seen after having looked at a moving body. *London and Edinburgh Philosophical Magazine and Journal of Science,* 1834, **5,** 373–374.

Adamson, R. W., & Taylor, D. W. Functional fixedness as related to elapsed time and to set. *Journal of Experimental Psychology,* 1954, **47,** 122–126.

Adey, W. R. The sense of smell. In J. Field (Ed.), *Handbook of physiology,* Sec. 1: *Neurophysiology.* Vol. I. Washington, D.C.: American Physiological Society, 1959.

A dictionary of mnemonics. London: Eyre Methuen, 1972.

Adorno, T. W., Frenkel-Brunswik, E., Levinson, D. J., & Sanford, R. N. *The authoritarian personality.* New York: Harper, 1950.

Agranoff, B. W. Biological effects of anti-metabolites used in behavioral

327

studies. In D. H. Efron *et al.* (Eds.), *Psychopharmacology: A review of progress.* PHS Publ. No. 1836, 909–917. Washington, D.C.: U.S. Govt. Printing Office, 1968.

Alexander, C. *Notes on the synthesis of form.* Cambridge, Massachusetts: Harvard Univ. Press, 1964.

Allport, G. W., & Pettigrew, T. F. Cultural influence on the perception of movement: The trapezoidal illusion among Zulus. *Journal of Abnormal and Social Psychology*, 1957, **55**, 104–113.

Allport, G. W., & Postman, L. J. The basic psychology of rumor. *Transactions of the New York Academy of Science*, Series II, 1945, **VIII**, 61–81.

Alpern, M., Lawrence, M., & Wolsk, D. *Sensory processes.* Belmont, California: Brooks/Cole, 1967.

Anderson, B. F. *The psychology experiment.* (2d ed.) Belmont, California: Brooks/Cole, 1971.

Anderson, B. F., & Johnson, W. L. Two kinds of set in problem solving. *Psychological Reports*, 1966, **19**, 851–858. (a)

Anderson, B. F., & Johnson, W. L. Two methods of presenting information and their effects on problem solving. *Perceptual & Motor Skills*, 1966, **23**, 851–856. (b)

Anderson, B. F., & Johnson, W. L. Parallel and serial processing in stimulus matching. Unpublished research, Univ. of Oregon, 1968.

Anderson, J. R., & Bower, G. H. *Human associative memory.* Washington, D.C.: Winston, 1973.

Anderson, N. H. Application of an additive model to impression formation. *Science*, 1962, **138**, 817–818.

Anderson, N. H., & Hubert, S. Effects of concomitant verbal recall on effects in personality impression formation. *Journal of Verbal Learning and Verbal Behavior*, 1963, **2**, 379–391.

Anderson, N. H., & Jacobson, A. Effect of stimulus inconsistency and discounting instructions in personality impression formation. *Journal of Personal Social Psychology*, 1965, **2**, 531–539.

Aristotle. De memoria. In R. M. Hutchins (Ed.), *Great books of the Western world.* London: Encyclopaedia Britannica, 1952.

Aristotle. On the soul. In R. M. Hutchins (Ed.), *Great books of the Western world.* London: Encyclopaedia Britannica, 1952.

Antrobus, J. S., Singer, J. L., Goldstein, S., & Fortgang, M. Mind-wandering and cognitive structure. *Transactions of the New York Academy of Science*, 1970, **32**, 242–252.

Archer, E. J. A re-evaluation of the meaningfulness of all possible CVC trigrams. *Psychological Monographs*, 1960, **74** (Whole No. 497).

Aronson, E., & Carlsmith, J. M. Effect of severity of threat on the valuation of forbidden behavior. *Journal of Abnormal Social Psychology*, 1963, **66**, 684–688.

Asch, S. E. Forming impressions of personality. *Journal of Abnormal and Social Psychology*, 1946, **41**, 258–290.

Asch, S. E. The doctrinal tyranny of associationism: Or what is wrong with rote learning. In T. R. Dixon & D. L. Horton (Eds.), *Verbal behavior and general behavior theory.* Englewood Cliffs, New Jersey: Prentice-Hall, 1968.

Asch, S. E., Ceraso, J., & Heimer, W. Perceptual conditions of association. *Psychological Monographs*, 1960, **74** (Whole No. 490).

Ashby, W. R. *Introduction to cybernetics.* New York: Wiley, 1956.

Ashby, W. R. *Design for a brain.* (2d ed.) New York: Wiley, 1960.

Atkinson, J. W., & Litwin, G. H. Achievement motive and test anxiety conceived as motive to approach success and motive to avoid failure. *Journal of Abnormal & Social Psychology*, 1960, **60**, 52–63.

Attneave, F. *Applications of information theory to psychology.* New York: Holt, 1959.

Attneave, F. Representation of physical space. In A. W. Melton & E. Martin (Eds.), *Coding processes in human memory.* New York: Winston, 1972.

Atwood, G. The logic of interpersonal attitudes: A genetic study. Unpubl. Masters Thesis, Univ. of Oregon, 1967.

Avant, L. L. Vision in the ganzfeld. *Psychological Bulletin*, 1965, **64**, 246–258.

Averbach, E., & Sperling, G. Short-term storage of information in vision. In C. Cherry (Ed.), *Symposium on information theory.* London: Butterworth, 1961. [Also in R. N. Haber (Ed.), *Contemporary theory and research in visual perception.* New York: Holt, 1968.]

Bachem, A. Tone height and tone chroma as two different qualities. *Acta Psychologica*, 1950, **7**, 80–88.

Bacon, F. Advancement of learning. *Novum organum.* New Atlantis. Chicago: Encyclopædia Britannica, 1952.

Bahrick, H. P., Fitts, P. M., & Rankin, R. E. Effect of incentives upon reactions to peripheral stimuli. *Journal of Experimental Psychology*, 1952, **44**, 400–406.

Ball, G. G., & Adams, D. W. Intracranial stimulation as an avoidance or escape response. *Psychonomic Science*, 1965, **3**, 39–40.

Bandura, A. *Principles of behavior modification.* New York: Holt, 1969.

Bandura, A. Relationship of family patterns to child behavior disorders. Progress Report, 1960. Stanford Univ., Project No. M-1734, U.S. Public Health Service.

Bandura, A., & Walters, R. H. *Adolescent aggression.* New York: Ronald Press, 1959.

Barber, B., & Fox, R. C. The case of the floppy-eared rabbits: An instance of serendipity gained and serendipity lost. *American Journal of Society*, 1958, **64**, 128–136.

Bar-Hillel, Y. The present status of automatic translation of languages. In F. L. Alt (Ed.), *Advances in computers*, Vol. I. New York: Academic Press, 1960.

Barnett, L. *The universe and Dr. Einstein.* (2d rev. ed.) New York: William Sloane Assocs., 1957.

Barondes, S. H. Effects of inhibitors of cerebral protein synthesis on "long-term" memory in mice. In D. H. Efron *et al.* (Eds.), *Psychopharmacology: A review of progress.* PHS Publ. No. 1836, 905–908. Washington, D.C.: U.S. Govt. Printing Office, 1968.

Barron, F. The disposition toward originality. *Journal of Abnormal & Social Psychology*, 1955, **51**, 478–485.

Barron, F. The psychology of creativity. In *New directions in psychology*, II. New York: Holt, 1965.

Bartlett, F. C. *Remembering.* Cambridge, England: Cambridge Univ. Press, 1932.

Battig, W. F. Paired-associate learning. In T. R. Dixon & D. L. Horton (Eds.), *Verbal behavior and general behavior theory.* Englewood Cliffs, New Jersey: Prentice-Hall, 1968.

Beck, J. Perceptual grouping produced by line figures. *Perception & Psychophysics*, 1967, **2**, 491–495.

Beh, H. C., & Barratt, P. E. H. Discrimination and conditioning during sleep as indicated by the electroencephalogram. *Science,* 1965, **147,** 1470–1471.

Békésy, G. v. *Sensory inhibition.* Princeton, New Jersey: Princeton Univ. Press, 1967.

Bellman, R. Control theory. *Scientific American,* 1964, **211,** No. 3, 186–201.

Berlyne, D. E. A theory of human curiosity. *British Journal of Psychology,* 1954, **45,** 180–191.

Berlyne, D. E. Uncertainty and epistemic curiosity. *British Journal of Psychology,* 1962, **53,** 27–34.

Berlyne, D. E. *Structure and direction in thinking.* New York: Wiley, 1965.

Berlyne, D. E., Borsa, D. M., Craw, M. A., Gelman, R. S., & Mandell, E. E. Effects of stimulus complexity and induced arousal on paired-associate learning. *Journal of Verbal Learning and Verbal Behavior,* 1965, **4,** 291–299.

Berlyne, D. E., Borsa, D. M., Hamacher, J. H., & Koenig, I. D. Paired-associate learning and the timing of arousal. *Journal of Experimental Psychology,* 1966, **72,** 1–6.

Berlyne, D. E., & Carey, S. T. Incidental learning and the timing of arousal. *Psychonomic Science,* 1968, **13,** 103–104.

Bernbach, H. A. A multiple-copy model for postperceptual memory. In D. A. Norman (Ed.), *Models of human memory.* New York: Academic Press, 1970.

Bertalanffy, L. v. General system theory. In *General systems,* Yearbook of the Society for the Advancement of General System Theory, Vol. 1, 1956, 1–10.

Bettelheim, B. Individual and mass behavior in extreme situations. *Journal of Abnormal & Social Psychology,* 1943, **38,** 417–452.

Bever, T. G., Fodor, J. A., & Garrett, M. A. A formal limitation of associationism. In T. R. Dixon & D. L. Horton (Eds.), *Verbal behavior and general behavior theory.* Englewood Cliffs, New Jersey: Prentice-Hall, 1968.

Bexton, W. H., Heron, W., & Scott, T. H. Effects of decreased variation in the sensory environment. *Canadian Journal of Psychology,* 1954, **8,** 70–76.

Bilodeau, I. McD., & Schlosberg, H. Similarity in stimulating conditions as a variable in retroactive inhibition. *Journal of Experimental Psychology,* 1951, **41,** 199–204.

Birch, H. G. The relation of previous experience to insightful problem-solving. *Journal of Comparative Psychology,* 1945, **38,** 367–383.

Bitterman, M. E. Toward a comparative psychology of learning. *American Psychologist,* 1960, **15,** 704–712.

Blum, G. S. An experimental reunion of psychoanalytic theory with perceptual vigilance and defense. *Journal of Abnormal & Social Psychology,* 1954, **49,** 94–98.

Bobbitt, J. M. An experimental study of the phenomenon of closure as a threshold function. *Journal of Experimental Psychology,* 1942, **30,** 273–294.

Boomer, D. Hesitation and grammatical encoding. *Language and Speech,* 1965, **8,** 148–158.

Bootzin, R. R., & Natsoulas, T. Evidence for perceptual defense uncontaminated by response bias. *Journal of Personal & Social Psychology,* 1965, **1,** 461–468.

Boring, E. G. *A history of experimental psychology.* New York: Appleton, 1929.

Boring, E. G. *The physical dimensions of consciousness.* New York: Appleton, 1933.

Boring, E. G., Langfeld, H. S., & Weld, H. P. *An introduction to psychology.* New York: Wiley, 1939.

Bousfield, W. A. The occurrence of clustering in the recall of randomly arranged associates. *Journal of General Psychology*, 1953, **49**, 229–240.

Bousfield, W. A., & Barclay, W. D. The relationship between order and frequency of occurrence of restricted associative responses. *Journal of Experimental Psychology*, 1950, **40**, 643–647.

Bousfield, W. A., Cohen, B. H., & Whitmarsh, G. A. Associative clustering in the recall of different taxonomic frequencies of occurrence. *Psychological Reports*, 1958, **4**, 39–44.

Bousfield, W. A., & Sedgewick, C. An analysis of the sequences of restricted associative responses. *Journal of General Psychology*, 1944, **30**, 149–165.

Bower, G. H. Application of a model to paired-associate learning. *Psychometrika*, 1961, **26**, 255–280.

Bower, G. H. A multicomponent theory of the memory trace. In K. W. Spence & J. T. Spence (Eds.), *The psychology of learning and motivation*, Vol. I. New York: Academic Press, 1967.

Bower, G. H., & Bostrum, A. Absence of within-list PI and RI in short-term recognition memory. *Psychonomic Science*, 1968, **10**, 211–212.

Bower, G. H., & Trabasso, T. Concept identification. In R. C. Atkinson (Ed.), *Studies in mathematical psychology*. Stanford, California: Stanford Univ. Press, 1964.

Bower, G. H., & Winzenz, D. Group structure, coding, and memory for digit series. *Journal of Experimental Psychology Monographs*, 1969, **80**, No. 2, Part 2, 1–17.

Bower, T. G. R. Discrimination of depth in premotor infants. *Psychonomic Science*, 1964, **1**, 368.

Bower, T. G. R. Stimulus variables determining space perception in infants. *Science*, 1965, **149**, 88–89.

Brand, J. Classification without identification in visual search. *Quarterly Journal of Experimental Psychology*, 1971, **23**, 178–186.

Bransford, J. D., & Franks, J. J. The abstraction of linguistic ideas. *Cognitive Psychology*, 1971, **2**, 331–350.

Breger, L. Dream function: An information processing model. In L. Breger (Ed.), *Clinical–cognitive psychology*. Englewood Cliffs, New Jersey: Prentice-Hall, 1969.

Bregman, A. S., & Charness, N. "Schema plus transformations" in visual pattern recognition. Paper presented at Eastern Psychological Association, Atlantic City, New Jersey, 1970.

Brehm, J. W., & Cohen, A. R. *Explorations in cognitive dissonance*. New York: Wiley, 1962.

Bridgman, P. W. *The logic of modern physics*. New York: Macmillan, 1927.

Broadbent, D. E. *Perception and communication*. Oxford: Pergamon Press, 1958.

Broadbent, D. E. *Decision and stress*. London: Academic Press, 1971.

Brooks, L. R. The suppression of visualization in reading. *Quarterly Journal of Experimental Psychology*, 1967, **19**, 289–299.

Brooks, L. R. Spatial and verbal components of the act of recall. *Canadian Journal of Psychology*, 1968, **22**, 349–368.

Brown, J. S. Gradients of approach and avoidance responses and their relation to motivation. *Journal of Comparative & Physiological Psychology*, 1948, **41**, 450–465.

Brown, R. *Words and things*. New York: The Free Press of Glencoe, 1958.

Brown, R. *Social psychology*. New York: The Free Press of Glencoe, 1965.

Brown, R., & Bellugi, U. Three processes in the child's acquisition of syntax. *Harvard Educational Review*, 1964, **34**, 133–151.

Brown, R., & Lenneberg, E. H. A study in language and cognition. *Journal of Abnormal & Social Psychology*, 1954, **49**, 454–462.

Brown, T. *Lectures on the philosophy of the human mind*. Hallowell, Maine: Masters Smith, 1854.

Bruner, J. S. Going beyond the information given. In *Contemporary approaches to cognition*. Cambridge, Massachusetts: Harvard Univ. Press, 1957. (a)

Bruner, J. S. On perceptual readiness. *Psychological Review*, 1957, **64**, 123–152. (b)

Bruner, J. S. *The process of education*. New York: Random House, 1960.

Bruner, J. S. *On knowing: Essays for the left hand*. Cambridge, Massachusetts: Belknap Press, 1964.

Bruner, J. S. Constructive cognitions. *Contemporary Psychology*, 1970, **15**, 81–83.

Bruner, J. S., Goodnow, J. J., & Austin, G. A. *A study of thinking*. New York: Science Editions, 1962.

Bruner, J. S., Mandler, J. M., O'Dowd, D., & Wallach, M. A. The role of overlearning and drive level in reversal learning. *Journal of Comparative & Physiological Psychology*, 1958, **51**, 607–613.

Bruner, J. S., Olver, R. R., Greenfield, P. M., Hornsby, J. R., Kenney, H. J., Maccoby, M., Modiano, N., Mosher, F. A., Olson, D. R., Potter, M. C., Reich, L. C., Sonstroem, A. McK. *Studies in cognitive growth*. New York: Wiley, 1966.

Bruner, J. S., & Postman, L. On the perception of incongruity: A paradigm. *Journal of Personality*, 1949, **18**, 206–223.

Bruner, J. S., Postman, L., & Rodrigues, J. Expectation and the perception of color. *American Journal of Psychology*, 1951, **64**, 216–227.

Bruner, J. S., & Potter, M. C. Interference in visual recognition. *Science*, 1964, **144**, 424–425.

Brunswik, E. Statistical separation of perception, thinking, and attitudes. *American Psychology*, 1951, **64**, 216–227.

Brunswik, E. "Ratiomorphic" models of perception and thinking. *Proceedings of the XIV International Congress of Psychology*, Montreal, 1954.

Bugelski, B. R., & Cadwallader, T. C. A reappraisal of the transfer and retroaction surface. *Journal of Experimental Psychology*, 1956, **52**, 360–365.

Bunch, M. E. The amount of transfer in rational learning as a function of time. *Journal of Comparative Psychology*, 1936, **22**, 325–337.

Bunch, M. E., & Lang, E. S. The amount of transfer of training from partial learning after varying intervals of time. *Journal of Comparative Psychology*, 1939, **27**, 449–459.

Bunch, M. E., & McCraven, V. G. The temporal course of transfer in the learning of memory material. *Journal of Comparative Psychology*, 1938, **25**, 481–496.

Burkamp, W. Versuche uber das Farbenwiedererkennen der Fische. *Archiv der Sinnesphysiologie*, 1923, **55**, 133–170.

Buschke, H. Relative retention in immediate memory determined by the missing scan method. *Nature*, 1963, **200**, 1129–1130. (a)

Buschke, H. Retention in immediate memory estimated without retrieval. *Science*, 1963, **140**, 56–57. (b)

Butler, B. E., & Merikle, P. M. Uncertainty and meaningfulness in paired-associate learning. *Journal of Verbal Learning & Verbal Behavior*, 1970, **9**, 634–641.

Butler, R. A. Discrimination learning by rhesus monkeys to visual-exploration motivation. *Journal of Comparative & Physiological Psychology*, 1953, **46**, 95–98.

Butler, R. A. Incentive conditions which influence visual exploration. *Journal of Experimental Psychology*, 1954, **48**, 19–23.

Callaway, E., & Stone, G. Re-evaluating the focus of attention. In L. Uhr & J. G. Miller (Eds.), *Drugs and behavior*. New York: Wiley, 1960.

Campbell, D. T. Blind variation and selective retention in creative thought as in other knowledge processes. *Psychological Review*, 1960, **67**, 380–400.

Carmichael, L., Hogan, H. P., & Walter, A. A. An experimental study of the effect of language on the reproduction of visually perceived form. *Journal of Experimental Psychology*, 1932, **15**, 73–86.

Cattell, R. B., & Drevdahl, J. E. A comparison of the personality profile (16 P.F.) of eminent researchers with that of eminent teachers and administrators, and of the general population. *British Journal of Psychology*, 1955, **46**, 248–261.

Chapanis, A., & McCleary, R. A. Interposition as a cue for the perception of relative distance. *Journal of General Psychology*, 1953, **48**, 113–132.

Chase, W. G., Graham, F. K., & Graham, D. T. Components of HR response in anticipation of reaction time and exercise tasks. *Journal of Experimental Psychology*, 1968, **76**, 642–648.

Cherkin, A. Kinetics of memory consolidation: Role of amnesic treatment parameters. *Proceedings of the National Academy of Science*, 1969, **63**, 1094–1101.

Cherry, E. C. *On human communication*. Cambridge, Massachusetts: MIT Press, 1965.

Chomsky, N. *Syntactic structures*. The Hague: Mouton, 1957.

Chomsky, N. A review of *Verbal Behavior* by B. F. Skinner. *Language*, 1959, **35**, 26–58.

Chomsky, N. *Aspects of the theory of syntax*. Cambridge, Massachusetts: MIT Press, 1965.

Chomsky, N., & Halle, M. *The sound pattern of English*. New York: Harper, 1968.

Christensen, P. R., Guilford, J. P., & Wilson, R. C. Relations of creative responses to working time and instructions. *Journal of Experimental Psychology*, 1957, **53**, 82–88.

Clark, H. H. Linguistic processes in deductive reasoning. *Psychological Review*, 1969, **76**, 387–404. (a)

Clark, H. H. The influence of language in solving three-term series problems. *Journal of Experimental Psychology*, 1969, **82**, 205–215. (b)

Clark, H. H. Semantics and comprehension. In T. A. Sebeok (Ed.), *Current trends in linguistics*. Vol. 12: *Linguistics and adjacent arts and sciences*. The Hague: Mouton, 1972.

Clark, H. H., & Card, S. K. The role of semantics in remembering comparative sentences. *Journal of Experimental Psychology*, 1969, **82**, 545–553.

Clark, H. H., Carpenter, P. A., & Just, M. A. On the meeting of semantics and perception. In W. G. Chase (Ed.), *Visual information processing*. New York: Academic Press, 1973.

Codelia, F. Free classification of words and pictures: A replication. Unpublished Research, Portland State Univ., Portland, Oregon, 1973.

Cofer, C. N. Verbal behavior in relation to reasoning and values. In H. Guetzkow (Ed.), *Groups, leadership, and men.* Pittsburgh: Carnegie Press, 1951.

Cohen, B. H., & Bousfield, W. A. The effects of a dual-level stimulus-word list on the occurrence of clustering in recall. *Journal of General Psychology,* 1956, **55,** 51–58.

Coleman, H. The dependence on learning of judgments of the "impossibility" of figures. Unpubl. Research, Pierce College, Athens, Greece, 1973.

Collier, G., & Marx, M. H. Changes in performance as a function of shifts in The magnitude of reinforcement. *Journal of Experimental Psychology,* 1959, **57,** 305–309.

Collins, A., & Quillian, M. R. Retrieval time from semantic memory. *Journal of Verbal Learning & Verbal Behavior,* 1969, **8,** 240–247.

Collins, A. M., & Quillian, M. R. How to make a language user. In E. Tulving & W. Donaldson (Eds.), *Organization of memory.* New York: Academic Press, 1972.

Conrad, C. Cognitive economy in semantic memory. *Journal of Experimental Psychology,* 1972, **92,** 149–154.

Conrad, R. Errors of immediate memory. *British Journal of Psychology,* 1959, **50,** 349.

Conrad, R. Acoustic confusions in immediate memory. *British Journal of Psychology,* 1964, **55,** 75–84.

Coombs, C. H., Dawes, R. M., & Tversky, A. *Mathematical psychology.* Englewood Cliffs, New Jersey: Prentice-Hall, 1970.

Corbin, H. H. The perception of grouping and apparent movement in visual depth. *Archives of Psychology,* 1942, No. 273.

Corso, J. F. *The experimental psychology of sensory behavior.* New York: Holt, 1967.

Corteen, R. S. Skin conductance changes and word recall. *British Journal of Psychology,* 1969, **60,** 81–84.

Courts, F. A. Relations between experimentally induced muscular tension and memorization. *Journal of Experimental Psychology,* 1939, **25,** 235–256.

Covington, M. V., & Crutchfield, R. S. An experiment in the use of programmed instruction for the facilitation of creative problem solving. *Programmed Instruction,* 1965, **4,** 3–10.

Crespi, L. P. Amount of reinforcement and level of performance. *Psychological Review,* 1944, **51,** 341–357.

Davidson, D., Suppes, P., & Siegel, S. *Decision making: An experimental approach.* Stanford, California: Stanford Univ. Press, 1957.

Dawes, R. M. Memory and distortion of meaningful written material. *British Journal of Psychology,* 1966, **57,** 77–86.

Deese, J. On the prediction of occurrence of particular verbal intrusions in immediate recall. *Journal of Experimental Psychology,* 1959, **58,** 17–22.

Deese, J. Frequency of usage and number of words in free recall: The role of associations. *Psychological Reports,* 1960, **7,** 337–344.

Deese, J. *The structure of associations in language and thought.* Baltimore: The Johns Hopkins Press, 1965.

De Jong, R. N., Itabashi, H. H., & Olson, J. R. "Pure" memory loss with hippocampal lesions: A case report. *Transactions of the American Neurological Association,* 1968, **93,** 31–34.

Delin, P. S. Learning and retention of English words with successive approximations to a complex mnemonic instruction. *Psychonomic Science,* 1969, **17,** 87–89.

Dement, W. C. An essay on dreams. In F. Barron, W. C. Dement, W. Edwards, H. Lindman, L. D. Phillips, J. Olds, & M. Olds. *New Directions in psychology II.* New York: Holt, 1965.

Denti, A., McGaugh, J. L., Landfield, P. W., & Shinkman, P. Further study of the effects of post-trial electrical stimulation of the mesencephalic reticular formation on avoidance learning in rats. *Physiological Behavior,* 1970, **5,** 659–662.

DeRivera, J. H. *The psychological dimension of foreign policy.* Columbus, Ohio: Charles E. Merrill, 1968.

Descartes, R. Rules for the direction of the mind. In R. M. Hutchins (Ed.), *Great books of the Western world.* Chicago: Encyclopaedia Britannica, 1952.

De Soto, C. B. Learning a social structure. *Journal of Abnormal & Social Psychology,* 1960, **60,** 417–421.

De Soto, C. B. The predilection for single orderings. *Journal of Abnormal & Social Psychology,* 1961, **62,** 16–23.

De Soto, C. B., & Albrecht, F. Cognition and social orderings. In R. P. Abelson, E. Aronson, W. J. McGuire, T. M. Newcomb, M. J. Rosenberg, & P. H. Tannenbaum (Eds.), *Theories of cognitive consistency.* Chicago: Rand McNally, 1968.

De Soto, C. B., London, M., & Handel, S. Social reasoning and spatial paralogic. *Journal of Personal & Social Psychology,* 1965, **2,** 513–521.

DeValois, R. L., & Jacobs, G. H. Primate color vision. *Science,* 1968, **162,** 533–540.

Dill, W. R., Hilton, T. L., & Reitman, W. R. *The new managers.* Englewood Cliffs, New Jersey: Prentice-Hall, 1962.

Dollard, J., & Miller, N. E. *Personality and psychotherapy.* New York: McGraw-Hill, 1950.

Donaldson, M., & Wales, R. J. On the acquisition of some relational terms. In J. R. Hayes (Ed.), *Cognition and the development of language.* New York: Wiley, 1970.

Doyle, A. C. Silver blaze. In M. Daly, *My favorite suspense stories.* New York: Dodd, Mead, 1968.

Duncan, C. P. The retroactive effects of electroshock on learning. *Journal of Comparative & Physiological Psychology,* 1949, **42,** 32–34.

Duncker, K. On problem-solving. *Psychological Monographs,* 1945, **58,** 5 (Whole No. 270).

Dunnette, M., Campbell, J. P., & Jaastad, K. The effect of group participating on brainstorming effectiveness for two industrial samples. *Journal of Applied Psychology,* 1963, **47,** 30–37.

Easterbrook, J. A. The effect of emotion on cue utilization and the organization of behavior. *Psychological Review,* 1959, **66,** 183–201.

Ebbinghaus, H. *Memory: A contribution to experimental psychology.* (Trans. by H. A. Ruger & C. E. Bussenius.) New York: Teachers College, Columbia Univ., 1913.

Eden, M. Handwriting and pattern recognition. *I. R. E. Transactions on Information Theory,* IT-8, 1962, 160–166.

Edwards, W., Lindman, H., & Phillips, L. D. Emerging technologies for making decisions. In *New Directions in Psychology II.* New York: Holt, 1965.

Egeth, H. E. Parallel versus serial processes in multidimensional stimulus discrimination. *Perception & Psychophysics,* 1966, **1,** 245–252.

Eimas, P. D., Siqueland, E. R., Jusczyk, P., & Vigorito, J. Speech perception in infants. *Science*, 1971, **171**, 303–306.

Einstein, A. Letter to Jacques Hadamard. In B. Ghiselin (Ed.), *The creative process*. Berkeley, California: Univ. of Calif. Press, 1952.

Eisenberg, P., & Lazarsfeld, P. F. The psychological effects of unemployment. *Psychological Bulletin*, 1938, **35**, 358–390.

Emmert, E. Grossenverhaltnisse der Nachbilder. *Klinisches Monatsblatt der Augenheilkunde*, 1881, **19**, 443–450.

Erickson, E. M. Critical comments on Hibler's presentation of his work on negative after images of hypnotically induced hallucinated colors. *Journal of Experimental Psychology*, 1941, **29**, 164–170.

Eriksen, C. W., & Hoffman, J. E. Some characteristics of selective attention in visual perception determined by vocal reaction time. *Perception & Psychophysics*, 1972, **11**, 169–171.

Eriksen, C. W., & Rohrbaugh, J. W. Some factors determining efficiency of selective attention. *American Journal of Psychology*, 1970, **83**, 330–342.

Erikson, E. H. The problem of ego identity. *Journal of the American Psychoanalytic Association*, 1956, 4, 56–121.

Estes, W. K. All-or-none processes in learning and retention. *American Psychologist*, 1964, **19**, 16–25.

Fairweather, G. W., Sanders, D. H., Maynard, H., Cressler, D. L., & Jennings, R. D. The effect of group membership on community adjustment: Maintaining productive groups in the community. Workshop presentation: Research utilization study. NIMH Grant No. MH09251. 1968.

Fehrer, E., & Raab, D. Reaction time to stimuli masked by metacontrast. *Journal of Experimental Psychology*, 1962, **63**, 143–147.

Festinger, L. A *theory of cognitive dissonance*. Evanston, Ill.: Row, Peterson, 1957.

Festinger, L., & Carlsmith, J. M. Cognitive consequences of forced compliance. *Journal of Abnormal & Social Psychology*, 1959, **58**, 203–210.

Festinger, L., Riecken, H. W., & Schachter, S. *When prophecy fails*. Minneapolis: Univ. of Minnesota Press, 1956.

Fields, P. E. Studies in concept formation. I. The development of the concept of triangularity by the white rat. *Comparative Psychological Monographs*, 1932, **9**, 1–70.

Fillmore, C. J. The case for case. In E. Bach & R. T. Harms (Eds.), *Universals in linguistic theory*. New York: Holt, 1968.

Fitts, P. M. Perceptual–motor skill learning. In A. W. Melton (Ed.), *Categories of human learning*. New York: Academic Press, 1964.

Flavell, J. H. *The developmental psychology of Jean Piaget*. New York: Van Nostrand, 1963.

Flavell, J. H., & Draguns, J. A microgenetic approach to perception and thought. *Psychological Bulletin*, 1957, **54**, 197–217.

Fleishman, E. A., & Hemple, W. E., Jr. Changes in factor structure of a complex psychomotor test as a function of practice. *Psychometrika*, 1954, **19**, 239–252.

Forgus, R. H. The effect of early perceptual learning on the behavior organization of adult rats. *Journal of Comparative & Physiological Psychol.*, 1954, **47**, 331–336.

Forgus, R. H. *Perception*. New York: McGraw-Hill, 1966.

Foss, D. Decision processes during sentence comprehension: Effects of lexical item difficulty and position upon decision times. *Journal of Verbal Learning & Verbal Behavior*, 1969, **8**, 457–462.

Fraisse, P., & Elkin, E. H. Etude genetique de l'influence des modes de presentation sur le seuil de reconnaissance d'objects familiers. *L'Annee Psychologique*, 1963, **63**, 1–12.

Freedman, J. L. Long-term behavioral effects of cognitive dissonance. *Journal of Experimental & Social Psychology*, 1965, **1**, 145–155.

Freeman, G. L. An experimental study of the perception of objects. *Journal of Experimental Psychology*, 1929, **12**, 241–258.

Frenkel-Brunswik, E. Intolerance of ambiguity as an emotional and perceptual personality variable. *Journal of Personality*, 1949, **18**, 108–143.

Frenkel-Brunswik, E. Further explorations by a contributor to "The authoritarian personality." In R. Christie & M. Jahoda (Eds.), *Studies in the scope and method of "The authoritarian personality."* New York: Free Press, 1954.

Freud, A. *The ego and the mechanisms of defense.* London: Hogarth Press, 1937.

Freud, S. *An outline of psychoanalysis.* (Transl. by J. Strachey.) New York: Norton, 1949.

Freud, S. *The interpretation of dreams.* New York: Basic Books, 1955.

Fuortes, M. G. F. Electric activity of cells in the eye of limulus. *American Journal of Ophthalmology*, 1958, **46**, 210–223.

Furedy, J. J., & Scull, J. Orienting-reaction theory and an increase in the human GSR following stimulus change which is unpredictable but not contrary to prediction. *Journal of Experimental Psychology*, 1971, **88**, 292–294.

Furth, H. G. *Thinking without language.* New York: Free Press, 1966.

Fuster, J. M. Effects of stimulation of brain stem on tachistoscopic perception. *Science*, 1958, **127**, 150.

Gagne, R. M., & Smith, E. C. A study of the effects of verbalization on problem solving. *Journal of Experimental Psychology*, 1962, **63**, 12–18.

Gardner, R. A., & Gardner, B. T. Teaching sign language to a chimpanzee. *Science*, 1969, **165**, 664–672.

Garner, W. R. An informational analysis of absolute judgments of loudness. *Journal of Experimental Psychology*, 1953, **46**, 373–380.

Garner, W. R. *Uncertainty and structure as psychological concepts.* New York: Wiley, 1962.

Garner, W. R. The stimulus in information processing. *American Psychologist*, 1970, **25**, 350–358.

Garner, W. R., & Felfoldy, G. L. Integrality of stimulus dimensions in various types of information processing. *Cognitive Psychology*, 1970, **1**, 225–241.

Garrett, M., Bever, T., & Fodor, J. The active use of grammar in speech perception. *Perception and Psychophysics*, 1966, **1**, 30–32.

Gates, A. I. Recitation as a factor in memorizing. *Archives of Psychology, New York*, 1917, No. 40.

Geldard, F. A. *The human senses.* New York: Wiley, 1953.

Gelman, R. Conservation, attention, and discrimination. Unpubl. doctoral dissert., Univ. Calif. L.A., 1967.

Gerard, H. B., & Mathewson, G. C. The effects of severity of initiation on liking for a group: A replication. *Journal of Experimental Social Psychology*, 1966, **2**, 278–287.

Gergonne, J. D. Essai de dialectic rationelle. *Annales des mathematiques pures et appliques*, 1817, **7**.

Geschwind, N. Language and the brain. *Scientific American*, 1972, **226** (April), 76–83.

Ghiselin, B. (Ed.) *The creative process.* Berkeley, California: Univ. Calif. Press, 1952.

Gibson, E. J. A systematic application of the concepts of generalization and differentiation to verbal learning. *Psychological Review*, 1940, **47**, 196–229.

Gibson, E. J. A re-examination of generalization. *Psychological Review*, 1959, **66**, 340–342.

Gibson, E. J. *Principles of perceptual learning and development*. New York: Appleton, 1969.

Gibson, J. J. Adaptation, after-effect and contrast in the perception of curved lines. *Journal of Experimental Psychology*, 1933, **16**, 1–31.

Gibson, J. J. Adaptation, after-effect and contrast in the perception of tilted lines. II. Simultaneous contrast and the areal restriction of the after-effect. *Journal of Experimental Psychology*, 1937, **20**, 553–569.

Gibson, J. J. *The perception of the visual world*. Cambridge: Houghton-Mifflin, 1950.

Ginsburg, H., & Opper, S. *Piaget's theory of intellectual development*. Englewood Cliffs, New Jersey: Prentice-Hall, 1969.

Gleitman, H. Forgetting in animals: Phenomena and explanatory theories. In W. K. Honig & P. H. R. James (Eds.), *Animal memory*. New York: Academic Press, 1970.

Glickman, S. E., & Schiff, B. A biological theory of reinforcement. *Psychological Review*, 1967, **74**, 81–109.

Glucksburg, S., & Danks, J. H. Effects of discriminative labels and of nonsense syllables upon availability of novel function. *Journal of Verbal Learning and Verbal Behavior*, 1968, **7**, 72–77.

Glucksburg, S., & Weisberg, R. W. Verbal behavior and problem solving: Some effects of labeling in a functional fixedness problem. *Journal of Experimental Psychology*, 1966, **71**, 659–664.

Goldberg, L. R. Diagnosticians versus diagnostic signs: The diagnosis of psychosis versus neurosis from the MMPI. *Psychological Monographs*, 1965, **79** (Whole No. 602).

Goldberg, L. R. Simple models or simple processes? *American Psychologist*, 1968, **23**, 483–496.

Goldstein, K., & Scheerer, M. Abstract and concrete behavior: An experimental study with special tests. *Psychological Monographs*, 1941, **53**, No. 239.

Gopher, D. Patterns of eye movement in auditory tasks of selective attention. Ph.D. Dissertation, Hebrew Univ., Jerusalem, 1971.

Gordon, W. J. *Synectics*. New York: Harper & Row, 1961.

Gottschaldt, K. Gestalt factors in repetition. In W. D. Ellis (Ed.), *A sourcebook on Gestalt psychology*. New York: Humanities Press, 1938.

Grant, D. A., & Curran, J. F. Relative difficulty of number, form, and color concepts of a Weigl-type problem using unsystematic number cards. *Journal of Experimental Psychology*, 1952, **43**, 408–413.

Greenberg, J. H. Some universals of grammar with particular reference to the order of meaningful elements. In J. H. Greenberg (Ed.), *Universals of language*. Cambridge, Massachusetts: MIT Press, 1962.

Greenspoon, J., & Ranyard, R. Stimulus conditions and retroactive inhibition. *Journal of Experimental Psychology*, 1957, **53**, 55–59.

Gregory, R. L. Distortion of visual space as inappropriate constancy scaling. *Nature*, 1963, **119**, 678.

Gregory, R. L. *The intelligent eye*. New York: McGraw-Hill, 1970.

Gregory, R. L. *Eye and Brain*. (2d ed.) New York: McGraw-Hill, 1973.

Grossman, S. P. *A textbook of physiological psychology*. New York: Wiley, 1967.

Guilford, J. P. *The nature of human intelligence.* New York: McGraw-Hill, 1967.

Guthrie, E. R. *The psychology of learning,* Revised. New York: Harper & Row, 1952.

Guthrie, E. R., & Horton, G. P. *Cats in a puzzle box.* New York: Holt, 1946.

Guthrie, G. D. Changes in cognitive functioning under stress: A study of plasticity in cognitive controls. Unpublished doctoral dissertation. Worcester, Massachusetts: Clark Univ., 1966.

Guy, D. E. Developmental study of performance on conceptual problems involving a rule shift. *Journal of Experimental Psychology,* 1969, **82,** 242–249.

Guzmán, A. Computer recognition of three-dimensional objects in a visual scene. MIT Artificial Intelligence Laboratory Project MAC-TR-59, 1968.

Haber, R. N. The effects of coding strategy on perceptual memory. *Journal of Experimental Psychology,* 1964, **68,** 257–262.

Haber, R. N., & Haber, R. B. Eidetic imagery: I. frequency. *Perceptual & Motor Skills,* 1964, **19,** 131–138.

Hadamard, J. *The Psychology of invention in the mathematical field.* New York: Dover, 1945.

Hake, H. W., & Garner, W. R. The effect of presenting various numbers of discrete steps on scale reading accuracy. *Journal of Experimental Psychology,* 1951, **42,** 358–366.

Halle, M., & Stevens, K. N. Analysis by synthesis. In W. Wathen-Dunn & L. E. Woods (Eds.), *Proceedings of the seminar on speech compression and processing.* Bedford, Massachusetts: Air Force Cambridge Research Labs., 1959.

Hammond, K. R., & Summers, D. A. Cognitive dependence on linear and non-linear cues. *Psychological Review,* 1965, **72,** 215–224.

Hanfman, E., & Kasanin, J. A method for the study of concept formation. *Journal of Psychology,* 1937, **3,** 521–540.

Hanfman, E., & Kasanin, J. Conceptual thinking in schizophrenia. *Nervous & Mental Diseases Monograph,* 1942, **67.**

Harlow, H. F. The formation of learning sets. *Psychological Review,* 1949, **56,** 51–56.

Harlow, H. F. The nature of love. *American Psychologist,* 1958, **13,** 673–685.

Harlow, H. F., McGaugh, J. L., & Thompson, R. F. *Psychology.* San Francisco: Albion, 1971.

Harper, R. S. The perceptual modification of colored figures. *American Journal of Psychology,* 1953, **66,** 86–89.

Harris, C. S., & Haber, R. N. Selective attention and coding in visual perception. *Journal of Experimental Psychology,* 1963, **65,** 328–333.

Hartley, E. L. *Problems in prejudice.* New York: King's Crown Press, 1946.

Hartman, E. B. The influence of practice and pitch-distance between tones on the absolute identification of pitch. *American Journal of Psychology,* 1954, **67,** 1–14.

Haygood, R. C., & Bourne, L. E., Jr. Attribute- and rule-learning aspects of conceptual behavior. *Psychological Review,* 1965, **72,** 175–195.

Head, H. *Studies in neurology.* New York & London: Oxford Univ. Press, 1920.

Heath, R. G., & Mickle, W. A. Evaluation of seven years' experience with depth electrode studies in human patients. In Ramey & O'Doherty (Eds.), *Electrical studies on the unanesthetized brain.* New York: Harper, 1960.

Hebb, D. O. *The organization of behavior.* New York: Wiley, 1949.

Hebb, D. O. Concerning imagery. *Psychological Review,* 1968, **75,** 466–477.

Hebb, D. O., & Penfield, W. Human behavior after extensive bilateral removals from the frontal lobes. *Archives of Neurology & Psychiatry*, 1940, **44**, 421–438.

Heidbreder, E., Bensley, M. L., & Ivy, M. The attainment of concepts: IV. Regularities and levels. *Journal of Psychology*, 1948, **25**, 299–329.

Heider, F. *The psychology of interpersonal relations*. New York: Wiley, 1958.

Helson, H. *Adaptation-level theory*. New York: Harper, 1964.

Henning, H. *Der Geruch*. Leipzig: Barth, 1924.

Hering, E. *Grundzuge der Lehre vom Lichtsinn*. Berlin: Springer, 1920.

Hernández-Péon, R. Psychiatric implications of neurophysiological research. *Bulletin of the Menninger Clinic*, 1964, **28**, 165–185.

Heron, W. The pathology of boredom. *Scientific American*, 1957, **196**, No. 1, 52–56.

Hess, E. H. Imprinting. *Science*, 1959, **130**, 133–141.

Hibler, F. W. Note on Mrs. Erickson's comments on Hibler's work on negative after images of hypnotically induced hallucinated colors. *Journal of Experimental Psychology*, 1941, **29**, 170–173.

Hilgard, E. R. *The experience of hypnosis*. New York: Harcourt, 1968.

Hilgard, E. R., Atkinson, R. C., & Atkinson, R. L. *Introduction to psychology*. (5th ed.) New York: Harcourt, 1971.

Hilgard, E. R., & Bower, G. H. *Theories of learning*. 3d ed. New York: Appleton, 1966.

Hilgard, E. R., & Hilgard, J. R. Hypnosis: Its place in a science of behavior. *The Stanford Observer*, February, 1972.

Hinckley, E. D., & Rethlingshafer, E. Value judgments of heights of men by college students. *Journal of Psychology*, 1951, **31**, 257–262.

Hinde, R. A. *Animal behaviour*. New York: McGraw-Hill, 1966.

Hochberg, J. E. Effects of the Gestalt revolution: The Cornell symposium on perception. *Psychological Review*, 1957, **64**, 73–84.

Hochberg, J. E. *Perception*. Englewood Cliffs, New Jersey: Prentice-Hall, 1964.

Hochberg, J. E. In the mind's eye. In R. N. Haber (Ed.), *Contemporary theory and research in visual perception*. New York: Holt, 1968.

Hochberg, J., & Brooks, V. The psychophysics of form: Reversible perspective drawings of spatial objects. *American Journal of Psychology*, 1960, **73**, 337–354.

Hochberg, J., & Brooks, V. Pictorial recognition as an unlearned ability: A study of one child's performance. *American Journal of Psychology*, 1962, **75**, 624–628.

Hockett, C. D. The origin of speech. *Scientific American*, 1960, **203**, 88–96.

Hoffman, P. J. The paramorphic representation of clinical judgment. *Psychological Bulletin*, 1960, **57**, 116–131.

Hoffman, P. J., Slovic, P., & Rorer, L. G. An analysis-of-variance model for the assessment of configural cue utilization in clinical judgment. *Psychological Bulletin*, 1968, **69**, 338–349.

Honzik, C. H. Delayed reaction in rats. *University of California Publications in Psychology*, 1931, **4**, 307–318.

Hoppe, F. Erfolg und Misserfolg. *Psychologische Forschung*, 1930, **14**, 1–62.

Horwitz, W. A., Kestenbaum, C., Person, E., & Jarvik, L. Identical twin-"idiot savants"-calendar calculators. *American Journal of Psychology*, 1965, **121**, 1075–1079.

Houston, B. K. Noise, task difficulty, and Stroop color-word performance. *Journal of Experimental Psychology*, 1969, **82**, 403–404.

Hovland, C. I. Experimental studies in rote-learning theory: VII. Distribution of practice with varying lengths of list. *Journal of Experimental Psychology,* 1940, **27,** 271–284.

Hovland, C. I., Harvey, O. J., & Sherif, M. Assimilation and contrast effects in reaction to communication and attitude change. *Journal of Abnormal & Social Psychology,* 1957, **55,** 244–252.

Hubel, D. H., & Wiesel, T. N. Receptive fields, binocular interaction and functional architecture in the cat's visual cortex. *Journal of Physiology,* 1962, **160,** 106–154.

Hubel, D. H., & Wiesel, T. N. Receptive fields of cells in striate cortex of very young, visually inexperienced kittens. *Journal of Neurophysiology,* 1963, **26,** 994–1002.

Hubel, D. H., & Wiesel, T. N. Receptive fields and functional architecture of the monkey striate cortex. *Journal of Physiology,* 1968, **195,** 215–243.

Hull, C. L. *A behavior system.* New Haven: Yale Univ. Press, 1952.

Hulse, S. H., & Firestone, R. J. Mean amount of reinforcement and instrumental response strength. *Journal of Experimental Psychology,* 1964, **67,** 417–422.

Humphrey, G. *Thinking.* London: Methuen, 1951.

Hunt, E. B. *Concept learning.* New York: Wiley, 1962.

Hunt, E., & Love, T. How good can memory be? In A. W. Melton & E. Martin (Eds.), *Coding processes in human memory.* New York: Winston, 1972.

Hunter, I. M. L. *Memory.* Baltimore: Penguin, 1957.

Hunter, W. S. The delayed reaction in animals and children. *Animal Behavior Monographs,* 1913, **2,** 1–86.

Hunter, W. S. The temporal maze and kinaesthetic sensory processes in the white rat. *Psychobiology,* 1920, **2,** 1–18.

Huttenlocher, J. Constructing spatial images: A strategy in reasoning. *Psychological Review,* 1968, **75,** 550–560.

Hyman, R. Stimulus information as a determinant of reaction time. *Journal of Experimental Psychology,* 1953, **45,** 188–196.

Hyman, R. Creativity and the prepared mind: The role of information and induced attitudes. In C. W. Taylor (Ed.), *Widening horizons in creativity.* New York: Wiley, 1964.

Hyman, R., & Well, A. Perceptual separability and spatial models. *Perception & Psychophysics,* 1968, **3,** 161–165.

Inhelder, B., & Piaget, J. *The growth of logical thinking.* New York: Basic Books, 1958.

Jacobson, E. *Progressive relaxation.* Chicago: Univ. of Chicago Press, 1938.

Jaensch, E. R. *Die Eidetik.* Leipzig: Quell & Meyer, 1925.

Jakobson, R., & Halle, M. *Fundamentals of language.* The Hague: Mouton, 1956.

James, W. *Principles of psychology.* New York: Holt, 1890.

Janis, I. L., & Frick, F. The relationship between attitudes toward conclusions and errors in judging logical validity of syllogisms. *Journal of Experimental Psychology,* 1943, **33,** 73–77.

Jenkins, H. M., & Ward, W. C. The judgment of contingency between response and outcomes. *Psychological Monographs,* 1965, **79** (Whole No. 594).

Jenks, R. S., & Deane, G. E. Human heart rate responses during experimentally induced anxiety: A follow-up. *Journal of Experimental Psychology,* 1963, **65,** 109–112.

Johannson, G. *Configurations in event perception.* Uppsala: Almquist & Wiksell, 1950.

Johnsgard, K. W. Check-reading as a function of pointer symmetry and uniform alignment. *Journal of Applied Psychology,* 1953, **37,** 407–411.

Johnson, D. M. *The psychology of thought and judgment.* New York: Harper & Row, 1955.

Johnson, N. F. The psychological reality of phrase structure rules. *Journal of Verbal Learning & verbal Behavior,* 1965, **4,** 469–475.

Johnson, N. F. Chunking and organization in the process of recall. In G. H. Bower (Ed.), *The psychology of learning and motivation,* Vol. 4. New York: Academic Press, 1970.

Johnson, T. J., & Van Mondfrans, A. P. Order of solutions in ambiguous anagrams as a function of word frequency of the solution words. *Psychonomic Science,* 1965, **3,** 565–566.

Johnson-Laird, P. N., Legrenzi, P., & Legrenzi, M. Reasoning and a sense of reality. *British Journal of Psychology,* 1972, **63,** 395–400.

Johnson-Laird, P. N., & Tagart, J. How implication is understood. *American Journal of Psychology,* 1969, **82,** 367–373.

Jones, E. E., & Bruner, J. S. Expectancy in apparent visual movement. *British Journal of Psychology,* 1954, **45,** 157–165.

Jones, S. Visual and verbal processes in problem-solving. *Cognitive Psychology,* 1970, **1,** 201–214.

Judson, A. J., & Cofer, C. N. Reasoning as an associative process: I. "Direction" in a simple verbal problem. *Psychological Reports,* 1956, **2,** 469–476.

Judson, A. J., Cofer, C. N., & Gelfand, S. Reasoning as an associative process: II. "Direction" in problem solving as a function of prior reinforcement of relevant responses. *Psychological Reports,* 1956, **2,** 501–507.

Kahneman, D. Method, findings, and theory in studies of visual masking. *Psychol. Bull.,* 1968, **70,** 404–425.

Kahneman, D. *Attention and effort.* Englewood Cliffs, N.J.: Prentice-Hall, 1973.

Kahneman, D., & Beatty, J. Pupil diameter and load on memory. *Science,* 1966, **154,** 1583–1585.

Kahneman, D., & Beatty, J. Pupillary responses in a pitch-discrimination task. *Perc. & Psychophysics,* 1967, **2,** 101–105.

Kahneman, D., Peavler, W. S., & Onuska, L. Effects of verbalization and incentive on the pupillary response to mental activity. *Canad. J. Psychol.,* 1968, **22,** 186–196.

Kahneman, D., & Tversky, A. On the psychology of prediction. *Psychological Review,* 1973, **80,** 237–251.

Kaplan, M. F., & Singer, E. Dogmatism and sensory alienation: An empirical investigation. *J. consult. Psychol.,* 1963, **27,** 486–491.

Karwoski, T. F., Gramlich, F. W., & Arnott, P. An experiment to determine the responses to stimuli representing three levels of abstraction. *J. soc. Psychol.,* 1944, **20,** 233–247.

Katona, G. *Organizing and memorizing.* New York: Columbia Univ. Press, 1940.

Keele, S. W. Attention demands of memory retrieval. *Journal of Experimental Psychology,* 1972, **93,** 245–248.

Keele, S. W. *Attention and human performance.* Pacific Palisades, Calif.: Goodyear, 1973.

Kendler, T. S., & Kendler, H. H. Reversal and nonreversal shifts in kindergarten children. *Journal of Experimental Psychology,* 1959, **58,** 56–60.

Kendler, T. S., & Kendler, H. H. An ontogeny of optimal shift behavior. *Child Development,* 1970, **41,** 1–27.

Kilpatrick, F. P. Two processes in perceptual learning. *Journal of Experimental Psychology*, 1954, **47**, 362–370.

Kimble, D. P. The effects of bilateral hippocampal lesions in rats. *Journal of Comparative & Physiological Psychology*, 1963, **56**, 273–283.

Kintsch, W. Habituation of the GSR component of the orienting reflex during paired-associate learning before and after learning has taken place. *Journal of Mathematical Psychology*, 1965, **2**, 330–341.

Kintsch, W. Models for free recall and recognition. In D. A. Norman (Ed.), *Models of human memory*. New York: Academic Press, 1970.

Klein, G. S., Gardner, R. W., & Schlesinger, H. J. Tolerance for unrealistic experiences: A study of the generality of cognitive control. *British Journal of Psychology*, 1962, **53**, 41–55.

Kleinsmith, L. J., & Kaplan, S. Paired-associate learning as a function of arousal and interpolated activity. *Journal of Experimental Psychology*, 1963, **65**, 190–193.

Kleinsmith, L. J., & Kaplan, S. Interaction of arousal and recall interval in nonsense-syllable paired-associate learning. *Journal of Experimental Psychology*, 1964, **67**, 124–126.

Kluever, H. Studies on the eidetic type and eidetic imagery. *Psychological Bulletin*, 1928, **25**, 69–104.

Kluver, H., & Bucy, P. C. An analysis of certain effects of bilateral temporal lobectomy in the rhesus monkey with special reference to "psychic blindness." *Journal of Psychology*, 1938, **5**, 33–54.

Kohler, W. *The mentality of apes*. New York: Harcourt, 1925.

Kohler, W. *Gestalt psychology*. New York: Liveright, 1929.

Kolers, P. A. Bilingualism and information processing. *Scientific American*, 1968, **218**, No. 3, 78–89.

Kopfermann, H. Psychologische Untersuchungen uber die Wirking zweidimensionaler Darstellungen Korperlich Gebilde. *Psychologisches Forschung*, 1930, **13**, 293–364.

Korte, A. Kinematoscopische Untersuchungen. *Zeitschrift für Psychologie*, 1915, **72**, 194–296.

Kozielecki. 1961. Cited by W. M. Du Charme & C. R. Peterson. Proportion estimation as a function of proportion and sample size. *Journal of Experimental Psychology*, 1969, **81**, 536–541.

Krech, D., & Crutchfield, R. S. *Elements of psychology*. New York: Knopf, 1958.

Krech, D., Crutchfield, R. S., & Livson, N. *Elements of psychology*. (2d ed.) New York: Knopf, 1969.

Krivanek, J., & McGaugh, J. L. Effects of pentylenetetrazol on memory storage in mice. *Psychopharmacologia*, 1968, **12**, 303–321.

Kroeber, T. C. The coping functions of the ego mechanisms. In R. W. White (Ed.), *The study of lives*. New York: Atherton, 1963.

Kuhn, T. S. *The structure of scientific revolutions*. Chicago: Univ. of Chicago Press, 1962.

Lacey, B. C., & Lacey, J. I. Cardiac deceleration and simple visual reaction time in a fixed foreperiod experiment. Paper presented at the meeting of the Society for Psychophysiological Research, Washington, D.C., October, 1964.

Lacey, B. C., & Lacey, J. I. Change in cardiac response and reaction time as a function of motivation. Paper presented at the meeting of the Society for Psychophysiological Research, Denver, October, 1966.

Lacey, J. I. Somatic response patterning and stress: Some revisions of activation theory. In M. H. Appley & R. Trumbull (Eds.), *Psychological stress*. New York: Appleton, 1967.

Lacey, J. I., Kagan, J., Lacey, B. C., & Moss, H. A. The visceral level: Situational determinants and behavioral correlates of autonomic response patterns. In *Expression of the emotions of man*. New York: International Universities Press, 1963.

Lashley, K. S. An examination of the "continuity theory" as applied to discrimination learning. *Journal of General Psychology*, 1942, **26**, 241–265.

Lashley, K. S. The problem of serial order in behavior. In L. A. Jeffress (Ed.), *Cerebral mechanisms in behavior—The Hixon symposium*. New York: Wiley, 1951.

Lawrence, D. H. The nature of a stimulus. In S. Koch (Ed.), *Psychology: A study of a science*. Study II, Vol. 5. *Process areas*. New York: McGraw-Hill, 1963.

Lawrence, D. H., & Festinger, L. *Deterrents and reinforcement: The psychology of insufficient reward*. Stanford, California: Stanford Univ. Press, 1962.

Lecky, P. *Self-consistency: A theory of personality*. New York: Island Press, 1945.

Leeper, R. A study of a neglected portion of the field of learning—the development of sensory organization. *Journal of Genetic Psychology*, 1935, **46**, 41–75.

Lenneberg, E. H. *Biological foundations of language*. New York: Wiley, 1967.

Lettvin, J. Y., Maturana, H. R., McCulloch, W. S., & Pitts, W. H. What the frog's eye tells the frog's brain. *Proceedings of the I.R.E.*, 1959, **47**, 1940–1951.

Levine, M. Human discrimination learning: The subset-sampling assumption. *Psychological Bulletin*, 1970, **74**, 397–404.

Levine, M., Levinson, B., & Harlow, H. F. Trials per problem as a variable in the acquisition of discrimination learning set. *Journal of Comparative & Physiological Psychology*, 1959, **52**, 396–398.

Lewis, D. J. Sources of experimental amnesia. *Psychological Review*, 1969, **76**, 461–472.

Lewis, D. J., & Maher, B. A. Neural-consolidation and electro-convulsive shock. *Psychological Review*, 1965, **72**, 225–239.

Lewis, J. L. Semantic processing of unattended messages using dichotic listening. *Journal of Experimental Psychology*, 1970, **85**, 225–228.

Liberman, A. M., Mattingly, I. G., & Turvey, M. T. Language codes and memory codes. In A. W. Melton & E. Martin (Eds.), *Coding processes in human memory*. New York: Winston, 1972.

Lindsay, P. H. Multichannel processing in perception. In D. I. Mostofsky (Ed.), *Attention: Contemporary theory and analysis*. New York: Appleton, 1970.

Lindsay, P. H., & Norman, D. A. *Human information processing*. New York: Academic Press, 1972.

Lindsay, R. K., & Lindsay, J. M. Reaction time and serial versus parallel information processing. *Journal of Experimental Psychology*, 1966, **71**, 294–303.

Lindsley, D. B. The reticular system and perceptual discrimination. In H. H. Jasper *et al.* (Eds.), *Reticular formation of the brain*. Boston: Little, Brown, 1958.

Lindsley, D. B., Schreiner, L. H., Knowles, W. B., & Magoun, H. W. Behavioral and EEG changes following chronic brain stem lesions in the cat. *EEG of Clinical Neurophysiology*, 1950, **2**, 483–498.

Locke, J. *An essay concerning human understanding.* New York: Dover, 1959.

Lockhart, R. S. Stimulus selection and meaningfulness in paired-associate learning with stimulus items of high formal similarity. *Journal of Experimental Psychology,* 1968, **78,** 242–246.

Lockhead, G. R. Identification and the form of multidimensional discrimination space. *Journal of Experimental Psychology,* 1970, **85,** 1–10.

Logan, F. A., Beier, E. M., & Ellis, R. A. Effect of varied reinforcement on speed of locomotion. *Journal of Experimental Psychology,* 1955, **49,** 260–266.

Loisette, A. *Assimilative memory or how to attend and never forget.* New York: Funk & Wagnalls, 1896.

Long, B. H., & Ziller, R. C. Dogmatism and predecisional information search. *Journal of Applied Psychology,* 1965, **49,** 376–378.

Lorens, S. A., & Darrow, C. W. Eye movements, EEG, GSR, and EKG during mental manipulations. *Electroencephalography & Clinical Neurophysiology,* 1962, **14,** 739–746.

Lorenz, K. Der Kumpan in der Umwelt des Vogels. *Journal fuer Ornithologie,* 1935, **83,** 137–213, 289–413.

Lovejoy, A. O. *The great chain of being.* Cambridge, Massachusetts: Harvard Univ. Press, 1936.

Luchins, A. S. Mechanization in problem solving. *Psychological Monographs,* 1942, **54,** No. 248.

Luria, A. R. *The role of speech in the regulation of normal and abnormal behavior.* New York: Liveright, 1961.

Luria, A. R. *The mind of a mnemonist.* New York: Basic Books, 1968.

Luria, A. R., & Homskaya, E. D. Disturbance in the regulative role of speech with frontal lobe lesions. In J. M. Warren & K. Akert (Eds.), *The frontal granular cortex and behavior.* New York: McGraw-Hill, 1964.

MacCorquodale, K., & Meehl, P. E. On a distinction between hypothetical constructs and intervening variables. *Psychological Review,* 1948, **55,** 95–107.

Mach, E. *The analysis of sensations.* New York: Dover, 1959.

MacKay, D. M. Towards an information-flow model of human behavior. *British Journal of Psychology,* 1956, **47,** 30–43.

MacKinnon, D. W. The personality correlates of creativity: A study of American architects. In *Proceedings of 14th Congress on Applied Psychology,* 1962, **2,** 11–39.

MacKinnon, D. W. The nature and nurture of creative talent. *American Psychologist,* 1962, **17,** 484–495.

MacKinnon, D. W., & Dukes, W. F. Repression. In L. Postman (Ed.), *Psychology in the making.* New York: Knopf, 1964.

Mackworth, J. F. Interference and decay in very short-term memory. *Journal of Verbal Learning & Verbal Behavior,* 1964, **3,** 300–308.

Mackworth, N. H. In 6th Annual Report, The Center for Cognitive Studies, Harvard Univ., 1965–1966.

MacLean, P. D. The limbic system with respect to self-preservation and the preservation of the species. *Journal of Nervous & Mental Diseases,* 1958, **127,** 1–11.

MacNichol, E. F., Jr. Three-pigment color vision. *Scientific American,* 1964, **211,** No. 6, 48–56.

Maier, N. R. F. Reasoning in humans. I. On direction. *Journal of Comparative Psychology,* 1930, **10,** 115–143.

Maier, N. R. F. Reasoning in humans. II. The solution of a problem and its appearance in consciousness. *Journal of Comparative Psychology*, 1931, **12**, 181–194. (a)

Maier, N. R. F. Reasoning and learning. *Psychological Review*, 1931, **38**, 332–346. (b)

Maier, N. R. F. An aspect of human reasoning. *British Journal of Psychology*, 1933, **24**, 144–155.

Maier, N. R. F. *Problem solving and creativity in individuals and groups.* Belmont, California: Brooks/Cole, 1970.

Malmo, R. B. Interference factors in delayed response in monkeys after removal of frontal lobes. *Journal of Neurophysiology*, 1942, **5**, 295–308.

Maltzman, I. On the training of originality. *Psychological Review*, 1960, **67**, 229–242.

Maltzman, I., Belloni, M., & Fishbein, M. Experimental studies of associative variables in originality. *Psychological Monographs*, 1964, **78**, 3 (Whole No. 580).

Maltzman, I., Harris, L., Ingram, E., & Wolff, C. A primary effect in the orienting reflex to stimulus change. *Journal of Experimental Psychology*, 1971, **87**, 202–206.

Mandler, G. Organization and memory. In K. W. Spence & J. R. Spence (Eds.), *The psychology of learning and motivation*, Vol. 1. New York: Academic Press, 1967.

Manske, M. E., & Davis, G. A. Effects of simple instructional biases upon performance in the Unusual Uses Test. *Journal of General Psychology*, 1968, **78**, 25–33.

Marbe, K. *Experimentell-psychologische Untersuchungen uber das Urteil eine Einleitung in die Logik.* Leipzig: Engelman, 1901.

Marks, E. S. Skin color judgments of negro college students. *Journal of Abnormal & Social Psychology*, 1943, **38**, 370–376.

Martin, C. J., Boersma, F. J., & Cox, D. L. A classification of associative strategies in paired-associates learning. *Psychonomic Science*, 1965, **3**, 463–464.

Martin, E., & Roberts, K. Grammatical factors in sentence retention. *Journal of Verbal Learning & Verbal Behavior*, 1966, **5**, 211–218.

Masserman, J. H. *Principles of dynamic psychiatry.* Philadelphia: Saunders, 1946.

Mattingly, I. G. Speech cues and sign stimuli. *American Scientist*, 1972, **60**, 327–337.

Mawardi, B. H. Industrial invention: A study in group problem solving. Unpublished doctoral dissertation, Harvard Univ., 1959.

Max, L. W. Experimental study of the motor theory of consciousness. IV. Action-current responses of the deaf during awakening, kinesthetic imagery, and abstract thinking. *Journal of Comparative Psychology*, 1937, **24**, 301–344.

May, R. *Love and will.* New York: Norton, 1969.

McClelland, D., Atkinson, J., Clark, B., & Lowell, E. *The achievement motive.* New York: Appleton, 1953.

McCullough, C. Color adaptation of edge-detectors in the human visual system. *Science*, 1965, **149**, 1115–1116.

McGaugh, J. L. Facilitation of memory storage processes. In S. Bogoch (Ed.), *The future of the brain sciences.* New York: Plenum, 1969.

McGaugh, J. L. *Learning and memory.* San Francisco: Albion, 1973.

McGaugh, J. L., & Hostetter. Unpubl. Research. Cited in E. R. Hilgard, R. C. Atkinson, & R. L. Atkinson. *Introduction to psychology* (5th ed.) New York: Harcourt, 1971. Pp. 262f.

McGaugh, J. L., & Krivanek, J. Strychnine effects on discrimination learning in mice: Effects of dose and time of administration. *Physiology and Behavior*, 1970, **5**, 798–803.

McGeoch, J. A., & Irion, A. L. *The psychology of human learning.* New York: Longmans, 1952.

McGinnies, E. Emotionality and perceptual defense. *Psychological Review*, 1949, **56**, 244–251.

McGuire, W. J. The nature of attitudes and attitude change. In G. Lindzey & E. Aronson (Eds.), *The handbook of social psychology.* (2d ed.) Reading, Massachusetts: Addison-Wesley, 1968.

McKellar, P. *Imagination and thinking.* New York: Basic Books, 1957.

McNeill, D. Developmental psycholinguistics. In F. Smith & G. A. Miller (Eds.), *The genesis of language: A psycholinguistic approach.* Cambridge, Massachusetts: MIT Press, 1966.

Mednick, S. A. Associative basis of the creative process. *Psychological Review*, 1962, **69**, 220–232.

Melton, A. The situation with respect to the spacing of repetitions and memory. *Journal of Verbal Learning & Verbal Behavior*, 1970, **9**, 596–606.

·Meyer, D. E. On the representation and retrieval of stored semantic information. *Cognitive Psychology*, 1970, **1**, 242–299.

Miles, R. C. Discrimination-learning sets. In A. M. Schrier, H. F. Harlow, & F. Stollnitz (Eds.), *Behavior of nonhuman primates.* New York: Academic Press, 1965.

Milgram, S. Behavioral study of obedience. *Journal of Abnormal & Social Psychology*, 1963, **67**, 371–378.

Mill, J. S. *System of logic.* New York: Longmans, 1930.

Miller, G. A. The magical number seven, plus or minus two: Some limits on our capacity for processing information. *Psychological Review*, 1956, **63**, 81–97.

Miller, G. A. The organization of lexical memory: Are word associations sufficient? In G. A. Talland & N. C. Waugh (Eds.), *The pathology of memory.* New York: Academic Press, 1969.

Miller, G. A. *The psychology of communication.* New York: Basic Books, 1967.

Miller, G. A. English verbs of motion: A case study in semantics and lexical memory. In A. W. Melton & E. Martin (Eds.), *Coding processes in human memory.* New York: Winston, 1972.

Miller, G. A., Galanter, E., & Pribram, K. H. *Plans and the structure of behavior.* New York: Holt, 1960.

Miller, G. A., Heise, G. A., & Lichten, W. The intelligibility of speech as a function of the context of the text materials. *Journal of Experimental Psychology*, 1951, **41**, 329–335.

Miller, G. A., & McNeill, D. Psycholinguistics. In G. Lindzey & E. Aronson (Eds.), *The handbook of social psychology*, Vol. III. (2d ed.) Reading, Massachusetts: Addison-Wesley, 1969.

Miller, G. A., Teller, V., & Rubenstein, H. In Seventh Annual Report, The Center for Cognitive Studies, Harvard Univ., 1966–1967.

Miller, N. E. Experimental studies of conflict. In J. McV. Hunt (Ed.), *Personality and the behavior disorders.* New York: Ronald Press, 1944.

Miller, N. E. Learning of visceral and glandular responses. *Science*, 1969, **163**, 434–445.

Miller, N. E., & Banuazizi, A. Instrumental learning by curarized rats of a specific visceral response, intestinal or cardiac. *Journal of Comparative & Physiological Psychology*, 1968, **65**, 1–7.

Millward, R. Latency in a modified paired-associate learning experiment. *Journal of Verbal Learning & Verbal Behavior*, 1964, **3**, 309–316.

Milner, B. Intellectual function of the temporal lobes. *Psychological Bulletin*, 1954, **51**, 52–62.

Milner, B. Effects of different brain lesions on card sorting. *Archives of Neurology*, 1963, **9**, 90–100.

Milner, B. Some effects of frontal lobectomy in man. In J. M. Warren & K. Akert (Eds.), *The frontal granular cortex and behavior*. New York: McGraw-Hill, 1964.

Milner, B. Visually-guided maze learning in man: Effects of bilateral hippocampal, bilateral frontal, and unilateral cerebral lesions. *Neuropsychologia*, 1965, **3**, 317.

Milner, B. Interhemispheric differences and psychological processes. *British Medical Bulletin*, 1971, **27**, 272–277.

Milner, B., & Teuber, H. L. Alternation of perception and memory in man: Reflections on methods. In L. Weiskrantz (Ed.), *Analysis of behavioral change*. New York: Harper & Row, 1968.

Milner, P. M. *Physiological psychology*. New York: Holt, 1970.

Minsky, M. Steps toward artificial intelligence. *Proceedings of the IRE*, 1961, **49**, 8–29.

Minsky, M. Mechanisms and images. Condon Lecture Series, Portland State University, Portland, Oregon, 1970.

Mischel, W. *Personality and assessment*. New York: Wiley, 1968.

Mittelstaedt, H. Basic control patterns of orientational homeostasis. *Symposium of the Society for Experimental Biology*, 1964, **18**, 365–386.

Morgan, C. T. *Physiological psychology*. (3d ed.) New York: McGraw-Hill, 1965.

Morin, R. E., DeRosa, D. V., & Stultz, V. Recognition memory and reaction time. *Acta Psychologica*, 1967, **27**, 298–305.

Morton, J. Repeated items and decay in memory. *Psychon. Sci.*, 1968, **10**, 219–220.

Morton, J. A functional model for memory. In D. A. Norman (Ed.), *Models of human memory*. New York: Academic Press, 1970.

Muenzinger, K. F. Motivation in learning. I. Electric shock for correct response in the visual discrimination habit. *Journal of Comparative Psychology*, 1935, **17**, 267–277.

Muenzinger, K. F. Vicarious trial and error at a point of choice. I. A general survey of its relation to learning efficiency. *Journal of Genetic Psychology*, 1938, **53**, 75–86.

Muller, G. E., & Pilzecker, A. Experimentelle Beitrage zur Lehre vom Gedachtnis. *Zeitschrift für Psychologie*, 1900, Ergbd. I.

Muller, G. E., & Schumann, F. Experimentelle Beitrage zur Untersuchung des Gedachtnisses. *Zeitschrift für Psychologie*, 1894, **6**, 81–190, 257–339.

Munn, N. L. *Psychology*. (4th ed.) Boston: Houghton Mifflin, 1961.

Murch, G. M. Binocular relationships in a size and color orientation specific aftereffect. *Journal of Experimental Psychology*, 1972, **93**, 30–34.

Murch, G. M. Color contingent motion aftereffects: Single or multiple levels of processing? *Vision Research*, 1974, **14**.

Murdock, B. B., Jr. The retention of individual items. *Journal of Experimental Psychology*, 1961, **62**, 618–625.

Murdock, B. B., Jr. The serial position effect in free recall. *Journal of Experimental Psychology*, 1962, **64**, 482–488.

Murdock, B. B., Jr. Signal detection theory and short-term memory. *Journal of Experimental Psychology*, 1965, **70**, 443–447.

Murray, D. J. The effect of white noise on the recall of vocalized lists. *Canadian Journal of Psychology*, 1965, **19**, 333–345.

Murray, F. B. Acquisition of conservation through social interaction. *Developmental Psychology*, 1972, **6**, 106.

Neisser, U. Decision-time without reaction-time: Experiments in visual scanning. *American Journal of Psychology*, 1963, **76**, 376–385.

Neisser, U. *Cognitive psychology*. New York: Appleton, 1967.

Neisser, U., & Weene, P. Hierarchies in concept attainment. *Journal of Experimental Psychology*, 1962, **64**, 644–645.

Newell, A. (Ed.) *Information Processing Language V Manual*. Englewood Cliffs, New Jersey: Prentice-Hall, 1961.

Newell, A., Shaw, J. C., & Simon, H. A. Elements of a theory of human problem solving. *Psychological Review*, 1958, **65**, 151–166.

Newell, A., Shaw, J. C., & Simon, H. A. The process of creative thinking. In H. E. Gruber, G. Terrell, & M. Wertheimer (Eds.), *Contemporary approaches to creative thinking*. New York: Atherton, 1962.

Newell, A., & Simon, H. A. *Human problem solving*. Englewood Cliffs, New Jersey: Prentice-Hall, 1972.

Norman, D. A. *Memory and attention*. New York: Wiley, 1969.

Obrist, P. A. Heart rate and somatic-motor coupling during classical aversive conditioning in humans. *Journal of Experimental Psychology*, 1968, **77**, 180–193.

Obrist, P. A., Webb, D. M., Sutterer, J. R., & Howard, J. L. Cardiac deceleration and reaction time: An evaluation of two hypotheses. *Psychophysiology*, 1970, **6**, 695–706.

Olds, J. Adaptive functions of paleocortical and related structures. In H. F. Harlow & C. N. Woolsey (Eds.), *Biological and biochemical bases of behavior*. Madison, Wisconsin: Univ. of Wisconsin Press, 1958.

Olds, J., & Olds, M. Drives, rewards, and the brain. In *New directions in psychology II*. New York: Holt, 1965.

Oleron, P. *Recherches sur le developpement mental des sourds-muets: Contribution a l'etude du probleme "langue et pensee."* Paris: Centre National de la Recherche Scientifique, 1957.

Oleron, P., Gumusyan, S., & Moulinou, M. Extension des concepts et usage du langage. *Revue Psychologie Francaise*, 1966, **11**, 149–161.

Olson, R. K., & Attneave, F. What variables produce similarity grouping? *American Journal of Psychology*, 1970, **83**, 1–21.

Oltman, P. K. Field dependence and arousal. *Perceptual & Motor Skills*, 1964, **19**, 441.

Osborn, A. F. *Applied imagination*. New York: Scribners, 1953.

Osgood, C. E. *Method and theory in experimental psychology*. New York and London: Oxford Univ. Press, 1953.

Osgood, C. E. Toward a wedding of insufficiencies. In T. R. Dixon & D. L. Horton (Eds.), *Verbal behavior and general behavior theory*. Englewood Cliffs, New Jersey: Prentice-Hall, 1968.

Osgood, C. E., Suci, G. J., & Tannenbaum, P. H. *The measurement of meaning*. Urbana, Illinois: Univ. of Illinois Press, 1957.

Osgood, C. E., & Tannenbaum, P. H. The principle of congruity in the prediction of attitude change. *Psychological Review*, 1955, **62**, 42–55.

Oyama, T. Figure-ground dominance as a function of sector angle, brightness, hue, and orientation. *Journal of Experimental Psychology*, 1960, **60**, 299–305.

Paivio, A. *Imagery and verbal processes*. New York: Holt, 1971.

Paivio, A., & Csapo, K. Concrete-image and verbal memory codes. *Journal of Experimental Psychology*, 1969, **80**, 279–285.

Papez, J. W. A proposed mechanism of emotion. *Archives of Neurology & Psychiatry, Chicago*, 1937, **38**, 725–743.

Parducci, A. Range-frequency compromise in judgment. *Psychological Monographs*, 1963, **77** (Whole No. 565).

Parducci, A. Category judgment: A range-frequency model. *Psychological Review*, 1965, **72**, 407–418.

Parducci, A. The relativism of absolute judgments. *Scientific American*, 1968, **219**, No. 6, 84–93.

Parducci, A., Calfee, R. C., Marshall, L. M., & Davidson, L. P. Context effects in judgment: Adaptation level as a function of the mean, midpoint, and medan of the stimuli. *Journal of Experimental Psychology*, 1960, **60**, 65–77.

Parrott, G. L. The effects of premise content on accuracy and solution time in syllogistic reasoning. Unpublished master's thesis, Michigan State Univ., 1967. [Cited in D. M. Johnson, *Systematic introduction to the psychology of thinking*. New York: Harper & Row, 1972. P. 239.]

Pavlov, I. P. *Conditioned reflexes*. (G. V. Anrep, Trans.) New York: Dover, 1927.

Penfield, W. Consciousness, memory, and man's conditioned reflexes. In K. Pribram (Ed.), *On the biology of learning*. New York: Harcourt, 1969.

Penfield, W., & Rasmussen, T. *The cerebral cortex of man*. New York: Macmillan, 1950.

Perky, C. W. An experimental study of imagination. *American Journal of Psychology*, 1910, **21**, 422–542.

Peterson, C. R., & Beach, L. R. Man as an intuitive statistician. *Psychological Bulletin*, 1967, **68**, 29–46.

Peterson, L. R. Search and judgment in memory. In B. J. Kleinmuntz (Ed.), *Concepts and the structure of memory*. New York: Wiley, 1967.

Peterson, L. R., & Peterson, M. J. Short-term retention of individual verbal items. *Journal of Experimental Psychology*, 1959, **58**, 193–198.

Pew, R. W. Acquisition of hierarchical control over the temporal organization of a skill. *Journal of Experimental Psychology*, 1966, **71**, 764–771.

Pfaffman, C. The sense of taste. In J. Field (Ed.), *Handbook of physiology*, Sec. 1: *Neurophysiology*. Vol. I. Washington, D.C.: American Physiological Society, 1959.

Piaget, J. *The origins of intelligence in children*. New York: International Universities Press, 1952. (a)

Piaget, J. *The child's conception of number*. New York: Humanities, 1952. (b)

Piaget, J. The stages of the intellectual development of the child. *Bulletins of the Menninger Clinic*, 1962, **26**, 120–128.

Piaget, J. *The early growth of logic in the child*. London: Routledge & Kegan Paul, 1964.

Piaget, J., & Inhelder, B. *Le developpement des quantities physiques chez l'enfant*. (2nd rev. ed.) Neuchatel, Switzerland: Delachauz & Niestle, 1962.

Platt, J. R. Strong inference. *Science*, 1964, **146**, 347–353.

Podell, H. A. Two processes of concept formation. *Psychological Monographs*, 1958, **72** (Whole No. 468).

Poincaré, H. Mathematical creation. In G. B. Halsted (Transl.), *The foundations of science*. New York: Science Press, 1913.

Pollack, I. The information of elementary auditory displays. *Journal of the Acoustical Society of America*, 1952, **24**, 745–749.

Pollack, I. The information of elementary auditory displays. II. *Journal of the Acoustical Society of America*, 1953, **25**, 765–769.

Pollack, I. Structure of memory search. In Mental Health Research Institute 12th Annual Report. Ann Arbor, Mich.: Univ. of Michigan, 1967. Pp. 20–21.

Pollio, H. R. Some semantic relations among word-associates. *American Journal of Psychology*, 1964, **77**, 249–256.

Pollio, H. R. *The structural basis of word association behavior*. The Hague: Mouton, 1966.

Polson, M. C., Restle, F., & Polson, P. G. Association and discrimination in paired-associate learning. *Journal of Experimental Psychology*, 1965, **69**, 47–55.

Polya, G. *How to solve it*. Garden City, New York: Doubleday (Anchor), 1957.

Posner, M. I. Information reduction in the analysis of sequential tasks. *Psychological Review*, 1964, **76**, 491–504.

Posner, M. I. Components of skilled performance. *Science*, 1966, **152**, 1712–1718.

Posner, M. I. Abstraction and the process of recognition. In G. H. Bower & J. T. Spence (Eds.), *The psychology of learning and motivation*, Vol. 3. New York: Academic Press, 1969.

Posner, M. I. On the relationship between letter names and super-ordinate categories. *Quarterly Journal of Experimental Psychology*, 1970, **22**, 279–287.

Posner, M. I. *Cognition: An introduction*. Glenview, Ill.: Scott, Foresman, 1973.

Posner, M. I., & Boies, S. J. Components of attention. *Psychological Review*, 1971, **78**, 391–408.

Posner, M. I., & Rossman, E. The effect of size and location of informational transforms upon short-term retention. *Journal of Experimental Psychology*, 1965, **70**, 496–505.

Postman, L. The effects of language habits on the acquisition and retention of verbal associations. *Journal of Experimental Psychology*, 1962, **64**, 7–19.

Postman, L. Does interference theory predict too much forgetting? *Journal of Verbal Learning & Verbal Behavior*, 1963, **2**, 40–48.

Postman, L. Short-term memory and incidental learning. In A. W. Melton (Ed.), *Categories of human learning*. New York: Academic Press, 1964.

Postman, L. Association and performance in the analysis of verbal learning. In T. R. Dixon & D. L. Horton (Eds.), *Verbal behavior and general behavior theory*. Englewood Cliffs, New Jersey: Prentice-Hall, 1968.

Postman, L., & Stark, K. Role of response availability in transfer and interference. *Journal of Experimental Psychology*, 1969, **79**, 168–177.

Pratt, R. W. Cognitive processing of uncertainty: Its effects on pupillary dilation and preference ratings. *Perception & Psychophysics*, 1970, **8**, 193–198.

Pribram, K. The neurophysiology of remembering. *Scientific American*, 1969, **220**, No. 1, 73–86.

Pribram, K. *Languages of the brain*. Englewood Cliffs, New Jersey: Prentice-Hall, 1971.

Pribram, K., & Tubbs, W. E. Short-term memory, parsing and the primate frontal cortex. *Science*, 1967, **156**, 1765–1767.

Quastler, H., & Wulff, V. J. Human performance in information transmission. Part one: simple sequential routinized tasks. Unpublished Manuscript. [Cited in F. Attneave, *Applications of information theory to psychology*. New York: Holt, 1959.]

Raphelson, A. C. The relationship between imaginative, direct, verbal, and physiological measures of anxiety in an achievement situation. *Journal of Abnormal & Social Psychology*, 1957, **54**, 13–18.

Razran, G. The observable unconscious and the inferable conscious in current Soviet psychophysiology: Introceptive conditioning, semantic conditioning, and the orienting reflex. *Psychological Review*, 1961, **68**, 81–147.

Razran, G. *Mind in evolution*. Boston: Houghton-Mifflin, 1971.

Reitman, W. R. *Cognition and thought*. New York: Wiley, 1965.

Restle, F. Discrimination of cues in mazes: A resolution of the "place-vs.-response" question. *Psychological Review*, 1957, **64**, 217–228.

Restle, F. The selection of strategies in cue learning. *Psychological Review*, 1962, **69**, 329–343.

Rethlingshafer, D., & Hinckley, E. D. Influence of judge's characteristics upon adaptation level. *American Journal of Psychology*, 1963, **76**, 16–23.

Riggs, L. A., Ratliff, F., Cornsweet, J. C., & Cornsweet, T. N. The disappearance of steadily fixated test objects. *Journal of the Optical Society of America*, 1953, **43**, 495–501.

Riklan, M., & Levita, E. *Subcortical correlates of human behavior*. Baltimore: Williams & Wilkins, 1969.

Ripley, A. *Minute mysteries*. New York: Pocket Books, 1949.

Rips, L. J., Shoben, E. J., & Smith, E. E. Semantic distance and the verification of semantic relations. *Journal of Verbal Learning & Verbal Behavior*, 1973, **12**, 1–20.

Rizzolatti, G., Umilta, C., & Berlucchi, G. Opposite superiorities of the right and left cerebral hemispheres in discriminative reaction time to physiognomical and alphabetical material. *Brain*, 1971, **94**, 431–442.

Robertson, J. *A two year old goes to the hospital* (film). Condon. Released in the United States by New York Univ. Film Library, 1953.

Rock, I. The role of repetition in associative learning. *American Journal of Psychology*, 1957, **70**, 186–193.

Rodieck, R. W. Quantitative analysis of cat retinal ganglion cell response to visual stimuli. *Vision Research*, 1965, **5**, 583–601.

Rosenzweig, S. The investigation of repression as an instance of experimental idiodynamics. *Psychological Review*, 1952, **59**, 339–345.

Rosenzweig, S. The experimental study of repression. In H. A. Murray (Ed.), *Explorations in personality*. New York: Wiley, 1962.

Rudel, R. G. Transposition of response by children trained in intermediate sized problems. *Journal of Comparative Physiology and Psychology*, 1957, **50**, 292–295.

Rumelhart, D. E., Lindsay, P. H., & Norman, D. A. A process model for long-term memory. In E. Tulving & W. Donaldson (Eds.), *Organization and memory*. New York: Academic Press, 1972.

Russell, B. *Our knowledge of the external world as a field for scientific method in philosophy*. London: Allen & Unwin, 1926.

Ryan, T. A., & Schwartz, C. B. Speed of perception as a function of mode of representations. *American Journal of Psychology*, 1956, **69**, 60–69.

Salapatek, P., & Kesson, W. Visual scanning of triangles by the human newborn. *Journal of Experimental Child Psychology*, 1966, **3**, 155–167.

Saltz, E. *The cognitive bases of human learning*. Homewood, Illinois: The Dorsey Press, 1971.

Saporta, S., Blumenthal, A. L., & Rieff, D. G. Grammatical models and language learning. *Monographs of the Series on Language & Linguistics*, 1963, **16**, 133–142.

Saugstad, P. An analysis of Maier's pendulum problem. *Journal of Experimental Psychology*, 1957, **54**, 168–179.

Schacter, A., & Singer, J. E. Cognitive, social and physiological determinants of emotional state. *Psychological Review*, 1962, **69**, 379–399.

Schaeffer, B., & Wallace, R. The comparison of word meanings. *Journal of Experimental Psychology*, 1970, **86**, 144–152.

Schank, R. C. Intention, memory and computer understanding. Stanford Artif. Intell. Project Memo. No. AIM-140, Stanford Univ., 1971.

Schank, R. C., Tesler, L., & Weber, S. Spinoza II: Conceptual case-based natural language analysis. Stanford Artif. Intell. Project Memo. No. AIM-109, Stanford Univ., 1970.

Schein, E. H. The Chinese indoctrination program for prisoners of war. *Psychiatry*, 1956, **19**, 149–172.

Schleidt, W. M. Reaktionen fur Truthuhnern auf fliegende Raubvogel und Versuche zur Analyse ihrer AAM's. *Zeitschrift für Tierpsychologies*, 1961, **18**, 534–560.

Schlosberg, H. The description of facial expressions in terms of two dimensions. *Journal of Experimental Psychology*, 1952, **44**, 229–237.

Schneider, G. E. Contrasting visuomotor functions of tectum and cortex in the golden hamster. *Psychologische Forschung*, 1967/1968, **31**, 52–62.

Sears, R. R. Experimental studies of projection: I. Attribution of traits. *Journal of Social Psychology*, 1936, **7**, 151–163.

Segal, M. H., Campbell, T. D., & Herskovitz, M. J. *The influence of culture on visual perception*. New York: Bobbs-Merrill, 1966.

Selfridge, O., & Neisser, U. Pattern recognition by machine. *Scientific American*, 1960, **203**, 60–79.

Shannon, C. E., & Weaver, W. *The mathematical theory of communication*. Urbana: Univ. of Illinois Press, 1949.

Shepard, R. N., Hovland, C. I., & Jenkins, H. M. Learning and memorization of classifications. *Psychological Monographs*, 1961, **75** (Whole No. 517).

Shepard, R. N., & Metzler, J. Mental rotation of three-dimensional objects. *Science*, 1971, **171**, 701–703.

Shor, R. E. Hypnosis and the concept of the generalized reality-orientation. *American Journal of Psychotherapy*, 1959, **13**, 582–602.

Shor, R. E. Three dimensions of hypnotic depth. In R. E. Schor & M. T. Orne (Eds.), *The nature of hypnosis*. New York: Holt, 1965.

Silviera, J. M. Incubation: The effect of interruption timing and length on problem solution and quality of problem processing. Unpublished Ph.D. Dissertation, Univ. of Oregon, 1971.

Simon, C. W., & Emmons, W. EEG, consciousness, and sleep. *Science*, 1956, **124**, 1066–1069.

Simon, H. A. *Models of man*. New York: Wiley, 1957.

Simon, H. A. *The shape of automation for men and management*. New York: Harper & Row, 1965.

Simon, H. A. *The sciences of the artificial*. Cambridge, Massachusetts: MIT Press, 1969.

Skaife, A. M. Role of deviation and complexity in changing musical taste. *Proceedings of the 75th Annual Convention of APA*, 1967, **2**, 25–26.

Skinner, B. F. *Science and human behavior*. New York: Macmillan, 1953.

Slobin, D. I. The acquisition of Russian as a native language. In F. Smith & G. A. Miller (Eds.), *The genesis of language: A psycholinguistic approach*. Cambridge, Massachusetts: MIT Press, 1966.

Slovic, P. Cue-consistency and cue-utilization in judgment. *American Journal of Psychology*, 1966, **79**, 427–434.

Slovic, P. Analyzing the expert judge: A descriptive study of a stockbroker's decision process. *Journal of Applied Psychology*, 1969, **53**, 255–263.

Slovic, P., Lichtenstein, S., & Edwards, W. Boredom-induced changes in preferences among bets. *American Journal of Psychology*, 1965, **78**, 208–217.

Smedslund, J. The acquisition of conservation of substance and weight in children. V. Practice in conflict situations without external reinforcement. *Scandinavian Journal of Psychology*, 1961, **2**, 156–160. (a)

Smedslund, J. The acquisition of conservation of substance and weight in children. VI. Practice on continuous versus discontinuous material in conflict situations without external reinforcement. *Scandinavian Journal of Psychology*, 1961, **2**, 203–210. (b)

Smith, D. D. *Mammalian learning and behavior*. Philadelphia: W. B. Saunders, 1965.

Smith, E. E. The power of dissonance techniques to change attitudes. *Public Opinion Quarterly*, 1961, **25**, 629–639.

Smith, E. E., Shoben, E. J., & Rips, L. J. Structure and process in semantic memory: A featural model for semantic decisions. *Psychological Review*, 1974, **81**, 214–241.

Smith, S. M., Brown, H. O., Toman, J. E. P., & Goodman, L. S. The lack of cerebral effects of d-tubocurarine. *Anesthesiology*, 1947, **8**, 1–4.

Sokolov, E. N. *Perception and the conditioned reflex*. (S. W. Waydenfold, Trans.) Oxford: Pergamon Press, 1963.

Sokolov, E. N. The orienting reflex as a regulator of information. In E. N. Sokolov (Ed.), *The orienting reflex and problems of normal and pathological reception*. Moscow: Prosveshicheniye, 1964.

Sokolov, E. N. The orienting reflex, its structure and mechanisms. In L. G. Voronin, A. N. Leontiev, A. R. Luria, E. N. Sokolov, & O. S. Vinogradova (Eds.), *Orienting reflex and exploratory behavior*. Russian Monographs on Brain and Behav., 3. Amer. Inst. of Bio. Sci., Washington, D.C., 1965.

Sokolov, E. N. The modeling properties of the nervous system. In M. Cole & I. Maltzman (Eds.), *A handbook of contemporary Soviet psychology*. New York: Basic Books, 1969.

Solarz, A. K. Latency of instrumental responses as a function of compatibility with the meaning of eliciting verbal signs. *Journal of Experimental Psychology*, 1960, **59**, 239–245.

Sommerhoff, G. The abstract characteristics of living systems. In F. E. Emery (Ed.), *Systems thinking*. Baltimore: Penguin, 1969.

Spearman, C., & Jones, L. W. *Human ability*. New York: Macmillan, 1950.

Spencer, T. J. Some effects of different masking stimuli on iconic storage. *Journal of Experimental Psychology*, 1969, **81**, 132–140.

Sperry, R. W. The great cerebral commisure. *Scientific American*, 1964 (January).

Sperry, R. W., & Gazzaniga, M. S. Language following surgical disconnection of the hemispheres. In F. L. Darley (Ed.), *Brain mechanisms underlying speech and language*. New York: Grune & Stratton, 1967.

Stern, W. *Psychologie der fruehen Kindheit*. Leipzig: Quelle & Meyer, 1914.

Stern, C. u. W. *Die Kindersprache*. Leipzig: J. A. Barth, 1928.

Sternberg, S. High-speed scanning in human memory. *Science*, 1966, **153**, 652–654.

Stevens, S. S. The psychophysics of sensory function. *American Scientist*, 1960, **48**, 226–253.

Stolz, W. S. A study of the ability to decode grammatically novel sentences. *Journal of Verbal Learning & Verbal Behavior*, 1967, **6**, 867–873.

Stromeyer, C. F., III. Eidetikers. *Psychology Today*, 1970, **4** (November), 76–81.

Stromeyer, C. F., III, & Mansfield, R. J. Colored aftereffects produced with moving images. *Perception & Psychophysics*, 1970, **7**, 108–114.

Stromeyer, C. F., III, & Psotka, J. The detailed texture of eidetic images. *Nature*, 1970, **225**, 346–349.

Suchman, J. R. Inquiry training: Building skills for autonomous discovery. *Merrill-Palmer Quarterly*, 1961, 147–169.

Suppes, P. Stimulus-response theory of finite automata. *Journal of Mathematical Psychology*, 1969, **6**, 327–355.

Suppes, P., & Ginsberg, R. A. Application of a stimulus sampling model to children's concept formation with and without correction of responses. *Journal of Experimental Psychology*, 1962, **63**, 330–336.

Suppes, P., & Ginsberg, R. A. A fundamental property of all-or-none models, binomial distribution of responses prior to conditioning, with application to concept formation in children. *Psychological Review*, 1963, **70**, 139–161.

Suppes, P., Groen, G., & Schlag-Rey, M. A model for response latency in paired-associate learning. *Journal of Mathematical Psychology*, 1966, **3**, 99–128.

Swets, J. A. Is there a sensory threshold? *Science*, 1961, **134**, 168–177.

Szekely, L. Zur Psychologie des Geistigen Schaffens. *Schweitzerische Zeitschrift für Psychologie und ihre Anwendungen*, 1945, **4**, 110–124.

Taylor, C. W., & Barron, F. (Eds.), *Scientific creativity: Its recognition and development*. New York: Wiley, 1963.

Taylor, D. W., & Faust, W. L. Twenty questions: Efficiency in problem solving as a function of size of group. *Journal of Experimental Psychology*, 1952, **44**, 360–367.

Taylor, J. A. The relationship of anxiety to the conditioned eyelid response. *Journal of Experimental Psychology*, 1951, **41**, 81–92.

Taylor, J. A. Drive theory and manifest anxiety. *Psychological Bulletin*, 1956, **53**, 303–320.

Taylor, K. W., Berry, P. C., & Block, C. H. Does group participation when using brainstorming facilitate or inhibit creative thinking? Yale Univ. Dept. of Psychol., Office of Naval Research, Tech. Rept. No. 1, 1957.

Taylor, R. L., & Posner, M. I. Retrieval from visual and verbal memory codes. Paper presented at the meeting of the Western Psychological Association, San Diego, 1968.

Teitelbaum, P. *Physiological psychology*. Englewood Cliffs, N.J.: Prentice-Hall, 1967.

Tennyson, A. T. *The poems of Alfred, Lord Tennyson*. London: J. M. Dent & Sons, 1906.

Terzian, H., & Dalle Ore, G. Syndrome of Kluver and Bucy reproduced in man by bilateral removal of the temporal lobes. *Neurology*, 1955, **5**, 373–380.

Teuber, H. L. Perception. In J. Field (Ed.), *Handbook of physiology*, Vol. 3. *Neurophysiology*. Washington, D.C.: American Physiological Society, 1960.

Teuber, H.-L., & Mishkin, M. Judgment of visual and postural vertical after brain injury. *Journal of Psychology*, 1954, **38**, 161–175.

Thigpen, C. H., & Cleckley, H. M. *The three faces of Eve*. New York: McGraw-Hill, 1957.

Thistlethwaite, D. L. A critical review of latent learning and related experiments. *Psychological Bulletin*, 1951, **48**, 97–129.

Thompson, R. Transposition in the white rat as a function of stimulus comparison. *Journal of Experimental Psychology*, 1955, **50**, 185–190.

Thorndike, E. L. *Animal intelligence*. New York: Macmillan, 1911.

Thorndike, E. L., & Lorge, I. *The teacher's word book of 30,000 words*. New York: Teachers College Press, Teachers College, Columbia Univ., 1944.

Thurstone, L. L. *Multiple-factor analysis: A development and expansion of the vectors of mind*. Chicago: Univ. of Chicago Press, 1947.

Tinbergen, N. *The study of instinct*. Oxford: Clarendon Press, 1951.

Tinbergen, N. *The Herring Gull's world*. London: Collins, 1953.

Tolman, E. C. *Purposive behavior in animals and men*. New York: Appleton, 1932.

Treisman, A. M. Contextual cues in selective listening. *Quarterly Journal of Experimental Psychology*, 1960, **12**, 242–248.

Treisman, A. M. Monitoring and storage of irrelevant messages in selective attention. *Journal of Verbal Learning & Verbal Behavior*, 1964, **3**, 449–459.

Tresselt, M. E., & Leeds, D. S. The Einstellung effect in immediate and delayed problem-solving. *Journal of General Psychology*, 1953, **49**, 87–95.

Truex, R. C., & Carpenter, M. B. *Human neuroanatomy*. Baltimore: Williams & Wilkins, 1964.

Tulving, E. Episodic and semantic memory. In E. Tulving & W. Donaldson (Eds.), *Organization of memory*. New York: Academic Press, 1972.

Tulving, E., & Patkau, J. E. Concurrent effects of contextual constraint and word frequency on immediate recall and learning of verbal material. *Canadian Journal of Psychology*, 1962, **16**, 83–95.

Turner, E. A., & Wright, J. Effects of severity of threat and perceived availability on the attractiveness of objects. *Journal of Personality & Social Psychology*, 1965, **2**, 128–132.

Tursky, B., Schwartz, G. E., & Crider, A. Differential patterns of heart rate and skin resistance during a digit-transformation task. *Journal of Experimental Psychology*, 1970, **83**, 451–457.

Tversky, A., & Kahneman, D. Availability: A heuristic for judging frequency and probability. *Cognitive Psychology*, 1973, **5**, 207–232.

Umilta, C., Rizzolatti, G., Marzi, C., Zamboni, G., Franzini, C., Camarda, R., & Berlucchi, G. Hemispheric differences in the discrimination of line orientation. Paper presented at the 1972 Annual Meeting of the European Brain and Behavior Society and at the Third Intensive Study Program of the Neuroscience Research Program, Boulder, Colorado.

Underwood, B. J. Ten years of massed practice on distributed practice. *Psychological Review*, 1961, **68**, 229–247.

Underwood, B. J. Degree of learning and the measurement of forgetting. *Journal of Verbal Learning & Verbal Behavior*, 1964, **3**, 112–129.

Underwood, B. J. False recognition produced by implicit verbal responses. *Journal of Experimental Psychology*, 1965, **70**, 122–129.

Underwood, B. J. Attributes of memory. *Psychological Review*, 1969, **76**, 559–573.

Underwood, B. J., & Keppel, G. One-trial learning? *Journal of Verbal Learning & Verbal Behavior,* 1962, **1,** 1–13.

Underwood, B. J., & Schulz, R. W. *Meaningfulness and verbal learning.* Philadelphia: J. B. Lippincott Co., 1960.

Unger, S. M. Habituation of the vasoconstrictive orienting reaction. *Journal of Experimental Psychology,* 1964, **67,** 11–18.

Uttal, W. R. Emerging principles of sensory coding. *Perspectives in Biology and Medicine,* 1969, **12,** 344–368.

Voss, J. F. On the relationship of associative and organizational processes. In E. Tulving & W. Donaldson (Eds.), *Organization of memory.* New York: Academic Press, 1972.

Vygotsky, L. S. *Thought and language.* Cambridge, Mass.: MIT Press, 1962.

Walker, E. L., & Tarte, R. D. Memory storage as a function of time with homogeneous and heterogeneous lists. *Journal of Verbal Learning & Verbal Behavior,* 1963, **2,** 113–119.

Wallace, R. K. Physiological effects of transcendental meditation. *Science,* 1970, **167,** 1751–1754.

Wallace, R. K., & Benson, H. The physiology of meditation. *Scientific American,* 1972, **226,** No. 2, 84–91.

Wallace, W. H., Turner, S. H., & Perkins, C. C. Preliminary studies of human information storage. Signal Corps Project No. 132C, Institute for Cooperative Research, Univ. Penn., December, 1957.

Wallach, H. Brightness constancy and the nature of achromatic colors. *Journal of Experimental Psychology,* 1948, **38,** 310–324.

Wallach, H., & O'Connell, D. N. The kinetic depth effect. *Journal of Experimental Psychology,* 1953, **45,** 205–217.

Wallach, M. A., & Kogan, N. *Modes of thinking in young children.* New York: Holt, 1965.

Wallas, F. *The art of thought.* New York: Harcourt Brace Jovanovich, 1926.

Ward, W. C., & Jenkins, H. M. The display of information and the judgment of contingency. *Canadian Journal of Psychology,* 1965, **19,** 231–241.

Warren, J. M. Primate learning in comparative perspective. In A. M. Schrier, H. F. Harlow, & F. Stollnitz (Eds.), *Behavior of nonhuman primates,* Vol. 1. New York: Academic Press, 1965.

Warren, R. M., & Gregory, R. L. An auditory analogue of the visual reversible figure. *American Journal of Psychology,* 1958, **71,** 612–613.

Wason, P. C. On the failure to eliminate hypotheses in a conceptual task. *Quarterly Journal of Experimental Psychology,* 1960, **12,** 129–140.

Wason, P. C. Response to affirmative and negative binary statements. *British Journal of Psychology,* 1961, **52,** 133–142.

Wason, P. C. The effect of self-contradiction on fallacious reasoning. *Quarterly Journal of Experimental Psychology,* 1964, **16,** 30–34.

Wason, P. C. Reasoning about a rule. *Quarterly Journal of Experimental Psychology,* 1968, **20,** 273–281.

Wason, P. C. Regression in reasoning? *British Journal of Psychology,* 1969, **60,** 471–480.

Wason, P. C., & Johnson-Laird, P. N. A conflict between selecting and evaluating information in an inferential task. *British Journal of Psychology,* 1970, **61,** 509–515.

Wason, P. C., & Johnson-Laird, P. N. *Psychology of reasoning.* Cambridge, Massachusetts: Harvard Univ. Press, 1972.

Watt, H. J. Experimental contribution to a theory of thinking. *Journal of Anatomy & Physiology,* 1905–1906, **40,** 257–266.

Waugh, N. C., & Norman, D. A. Primary memory. *Psychological Review*, 1965, **72**, 89–104.

Webb, R. A., & Obrist, P. A. The physiological concomitants of reaction time performance as a function of preparatory interval series. *Psychophysiology*, 1970, **6**, 389–403.

Weinberg, H. Evidence suggesting the acquisition of a simple discrimination during sleep. *Canadian Journal of Psychology*, 1966, **20**, 1–11.

Welsh, G. *Welsh Figure Preference Test*. Consulting Psychologists Press, 1959.

Werner, H., & Wapner, S. Toward a general theory of perception. *Psychological Review*, 1952, **59**, 324–338.

Wertheimer, M. Untersuchungen zur Lehre von der Gestalt. *Psychologisches Forschung*, 1923, **4**, 301–350.

Wertheimer, M. *Productive thinking*. New York: Harper & Row, 1945.

Wertheimer, M. Principles of perceptual organization. In D. C. Beardslee & M. Wertheimer, *Readings in perception*. Princeton, New Jersey: Van Nostrand–Reinhold, 1958.

Wertheimer, M. On discrimination experiments. I. Two logical structures. *Psychological Review*, 1959, **66**, 252–266.

White, R. W. Motivation reconsidered: The concept of competence. *Psychological Review*, 1959, **66**, 297–333.

Whitehead, A. N., & Russell, B. *Principia mathematica*. Cambridge: University Press, 1935.

Wicker, F. W. On the locus of picture-word differences in paired-associate learning. *Journal of Verbal Learning & Verbal Behavior*, 1970, **9**, 52–57.

Wickelgren, W. A. Distinctive features and errors in short-term memory for English vowels. *Journal of the Acoustical Society of America*, 1965, **38**, 583–588.

Wickelgren, W. A. Distinctive features and errors in short-term memory for English consonants. *Journal of the Acoustical Society of America*, 1966, **39**, 388–398.

Wickelgren, W. A. Exponential decay and independence from irrelevant associations in short-term memory for serial order. *Journal of Experimental Psychology*, 1967, **73**, 165–171.

Wickelgren, W. A. Multitrace strength theory. In D. A. Norman (Ed.), *Models of human memory*. New York: Academic Press, 1970.

Wiesel, T. N., & Hubel, D. H. Spatial and chromatic interactions in the lateral geniculate body of the rhesus monkey. *Journal of Neurophysiology*, 1966, **29**, 1115–1156.

Wilkins, M. C. The effect of changed material on the ability to do formal syllogistic reasoning. *Archives of Psychology*, 1928, **16**, No. 102.

Winkelman, J., & Schmidt, J. Associative confusions in mental arithmetic. *Journal of Experimental Psychology*. In Press.

Winograd, T. Understanding natural language. *Cognitive Psychology*, 1972, **3**, 1–191.

Wiseman, G., & Neisser, U. Perceptual organization as a determinant of visual recognition memory. Paper presented at meeting of the Eastern Psychol. Assoc., Spring, 1971.

Witkin, H. A. The perception of the upright. *Scientific American*, 1959, **200**, No. 2, 50–56.

Witkin, H. A. Psychological differentiation and forms of pathology. *J. abnorm. Psychol.*, 1965, **70**, 317–336.

Witkin, H. A., Lewis, H. B., Hertzman, M., Machover, K., Meissner, P. B., & Wapner, S. *Personality through perception*. New York: Harper & Row, 1954.

Wittgenstein, L. *Philosophical investigations.* New York: Macmillan, 1953.

Wood, D. J. The nature and development of problem-solving strategies. Unpublished doctoral dissertation, Univ. of Nottingham, 1969.

Woodrow, H., & Lowell, F. Children's association frequency tables. *Psychological Monographs*, 1916, **22** (Whole No. 97).

Woodworth, R. S. *Experimental psychology.* New York: Holt, 1938.

Woodworth, R. S., & Sells, S. B. An atmosphere effect in formal syllogistic reasoning. *Journal of Experimental Psychology*, 1935, **18**, 451–460.

Worthen, B. R. Discovery and expository task presentation in elementary mathematics. *Journal of Educational Psychology Monograph Supplement*, 1968, **59** (No. 1, Part 2).

Wundt, W. *Grundriss der Psychologie.* Leipzig: Engelman, 1896.

Yasukochi, G. Emotional response elicited by electrical stimulation of the hypothalamus in cat. *Folia Psychiatrica Neurologica Japonica*, 1960, **14**, 260–267.

Yerkes, R. M., & Yerkes, D. N. Concerning memory in the chimpanzee. *Journal of Comparative Psychology*, 1928, **8**, 237–271.

Yngve, V. The depth hypothesis. In R. Jakobson (Ed.), *Structure of language in its mathematical aspects.* Providence, Rhode Island: American Mathematical Society, 1961.

Young, R. K. Tests of three hypotheses about the effective stimulus in serial learning. *Journal of Experimental Psychology*, 1962, **63**, 307–313.

Young, T. On the mechanism of the eye. *Philosophical Transactions of the Royal Society (London)*, 1801, **91**, Part 1, 23–88.

Youssef, Z. I. Association and integration in serial learning. *American Journal of Psychology*, 1967, **80**, 355–362.

Yuille, J. C., & Paivio, A. Abstractness and recall of connected discourse. *Journal of Experimental Psychology*, 1969, **82**, 467–471.

Zajonc, R. B. The process of cognitive tuning in communication. *Journal of Abnormal & Social Psychology*, 1960, **61**, 159–167.

Zajonc, R. B. Response suppression in perceptual defense. *Journal of Experimental Psychology*, 1962, **64**, 206–214.

Zeaman, D. Response latency as a function of the amount of reinforcement. *Journal of Experimental Psychology*, 1949, **24**, 294–304.

Zeigarnik, B. Uber das behalten von erledigten und unerledigten Handlungen. *Psychologisches Forschung*, 1927, **9**, 1–85. [An English description may be found in D. Cartwright (Ed.), *Field theory in social science.* New York: Harper & Row, 1951.]

Zeiler, M. D. The ratio theory of intermediate size discrimination. *Psychological Review*, 1963, **70**, 516–533.

Zimbardo, P. G. The effect of effort and improvisation on self-persuasion produced by role-playing. *Journal of Experimental Psychology*, 1965, **1**, 217–219.

Zimbardo, P. G., Weisenberg, M., Firestone, I., & Levy, B. Communicator effectiveness in producing public conformity and private attitude change. *Journal of Personality & Social Psychology*, 1965, **33**, 233–256.

Zinchenko, V. P., van Chzhi-Tsin, & Tarakonov, V. V. The formation and development of perceptual activity. *Soviet Psychology & Psychiatry*, 1963, **2**, 2–12.

Author Index

361

Subject Index

and rigidity of thought processes, 300
Authority, obedience to, 318
Automatic activation of associations, 121, 123, 141
Automatic processes, voluntary vs., 124
Automatic processing, subordinate executive system and, 163
Automatization
    and cognitive development, 167
    and consciousness, 167
    degrees of, 166
    and practice, 164
    process of, 164
    and processing capacity, 169
    stage of learning, 164
Avoidance gradient, 312

B

Ballistic system, 14
Behavior, goal-directed, 157
Biased conflict reduction, 317
Biased thought, 314, 317, 319, 320
Bilateral parallax, 57
Binary connectives, 189
Binocular parallax, 56, 57
Binocular transfer, 39, 41
Bipolar layer of retina, 34
Bivalent variables, 225,
    and reasoning about relationships, 257
Blind men and elephant, story of, 201
Blindspot, 46
Blood pressure
    conditioning of, 171
    hypnotic control of, 171
Boredom, conflict motivation and, 293
Brain, 37
Brain waves, 68
Brainstorming, 146
Brightness
    adaptation, 39
    constancy, 57, 58, 60, 72, 74
    discrimination, 37
    simplicity and, 56
British associationists, 144, 145
Bug detector, 13
Bulb-board task, 227, 228, 270

C

Calculators
    calendar, 191
    lightning, 159
        rate of information processing, 159
        STM in, 159
Capacity
    processing, 244, 258
    of STM, 159, 206
Causal implications, 190
Casual relationships, 189
Causal variable
    many, 258
    single, 253
Causality multiple, 258
Cause–effect reasoning, 190
Cause–effect order, subject–object order and, 184
Cell assembly, 133
    consciousness and, 133
Central processing, 122, 152
    probe reaction time and, 123, 124
Central processor, 153
Change of energy, 65
    in amount, 65
    in kind, 65
Change of direction, 147
Chemical stimuli, 28
Choice
    after the, 314
    among ends, 311, 313
    multidimensional thought and, 308
    among means, 303, 306
    probability and, 306
    riskless, 305
    risky, 305
    unidimensional thought and, 308
    utility and, 306
Choosing a less connected start, heuristic of, 273
Choosing highest probability of winning, strategy of, 308
Chunking, 170, 206
    as a function of practice, 206, 207
    and memorizing, 212
    and recall vs. recognition, 207
Circular reactions, 168, 207
    primary, 168, 207

Date Due